THE
DIACONATE

THE
DIACONATE

A
FULL
AND EQUAL
ORDER

A Comprehensive and Critical Study
of the Origin, Development, and
Decline of the Diaconate in the Context
of the Church's Total Ministry
and
The Renewal of the Diaconate Today
with Reflections for the Twenty-First Century

REVISED EDITION

James Monroe Barnett

Trinity Press International
Harrisburg, Pennsylvania

Unless otherwise noted, quotations from Scripture are from the
New Revised Standard Version (NRSV).

Revised edition
Trinity Press International
P.O. Box 1321
Harrisburg, PA 17105
Trinity Press International is a division of the Morehouse Group.

Library of Congress Cataloging-in-Publication Data

Barnett, James Monroe.
    The diaconate—a full and equal order : a comprehensive and
critical study of the origin, development, and decline of the
diaconate in the context of the church's total ministry and the
renewal of the diaconate today with reflections for the twenty-first
century / James Monroe Barnett. — Rev. ed.
        p.   cm.
    Includes bibliographical references and index.
    ISBN 1-56338-093-5
    1. Deacons—History of doctrines. 2. Deacons.   I. Title.
BV680.B37   1995
262'.14—dc20   94-4923
                                                    CIP

Printed in the United States of America

99   00   01   02   10   9   8   7   6   5   4   3

This edition is respectfully dedicated
To the faithful deacons of the Church today
and
In thanksgiving for their ministries.

Contents

Part One

The Origin, Development, and Decline of the Diaconate

Part Two

The Renewal of the Diaconate Today
with Reflections for the Twenty-first Century

Chapter 10
The Character and Place of the Diaconate 165

Chapter 11
Some Considerations Regarding Qualifications 182

Chapter 12
The Functions and Training of the Deacon 190

Chapter 13
The Wholeness of the Church 217

Appendix 218

Select Bibliography 229

Index 245

Foreword to the First Edition

From time to time I am invited to preach a sermon at the ordination of a deacon. The old Episcopal Prayer Book of 1928 prescribed the subjects of the sermon which I always tried to follow conscientiously. The preacher was required to declare *inter alia* "how necessary that Order is in the Church of Christ" (BCP 1928, p. 530). I always longed to say, Yes, so necessary that in many dioceses there are no deacons around to speak of between Christmas and Trinity! No wonder that excellent rubric has (however regrettably) been removed from the new Prayer Book! It was sheer hypocrisy to claim that we regarded the diaconate as "necessary" to the Church. Another thing I wanted to say was that the Presbyterians and Baptists were in this instance more Catholic than we were: if they had lost episcopacy they had at least restored something more like the diaconate as it was in the Primitive Church. The German Lutherans also have a genuinely caritative diaconate, doing social service in parishes and running charitable institutions like Bethel, Bielefeld, for epileptics and other handicapped people.

The removal of that embarrassing rubric and of the post-communion prayer which referred to the diaconate as "this inferior office" (BCP 1928, p. 555) has not improved matters all that much. Now the overall impression is that a person being ordained to the diaconate is being ordained primarily to a ministry of the word. See the New Testament reading from 2 Corinthians 4:1–6, which is all about the apostolic ministry of preaching the Word. And then, as the Bishop hands the newly ordained person the Bible, he says, "Receive this Bible as a sign of your authority [*sic*] to proclaim God's word . . ." Worse than that, every preacher, Roman Catholic or Episcopalian, who exalts the importance of the *diakonia* in the Church of him who came among us as One who serves knows full well that this person in front of him, now being ordained with such solemnity, will to all intents and purposes have to go through it all again in six months or a year's time to be ordained as a priest. Of course, we say, "Once a deacon, always a deacon," but that is pious fiction. The ordination of a deacon, as at present practiced, is usually little more than a farce. In the Roman Catholic Church, as with us, the diaconate — despite some attempts since Vatican II — is still seen primarily as a stepping stone to the priesthood.

Dr. Barnett's scholarly study, drawing from Scripture and Antiquity, points

the way to the abolition of the apprentice diaconate and the recovery of the Office in its primitive authenticity. I commend his work to all who on the one hand are concerned for the Catholicity of the Church, and to all who on the other hand accept the Reformation principle, *ecclesia semper reformanda.*

REGINALD H. FULLER
Virginia Theological Seminary
Alexandria, Va.

Preface to the Revised Edition

The original edition of *The Diaconate*, published in 1981, went through four printings, the first two by Seabury Press and one each by Winston-Seabury and Harper and Row, now HarperCollins, as these publishing houses merged or were acquired by one another. Seabury Press predicted at its initial publication that it would become the definitive work on the subject, and I have been told that it is. It is at least a standard text and reference work in many seminaries and diaconal training programs.

For me, the diaconate has become the most glorious order within a splendid ministry when it is viewed in the context of the whole and seen as it can and should be — the order that informs all orders of the primary work we are all sent to do, though in different ways with varying functions.

This study is, I believe, the most thorough, accurate, and complete work that has been done. Although a number of books have been published since this book was first released, none has been a comprehensive study of the office as it appears in the New Testament and as it developed in the Church. Of equal importance, none either has attempted to deal with the diaconate in the context of the nature of the Church and its total ministry. Further, working from the original sources has in some instances led to conclusions at variance with those that have been widely accepted. A notable example is that preaching was not a function of the diaconate in the early Church, an error involving among other things a confusion of orders. Another, which has been widely affirmed since the study was originally published, is that *cursus honorum* as a rule and requirement actually came about many centuries later and for far different reasons than has frequently been thought.

In the years between the original edition and this one, the diaconate has flourished, particularly in the Roman Catholic and Episcopal churches in the United States. Interest has significantly increased as well in various denominations, as is seen by such events as the two conferences on "The Diaconate and Diaconal Ministry" sponsored by the Faith and Order Commission of the National Council of Churches in the United States. In addition, the renewal of the Church has proceeded apace with profound theological insights relating to its total ministry, the most notable being a biblical and patristic understanding of Baptism.

This revision includes numerous additions in both the historical and contemporary areas in order to facilitate a better understanding of the whole of the

Church's ministry with the diaconate set firmly in this context and to focus and offer some insight into problems that have arisen or become more evident in the developing diaconate. *The Diaconate* is about far more than the office of a deacon. It is about what the Church is or should be; what Baptism means for the Church's ministry and what that ministry should be; what orders are and how they relate to each other and to the body of the baptized; the popular heresy of "sacred" and "secular" places, people, and things; clericalism and its symbols; the authority of the Church to alter its structures; and much else.

A major reason for revising *The Diaconate* was the need to deal more directly with some of the important ramifications suggested in the original. I received a letter following the original publication from Robert H. Platman, Ph.D., a seminary professor and parish priest, who wrote, "I've just finished reading *The Diaconate*. . . . What is particularly interesting to me is the group of implications with which you don't deal, but hint at. Clearly, you have demolished the arguments against the ordination of women and those for a particular 'clerical' life-style." In giving lectures and leading conferences on the diaconate throughout the United States, I have become increasingly aware that the implications, including those Dr. Platman mentions, escape the notice of many readers. I have always considered those implications an important part of the study. One of greatest importance is the emerging concept of the centrality of Baptism in the Church's life and ministry. Another is the change in the roles of the bishop and the presbyter in the late third and early fourth centuries. Although usually overlooked, the change has important ramifications for the place of the deacon in today's structure and his or her relationship with the other orders.

There are also the problems created by the conflict of imposing a hierarchical structure on the New Testament and pre-Nicene organic horizontal structure of the Church, with their accompanying theologies, and somewhat similar anomalies relating to imposing ceremonial accretions on the reformed rites. Others include the plague of clericalism with its subtle symbols and the "omnivorous priesthood" of the past as the real problem with both lay and diaconal ministry, indeed also of an impossibly overburdened presbyteral ministry. There are, too, such things as the mistaken conception of the diaconate as a ministry properly only outwardly directed in the world beyond the Church, terminology such as "the celebrant" carried over from the past, and voting by deacons in diocesan or comparable structures of democratically governed churches.

Additions made to the historical information range from the origin of status symbols the Church took over from imperial Rome for its clergy along with the implications involved and of *cursus honorum* to additional information concerning the meaning of *diakonia* in light of a recent extensive, but misleading, word study. Other additions include a brief section dealing with liturgical practices related to the diaconate, suggesting that ceremonial practice be conformed to the theology emerging or reemerging in the contemporary Church. For example, the importance of the deacon participating not only in the Sunday Eucharists but also in weddings, funerals, and other services as well sets forth the fullness of the Church's ordained ministry. Or, liturgically, the reading of the Gospel at the Eucharist, not the sermon, is the apex of the ministry of the word.

Among the practical additions are two sample "letters of agreement" for use as a starting point to establish a clear relationship between the deacon and the parish and/or diocese.

I do wish to thank the many deacons whom I have met and learned much from in the years intervening between the two editions. They range from the fine deacon in my parish, Sylvia Landers, ordained a few years ago, to many across the land whom I have met at workshops and conferences in the Episcopal, Roman Catholic, Lutheran, and other churches. My fascination with and love for the diaconate has only increased as I have come to know these living icons of our Servant-Lord. Joined to this is now my utmost respect for these vivid symbols of Christ in the midst of his and our world.

I am happy that Trinity Press International wants to publish this revised edition, and I especially thank Harold Rast, Th.D., its director, for his patience and help.

JAMES BARNETT
September 1, 1994
Feast of David Pendleton Oakerhater, Deacon,
"God's Warrior," Missionary of the Cheyenne

Acknowledgments

I do wish to acknowledge and to express my appreciation to many who most graciously helped me in the research and writing of this study, notably to:

The late Dr. Massey H. Shepherd Jr. for suggesting the diaconate as my area of study to fulfill the requirements of a graduate program, for his advice at the outset, and for reading the original manuscript and making invaluable notes and comments.

Dr. Donald S. Armentrout, my advisor, for his generous help in my research and in reading the manuscript, giving many valuable suggestions.

Dr. Marion J. Hatchett for his counsel and advice and his warm friendship and support.

Thomas Edward Camp, Associate Librarian of the University of the South and Librarian of the School of Theology during my original research, for providing much assistance in finding and obtaining needed works.

Dr. Reginald Fuller for translating some references, reading the manuscript, and graciously writing a foreword for the first edition.

Fr. Ron Del Bene for reading an early draft of the manuscript, offering helpful comments and encouraging its publication.

Dr. O. C. Edwards, Dr. J. Robert Wright, Fr. Patrick McCaslin, Msgr. Ernest J. Fiedler, Bishop Joe Morris Doss, and Mel Hunke, for reading all or part of the original manuscript and making valuable suggestions from diverse viewpoints. Father McCaslin in addition shared at length some of his experience as Director of the Permanent Diaconate Program for the Archdiocese of Omaha and as national President of the Association of Diaconal Directors. Monseigneur Fiedler, Executive Director of the Bishops' Committee on the Permanent Diaconate of the National Conference of Catholic Bishops at the time of the original publication, also graciously supplied information and encouraged the publication of the work, as did his successor Deacon Constantino J. Ferriola Jr.

Dr. Laura Franklin, retired professor of English at Wayne State College, Wayne, Nebraska, for spending many hours checking and proofreading the manuscript.

Fr. Thomas McDermott, O.P., a Dominican and friend, now pastor of the Dominican work in Lagos, Nigeria, for spending many hours obtaining books and facilitating my research when a good theological library was not readily available.

Fr. Conrad L. Harkins, O.F.M., Director of the Franciscan Institute at Saint Bonaventure University; Fr. Edward H. Konerman, S.J., Secretary of the Catholic Theological Society of America; and Dr. Stanley T. Vandersall, Professor of the Department of Classics, the University of Nebraska–Lincoln.

The late Howard Galley, my original editor at the Seabury Press.

The library of Creighton University, Omaha, particularly for research assistance in the revision.

Therese D. Boyd, my editor at Trinity Press International, for her highly competent work and gracious manner.

Above all, my wife, Marian, for her constant and unfailing encouragement, understanding, support, and love during all the time I have spent on this project, and for the laborious task of typing the original manuscript more than once before the age of our computer.

Part One

The Origin, Development, and Decline of the Diaconate

Chapter 1

The Nature of the Church —
Truly Organic

The principle underlying the diaconate as an office and function in the Church is rooted in the nature of the Church itself as it was originally founded and lived in the pre-Nicene world. The first principle of that Church was that it was *laos,* the people of God. The Church was called into being by God and made "a chosen race, a royal priesthood, a holy nation, God's own people" (1 Pet. 2:9). All were *laos.* There was no word to distinguish, in the sense of today, between clergy and laity, because no word was needed or appropriate. The clergy were laity along with others who belonged to the people of God.[1]

Baptism was the creating sacrament of the Church and of its life and ministry as well. Baptism, replacing and standing in marked contrast to circumcision, created the *laos,* the people of God, in a new and dynamic way. In Baptism the Holy Spirit came anew to each, bestowing as he willed gifts for ministry, that together Christians might extend the presence of the living Lord and the fullness of his ministry throughout the world. From this empowerment and from these gifts to the *laos* all ministry flowed.

It is here that we must begin if we are to clarify our understanding of the Church's ministry, because we must first rethink our theology of the Church itself. As G. W. H. Lampe observed, the basic problem in many attempts to deal with the ministry is the failure to have dealt adequately first of all with the nature of the Church. He writes, "We have too often tried to put the hierarchical cart before the ecclesiastical horse, and, not unnaturally, failed to make progress."[2] While references in the New Testament and the post-apostolic generation to the origin and development of the ministry, and especially to what today we term

---

1. Reginald Fuller, "Early Catholicism in the New Testament," lectures at the Graduate School of Theology, Sewanee, Tenn., 1970. Cf. Ernst Käsemann, *Essays on New Testament Themes,* Studies in Biblical Theology 41 (London: SCM Press, 1964), 63–87 (hereafter cited as Käsemann, *N.T. Themes*).

2. G. W. H. Lampe, *Some Aspects of the New Testament Ministry* (London: SPCK, 1949), 3 (hereafter cited as Lampe, *N.T. Ministry*). Lampe rightly states that such is the case in much of English writing on the subject, from Charles Gore's *The Church and the Ministry* to *The Apostolic Ministry,* edited by Kenneth E. Kirk.

3

the "clerical ministry," are inadequate to provide a clear picture, the greater factor resulting in different interpretations of the Church's ministry has been the differing theological assumptions regarding the nature of the Church.[3]

Although it is far beyond the scope of this study to discuss in detail the nature of the Church, some consideration of several fundamental aspects of its nature is necessary here. We need first of all to recall the Church's corporate, organic constitution, which for centuries has been lost from sight and obscured in large measure by a "clericalism" that has dominated the churches, whether Protestant, Anglican, Orthodox, or Roman Catholic. The first Christians did not think in terms of having particular persons set aside, by whatever means, as "ministers" to do the Church's ministering. Even less did they think "primarily of a hierarchy and secondarily of a Church whose catholicity was guaranteed thereby"[4] as many Christians do today.

In fact, in the early Church we find no sacred persons or sacred places.[5] In Jesus there is the union of infinite God with the flesh of humanity in which the goodness and holiness of creation is forever affirmed. Therefore, from the outset the Church avoided taking over the false distinction from Judaism between the sacred and the secular. It saw all as sacred. This is not, of course, to say that those Christians did not hold and treat some things more reverently than others. But it is to say that they had new insight into the nature of the Church and its relationship to the world. They had the Eucharist wherever they happened to come together as the Church.[6] They avoided designating those who performed the various functions of the Church by titles that would have set them apart from or given them rank above the rest of the *laos*. As Hans Küng observes, the New Testament clearly avoids using the "current and obvious terms" which denote "primacy," "rank," or "the honour and dignity of office" in reference to Christian ministries. New words were needed because, as Küng notes, the Greek words then in use "all express a relationship of rulers and ruled."[7]

In emphasizing that the charisma given all Christians in Baptism excluded the possibility of sacred space, sacred time, and sacred persons in the primitive Church, Ernst Käsemann asks rhetorically,

> "Does not all this lead to the profanation of what is holy?" The answer is, that the opposite is true. The fenced-off boundaries of "religion" are broken through when grace invades the world and its everyday life. It is not mistrust of the cultic element as such which leads Paul to avoid as a general rule the terminology of Old Testament or heathen sacrifices. On the contrary, in Rom. 12:1f he deliberately resorts to cultic language of this kind in order to describe the sanctification

---

3. Massey H. Shepherd Jr., "Ministry, Christian," in *The Interpreter's Dictionary of the Bible,* ed. George A. Buttrick, 5 vols. (New York: Abingdon Press, 1962), 3:386,

4. Lampe, *N.T. Ministry,* 2.

5. Massey H. Shepherd Jr., "The Christian Year," lectures at the Graduate School of Theology, Sewanee, Tenn., Summer 1970. Cf. Käsemann, *N.T. Themes,* 78.

6. Shepherd, "The Christian Year."

7. Hans Küng, *The Church,* trans. Ray and Rosaleen Ockenden (New York: Sheed and Ward, 1976), 389.

of everyday life as the true sacrifice of Christendom. Thus sacramental worship stands at the very heart of the life of the Christian assembly.[8]

Sacramental worship, as it was conceived and practiced in the early Church, brought together and made sacred the whole of life.

As Jesus brought a new unity to the physical and the spiritual, so he also brings a new unifying principle to Israel in his own person. He used the analogy of the vine, saying, "I am the vine, you are the branches" (John 15:5). He likened the Church to a flock of sheep and himself to its shepherd (John 10:1–16, 21:15–17). Christ himself becomes the unifying principle of the Church, which is not simply commissioned and empowered, as has often been suggested in recent years, but is reconstituted into a truly organic society, the New Israel.

This understanding of the Church permeates the whole of the New Testament. The Church is said to be God's flock (Luke 12:32; Acts 20:28; 1 Pet. 5:2). Paul writes, "There is one body and one Spirit, just as you were called to the one hope of your calling, one Lord, one faith, one baptism, one God and Father of us all, who is above all and through all and in all" (Eph. 4:4–6). But perhaps the greatest of the New Testament analogies for the Church is that used by Paul when he terms it the "body of Christ," likening its members to the various parts of the human body.[9] Although a number of other figures are used for the Church in the New Testament, none serves to weaken those setting forth its organic nature.

Further, from the outset Christian initiation has been through the new birth of Baptism,[10] in which one is grafted into this body. And in a reference to the Eucharist Paul writes, "Because there is one bread, we who are many are one body, for we all partake of the one bread" (1 Cor. 10:17). The Eucharist continually renews the paschal mystery and is indeed seen from the beginning to be both a creator and symbol of the Church's organic oneness with and in Christ. Here Paul goes beyond analogy and says the Church's members "are one body." We see the primary importance of the Eucharist in this connection when Ignatius expresses the universal practice of the early Church:

> Be careful, then to observe a single Eucharist. For there is one flesh of our Lord, Jesus Christ, and one cup of his blood that makes us one, and one altar, just as there is one bishop along with the presbytery and deacons, my fellow slaves. In that way whatever you do is in line with God's will.[11]

One Eucharist in one place in one day remained the ideal of the Church until it was finally forgotten in the later Middle Ages. For centuries after the Church at Rome began to have Sunday Eucharists in the parish churches, fragments of the Bread consecrated at the pope's Eucharist were sent by acolytes to be placed in

---

8. Käsemann, *N.T. Themes,* 78.

9. 1 Cor. 12:12–27; Rom. 12:4–8; Col. 1:18, 24; 3:15.

10. John 3:3–8. Cf. Lampe, *N.T. Ministry,* 2.

11. Ignatius, *To the Philadelphians* 4.1, in "The Letters of Ignatius, Bishop of Antioch," *Early Christian Fathers,* ed. Cyril C. Richardson, Library of Christian Classics 1 (Philadelphia: Westminster Press, 1953), 105.

the chalice of every church, thereby symbolically making all Eucharists one as the Church is one and uniting all with Christ and one another.[12] Although obviously there must be more than one Eucharist in a city or town of any size, the multiplication of Eucharists in one church on one day contradicts, as the early Church clearly saw, the fundamental theology of its organic nature. The single Eucharist symbolized and created the oneness of the Christian community. Multiple Eucharists divided it symbolically and actually. Although the consequences of this contradiction are impossible to assess, they have undoubtedly been much more far-reaching and detrimental than is recognized.

In the practical realm, the multiplication of Eucharists has made possible the growth of many parishes until they are so large that the Christian community is more community in theory than in practice. In some large churches today an attempt has been made to address this problem by creating small groups or communities within the larger congregation. While laudable in its intent and perhaps the best that can be done at the moment in large parishes, given the historical circumstances, this strategy lacks the creative force both symbolically and pragmatically of one Eucharist in one place in one day. It has not been eminently successful. There is little sense of community, of belonging to one body or one family. Many in these churches remain uninvolved. Liturgical renewal today should work toward reducing the size of very large congregations, even if it means the loss of some monumental buildings. Success measured in terms of numbers of people alone is a value of the world, not of the Church, however much we often seem tempted to think and act otherwise.

But even smaller parishes have multiplied Eucharists for no other reason than convenience. Certainly this fragmentation of Christian communities is indicative of a marked failure to comprehend the fundamental nature of the Church, that it is one, as Christ's body is one, and to live out in the world all that this means.

Most Christians today seem to have little sense of being an integral and important part of a community — a caring, loving family — which needs each one of its members in all of his or her uniqueness to be whole. Some years ago an older woman in my parish told me with deep regret how, many years before, she and her husband had been upset by something in the parish and had stopped going to church for a number of years. She then added, "Of course, we only hurt ourselves." How often we think that way, failing to recognize the needed contribution of each to the life of the whole. Far fewer people are actively participating in the Church's work than would be were there a clear sense among Christians that all in their community are important to its life. Much of the Church's ministry goes undone. For example, one of the most frequent complaints of visitors to churches is that "no one spoke to [them]," or if someone did, they were not made to feel welcome. Few, if any of us, would treat a person visiting our home or family like this. Welcoming people is

---

12. Dom Gregory Dix, *The Shape of the Liturgy* (Westminster, England: Dacre Press, 1945), 21.

one of the easiest and simplest of ministries, yet even this is sorely neglected. The lack of community is probably the principal cause for the high rate of dropouts among adult converts experienced by the major churches in America in recent times.

It is worthy of note that the Church's organic nature and unity are but the reflection of God. God is within himself a community of persons who are united with one another in perfect harmony and oneness, yet each person of the Trinity individually possesses personality and function. God has called and constituted the Church to be such a community of persons in the world, realizing the oneness of humanity and expressing the unity in perfect harmony of life together as each member grows into his or her own fullness.

Something of the Church's nature is to be seen in the word "church" itself. Although the derivation of the English word "church" is from the Greek *kuriakon,* meaning "the Lord's house" or a building designated for Christian worship, it is not so in the New Testament. Reginald Fuller observes that in the New Testament "church" is the Greek *"ecclesia,"* a word which "always means an assembly of people and cannot mean a building." It is apparently for this reason that the Greek-speaking Christians chose *ecclesia* and not "synagogue" to designate the messianic community.[13] The name *ecclesia* was used to designate those whom God had called and who had responded to his call with faith and obedience to live in a divinely constituted community. The idea of community is fundamental to the nature of this *Ecclesia,* but it is a community that points in two directions. On the one hand, it is the assembly of those called by God to live together as his people and, more important, on the other hand of those who meet with and live together with God.[14]

Interestingly, Walter Lowrie also declares in his illuminating discussion of the meaning of *ecclesia* that "holy" was used to describe the actual character of those belonging to the *Ecclesia* by the New Testament writers and others afterwards.[15] Holiness in the Church was redefined to refer to the Church as an institution only after large numbers of half-converted people entered. He writes,

> Even in the early Catholic period the Church was still defined with sole reference to its true members; and so long as the character of the great majority of the disciples corresponded substantially with the ideal, it was possible to ignore the exceptions. It was only when widespread corruption forced men to *dwell* upon this incongruity, that they felt obliged to choose between a radical purification of the Church, or a new definition of it such as the trend of Catholic development

---

13. Reginald H. Fuller, "Church," in *A Theological Word Book of the Bible,* ed. Alan Richardson (New York: Macmillan, 1951), 46–47. Cf. Walter Lowrie, *The Church and Its Organization in Primitive and Catholic Times: An Interpretation of Rudolph Sohm's Kirchenrecht* (New York: Longmans, Green, 1904), 102–40. Lowrie discusses here at length and with profound insight the significance of the name *ecclesia,* Jesus' use of the term which he regards as genuine in Matt. 16:18ff and 18:17ff, and that of the New Testament writers.

14. Lowrie, *The Church and Its Organization,* 106.

15. Ibid., 106–7.

demanded, that is, as an *institute,* which enjoyed the character of holiness apart from any consideration of the character of its members.[16]

This does not mean, of course, that these Christians in the very early period did not sin. It does mean that their lives were substantially different from those of others outside the *Ecclesia,* so different the New Testament could unhesitatingly call them "saints," "holy ones." No small part of this difference was to be seen in the servant-ministry of all the people of God, which came to be exemplified in the diaconate.

Hans Küng notes that as Christianity spread, although *ecclesia* was used in the New Testament to mean a local church or a group of congregations, it was so used in the sense that "each single *ekklesia* was a copy of the original community, each represented the universal *ekklesia.*"[17] Walter Lowrie writes on this theme:

> Where the Lord is, the head of the body, there is Christendom; where two or three are gathered in Christ's name, there is the *people of Christ,* the New Testament Israel; there is *the whole of Christendom* with all of its promised privileges; for Christ is in the midst, and that is all in all. Where Christ is, there is the Ecclesia — the people of God.... Hence it is that *every assembly of Christians,* whether it be great or small, which is gathered in the name of the Lord is called Ecclesia.... The *whole* Church is not composed of individual Churches, neither is the individual Church regarded as a part of the whole.... There is but *one* Ecclesia, the assembly of *the whole of Christendom* but this one Ecclesia has innumerable manifestations.[18]

This view is in some important ways radically different from that commonly held regarding the nature of the Church and has the broadest of implications, far beyond the scope of our subject. But only in this context can we see the full extent of the Church's organic character. To think of the Church throughout the world as it exists today as the universal Church is great, but there is a sense in which it is even greater to think of the Church in any parish as being the universal Church, as being *the* Body of Christ with all of its power and gifts and life.

The hierarchical structure adopted by the Church in the fourth century significantly diminishes the importance the New Testament gives to local churches as the basic unit of the Church and as a manifestation and representative of the whole of Christendom. This does not mean that the New Testament churches were "congregational" in the sense the word is used today: that each is independent and free to determine its own doctrine and discipline. In fact, it is more the opposite: as a manifestation and representative of the whole, each is subject to the whole. The transition of the fourth century resulted in a shift from the local

---

16. Ibid., 108 (italics in original).
17. Hans Küng, *Structures of the Church,* trans. Salvator Attanasio (New York: Thomas Nelson & Sons, 1964), 11–12. Cf. Fuller, "Church," 47.
18. Lowrie, *The Church and Its Organization,* 136–37 (italics in original).

church to the diocese. Power, not *diakonia,* was involved. The power of rule in the local church moved from presbyteral councils to diocesan bishops.

Although the Church is far from returning to the New Testament model today, the renewal of the late twentieth century has moved in that direction. For example, after meeting for twelve years, the Anglican–Roman Catholic International Commission issued its final report in 1982. Following its release, Archbishop of Canterbury Robert Runcie issued a statement saying that the true significance of the report was its view that "the one Christian church is a communion of local churches, a view he called 'immensely important,' and a change from the 'monolithic institutional ecclesiology' of the past."[19]

Further, the Christian *Ecclesia* of the New Testament age saw itself as Israel. It was the remnant that had been called by God to be Israel and to live then, already, in the age to come.[20] As Jesus himself had worked within the system,[21] the primitive Church continued to do so. It regarded the whole system as essentially valid, continuing to worship in the Temple, attend the synagogues, and keep the Law. It formed no revolutionary party but saw its mission as being sent to call the whole of Israel into the Church, the true Israel of God.[22] Gradually it did come to see that the Church of God was a "reconstituted" Israel in which the sacrificial system (Heb. 10:1–25) and the Law (Acts 15:1–29), symbolized by circumcision, had been fulfilled by Christ and were no longer needed. Then, rejected finally by the Jews of the old Israel and cast out of the synagogues, c. 65 C.E., Christians were not only free to develop their own institutions apart from the Jews, but found it necessary.

It was only natural at the outset that the primitive Church was not greatly concerned with questions of organization and structure. It already had the organization and structure of the old Israel, which it was.[23] It also had the Twelve and the apostles, which seemed quite adequate for its needs. And when they were not, it had the authority and the flexibility to provide what was needed, as is seen by the appointment of the Seven in Acts 6. Further, it was "too near the heart of a vast explosion of spiritual power" to be concerned with such questions.[24] It had experienced not only the resurrection of Christ but the outpouring of the Holy Spirit (Acts 2). It had found the Holy Spirit to be the energizing principle of its life and knew itself to be "the Spirit-possessed body of the redeemed who had passed from death into life, who had received the earnest of the Spirit, and were now awaiting the imminent Parousia."[25] Therefore, since these Christians were not concerned with questions of constitutional order, the

---

19. *The Living Church* (Milwaukee, Wis.: Living Church Foundation, May 2, 1982), 6.

20. Lampe, *N.T. Ministry,* 2.

21. Eduard Schweizer, *Church Order in the New Testament,* trans. Frank Clarke (London: SCM Press, 1961), 34–38.

22. Pierson Parker, "Violence in the Gospels," lectures at the Graduate School of Theology, Sewanee, Tenn., Summer 1972.

23. Schweizer, *Church Order in the New Testament,* 47.

24. Lampe, *N.T. Ministry,* 2–3.

25. Ibid., 2.

answers to most questions about the nature of the ministry are not answered directly by the New Testament.

However, not only may certain inferences be made with confidence but the Scriptures do provide us with fundamental principles, some of which seem often to be overlooked, perhaps in some cases because of their very simplicity. We have already set forth the social nature, first of all, of God and then of the Church. The Church's fundamental nature is social and organic. Due to the highly individualistic philosophy of human nature that has permeated the thinking of the West in modern times but now seems to be waning, it might be well to note with Arnold Toynbee and others that humanity itself is primarily social by its nature. Only secondarily are we individuals apart from other human beings.[26] It follows then from human nature that for society to exist as such there must be order.

The fact that God is a God of order is to be seen throughout the universe: the stars stay in their courses; sugar is always sweet; acorns always produce oak trees and never puppies. So true is this basic principle that the disorder we do observe can be seen as evil, a perversion or privation of good, as Augustine taught.[27] The structure of ancient Israel reflects this order with its high priest and priesthood, sacrificial system, synagogues and their rulers, law, Sanhedrin, and theocratic monarchy. When we come to the Christian community called into being by God in Christ, we expect to find order, an order that in fact is evident from the beginning of the New Testament period, even with its eschatological outlook and charismatic ministries.[28] We see it in the replacement of Judas, in the appointment of the Seven, in the authority of the Twelve, in the "forms of leadership" or "administrators" of Paul, in the appointment of elders, in the authority of "the apostles and the elders" of Acts 15, and elsewhere.[29]

This is not to say that Jesus dictated every aspect of the structure of the Church any more than did God when he instituted the Old Covenant with Abraham or renewed it later with Moses. Evidence from the gospels indicates that Jesus gave few instructions for the Church's organizational structure.[30] John

---

26. Arnold Toynbee, *A Study of History,* 2 vols., abridgment by D. C. Somervell (New York: Oxford University Press, 1957), 2:79.

27. Augustine, *Concerning the Nature of the Good Against the Manichaeans (De Natura Boni)* 3, 4, in *St. Augustine: The Writings Against the Manichaeans and Against the Donatists,* in *Nicene and Post-Nicene Fathers of the Christian Church, A Select Library of the,* 1st ser., 14 vols., ed. Philip Schaff (Grand Rapids: Eerdmans, 1956), 4:352; *On the Morals of the Manichaeans (De Moribus Manichaeorum)* 5.7, in *Nicene and Post-Nicene Fathers,* 1st ser., 4:70; *City of God* 11.9, in *St. Augustine's City of God and Christian Doctrine,* trans. Marcus Dods, in *Nicene and Post-Nicene Fathers,* 1st ser., 2:210. Cf. Gerald Bonner, *St. Augustine of Hippo, Life and Controversies* (Philadelphia: Westminster Press, 1963), 199–201, 204–6.

28. Lampe, *N.T. Ministry,* 7. Cf. Schweizer, *Church Order in the New Testament,* 14, 178–79.

29. Acts 1–6, esp. 1:15–26 and 6:1–6; Mark 3:13–19; 1 Cor. 12:28; Acts 14:23 (cf. Acts 20:17).

30. "A Report on the Restoration of the Office of Deacon as a Lifetime State," by a Committee of the Catholic Theological Society of America, Edward Echlin, chairman. Published in the *American Ecclesiastical Review* 164, no. 3 (March 1971): par. 9, p. 193.

records that Jesus said, "I still have many things to say to you, but you cannot bear them now. When the Spirit of truth comes, he will guide you into all the truth; for he will not speak on his own, but will speak whatever he hears, and he will declare to you the things that are to come" (John 16:12–13).

There would not be the same imperative for Jesus to dictate during his incarnate life the details of organization as there would be for another, because he was to return in the person of the Spirit to be the energizing principle of the New Covenant Church. What Jesus did, it would seem probable (although we cannot expect the New Testament by its nature to provide adequate information), was to provide all the initial authority needed in his commissioning of the Twelve, of Paul, and perhaps of other apostles for those first years when the Church was to continue as part of the old Israel and to provide under the guidance of the Holy Spirit for its continuance thereafter. His emphasis was on the nature of the authority his disciples were to exercise, an authority of service.[31]

Käsemann strongly affirms the guidance of the Spirit in the primitive Church's transition from the charismatically called and authorized ministries of Paul's genuine letters, to the ordained and apostolically validated ministries found in the Lucan writings, the Pastorals, 1 Clement, and the Ignatian letters. He sees this "revolution" as an historical necessity because the Pauline understanding of "office, worship, Christian freedom and responsibility" encouraged an uncontrolled and apparently uncontrollable enthusiasm that threatened the gentile churches.[32] In the face of this danger Pauline Christianity turned to forms of church government already proven in Jewish Christianity. Käsemann continues:

> It is precisely in this respect, in my opinion, that the revolution can be called legitimate. For I think that the Holy Spirit manifests itself in the Church most clearly when, in the midst of the pressing need and perplexity of men, it awakes the courage and spiritual gifts for new ways which are appropriate to the situation. Apostles do not justify retaining old orders, when they can no longer serve contemporary life. That Church which does not stand ready at all times to break out of its traditional walls and is not willing to bear the risks inevitably associated therewith cannot seriously appeal to her Master for her stance.[33]

The Church must indeed adapt itself to the age in which it lives, and it has been given not only the latitude and freedom it needs but also the power of the Holy Spirit to guide it according to the times and circumstances.

The principle of the Spirit's guidance contains within itself the necessity for testing every direction and adaptation against the scriptural norms of God's revelation in Christ. For example, making "sacred persons" of the clergy is not in accord with the revelation in Christ, wherein the distinctions between the sacred

---

31. Ibid., par. 9, p. 11.
32. Ernst Käsemann, *New Testament Questions of Today* (London: SCM Press, 1969), 245–47 (hereafter cited in Käsemann, *N.T. Questions*).
33. Ibid.

and the secular of the old Israel are abolished and the unity of all creation is affirmed. In like manner the shift from a Church whose ministry encompassed all its people, each with a special function for the good of the whole, like the organs of a body, to a Church whose ministry was one of ascending grades characterized by rank, status, and power is to be found wanting when tested by the revelation in Christ. It is somewhat ironic that those pentecostal groups who put great emphasis today on the place of the Spirit in the Church often deny his guidance in those early years in this most vital area.

The commission given to the Twelve, as Massey Shepherd notes, "implies, at the least, the formation and governance of a specific historical community of Christian disciples."[34] They are to extend Jesus' work of preaching and healing, take the gospel to the world, baptize all nations, and forgive sins.[35] They are pictured in the first chapters of Acts directing the Church in its varied activities. This is true though, as many have observed, the Church's outlook was predominantly eschatological. The argument that since Jesus expected the eschaton to come immediately he could not have intended to found a Church is quickly and effectively countered by Reginald Fuller's assertion that the Church is eschatological: "*ecclesia* in NT usage is itself an eschatological term — the community which is promised the Kingdom of God."[36] Although the *parousia* (second coming) did not come within the lifetime of the apostles as they apparently at first expected, the Kingdom had been ushered in and they lived at the end of history.

---

34. Shepherd, "Ministry, Christian," 3:387.
35. Mark 3:14–15 and parallels; Luke 24:46–48; Acts 1:8; Matt. 28:19; John 20:23.
36. Fuller, "Church," 47.

Chapter 2

Ministry in the New Testament
SENT TO SERVE

The Varied Ministries Constituting the Ministry

In the New Testament period and throughout the pre-Nicene age the Church's ministry was that of the whole people of God. Each member exercised his or her function in and for the whole body. It is in this context that every ministry and office in the Church must be understood. Thus, the apostolic ministry of the Church is rightly conceived in terms that comprehend and envision the totality of the widely varied forms of ministry found in the New Testament and, by extension, those that developed later which were in accord with the principles found in the New Testament. It is not then limited to the narrow confines of the threefold ministry of bishops, presbyters, and deacons.

One of the greatest sources of misunderstanding of the ministry of the early Church stems from our looking back, preconditioned as we are, to that period and seeing the leadership of the Church then as "the ministry." This is to forget that all were "laity" (*laos*), even the leaders. More subtle perhaps, but closely connected, is the tendency to think in terms of a clerical ministry that guarantees the catholicity of the Church[1] or even constitutes it. The New Testament view is that the action of the clergy is the action of the Church. The clergy act for the Church just as other members act for the Church in doing other ministries. Baptism, not ordination, confers authority to be the Church. It is both interesting and significant that, as Baptism declined in importance in the Medieval period, rites originally connected with it were transferred to ordination. Marion Hatchett observes, "Ordination was in effect replacing baptism as initiation into the Church."[2]

A. T. Hanson rightly states that the New Testament does imply a distinction between clergy and laity in the modern sense of these terms but that the distinction is between

---

1. Lampe, *N.T. Ministry,* 2.
2. Marion J. Hatchett, *Commentary on the American Prayer Book* (New York: Seabury Press, 1980), 504.

those who lead in certain actions and those who are led. But the actions are not the actions of the clergy, but of the Church. Ordination does not confer authority to be the Church; it confers authority to act on behalf of the Church, and whatever the ordained man does (be it celebrating the Eucharist or granting absolution) the laity on behalf of whom he acts do it in some sense also through him.[3]

However, Hanson's statement that the idea of the clergy being a special group "marked out by the fact that they are empowered or permitted to perform certain actions which the laity are not permitted to perform" is "to introduce a distinction between clergy and laity which is quite alien to the New Testament" presses the evidence too far.[4] The very idea of an organic society implies that its various members have different functions, and it is quite clear that the gifts of the Spirit are distributed differentially among the baptized. Paul affirms this: "For as in one body we have many members, and not all the members have the same function, so we, who are many, are one body in Christ, and individually we are members one of another. We have gifts that differ according to the grace given to us" (Rom. 12:4–6). Paul then lists gifts such as prophecy, teaching, and ministering. There is little evidence in the New Testament to support such a confusion of ministries as is suggested by Hanson.

The basic argument here is essentially that of Eduard Schweizer, although he makes an exception of the office of "apostle":

> The New Testament agrees that God does not bestow all the gifts of grace on every Church member. . . . The apostle is marked out from the rest by his special call from the risen Lord; but he is the one who regards his ministry as teamwork with fully authorized fellow workers. . . . Except for the apostolic ministry, therefore, which is unique through a special call, no ministry in the New Testament is forbidden to any member of the Church. It is only in the Pastorals that women are excluded from preaching and that an age limit is fixed for widows. Otherwise, God decides by his gift what ministry is to be performed by one, what by another. The Church can confirm this by its order, but it must remain open to God's correction, and must not, through its order, completely exclude others from that ministry. . . . It is God's spirit who marks out in freedom the pattern that Church order afterwards recognizes; it is therefore functional, regulative, serving, but not constitutive, and that is what is decisive.[5]

There appears to be a subtle but fundamental contradiction in the position taken by Hanson and Schweizer. On the one hand, they do recognize and assert that God has called the varying members of the Church to different ministries and given them varying gifts for these ministries ("God does not bestow all the gifts of grace on every Church member") but on the other hand, they maintain that all

---

3. A. T. Hanson, "Shepherd, Teacher, and Celebrant in the New Testament Conception of the Ministry," in *New Forms of Ministry,* ed. David M. Paton, Research Pamphlets No. 12, World Council of Churches Commission on World Mission and Evangelism (London: Edinburgh House Press, 1965), 17.

4. Ibid.

5. Schweizer, *Church Order in the New Testament,* 203–4.

can perform the same function ("Except for the apostolic ministry . . . no ministry in the New Testament is forbidden to any member of the Church").

Yet an organic society is not so constituted. In the human body the eye cannot perform the function of the nose, nor the heart of the lungs. The same is true of the Church. Käsemann shows how often the watchword "To each his own" occurs in connection with charisma in the ministry of the primitive Church. The Spirit gives to each Christian what is needed for his or her particular ministry for the benefit of the whole: "There is differentiation in the divine generosity. . . . No one goes away empty, but no one has too much." Each is responsible to use the gifts given by the Spirit responsibly in accord with the particular grace given.[6]

More than anything else it is probably because the Church largely came to act as though the clerical ministry could perform all the functions of the Church's ministry that some have come to deny any special power or position to any ministry or function. Much theology has maintained in effect that the clerical ministry was the essence of the ministry, if not the whole ministry. Although we may tend to think of Catholic Christianity as being the offender here with its all-encompassing clerical ministry, certainly Protestant Christianity has not escaped from such clericalism. But as we shall see later, this type and degree of confusion of function was foreign to the pre-Nicene Church.

Further, it is to be noted that the Church has always sought to confirm by its order those whom God has chosen, although at times individuals within the Church have shown little regard for this concern. But to maintain, as Schweizer does, that church order is "functional, regulative, serving, but not constitutive, and that is what is decisive" would seem to lead to a kind of subjectivism that is not in accord with the record of Scripture and that serves to weaken the unity of the Church. The place of Judas was filled by Matthias through casting lots. He thereby became (although we are not told whether there was any other manner of appointment) one of the Twelve (Acts 1:21–26). This would appear constitutive. Acts 6 tells us that the people chose the Seven, who were to be appointed by the Twelve, to provide for the distribution to the Hellenist widows. (But note the discussion of Acts 6 regarding the reason for the appointment of the Seven in the next chapter.) Through prayer and the laying on of hands by the Twelve, Luke writes, they were constituted to their office with apparent effectiveness. We read immediately that Stephen, "full of grace and power, did great wonders and signs among the people" (Acts 6:8). Peter and John go from Jerusalem to Samaria to give apostolic approval to the converts of Philip in Samaria and bestow the Holy Spirit through the laying on of hands according to Acts 8:14–17. The elders of 1 Timothy 4:14 convey the Spirit through the laying on of hands and in verse 22 Timothy is warned about being hasty in laying on hands. Paul is said to have given Timothy the "gift of God" through the laying on of hands in 2 Timothy 1:6.

Even if the gift of the Spirit through the hands of the apostles in Acts 8 is

---

6. Käsemann, *N.T. Themes,* 76, 77.

the insertion of material from other sources by the Lukan author, as Käsemann convincingly argues,[7] and although the Pastorals are not genuinely Pauline, the instances are still part of the tradition of the Church recorded in canonical Scripture and do illustrate that church order is constitutive even in the New Testament.

A major concern of Schweizer and others is to maintain the freedom of the Holy Spirit to work in the Church. However, it is surely limiting the freedom of the Spirit to argue that he does not act here in a constitutive way. Further, this is not to say that this type of church order even concerned the whole of the Church's ministry. It did not. To say that God does act through his Church in answer to its prayers in granting the grace of particular functions is not to limit God to that only. Nor does it insure that the one who receives the grace will use it. But it does make order in the Church possible by providing a degree of objectivity.

Sent with Authority

Two words sum up the basic characteristics of the ministry both of Jesus and of those exercising the various ministries of the New Testament Church. They are "sent" (*apostellein*) and "serve" (*diakonein*).[8] So central is the first of these characteristics that Bishop Frank Wilson wrote at the outset of his book on church history, "Our Lord did not write a book; neither did He erect an organization. The one thing He did was to issue a Divine Commission to certain selected persons which Commission they were to perpetuate."[9] While this statement standing alone might be interpreted as neglecting particularly Jesus' empowering of the Church, it does serve to point out the essential "sentness" of the Church.

However, the divine commission that Jesus had and then transmitted to his disciples went beyond simply being "sent" as we would understand this today. Peder Borgen in an essay entitled "God's Agent in the Fourth Gospel"[10] discusses the Jewish concept of agentry as it was understood in the *halakah,* the name used for authoritative Jewish law seen as a way of life and for rabbinic literature dealing with the law.[11] Borgen says that the basic principle of agentry as an institution in Judaism was judicial and may be expressed as "an agent is like the one who sent him." This principle is similar to that of a "power of attorney" in American law today. The agent could act for the sender as though the agent

---

7. Ibid., 85–89.

8. Lampe, *N.T. Ministry,* 3. Cf. Shepherd, "Ministry, Christian," 386.

9. Frank E. Wilson, *The Divine Commission: A Sketch of Church History* (New York: Morehouse-Gorham, 1946), 3 (original in italics).

10. Peder Borgen, "God's Agent in the Fourth Gospel," in *Religions in Antiquity: Essays in Memory of Erwin Ramsdell Goodenough,* ed. Jacob Neusner, Studies in the History of Religions 14 (Leiden, Netherlands: E. J. Brill, 1968), 137–48.

11. *An Encyclopedia of Religion,* ed. Vergilius Ferm (New York: Philosophical Society, 1945), s.v. "Halakah," by Ben Zion Bokser.

were the sender, as in buying or selling property. However, Borgen says that this concept was developed by rabbis into a "judicial mysticism" in which "the agent is a person identical with the sender. Thus not only his authority and his function are derived from the sender, but also his qualities." But the identification is modified to the extent that the sender is seen to be superior to the agent. The agent was to be obedient to the sender, carrying out the mission given by the sender, and could transfer his agency to another.[12] When one dealt with the agent, one dealt with the sender. Their identities were virtually indistinguishable.

Borgen cites parallels between texts and ideas of agency in the Fourth Gospel and *halakhic* teaching. He convincingly concludes,

> Thus there are striking similarities between the halakhic principles of agency and ideas on the Fourth Gospel, as (a) the unity between the agent and his sender — (b) although the agent is subordinate, (c) the obedience of the agent to the will of the sender, (d) the task of the agent in the lawsuit, (e) his return and reporting back to the sender, and (f) his appointing of other agents as an extension of his own mission in time and space.[13]

Borgen's insight into agentry is helpful both in comprehending Jesus' self-understanding in relation to the Father and his commissioning his disciples — the Twelve, the Seventy, and us.

Jesus first of all knew himself to have been sent. Luke records the incident in the synagogue at Nazareth at the outset of Jesus' ministry when he stood up and read from Isaiah, " 'The Spirit of the Lord is upon me, because he has anointed me to bring good news to the poor. He has sent me to proclaim release to the captives and recovery of sight to the blind.' " Afterwards, he said, "Today this scripture has been fulfilled in your hearing" (Luke 4:16–21). He was "sent for this purpose," to "proclaim the good news of the kingdom of God to the other cities also" (Luke 4:43; cf. Matt. 15:24). In another context he says, "Whoever welcomes me welcomes not me but the one who sent me" (Mark 9:37). It is the Father who has sent him: "The works that the Father has given me to complete, the very works that I am doing, testify on my behalf that the Father has sent me."[14]

Jesus then sent the Twelve. In what appears to be a training mission, Matthew tells us that they are sent at this point only to "the lost sheep of the house of Israel," but their commission is later made universal.[15] They are to extend Jesus' work of healing and casting out demons (Matt. 10:1, 8). Mark reports that they are also to "proclaim the message" (Mark 3:14). Luke records the appointment and sending first of the Twelve and then of the Seventy, indicating that Jesus extended the number of those sent to do his work in the world beyond the Twelve, whatever the meaning of the number seventy (or seventy-two)

---

12. Borgen, "God's Agent in the Fourth Gospel," 138–40, 143.
13. Ibid., 143–44.
14. John 5:36ff. Cf. Acts 3:26; 1 John 4:9, 10, 14; John 3:16–17; 6:29, 57; 7:29 et al.
15. Matt. 10:5–6 (cf. Mark 6:7–13); Matt. 28:16–20 (cf. Acts 1:8).

(Luke 9:1–6, 10:1–12). The Spirit sends Barnabas and Saul after selecting them (Acts 13:2–4). Paul speaks of himself as one who is sent: "For Christ did not send me to baptize but to proclaim the gospel" (1 Cor. 1:17; cf. Acts 26:16–17). Indeed, the idea that Jesus has sent his Church into the world is implied in the fact that the principal forms of ministry are gifts to the Church: apostles, prophets, evangelists, pastors, and teachers (Eph. 4:11). The idea underlies the whole of New Testament thought.[16]

Jesus possessed both power and authority from God, so much so that people were amazed (Mark 1:22, 27). He corrected the Mosaic Law, which was to the Jews of ancient Israel divinely instituted (Matt. 5:22, 28, 32, 34, 39, 44). He exorcised demons, which was either a divine or demonic activity (Luke 11:14–20), and healed all manner of disease.[17] He forgave sins, a prerogative belonging only to God.[18] He claimed authority over life and death, as given to him by his Father (John 10:18). The power to give eternal life to humanity had been committed to him by his Father (John 17:2). Indeed, he had been given "all authority in heaven and on earth" (Matt. 28:18; cf. Eph. 1:21–23). The idea of "sending" is closely related to that of "authority" in the sending of the disciples, and especially of the Twelve, as it is with Jesus' own commission. The Twelve are given authority specifically to heal the sick and cast out demons, to preach, and to baptize.[19] The Seventy are sent with power to heal and have "authority . . . over all the power of the enemy" (Luke 10:9, 19). Peter is given the authority to "bind" and to "loose," an authority that is later extended to "the disciples" (Matt. 16:19, 18:18). In John's gospel the Holy Spirit is given to "the disciples" on Easter Day and is associated with the apostolic mission, "defined here, however, not as kerygma but as the forgiving and retaining of sins," the latter being a probable reference to Baptism, not the sacrament of penance.[20]

Jesus sends the disciples forth with his own power and authority, "As the Father has sent me, so I send you" (John 20:21–23). We might note also that Paul as well was given authority (2 Cor. 10:8), having been called to be an apostle (Rom. 1:1; Gal. 1:1).

---

16. Lampe, *N.T. Ministry,* 5.

17. Matt. 4:23–24; Mark 1:23–45; Luke 4:23, 33ff; John 4:46ff.

18. Mark 2:3–12. Cf. Matt. 9:1–8; Luke 5:17–26.

19. Mark 3:14–15, 6:7; Matt. 10:7–8, 28:19 (where it is the Eleven); Luke 9:1–2, 21.

20. John 20:23. Reginald Fuller states that in this passage as in Acts

the Spirit empowers the Church for its mission ("even as I send you"). The mission is defined here, however, not as kerygma but as the forgiving and retaining of sins. The traditional Catholic and High Anglican interpretation of this has seen it as a reference to the sacrament of penance, but this is probably an anachronism as far as the evangelist is concerned. In the New Testament, forgiveness of sins is baptismal language (see Luke 24:47), and what we have here is the Johannine version of the tradition, which includes in the appearance stories the command to baptize.

Preaching the Lectionary: The Word of God for the Church Today, rev. ed. (Collegeville, Minn.: Liturgical Press, 1984), 99.

To Serve

The thing that stands out above all else in the sending forth of the Church then is that it is sent with power and authority to extend the work of Jesus in the world. This work is service, *diakonia,* the second great characteristic of the ministry of Jesus and of the Church.

The word *diakonos* (deacon) literally means a servant and in particular a waiter.[21] However, this literal meaning of "waiter" should not mislead one to see the diaconate, either in its origin or as it emerged in the early Church, as an office simply of menial service or even one limited to works of mercy and charity. The meaning of "waiter" signifies that the attitude of the disciples of Jesus is ever to be one of humility in serving others.

Most of the New Testament uses of *diakonos, diakonia,* and *diakoneō* clearly bear the general meaning of service and were applied to Christ and to all sorts of others.[22] In its noun form, *diakonos* occurs thirty times in the New Testament and ranges in meaning from the most menial service, as in Mark 9:35, to the highest service of God, as in Colossians 1:23.[23] Jesus uses the word of himself: "I am among you as one who serves (*diakoneō*)" (Luke 22:27), the context emphasizing the kind of service denoted by "serving at tables." Again when James and John asked for the chief places of honor, Jesus contrasted the way of the world with the example of his life, saying that "whoever wishes to become great among you must be your servant, and whoever wishes to be first among you must be slave of all. For the Son of Man came not to be served but to serve (*diakoneō*)."[24] He also by implication again applies the term to himself by saying that when the master of the house returns from the wedding feast and finds his servants waiting, "he will fasten his belt and have them sit down to eat, and he will come and serve (*diakoneō*) them" (Luke 12:37).

Paul says that Jesus became a "servant" (*diakonos*) to the Jews to show God's truthfulness in order that the promises given to the patriarchs might be confirmed and the Gentiles might glorify God (Rom. 15:8). He applies the word *diakonos* again to Jesus in asking if his critics would be right under the circumstances in claiming that Christ is a "servant (*diakonos*) of sin" (Gal. 2:17).

Paul also uses this term to describe himself and his own ministry: He was made "a servant" (*diakonos*) of the gospel (Eph. 3:7; cf. Gal. 1:23) and also of the Church (Col. 1:23, 25). He describes Epaphrus as a "servant" (*diakonos*) of Christ and Timothy as his "co-worker [*diakonos*] for God" (Col. 1:7; 1 Thess. 3:2) and uses the term in the plural of himself and others.[25] He also describes

---

21. Hans Lietzmann, *A History of the Early Church.* Vol. 1, *The Beginnings of the Christian Church.* Vol. 2, *The Founding of the Church Universal,* trans. Bertram Lee Woolf (New York: World Publishing, Meridian Books, 1961), 155. Cf. Lampe, *N.T. Ministry,* 5–6.

22. C. F. D. Moule, "Deacons in the New Testament," *Theology* 58 (1955): 405–7.

23. Burton Scott Easton, *The Pastoral Epistles* (New York: Scribner's, 1947), 181.

24. Mark 10:43–45. Cf. Matt. 20:26–28; Luke 22:24–27; Mark 9:35.

25. 1 Cor. 3:5; 2 Cor. 3:6, 6:4, 11:23.

the civil authority as "God's servant" (*diakonos*) (Rom. 13:4) and uses the term elsewhere for the servants of Satan (2 Cor. 11:15).

The "ministry" of the Twelve is referred to as *diakonia* in reference to filling the place of Judas (Acts 1:17, 25). The "varieties of services" (*diakonia*) mentioned by Paul include "serving [*diakonia*] the word," "the ministry [*diakonia*] of reconciliation," and "the ministry [*diakonia*] of the Spirit."[26] In Romans Paul refers to his "ministry" to Jerusalem as *diakonia* (15:31) and in 2 Corinthians calls the "ministry" of the Church at Corinth for that at Jerusalem *diakonia* (9:1).

In the Gospels certain women of Galilee are said to have "provided [*diakoneō*] for" Jesus (Mark 15:41; cf. Matt. 27:55). The "service of tables" is implied by Luke in connection with Martha's work (10:40) and made explicit in this regard by John (12:2). There is a definite financial connotation when Luke records that a number of women "provided for" (*diakoneō*) Jesus and the Twelve "out of their resources" (8:3) and again when Paul goes to Jerusalem "in a ministry [*diakoneō*] to the saints" (Rom. 15:25). Timothy and Erastus are those who help (*diakoneō*) Paul (Acts 19:22).

From these references it becomes clear that the word "service" (*diakonia*) has broad application including widely varied forms of service and is the key New Testament word for the ministry of the Church and the word "servant" (*diakonos*) is key for those who exercise the function of ministry.[27] It is also readily apparent that this ministry points in two directions at the same time.[28] It has first of all been sent by God in Christ and therefore has God as its source and reference point. Second, it has been sent to serve others, all others, but especially those in the Church (Gal. 6:10; John 13:34).

In his recent work John N. Collins, an Australian "laicised" Roman Catholic priest who teaches religious education, maintains that contemporary conceptualization of *diakonia* and its cognates derives from the work of Wilhelm Brandt and H. W. Beyer, the latter being the more influential through his word study of *diakonia* in Kittel's *Theological Dictionary of the New Testament,* originally published in German in 1935.[29] In the words of H. W. Beyer, who acknowledged his indebtedness to Brandt, *diakonia* is narrowly defined as "active Christian love for the neighbor." In this view, *diakonia* is more or less limited to "a service of love" in the doing of works of mercy and charity, often with menial or servile connotations. Collins writes, "In fact all advocacy of 'diakonia' is

---

26. 1 Cor. 12:5; Acts 6:4; 2 Cor. 5:18, 3:8.

27. Cf. Moule, "Deacons in the New Testament," 405; Lampe, *N.T. Ministry,* 6; Urban T. Holmes III, *The Future Shape of Ministry: A Theological Projection* (New York: Seabury Press, 1971), 17 (hereafter cited as Holmes, *Future Shape*); J. C. Lambert and George Johnston, "Minister," in *Dictionary of the Bible,* ed. James Hastings, rev. ed. Frederick C. Grant and H. H. Rowley (New York: Scribner's, 1963), 662.

28. Lampe, *N.T. Ministry,* 6.

29. John N. Collins, *Diakonia: Re-interpreting the Ancient Sources* (New York: Oxford University Press, 1990), 6. The reference is to Gerhard Kittel's *Theological Dictionary of the New Testament,* trans. and ed. Geoffrey W. Bromiley (Grand Rapids: Eerdmans, 1964–76).

ultimately founded on the work of one or the other of these writers."[30] Certainly, this is an overstatement. The restoration of the diaconate in the Roman Catholic, Anglican, and American Evangelical Lutheran churches is founded on knowledge of the diaconate in the early Church, and it envisions and includes liturgical functions and other types of pastoral and societal functions that would not be classified as works of mercy or charity as well.

Collins's linguistic study is of *diakonia* in late classical and early Christian writings. He finds *diakonia* and its related forms in three contexts, those of "message," "agency," and "attendance upon a person or in a household," and speaks of roles such as diplomatic messengers, servants of merchants or land owners who act as their agents in purchasing or legal matters, and maids sent to the market for household needs.[31] There is no doubt that an agency relationship exists in these functions, but an agent serves and acts as the servant of the person or group for whom the service is done. "Servant" and "service" have broader, more inclusive meanings than "agent" or "agency" and in the context of the New Testament generally convey more fully the meaning of *diakonos* and *diakonia*.

As we seek to discover the character of the diaconate and the meaning of *diakonia* in the early Church, word studies such as that by Collins may offer some insight, but the functions in which the deacons are involved are the more determinative factor. To the extent that Collins is correct in his observation that *diakonia* has been narrowly defined as charitable works, the modern conceptualization of *diakonia* is inadequate. It is true that the emphasis on charitable works to the exclusion of other types of service in the restoration of the diaconate has sometimes been excessive. For example, some diaconal programs require training in hospital ministry for all diaconal candidates and expect all diaconal candidates to develop ministries of a charitable nature. The deficiency in this narrow conceptualization is apparent from the use of the word with widely varied meanings in the New Testament and the writings of the fathers and the history of diaconal functions in the early Church.

No Christian ministry may rightly be seen as menial or servile. Collins indicates that these terms are descriptive of at least much of diaconal ministry as it has developed in this century, due, he believes, to the prevailing influence of Brandt and Beyer. Menial and servile are defined as meaning "lacking in dignity" or being "cravenly submissive."[32] To think in these terms is to adopt the values of the world, contrary to the spirit and teaching of Christ. His own ministry was a ministry of humble service, as he forcefully declared, but in no respect menial or servile. Although his washing the feet of his disciples at the Last Supper in the Johannine tradition might well be so interpreted by the world, certainly the Church sees it differently. Jesus' laying aside his garments was an acted parable of humiliation, symbolizing first his humbling himself to

---

30. Collins, *Diakonia*.
31. Ibid., 335, 79, 90, 97, 125.
32. *Webster's Ninth New Collegiate Dictionary* (Springfield, Mass.: Merriam-Webster, 1991), s.v. "menial," "servile."

become incarnate and then to die for the sins of humankind.[33] Christ intended that all Christian ministry, of whatever kind, be that of humble service. "Whoever wishes to be great among you must be your servant, and whoever wishes to be first among you must be your slave" (Matt. 20:26–27). Status is created in Baptism, making all Christians sons and daughters of God himself. The true meaning of this status makes all worldly pretensions fade into nothingness.

Regrettably, Collins believes that Baptism is not the basic sacrament of ministry. He writes,

> In their authentically modern way churches are increasingly speaking of a common call to ministry that does not depend on ordination. . . . A ministry is a charge put upon someone, and those who gave us the language took it originally from a broadly religious background because they wanted to speak of churchly charges: for most, their ministries were commissions handed out by church authorities; for a few — very few — there was a sense of a ministry received instead directly from God.[34]

While it is probable that the charismatically called ministries referred to in the New Testament, such as the prophets and teachers, were considered to have received their ministries "directly from God," ministries generally in the New Testament and early Church are correctly seen as commissions in the sense that individuals were both called and commissioned by ordination or otherwise by the Church, but their ministries were not "commissions handed out by church authorities." Nor did the apostolic Church want to speak of "churchly charges." They deliberated avoided "churchly" terminology. Collins puts back into this early period a theology of ministry and of church structure which arose later, much later. Elsewhere he writes of a "local hierarchy" in the time of Ignatius of Antioch around the turn of the first century and says that Ignatius is "practically a monarchical figure," ascribing to the time of Ignatius the results of developments which took place in the fourth century, as will be discussed later.[35]

Collins sees the embodiment of "a new low theology of official or ordained ministry," legitimized by the work of Brandt and Beyer, in the statement of an Anglican Working Party relating to the theology of the laity which says that for bishops, priests, and laity alike "the great sacrament of our common calling is our baptism." Then, Collins observes, the statement appears to include virtually all areas of the lives of Christians in ministry, which he says may rightly be described as *"diakonia"* or service, but not ministry. He continues,

> Saying this, however, is not the same as saying that all share in ministry, as if ministry were a global or churchwise reality that Christians are called to give

---

33. Fuller, *Preaching the Lectionary*, 60. Whether or not the incident is viewed as an act of the "historical Jesus," it is authoritative as canonical Scripture and does faithfully present a major aspect of the tradition found throughout the gospels arising from Jesus himself.

34. Collins, *Diakonia*, 258.

35. Ibid., 238–39.

expression to in their various activities and at different levels of the experience of life, or as if Christians were baptized into a ministerial condition.[36]

The recovery of an understanding of Baptism more in accord with that of the New Testament and early Church, one that might be called "a high theology" both of Baptism and of the laity, has led to a new understanding of the Church's ministry as belonging to all the baptized, and a reassessment, as yet incomplete, of the meaning of ordination. The recovery of this baptismal theology plus the realization that in the early Church and until the fourth century all the baptized were laity and the Church was structured horizontally rather than hierarchically have implications calling for theological concepts regarding the ministry and the structure of the Church different from those inherited from the Medieval period, which appear to underlie Collins' work.

There can be little doubt that Jesus intended to create a radically new consciousness in his disciples regarding their "ministry."[37] Under the Old Covenant all were well aware of the "service" they were to render to God in worship and obedience to his Law. However, they had little consciousness of being sent by God to serve the needs of their fellow human beings. Like the "Gentiles," they thought of greatness in terms of rank, power, and authority. Jesus clearly reversed this system of values:

> You know that the rulers of the Gentiles lord it over them, and their great ones are tyrants over them. It shall not be so among you; but whoever wishes to be great among you must be your servant, and whoever wishes to be first among you must be your slave; just as the Son of man came not to be served but to serve, and to give his life a ransom for many. (Matt. 20:25–28)

Again, in the great picture of the judgment Jesus makes humble service to others the crux of entrance into heaven. Those who fed the hungry, gave drink to the thirsty, welcomed the stranger, clothed the naked, and visited the sick and those in prison did it to Jesus: "Just as you did it to one of the least of these who are members of my family, you did it to me" (Matt. 25:31–46).

There is no doubt that the ministry implied here is to all those in need, regardless of who or what they are. However, an important point missed by a significant number of those involved with the diaconate today is that Jesus' command to love as recorded by John emphasizes loving fellow members of the Christian community. In his farewell discourse at the Last Supper, the new commandment he gives to the disciples is "that you love one another. Just as I have loved you, you also should love one another" (John 13:34). This speaks directly to the advocacy of a diaconate whose nonliturgical ministries are to be focused outside the Church to the exclusion of those directed toward the Christian community. When Christians are genuinely concerned to love one another with the love manifested in Jesus, this love overflows into the world and the

---

36. Ibid., 258.
37. Moule, "Deacons in the New Testament," 405.

world is drawn to seek the source of such love. Legitimate diaconal ministry certainly includes that directed both to the Church and to the world.

The quintessential character of Jesus' ministry and that of those who would follow him is epitomized in a most vivid and dramatic way at the Last Supper when he girded himself with a towel as the lowest household servant and washed the feet of his disciples, commanding his followers to do likewise (John 13:1–15). Jesus therein indelibly marked the character of the apostolic ministry as *diakonia*. This enacted parable from the thirteenth chapter of John's gospel could appropriately be read at the ordination of every deacon.

It is just here that we find a source of misunderstanding regarding Jesus' intention toward the organization and structure of his Church. He intended to change the character of the ministry of the Church under the New Covenant, that is of the whole body of the Church, from that of "exclusive privilege and ritual performance" to one of "lowly and devoted service" to others in the name of Christ.[38] But in speaking of this ministry and the word *diakonia* to describe it, Eduard Schweizer goes beyond affirming this point: "The very choice of the word, which still clearly involves the idea of humble activity, proves that the Church wishes to denote the attitude of one who is at the service of God and his fellow-men, not a position carrying with it rights and powers."[39]

The two ideas, an office created for humble service but possessing rights and powers, are not mutually exclusive. In fact, such things as the rights and powers given to the Twelve and exercised by them in Acts 16, the authority exercised by Paul over the churches he founded, the authority of the apostles and elders at Jerusalem in Acts 15, and the authority of other apostles, prophets, and teachers, among other factors, bear this out. Jesus certainly possessed authority and power and sent his disciples as he had been sent. He did not condemn or reject the order of the Old Covenant. He rather "fulfilled" it and established a new order in which service to God is service to others. The radically different thing is the attitude toward office and not the failure of an office to possess rights and authority. These, as we have seen, are necessary for order in any social organization.

It is not that Schweizer and others deny there were those in the Church who had rights and authority. Obviously, this was not the case even in the New Testament age. They instead hold that rights and authority were not attached to an office as such but rather simply belonged to those who exercised them. Schweizer avers,

> It is certainly quite true that the prophet has authority only as far and as long as his prophecy goes on. But exactly the same is true of the apostles and of the overseers, superintendents, elders, and whatever else they are called; for only where the apostle's words can really inwardly prevail in the Church do they become its real authority. It is certainly true that the Church acknowledges, or even

38. Lambert and Johnston, "Minister," 662.
39. Schweizer, *Church Order in the New Testament,* 177.

chooses, as its leaders those people from whom it has repeatedly experienced such authoritative guidance and who have proved themselves.[40]

The view here is not that of an organic society, where there is an inherent difference between members' functions. He maintains that every member of the Church can baptize, celebrate the Eucharist, and preach, arguing on this basis, "The assertion that the gift of grace is bestowed on *every* church member, and that therefore *every* member is called to service, is constant in the New Testament."[41]

It is true that in the New Testament every member of the Church has received the gift of grace and has been called to service; but what follows here is Paul's assertion, which runs throughout his writings, that all ministries are charismatic gifts of the Spirit. The gift of the Spirit's grace brings rather "varieties of service" (1 Cor. 12:5) such as we see in organic societies. In the natural family the father by virtue of his office can never fulfill the function either of the mother or of the child in that family, nor in the body can the hands do that of the vocal chords (1 Cor. 12:12–26). In the New Testament we find diversity of function and office, so that the Seven of Acts 6 are called to a special and apparently unique ministry and are appointed with prayer and the laying on of hands by the Twelve (Acts 6:1–6). Certainly in the Church at Jerusalem grace is bestowed by the Spirit for the office through the Church's prayer and the laying on of hands, even though the Spirit is not limited to the Church's selection and appointment to bestow gifts for various ministries within the Church.

The principle involved here is seen also in the Lukan tradition when Luke says the apostles at Jerusalem sent Peter and John to Samaria to investigate the preaching of the gospel there. According to the tradition, they prayed and laid hands on those who had been baptized for the receiving of the Holy Spirit, and they thereby did receive the Spirit (Acts 8:14–17), thus giving apostolic validation to the work of Philip.[42] Again in Acts Luke says that Paul baptized about twelve at Ephesus; and then, when he laid his hands on them, they received the Spirit (19:1–7). When the Spirit directed the prophets and teachers of the Church at Antioch to set apart Barnabas and Saul for the work he was calling them to do, they did so with fasting, prayer, and the laying on of hands. In this way apparently they were "sent out by the Holy Spirit" (Acts 13:1–4). The author of 1 Timothy speaks of not neglecting "the gift that is in you, which was given to you through prophecy with the laying on of hands by the council of elders" (1 Tim. 4:14).

The point in this connection is not so much about the laying on of hands (which is only the means) as the tradition recorded here.[43] Clearly, the Church

---

40. Ibid., 187.
41. Ibid., 187–88 (italics in original).
42. Käsemann, *N.T. Themes,* 166.
43. It is worth noting, however, that this is the means used by Jesus to bless the children (Mark 10:16) and to heal the sick at times (Mark 6:5; Luke 13:13).

was confident that God would give the Spirit to those upon whom its leaders laid their hands with prayer for specific purposes.

The New Testament does teach that ministerial function is given by the *charisma* of the Holy Spirit.[44] But it does not teach that the ministry of the Church is constituted as the wind, which "blows where it chooses, and you hear the sound of it, but you do not know where it comes from or where it goes." Jesus is speaking of the individual ("So it is with everyone who is born of the Spirit"; John 3:8) and the fact that the *source* of the inward power of the individual Christian is not apparent for the world to see. Rather than constituting the Church's ministry haphazardly, the Holy Spirit fills all the various ministries with his presence and power, at least to the degree that those exercising the ministries allow this chrism to be operative. It is this primary fact that we find expressed in Paul's writings. Although he speaks of the duty of his congregations to love, respect, and be subject to their leaders (1 Cor. 16:15–16; 1 Thess. 5:12–13), he has little to say about the "official ministries" of the Church other than that of apostle. He thought of ministry primarily as a function given by the grace of the Spirit and not in terms of office. And he saw it in the broadest terms: "It was an exercise by each and every member of the Church of his own charism of the Spirit to the edification of all. Even apostleship was to Paul a 'spiritual gift.' "[45]

Urban Holmes sees the most relevant text relating to Paul's conception of the ministry to be 1 Corinthians 12:28–31:

> And God has appointed in the church first apostles, second prophets, third teachers, then deeds of power, then gifts of healing, forms of assistance, forms of leadership, various kinds of tongues. Are all apostles? Are all prophets? Are all teachers? Do all work miracles? Do all possess gifts of healing? Do all speak in tongues? Do all interpret? But strive for the greater gifts.

He previously stated that, except for the "apostolate," the ministry for Paul is "essentially functional charismatic." He then states, "Here we do not have an authorized, ordained (i.e., a 'laying on of hands' by men in a certain office) ministry; but one whose validity was tested by its right teaching (1 Timothy 4:1, for example, is perhaps a reflection upon the dangers of a divisive charismatic ministry)."[46]

Holmes fails to make any distinction here between the first three "offices" and the others. Both C. K. Barrett and Reginald Fuller have noted that a twofold break in the sentence calls attention to an important distinction between the two groups.[47] The first three in the list refer to persons, the others to functions or gifts. Although the difference is somewhat blurred in the RSV and in many

---

44. Lampe, *N.T. Ministry,* 6.
45. Shepherd, "Ministry, Christian," 389.
46. Holmes, *Future Shape,* 14–15.
47. C. K. Barrett, *A Commentary on the First Epistle to the Corinthians* (New York: Harper & Row, 1968), 295 (hereafter cited as Barrett, *1 Corinthians*); Fuller, "Early Catholicism." Note the discussion on 1 Corinthians 12 in chap. 3, below, in the section, "Philippians 1:1."

other modern translations, it is made more apparent in the translation cited here from the NRSV. The King James Version follows more closely the Greek and reads "first apostles, secondarily prophets, thirdly teachers, after that helps, governments, diversities of tongues." Further, the numerical sequence ends after teachers, indicating that those which follow are of lesser consequence. Barrett notes that the first three have to do with the ministry of the word and observes, "This threefold ministry of the word is, according to Paul, the primary Christian ministry. By it the Church is founded, and built up."[48]

This certainly is not the picture that emerges in the second century with the monepiscopate, the term denoting the use of *episkopos* (bishop) to designate a single officer as president of the local Christian community, or even that in Acts and the Pastoral Epistles. However, Paul's concept of ministry in 1 Corinthians is more than that of a ministry "whose validity was tested by its right teaching." Right teaching is undoubtedly important to Paul. But the picture here starts with the apostle, who has been a witness to the resurrection and possessed authority, having been commissioned directly by the risen Christ.[49] The apostle may not have been ordained through the laying on of hands, but he was certainly authorized and commissioned.

The basis of the authority of prophets and teachers is not so apparent, but they undoubtedly do possess it in the Church. It is at least possible that, in light of the evidence we shall allude to in connection with the appointment of the bishops and deacons of Philippians 1:1 in the next chapter, the prophets and teachers at least were often appointed with the laying on of hands. If this is true, it might be interpreted more in the sense of connecting them with Paul and his authority and of Paul's recognition of their possessing the Spirit's charisma than of an ordination in which Paul conveyed the charisma. Those who worked miracles, healed, and spoke in tongues would need no special authority by the nature of their service. However, those who acted in administering the Church's affairs, if not also those who gave help to others, such as the needy, would need some form of authorization by the Church. These latter ministries are not concerned with teaching and so *could not* have been validated by "right teaching."

The important thing here is to see that the whole of the Church of the New Testament age was sent into the world with power and authority to serve. At least certain of its primary leaders were authorized and commissioned for special functions and held what may rightly be called "offices." However, the word *diakonia,* chosen by that Church to describe the ministry of all, is one that was under the Old Covenant unbiblical and nonreligious and excludes all pretensions to rank and status. All are sent for *diakonia,* for ministry that is exercised foremost in service to others.

---

48. Barrett, *1 Corinthians,* 295.
49. 1 Cor. 9; Rom. 1:1–6; 2 Cor. 10:8, 12:1–5.

Chapter 3

The Diaconate in the New Testament

Acts 6:1–6

It was natural that the specialized ministry of the deacon would develop to express in representative form the basic principle of the apostolic ministry which the whole Church was called upon to render.[1] The need for such an office developed very early in the life of the Church that had been "sent" into the world to "serve." The picture of the communal life of the Church in Jerusalem given in Acts shows that almost from the outset the Church found it necessary to appoint those who would assist in looking after its poor. The implication of Acts 6:1–6 is that the Christian community at Jerusalem had such "distributors" of food at the community's meals even before the appointment of the Seven.

The problem of the neglect of the "Hellenist" widows referred to in Acts 6:1 came about as "the disciples were increasing in number," Luke says, because those whom he calls "Hellenists" "complained against the Hebrews because their widows were being neglected in the daily distribution of food." The population of Jerusalem at that time included many Greek-speaking Jews ("Hellenists") who had been born abroad in the diaspora. Among these there were many devout Jews who had settled in Jerusalem toward the end of their lives in order to be buried near the Holy City. The Christian community had gained adherents from among these Jews, and there may have been a relatively large number of the Christian widows who were "Hellenists" and, therefore, were dependent upon charity, because they had no relatives in Jerusalem to take care of them.[2] Following Jewish custom, the Jerusalem Church apparently already had relief officers to distribute aid.[3]

---

1. Lukas Vischer, "The Problem of the Diaconate," in *The Ministry of Deacons,* ed. Department of Faith and Order (Geneva: World Council of Churches, 1965), 19. Cf. Moule, "Deacons in the New Testament," 405.

2. Ernst Haenchen, *The Acts of the Apostles: A Commentary* (Philadelphia: Westminster Press, 1971), 260–61.

3. Joachim Jeremias, *Jerusalem in the Time of Jesus* (Philadelphia: Fortress Press, 1969), 130–32. Cf. Haenchen, *The Acts of the Apostles,* 261–62. Kirsopp Lake, "The Communism of Acts 2 and 4–6 and the Appointment of the Seven," in *The Beginnings of Christianity,* vol. 5, pt. 1, *The Acts of the Apostles,* ed. F. J. Foakes Jackson and Kirsopp Lake (Grand Rapids: Baker Book House, 1979 5:148–49 (hereafter cited as Lake, "Communism of Acts 2 and 4–6").

The Twelve proposed the election of the Seven to the whole assembly of disciples. The reason they gave, according to Luke's account, that "it is not right that we should give up preaching the word of God to serve tables," does not imply that the Twelve had personally been handling the "daily distribution" but rather that they proposed the selection of others so that this would not become necessary for them in the future.[4] For the Twelve, prayer and the proclamation of the word are of first importance and must take precedence over social work.[5]

Critical study of this passage has led increasingly to the conclusion that a deeper problem existed in the Jerusalem Church than appears in Luke's account.[6] Lukas Vischer sees the activity of the Seven as "scarcely different from that of the apostles" and suspects that the Seven are appointed to "preserve unity" in a situation of tension much deeper than that noted in Acts between the Greek-speaking Christians ("Hellenists") and the Aramaic speaking Christians ("Hebrews") in Jerusalem.[7] Ernst Haenchen argues convincingly that this tension is basically due to the "Hellenists" led by Stephen, going far beyond the "Hebrews" in "the exercise of great freedom in relation to the law," so that in the Church's distributions to the poor, the "Hellenist" widows were deliberately neglected by the "Hebrews" in charge.[8]

Acts 6:12–14 gives evidence of such freedom of interpretation by recording that, when Stephen was arrested and brought before the council (the Sanhedrin), his accusers said, "This man never stops saying things against this holy place [the Temple, which was adjoined by the senate-house] and the law; for we have heard him say that this Jesus of Nazareth will destroy this place and will change the customs that Moses handed on to us." It is important to note that the Jews who objected to Stephen's teaching and instigated his arrest were not Palestinian Jews referred to as "Hebrews," but "Hellenists," those from the diaspora,[9] further indicating the distinctiveness of the "Hellenists." The destruction of the Temple and change of the customs given by Moses, which Stephen is accused of teaching, threatened "the whole Jewish system of civil and religious life."[10]

The freedom referred to is that taught by Jesus himself, as when his disciples broke the Mosaic Law by plucking ears of grain on the sabbath. Jesus justified this breach by saying, "The sabbath was made for humankind, and not humankind for the sabbath" (Mark 2:27). The Church generally would adopt

4. Haenchen, *The Acts of the Apostles,* 262. Cf. Richard B. Rackham, *The Acts of the Apostles,* 13th ed. (London: Methuen, 1947), 83.

5. Edward Echlin, *The Deacon in the Church Past and Future* (Staten Island, N.Y.: Alba House, Society of St. Paul, 1971), 8.

6. Haenchen gives a good detailed analysis of Acts 6:1–7 and a helpful summary of the history of criticism relative to the election of the Seven, in *The Acts of the Apostles,* 259–69.

7. Vischer, "The Problem of the Diaconate," 15–16.

8. Haenchen, *The Acts of the Apostles,* 268–69. Cf. G. W. H. Lampe, "Acts," in *Peake's Commentary of the Bible,* ed. Matthew Black and H. H. Rowley (London: Nelson, 1962), 893–94. Cf. Vischer, "The Problem of the Diaconate," 16. It might be observed, human nature being what it is, that in such a situation of tension the neglect could have been more imagined than real.

9. Haenchen, *The Acts of the Apostles,* 271. Cf. Rackham, *The Acts of the Apostles,* 89–90.

10. Rackham, *The Acts of the Apostles,* 91.

this freedom, but in the "Jewish period" of the Church, prior to the controversy over circumcision reported in Acts 15, there is ample evidence to indicate a much stricter view regarding the Law on the part of the Twelve and many other Jewish-Christians at Jerusalem, most of whom were probably Aramaic-speaking "Hebrews" in the sense of Acts 6.

Two such groups would explain why, immediately following the stoning of Stephen, in the "severe persecution" of the Jerusalem Church reported in Acts 8, "the apostles at Jerusalem" were *not* arrested. Stephen was killed, and then another of the Seven "Hellenist" leaders, Philip, is named as representing those who were "scattered" in this persecution and "went from place to place proclaiming the word" (Acts 8:4–5). Interestingly, Kirsopp Lake maintains that a major cause of the failure of the communal experiment of the Jerusalem Church, in which property was held in common, was that the Seven "administrators" were killed or driven out of Jerusalem.[11]

In contrast, Acts 8:14 clearly says that the apostles, including two of the Twelve, Peter and John, were still in Jerusalem, apparently living in peace. The inference, as drawn by Haenchen and others, that there were then two recognizably distinct groups within the primitive Christian community at Jerusalem — the "Hellenists" interpreting the Law with the freedom taught by Jesus and the "Hebrews" traditionally keeping the whole of the Mosaic Law — would explain first of all why the apostles were not touched by the persecution. At the same time it would also perhaps best account for the appointment of the Seven and their subsequent work as Acts describes it.[12] As Fuller suggests, the Seven were already leaders of the "Hellenists" at the time of their election, and their appointment stemmed from the concern of the Twelve to avoid a split between the two groups.[13]

The position of the Seven emerges then as one considerably different from that of those who wait on tables. The responsibility of the "daily distribution" for the Christian "Hellenist" widows was no doubt given them, but given them as the leaders of the "Hellenists" of the Christian community, not as those who personally distribute the food or act as table waiters. The evidence in Acts of the nature of the ministries of Stephen and Philip does lead to the conclusion, as Schweizer noted, that the Seven "stand out as men who have the gift of missionary preaching and a special insight into the new nature of the Church."[14]

The Seven then were chosen by the Church and commissioned for their work by the Twelve with prayer and the laying on of hands (Acts 6:5–6). The number "seven" could have suggested itself to the Twelve not only because it was a sacred number among the Jews[15] but also because in Jewish towns the lo-

---

11. Lake, "Communism of Acts 2 and 4–6," 141.
12. Haenchen, *The Acts of the Apostles,* 266–68. Cf. Fuller, *Preaching the Lectionary,* 82.
13. Fuller, *Preaching the Lectionary,* 82.
14. Schweizer, *Church Order in the New Testament,* 30.
15. Rackham, *The Acts of the Apostles,* 83.

cal council known as "the 'Seven of the Town' or 'Seven Best of the Town' " usually was composed of seven men.[16]

Vischer maintains that the appointment of the Seven gave them a special position, so that they worked "beside" and "not simply subordinate to" the apostles.[17] In the sense that they formed the leadership of the "Hellenists," a group sufficiently distinct so as to have been subject to severe persecution and scattered while the rest of the Christian community remained untouched, their position was "beside" the apostles. They functioned for the "Hellenist" Christians in the same role that the apostles did for the "Hebrew" Christians in Jerusalem. Their appointment by the Twelve with the laying on of hands, a practice taken from Judaism, "formally associated the seven with the twelve, as their deputies to discharge a special duty"[18] and was seen as directly transmitting to them blessing and power.[19] The Seven and the "Hellenists" were part of the larger primitive community and, as such, were subordinate to the Twelve. Their work appears to have been to act as delegates of the Twelve, perhaps foreshadowing such apostolic delegates as Timothy and Titus.

But the primitive Church did not think in terms of "subordination" as we do today. The subordination of the Seven is not that which was to develop later. We do not find rank and dignity of office there. Rather the subordination is one simply of authoritative leadership exercised for the welfare of the community.

Further, the Seven are not called "deacons" in Acts or elsewhere in the New Testament, and it is virtually certain that they did not hold that office.[20] Their office was unique and was not continued in the Church.[21] The word "deacon" is, in fact, never used in Acts.[22] In reviewing recent research on ministries in the New Testament, André Lemaire reports that the majority of scholars support this conclusion: the Seven were not deacons.[23]

However, although they were not deacons, they are significant to the diaconate in that from an early time the idea Luke conveys in Acts of the Seven

---

16. Haenchen, *The Acts of the Apostles*, 263.

17. Vischer, "The Problem of the Diaconate," 16.

18. F. F. Bruce, *Commentary on the Book of the Acts*, The New International Commentary on the New Testament (Grand Rapids: Eerdmans, 1956), 130–31. Reginald Fuller suggests that the laying on of hands reflects the practice at the time Luke wrote rather than that of the Jerusalem Church of the time, although stating that "ordination by the laying on of hands with prayer must have been introduced in a Palestinian-Jewish environment, for it reflects the practice of ordaining elders" (*Preaching the Lectionary*, 82).

19. Haenchen, *The Acts of the Apostles*, 264. Cf. Rackham, *The Acts of the Apostles*, 85.

20. Moule, "Deacons in the New Testament," 406–7. Cf. Haenchen, *The Acts of the Apostles*, 265–66; Rackham, *The Acts of the Apostles*, 86; Fuller, *Preaching the Lectionary*, 185; G. H. C. Macgregor, "Exegesis," "The Acts of the Apostles," in *The Interpreter's Bible*, 12 vols. (New York: Abingdon Press, 1954), 9:90–91; Echlin, *The Deacon in the Church Past and Future*, 7–8.

21. Vischer, "The Problem of the Diaconate," 16. Cf. Macgregor, "Exegesis," "The Acts of the Apostles," 9:90–91. But for an opposing view, see Easton, *The Pastoral Epistles*, 182–83.

22. Massey H. Shepherd Jr., "Deacon," in *The Interpreter's Dictionary of the Bible*, 5 vols. (New York: Abingdon Press, 1961), 4:785. Cf. Rackham, *The Acts of the Apostles*, 86.

23. André Lemaire, "The Ministries in the New Testament: Recent Research," *Biblical Theology Bulletin* 3, no. 2 (June 1973): 147.

as caring for the needs of the poor and less fortunate came to be looked to as a model for the diaconate.[24] The office held by the Seven, however, as it is described in the ministries of Stephen and Philip, does not serve as a model for the deacon either as it originated or developed in the early Church.

Irenaeus (c. 185) was the first of the early Church writers to call the Seven deacons. In writing of Stephen's speech to the Sanhedrin in his work *Against Heresies,* Irenaeus speaks of "Stephen, who was chosen the first deacon by the Apostles."[25] Irenaeus was apparently reading back into the history of the primitive Church at Jerusalem the idea that the Seven were deacons because of Luke's statement in Acts 6 that the Twelve said they should not neglect their ministry of the word to "wait tables" and that seven men should be selected by the community for the task.

Although many of the early fathers, following Irenaeus, did regard the Seven as deacons, the view was not universal and it does not appear to have significantly influenced the development of the office, probably due both to the fact that the basic character of the diaconate was already well established by the time the idea set forth by Irenaeus that the Seven were deacons became widely known and to its not having been accepted by many.

John Chrysostom wrote in one of his homilies and was later quoted with approval by the Council of Trullo (692) in reference to the question of their office:

> Was it that of deacons? But this office did not yet exist in the churches. But was it the dispensation of a presbyter? But there was not as yet any bishop, but only apostles, whence I think it is clear and manifest that neither of deacons nor of presbyters was there then the name.[26]

Canon 16 of Trullo concludes that "the Seven deacons are not to be understood as deacons who served at the mysteries" but were those who were entrusted with philanthropic works.

Since the Seven were called deacons by some of the early Church fathers and the philanthropic aspect of their office mentioned in Acts corresponds to some diaconal functions, facts about them recorded in Acts are worthy of our attention. First, we note that their qualifications are threefold: They are to be men of good reputation, full of the Spirit, and filled with wisdom (Acts 6:3). The only duty mentioned for them at their appointment is the responsibility to

---

24. Vischer, "The Problem of the Diaconate," 17.

25. Irenaeus, *Against Heresies* 3.12.10, in *The Apostolic Fathers with Justin Martyr and Irenaeus,* in *The Ante-Nicene Fathers: Translations of the Writings of the Fathers Down to A.D. 325,* ed. Alexander Roberts and James Donaldson, Amer. rpt. ed. A. Cleveland Coxe (Grand Rapids: Eerdmans, 1956), 1:434. Cf. 4.15.1, *Ante-Nicene Fathers,* 1:480, for an almost identical statement.

26. John Chrysostom, *Homily 14. On Acts 5:34,* in *St. Chrysostom: Homilies on the Acts of the Apostles and the Epistle to the Romans,* in *Nicene and Post-Nicene Fathers,* 1st ser., 11:90–91. However, the translation used here is a better rendering of the passage and is given in Canon 16 of Trullo, in *The Seven Ecumenical Councils,* ed. Henry R. Percival, in *Nicene and Post-Nicene Fathers of the Christian Church, A Select Library of the,* 2d ser., 14 vols., ed. Philip Schaff and Henry Wace (Grand Rapids: Eerdmans, 1956), 14:373.

see to the "daily distribution" for the "Hellenist" widows. This would have included "serving tables" at the common meal of the community as well as other distributions.[27] However, it is probable that the Seven fulfilled this responsibility through the assistance of others, just as it is assumed the Twelve did,[28] rather than making the actual distribution themselves. In this respect they might be termed "charity commissioners," as Kirsopp Lake calls them.[29]

However, the picture of the ministries of Stephen and Philip in Acts, which may well be illustrative of the Seven, is of another kind. Although Norbert Brockman says that what both Stephen and Philip are reported doing in Acts is essentially "catechetical instruction" and would be an appropriate type of witness for any good Christian,[30] they appear to function much like the apostles, particularly in the proclamation of the word and in working miracles (Acts 6:8). Not only does Stephen address the council (Sanhedrin) with what may be called a sermon (Acts 7:1–53), but the "false witnesses" set up against him accuse him of being one who "never ceases to speak words against this holy place and the law" (Acts 6:13). Philip goes down to Samaria to proclaim Christ, his mission being so effective that multitudes are reported to have heeded what he said, witnessed the miracles he did, and been baptized (Acts 8:4–13). He converts and baptizes the Ethiopian eunuch (Acts 8:26–40). Philip is also called an evangelist (Acts 21:8).

It is significant that, in spite of the important place preaching had in the ministries of Stephen and Philip, and even though the Seven were thought by some to have been deacons from the time of Irenaeus, preaching was not part of the deacon's function as the office developed in the Church of the sub-apostolic age so far as is known, and it did not become so in the early Church.

In light of the evidence from Scripture and the early Church and of recent scholarship regarding the controversy and appointment of the Seven in Acts 6, we must conclude that the Seven were *not* deacons.

Philippians 1:1

In the opening verse of Paul's letter to the Philippians he addresses "all the saints in Christ Jesus who are at Philippi, with the bishops and deacons." It is noteworthy that the NRSV gives "overseers and helpers," the English meaning of the Greek words, as an alternate translation for "bishops and deacons." Some authorities understand "bishops and deacons" to refer simply to the function of exercising oversight and of serving the Christian community.[31] Others, like F. W.

---

27. Acts 2:46 speaks of the daily meal; Acts 4:35 mentions other distributions.

28. Rackham, *The Acts of the Apostles,* 83.

29. Lake, "Communism of Acts 2 and 4–6," 149.

30. Norbert Brockman, *Ordained to Service: A Theology of the Permanent Diaconate* (Hicksville, N.Y.: Exposition Press, 1976), 8.

31. For example, Bo Reicke, "Deacons in the New Testament and in the Early Church," in *The Ministry of Deacons,* ed. Department of Faith and Order, 10. Cf. Lietzmann, *A History of the Early Church,* 1:146.

Beare, see them as officers but not in the technical sense.[32] It is true that Paul's inclusion of these terms in his address is unique here. But we must remember that in this period in which "status" has little meaning or place and the Church is characterized by a truly organic nature, it would have been natural simply to address the Church as a whole in a given place without mention of any particular officers, as we find in Paul's other letters. In this instance the occasion for singling out "bishops and deacons" probably arises from their special responsibility in collecting and sending the gift to Paul for which he thanks the Church there.[33] But that they were singled out is in itself a strong indication that they were recognized officials of the Church at Philippi.

Fuller asserts that the ministries of the Pauline churches are essentially charismatic, being "set" in the Church by God.[34] He interprets the "bishops and deacons" of Philippians 1:1 in the light of the list in 1 Corinthians 12:28, which he sees to be the most important of the charismatic lists because it is systematic. As we noted earlier, the first three of the list, apostles, prophets, and teachers, are people. The rest are gifts or powers, which are exercised temporarily and so do not attach themselves to persons. Among these are "governments" or "forms of leadership" corresponding to the "bishops" of Philippians 1:1 and "helps" or "forms of assistance" corresponding to the "deacons" of that passage.[35] Although Fuller sees these bishops and deacons to be charismatics, he rightly assigns a difference to them. First, although they correspond to the "governments" and "helps" of 1 Corinthians 12, they also correspond to the "apostle, prophets, and teachers" in that they are people. Therefore, the charismatic gifts tend to attach themselves to the persons, and the "bishops and deacons" exercise their functions on a more or less permanent basis. This difference, he asserts, is a step toward "Early Catholicism," the term denoting a time in which the traditional offices are already present.

It would also appear that officials always existed who exercised pastoral and administrative responsibilities side by side with the apostles, prophets, and teachers, to whom Paul assigns special precedence. They may have been volunteers at first, but gradually they must have acquired official recognition.[36]

The question of their appointment or commissioning through prayer and the laying on of hands must remain speculative. Fuller believes that there is no or-

---

32. F. W. Beare, *A Commentary of the Epistle to the Philippians* (New York: Harper & Brothers, 1959), 49; Ernest F. Scott, "The Epistle to the Philippians," in *The Interpreter's Bible,* 12 vols. (New York: Abingdon Press, 1955), 11:16.

33. J. Hugh Michael, *The Epistle of Paul to the Philippians,* The Moffatt New Testament Commentary (New York: Harper & Brothers, n.d.), 6–7. Cf. Shepherd, "Ministry, Christian," 3:390; Reicke, "Deacons in the New Testament and in the Early Church," 10.

34. Fuller, "Early Catholicism." Cf. Vischer, "The Problem of the Diaconate," 18; Käsemann, *N.T. Themes,* 63–94, esp. 81.

35. Cf. J. N. D. Kelly, *A Commentary on the Pastoral Epistles: 1 Timothy, 2 Timothy, Titus* (New York: Harper & Brothers, 1963), 81 (hereafter cited as Kelly, *Pastoral Epistles*).

36. Ibid., 71–72.

dination, as we know it, recorded in Paul's writings.[37] However, these Jewish Christians almost from the beginning seem to have used the long-revered Judaic sign of laying on of hands to authorize and empower those appointed to serve as leaders in the Church. Luke says the Seven of Acts 6 are so appointed by the Twelve with fasting and prayer after election by the Jerusalem community. When the Holy Spirit directs prophets at Antioch to "set apart" Barnabas and Saul for their missionary work, it is done by the laying on of hands after fasting and prayer (Acts 13:1–3). Although there is no question of ordination conveying power and authority for ministry here, but rather the sign of blessing for their work as they were sent forth, it does indicate its use and associate it with Paul. Luke's statement in Acts 14:23 that Barnabas and Paul appointed elders in every church with fasting and prayer represents a tradition of such long standing that Luke assumes it to have been true, although apparently he is reading the appointment of elders back into the founding of the Pauline churches.[38]

In light of such evidence it is not unreasonable to believe it even likely that Paul used this sign of appointment to recognize, authorize, and confirm charismatic ministries, especially the chief ones of prophet and teacher, as he founded his churches. It is certainly possible that the "bishops and deacons" of Philippians 1:1 were commissioned through the laying on of hands with prayer, although if this is true it is probable that it did not possess the full meaning of later ordination. As G. W. H. Lampe has stated,

> There is no sufficient evidence to suggest that the exercise of the ancient sign of delegation of authority (and of spiritual blessing), the imposition of hands, was confined to those possessing any particular status in the Church; until Christian unity began to be threatened, and until the ministry came to be associated with the Old Testament priesthood, the importance of the rite was probably not so overwhelmingly great as we should naturally expect it to be.[39]

Käsemann sees ordination with the same meaning it had in Judaism only in the Pastorals, 1 Timothy 4:14, 5:22, and 2 Timothy 1:6. Along with most Pauline scholars he regards these as not genuinely Pauline but rather as representing Christian communities with Pauline characteristics in the province of Asia. Here ordination originating in the Jewish-Christian communities is brought into the Pauline communities. As in Judaism, it bestows the Spirit and gives special authorization and power to administer the *depositum fide,* the faith as contained in the Pauline tradition.[40]

In addition, in view of Paul's failure to mention bishops and deacons anywhere else (in this connection at least), and of his use of different terms in his other letters for those who perform various tasks in the Church, it is reasonable to think that there was no uniform structure of offices in the Pauline churches of

---

37. Fuller, "Early Catholicism."
38. Haenchen, *The Acts of the Apostles,* 436.
39. Lampe, *N.T. Ministry,* 14–15.
40. Käsemann, *N.T. Themes,* 86–87.

the early New Testament period.[41] However, when we add the clear emergence of these offices in their technical sense by the late New Testament period and their probable origin in the Pauline churches to what has already been said, we must conclude that these "bishops and deacons" are officers of the Church at Philippi and not simply men exercising leadership.[42]

This is, however, not to say that either the diaconate or the episcopate of the Church at Philippi was the more fully developed office of the second century.[43] No mention is made here of the functions of the "bishops and deacons," so we cannot know the exact nature of their offices at this date, c. 60.[44] It is apparent that the deacons are associated with the bishops in the leadership of the Church. They represent the first stage of the office as it emerges in more developed form in the Pastoral Epistles. Philippians 1:1 is, then, to be considered the first reference in the New Testament to the specific office of deacon.[45]

1 Timothy 3:8–13

Scholars generally agree that by the time of the later strata of the New Testament the term "deacon" is used unquestionably to denote the office in the technical sense.[46] Most of the New Testament information regarding the office is to be found in 1 Timothy 3:8–13. Although there is considerable divergence regarding the date of this epistle, it probably should be put early in the second century.[47]

We should note here that the offices of bishop and of deacon probably originated in the Pauline or Hellenistic churches, which had no presbyters during Paul's lifetime,[48] and that the office of presbyter probably originated in the

---

41. Vischer, "The Problem of the Diaconate," 17.

42. Among those supporting this view: J. B. Lightfoot, *St. Paul's Epistle to the Philippians* (1913; rpt., Grand Rapids: Zondervan, 1963), 95–99; Michael, *The Epistle of Paul to the Philippians,* 4–6; J. Müller, *The Epistles of Paul to the Philippians and to Philemon,* The International Commentary on the New Testament (Grand Rapids: Eerdmans, 1955), 35; Echlin, *The Deacon in the Church Past and Future,* 9; Lambert and Johnston, "Minister," 662; Moule, "Deacons in the New Testament," 406; Vischer, "The Problem of the Diaconate," 17.

43. Joseph A. Fitzmyer, "The Letter to the Philippians," in *The Jerome Bible Commentary,* 2 vols., ed. Raymond E. Brown, Joseph A. Fitzmyer, and Roland E. Murphy (Englewood Cliffs, N.J.: Prentice-Hall, 1968), 2:249. Cf. Echlin, *The Deacon in the Church Past and Future,* 5.

44. Philippians is dated c. 55 (Michael, *The Epistle of Paul to the Philippians,* xxi) to c. 64 (Beare, *A Commentary on the Epistle to the Philippians,* 24), although the weight of evidence seems to favor the latter years.

45. J. J. O'Rourke, "Deacons — In the Bible," in *New Catholic Encyclopedia,* prepared by an editorial staff at the Catholic University of America (New York: McGraw-Hill, 1967), 4:667.

46. Vischer, "The Problem of the Diaconate," 19. Cf. Reicke, "Deacons in the New Testament and in the Early Church," 10.

47. Kelly, who makes a strong case for Pauline authorship, dates it c. 62–65 (pp. 34–36); Burton Scott Easton (*The Pastoral Epistles,* 21) sets it c. 105; Barrett put it between 90 and 125 (C. K. Barrett, *The Pastoral Epistles in the New English Bible* [London: Oxford University Press, 1963], 18; hereafter cited as Barrett, *Pastoral Epistles*); Titus sets the date between 100–150, suggesting c. 130 as likely (Eric Lane Titus, "The First Letter to Timothy," in *The Interpreter's One-Volume Commentary on the Bible,* ed. Charles M. Laymon [Nashville: Abingdon Press, 1971], 883).

48. Käsemann, *N.T. Themes,* 86.

Jewish-Christian churches, particularly at Jerusalem.[49] Lemaire reports in his survey of recent research in New Testament ministries that all studies relating to the presbyterate in the New Testament find its origin to be in the Jewish-Christian communities, where it is first attested. These communities borrowed the office directly from the traditional organizational structure of the Jewish synagogue. Like their Jewish counterparts, Christian presbyters (elders) were ordained by the laying on of hands to govern the community as part of the presbyteral council. And like their synagogue prototypes they were given places of honor at the liturgy.[50]

Reginald Fuller conjectures that presbyters came into being around the decade of the fifties at Jerusalem. They are mentioned there in Acts 21. A synthesis afterwards occurs. Presbyters are adopted by the Pauline churches and, as Vischer points out, are linked with the bishops, so that in Acts 20 the terms are interchangeable.[51] The bishops and deacons of the Pauline churches are joined with the presbyters of the Judaistic churches. The synthesis, Fuller maintains, had taken place by 110. There are then the three orders of bishops, presbyters, and deacons. He further sees the emergence of one bishop as head of the presbyteral council, or the monepiscopate, in the Ignatian bishops. The link in the "tunnel" period is seen in Timothy and Titus, who are "apostolic men" or "apostolic delegates" forming the link between the apostles and the Ignatian bishops.[52] This theory seems quite plausible and will provide a general framework at least into which the office of deacon fits as we find it in the later New Testament period.

When we turn to 1 Timothy 3, we find first of all that again the offices of bishop and deacon are mentioned together, indicating their close connection as they developed in the Church. Although the duties are not given for either office, the qualifications are listed and are nearly identical. Clearly, both offices are filled from respected men in the community. The requirements for deacons, no less than those for bishop, are "strict because of the dignity of the office."[53]

Considerable evidence indicates that the lists of virtues required for these offices are not of Christian origin but were in general use in the Hellenistic world and have here simply been applied to Church offices.[54] Martin Dibelius and Hans Conzelmann argue convincingly for this view and state emphatically,

49. This concept is briefly outlined by Vischer ("The Problem of the Diaconate," 17) but was set forth in detail by Fuller ("Early Catholicism"). Cf. the introduction by Cyril Richardson to "The Letters of Ignatius, Bishop of Antioch," in *Early Christian Fathers,* ed. Richardson, 177.

50. Lemaire, "The Ministries in the New Testament," 146, 147.

51. Vischer, "The Problem of the Diaconate," 17.

52. Käsemann, *N.T. Themes,* 87; Fuller, "Early Catholicism."

53. Easton, *The Pastoral Epistles,* 132–33. Cf. Echlin, *The Deacon in the Church Past and Future,* 84.

54. Barrett, *Pastoral Epistles,* 57. Cf. George A. Denzer, "The Pastoral Letters," in *The Jerome Biblical Commentary,* 2 vols. (Englewood Cliffs, N.J.: Prentice-Hall, 1968), 2:354.

"Such a schema underlies the teaching of duties in 1 Timothy 3. This explains why so little is mentioned which would especially characterize a bishop or deacon. For this reason the specifically Christian element is missing."[55]

Bearing this in mind, the use of these lists to shed light on the nature and duties of these offices must be quite limited. Further, the similarity of the two lists of qualifications is such that it seems unwise to attempt to draw too much from the differences,[56] although some comparison is in order.

First, let us examine the requirements for deacons which are directly paralleled by those for bishops. Deacons are to be "serious," which has to do with both inward temper and outward attitude and roughly corresponds to the requirements that the bishop be "sensible" and "dignified" or "respectable." They are to be "not indulging in much wine," the requirement condemning drunkenness, not the use of wine.[57] They are to be "not greedy for money," both because undue concern for money is inconsistent with Christian character and because the duties of the office relating to alms and other financial matters would create a temptation. In addition, deacons are "first [to] be tested." This testing is best understood in the sense of an examination of character and conduct prior to selection and not a probationary period, as some have thought.[58]

The meaning of the requirement for both offices that they be filled with men who are the "husband of one wife" is disputed. Although the phrase is translated in the NRSV as "married only once," the footnote states that the Greek says "husband of one wife." Some have interpreted it to mean "married to one wife," as against polygamy. E. K. Simpson finds this to be the obvious meaning, arguing that it was "practiced not uncommonly among the Jews of later days, and of course, excessively rife in pagan circles."[59] However, this was not a likely danger for Christians of any kind and would, therefore, be an improbable interpretation.[60]

Burton Scott Easton and J. N. D. Kelly are among those who see the meaning to be "married only once," the prohibition being against second marriage either after divorce or the death of a wife.[61] It is argued that there is abundant evidence from both literature and funerary inscriptions of antiquity to show that to remain unmarried under these circumstances was considered meritorious while to marry again was self-indulgent.[62] However, Dibelius and Conzelmann observe that this

55. Martin Dibelius and Hans Conzelmann, *The Pastoral Epistles,* trans. Philip Buttolph and Adela Yarbro, ed. Helmut Koester (Philadelphia: Fortress Press, 1972), 51.

56. W. J. Lawstuter, "The Pastoral Epistles: First and Second Timothy and Titus," in *The Abingdon Bible Commentary,* ed. Frederick Carl Eiselen, Edwin Lewis, and David G. Downey (New York: Abingdon Press, 1929), 1278.

57. Kelly, *Pastoral Epistles,* 81, 77.

58. Easton, *The Pastoral Epistles,* 10. Cf. Kelly, *Pastoral Epistles,* 84.

59. E. K. Simpson, *The Pastoral Epistles: The Greek Text with Introduction and Commentary* (Grand Rapids: Eerdmans, 1954), 50.

60. Barrett, *Pastoral Epistles,* 58.

61. Easton, *The Pastoral Epistles,* 10; Kelly, *Pastoral Epistles,* 84.

62. Kelly, *Pastoral Epistles,* 75.

attitude was "especially in contrast to a multiplicity of marriages as the result of separation."[63]

In the Roman Catholic and Eastern Orthodox churches, according to Norbert Brockman, it is this interpretation of the passage which has led to the prohibition of a second marriage for deacons. Although Brockman notes that a never-married deacon may not marry in either church, he does not explain how the text can be interpreted to encompass a meaning that prohibits even a first marriage. The interpretation, "married only once," does prohibit a widower remarrying. However, Brockman, while observing that this interpretation is not likely to be abandoned in the Roman Catholic Church today due particularly to the desire for rapprochement with the Orthodox, argues that the original meaning of the passage may better be understood to be that a deacon "be a man noted for fidelity to his wife, the example of an authentically Christian married life."[64]

The nature of the requirement set forth in this text, it is to be emphasized in light of New Testament thought, would not be limited to the Church's leaders but would be for all.[65] All are laity and there is but one standard for all the baptized. Simpson puts this aptly: "To postulate grades of official sanctity among members of the same spiritual body may be orthodox clericalism, but it is heterodox Christianity."[66] In this connection, the Pauline teaching that marriage is dissolved by the death of the spouse leaving the other free to remarry as is set forth in Romans 7:1–3 virtually rules out a prohibition against a second marriage. Although a double standard does develop with clerical celibacy later, Tertullian writes early in the third century, "Vain shall we be if we think that what is not lawful for priests is lawful for laics."[67]

In light of what has been said, the best understanding of this passage is that the requirement is one of fidelity to one's wife and might best be interpreted, as Barrett suggests, "faithful to his one wife"[68] or, as Jean-Paul Audet says, "a husband 'undividedly attached to his wife,'" a view also supported by André Lemaire.[69] The bishop or deacon is to have a stable and harmonious marriage, which will give assurance that he will perform the pastoral service of his office with dignity and efficiency.[70] This interpretation is strengthened by virtue of the fact that this list is in all probability one of virtues describing public office and

63. Dibelius and Conzelmann, *The Pastoral Epistles,* 52.

64. Brockman, *Ordained to Service,* 17–18.

65. Barrett, *Pastoral Epistles,* 58; Dibelius and Conzelmann, *The Pastoral Epistles,* 52.

66. Simpson, *The Pastoral Epistles,* 50.

67. Tertullian, *On Exhortation to Chastity* 7, *Tertullian, Part Fourth; Minucius Felix; Commodian; Origen, Parts First and Second,* in *Ante-Nicene Fathers,* ed. Roberts and Donaldson, 4:54. Quasten dates this at between 204–212 (Johannes Quasten, *Patrology,* vol. 2, *The Ante-Nicene Literature after Irenaeus* [Westminster, Md.: Newman Press, 1950], 305).

68. Barrett, *Pastoral Epistles,* 58–59.

69. Jean-Paul Audet, *Structures in Christian Priesthood: A Study of Home, Marriage, and Celibacy in the Pastoral Service of the Church,* trans. Rosemary Sheed (New York: Macmillan, 1967), 60. See also André Lemaire, "Pastoral Epistles: Redaction and Theology," *Biblical Theology Bulletin* 2, no. 1 (February 1972): 32, who affirms this view.

70. Audet, *Structures in Christian Priesthood,* 57–61.

not of specific Christian origin. The Christian author would in this connection have been saying that Christian bishops and deacons are required to have standards at least as high as public officials. The general meaning here would be that of fidelity in marriage.

Several requirements are listed for the deacon and not for the bishop. Deacons are to be "not double-tongued." The special responsibility of deacons in connection with the poor and other pastoral concerns of the Church makes it especially important that they be truthful and consistent in their dealings with others. The deacon also must "hold fast to the mystery of the faith with a clear conscience." Easton argues that this requirement is made for deacons alone because the bishops acted only as members of a council where one man's mistakes can easily be corrected by the group, but a deacon acted individually with the poor, "whom he could influence profoundly."[71] While interesting, this is perhaps pressing the differences unduly. Kelly puts the emphasis on "clear conscience," noting that sound faith without such a clear conscience is sterile. He asserts, and rightly, that this qualification of Christian conviction is the most important listed.[72]

The "women" mentioned here are probably wives of the deacons.[73] Although some scholars argue that these women are "women deacons," the Greek means only "women similarly" or "women likewise" and the reasons for selecting the other reading seem insufficient.[74] Their special mention would be due to their close association with their husbands in the pastoral and charitable work of the deacon. It may well be supposed that they often accompanied their husbands on visits to the homes of members of the Christian community. Therefore, they also would need to be "serious" and "not slanderers, but temperate, faithful in all things."

The qualifications for the bishop not given in the deacon's list are that the bishop is to be "hospitable, an apt teacher," and "not a recent convert," qualities that do not need additional comment for our purposes.

Up to this point nothing has been said regarding the relationship of the bishops and deacons. It seemed best to look first at the pertinent New Testament texts. These, as we have now seen, simply mention the two offices together, leaving us with little more than the order of first bishops and then deacons to note in this connection. And in light of subsequent development we correctly see here an order of precedence. However, such an order does not imply the later subordination of the deacon to the bishop based on rank and status, which has often been read back into this early period.

Easton rightly observes that, although the Greek word "deacon" means "servant" or "assistant," it would be misleading to translate it as such. The deacons were not the assistants of the bishops at this time but rather "dispensers of the

---

71. Easton, *The Pastoral Epistles,* 9.
72. Kelly, *Pastoral Epistles,* 82.
73. Moule, "Deacons in the New Testament," 406. Cf. Easton, *The Pastoral Epistles,* 132–33.
74. Kelly, *Pastoral Epistles,* 83–84.

Church's charities; they 'served' the poor and the sick," not the Church's primary leaders.[75] To think in terms of subordination to the bishops at this time is largely to forget the character of the Church of the late New Testament period.

Prototype for Deacons

The effort to find a prototype in Judaism or pagan religions for this office has met with scant success. The term "deacon" is used in Greek inscriptions to denote officials of pagan cults and other groups in all parts of the Mediterranean world. Here "deacon" frequently denotes a waiter, an inference drawn from the fact that it often refers to boys and cooks, but the evidence is insufficient to conclude that any such office provided a Christian prototype.[76] The ruler of the Jewish synagogue did have an assistant called a *hazzan* whose liturgical function is somewhat analogous but who had no similar pastoral or sacramental duties. Also, the title is entirely unlike that of "deacon." In classical Greek writings the word has the meaning of ordinary servants, messengers, and civil officials. Josephus and Epictetus at times use the term to refer to a "servant" of God.[77]

Although Edward Echlin states, "The similarity between Jewish levites and Christian deacons is striking,"[78] the evidence does not support the implication that they were prototypes. Henry Gwatkin sees "no likeness to the Levite, who was rather a porter of the temple, who looked after the beasts, and sang in the Choir." In his view the nearest Jewish parallel is the "collector of alms," although he does not find this office analogous.[79] Dom Gregory Dix sees a parallel

> between the deacon who placed the bread and mingled cup before the president [at the Eucharist], ministered the *lavabo* [a ceremony which he points out in a footnote is not attested to before the fourth century at the Eucharist] and ministered the elements to the communicants, and the Jewish "attendant" who ministered the ceremonial hand-washing, set the bread for breaking, and the mingled cup for blessing before the president of the *chabūrah* and served the food and drink of the religious meal.[80]

---

75. Easton, *The Pastoral Epistles,* 132.

76. Shepherd, "Ministry, Christian," 3:389–90. Cf. Schweizer, *Church Order in the New Testament,* 174.

77. Shepherd, "Deacon" and "Deaconess: KJV Servant," in *The Interpreter's Dictionary of the Bible,* 5 vols. (New York: Abingdon Press, 1961), 4:785–86; Shepherd, "Ministry, Christian," 3:389.

78. Echlin, *The Deacon in the Church Past and Future,* 4. (He gives Dom Gregory Dix, "The Ministry in the Early Church c. A.D. 90–410," in *The Apostolic Ministry: Essays on the History and the Doctrine of Episcopacy,* ed. Kenneth E. Kirk [London: Hodder & Stoughton, 1946]), as his reference here, but without a page number. I am unable to find the support.)

79. Henry M. A. Gwatkin, "Deacon," in *A Dictionary of the Bible: Dealing with Its Language, Literature, and Contents,* ed. James Hastings (New York: Scribner's, 1911), 1:574.

80. Dix, "Ministry in the Early Church," 246.

Again, although there may be some similarity of function, there seems to be no connection between this "attendant" and the Christian deacon. It is most probable that the office of deacon was without direct antecedents either in Judaism or paganism, growing out of the distinctive character of the *diakonia* Jesus gave to the nature of the Church and its ministry.

Chapter 4

Age of the Apostolic Fathers

The Golden Age: 100–600 C.E.

The five centuries from 100 to 600, or from Ignatius of Antioch to Gregory the Great, have been called the Golden Age of the diaconate.[1] As the diaconate developed in this period deacons flourished in numbers and in importance. They oversaw the pastoral care of the Church. They were administrators of the Church's charities. They were assistants of its bishops, often succeeding them in office. They had a major role in the Church's liturgies. They were the great symbol of the servant ministry to which the Church has been called by Christ.

Councils in the early fourth century, such as Arles and Nicaea, demonstrate the importance of the diaconate by admonishing deacons to "keep within their proper bounds"[2] as presbyters were growing in importance by assuming the functions of the pre-Nicene bishop. At Rome in the time of Pope Damasus, 366–384, Ambrosiaster could write his treatise "On the Boastfulness of Roman Deacons."[3] Jerome, writing in the late fourth or early fifth century, reports that presbyters at Rome are ordained only on recommendation of a deacon and are "less thought of."[4] Even the seventh-century Council of Toledo, 633, finds it necessary to direct that in choir deacons "are not to raise themselves above the presbyters."[5] There is no doubt, as we shall see, that their very importance, coupled with the lack of any clear definition of their relationship to the presbyter, was a major factor in their decline.

---

1. Edward R. Hardy, "The Deacon in History and Practice," in *The Diaconate Now,* ed. Richard T. Nolan (Washington, D.C.: Corpus Books, 1968), 15. Echlin (*The Deacon in the Church Past and Future,* 25, 57) refers to the golden age of the diaconate as being from Ignatius to Nicaea. Although the decline of the diaconate, or more properly, the root causes of its decline began in the fourth century, the diaconate continued to flourish long after.

2. Canon 18, Nicaea, in J. Stevenson, ed., *A New Eusebius: Documents Illustrative of the Church to A.D. 337* (New York: Macmillan, 1957), 363.

3. Introduction by Stanley L. Greenslade to *Letter 146* of Jerome, in *Early Latin Theology,* trans. S. L. Greenslade, Library of Christian Classics 5 (Philadelphia: Westminster Press, 1956), 383–84.

4. Jerome, *Epistle 146.2,* in *Early Latin Theology,* 5:388. The translator dates this letter after 388 (5:383–84). The evidence might suggest c. 400. Jerome died in 419 or 420 (5:286).

5. Charles Joseph Hefele, *A History of the Councils of the Church, from the Original Documents. A.D. 451 to A.D. 680,* trans. William R. Clark, in Hefele, *A History of the Councils of the Church* (Edinburgh: T. & T. Clark, 1895), 4:454.

Guided by the Holy Spirit

It is when we move outside of the New Testament into the sub-apostolic age that we see more clearly the character and function of the various offices within the Church as they underwent a transformation from the apostolic age. This change, however, is not to be considered simply a natural development in a human society. The charisma of the Holy Spirit was fully at work in the Church, guiding its development. Lampe reminds us, "Though in one aspect, the change was due to the natural pressure of altered circumstances, it did not happen without the guidance and authority of the Holy Spirit."[6]

The Letter of the Church at Rome
to the Church at Corinth (*1 Clement*)

References to the diaconate outside the New Testament in the sub-apostolic age are relatively plentiful. The first of these, the letter of Clement to the Church at Corinth (c. 96), provides the only other reference generally assigned to the New Testament period mentioning bishops and deacons.[7] This writing is of great importance, having been held in such esteem in antiquity that it was counted among the Scriptures by the Syrian Church and appended to the biblical *Codex Alexandrinus*.[8] Clement, the author, was listed by Irenaeus as the third bishop of Rome[9] but he can better be described as one of the leading presbyters or, possibly, presbyter-bishops of Rome. Irenaeus also says that Clement, along with many others still alive, had known the apostles and had "their traditions before his eyes."[10]

Cyril Richardson rightly points out that to call Clement the third bishop of Rome implies that the monepiscopate was already established at Rome, which is highly unlikely, since Clement himself refers to the Church rulers both as bishops and as presbyters, using the terms interchangeably. Richardson believes that a hint in the *Shepherd of Hermas* may indicate that Clement acted as a "kind of foreign secretary for the church." He adds, "It must suffice to call him a leading — perhaps the leading — presbyter-bishop of the Roman Church."[11] Echlin calls Clement "a leading Roman presbyter."[12] Shepherd says that the Roman Church at this time was governed by a council of presbyters, which probably had a chairman appointed by seniority.[13] Walter Lowrie's interpretation that in

6. Lampe, *N.T. Ministry,* 20.

7. Moule, "Deacons in the New Testament," 407.

8. Berthold Altaner, *Patrology,* trans. Hilda C. Graef (New York: Herder & Herder, 1960), 99.

9. Irenaeus, *Against Heresies* 3.3.3., in *Early Christian Fathers,* ed. Richardson, 372.

10. Ibid., 373.

11. Cyril C. Richardson, introduction to "The Letter of the Church of Rome to the Church of Corinth, Commonly called Clement's First Letter," in *Early Christian Fathers,* ed. Richardson, 36–37.

12. Echlin, *The Deacon in the Church Past and Future,* 14.

13. Massey H. Shepherd Jr., "Smyrna in the Ignatian Letters: A Study in Church Order," *Jour-*

1 Clement not all presbyters were bishops but only those *appointed to liturgize* probably reflects a concern of later times.[14]

Clement wrote anonymously but on behalf of the Church at Rome to help settle a controversy in which a group in the Corinthian Church had thrust their leaders out of office. He tells us that the apostles

> after receiving their orders and being fully convinced by the resurrection of our Lord Jesus Christ and assured by God's word, went out in the confidence of the Holy Spirit to preach the good news that God's Kingdom was about to come. They preached in country and city, and appointed their first converts, after testing them by the Spirit, to be bishops and deacons of future believers.[15]

Clement further writes in reference to the office of bishop that the apostles "appointed the officers we have mentioned. Furthermore, they later added a codicil to the effect that should these die, other approved men should succeed to their ministry." He also speaks of appointment being by the apostles "or later on and with the whole church's consent, by others of proper standing." Clement calls the leaders of the Church at Corinth "bishops and deacons," as we have seen, but he uses "presbyters" for these leaders elsewhere.[16] While it is apparent that the terms "bishops" and "presbyters" are used here interchangeably, a careful reading of the text does not enable us to say that the "deacons" are in that category. In light of what we know subsequently, it is probable that Clement means to include them here as important leaders of the Corinthian Church but not the same as the presbyter-bishops.

Dom Gregory Dix sees in this letter the first Christian description of the way in which the Eucharist was performed. He renders his own translation of the pertinent lines:

> Unto the high-priest (=the celebrant-bishop) his special "liturgies" have been appointed, and to the priests (=presbyters) their special place is assigned, and on the levites (=deacons) their special "deaconings" are imposed; the layman is bound by the ordinances for the laity. Let each of you, brethren, make eucharist to God according to his own order, keeping a good conscience and not transgressing the appointed rule of his "liturgy."[17]

This interpretation, however, is almost certainly reading back into Clement later thought. As we have seen, the Corinthian Church apparently had presbyter-bishops and deacons, but not yet the later threefold structure. The term "priest" was not then applied to any church official. The reference of Clement here would rather seem to be, when taken in context, to the order found in the religion of

---

nal of Religion 20 (1940): 156 (hereafter cited as Shepherd, "Ignatian Letters"). Cf. Richardson, Introduction to "Clement," 39.

14. Lowrie, *The Church and Its Organization,* 341–50. Lowrie, however, is probably not correct in arguing that the term *presbyter* ("elder") in *1 Clement* does not denote an office (348–52) except when they are called "appointed presbyters."

15. *1 Clement* 42 and 44, in *Early Christian Fathers,* ed. Richardson, 62–64.

16. *1 Clement* 44, 47, and 57, pp. 63–65, 69.

17. Dix, *Shape of the Liturgy,* 1. (Reference is to *1 Clement* 40 and 41.)

the Old Testament. He moves from that to speak of the order in the Church established by God through Jesus Christ.

As valuable as *1 Clement* is, it does not shed any light upon the function of the deacon at that time.[18] It does assert that apostolic authority and succession are to be transmitted in an orderly fashion by the direction of the apostles through the proper appointment of the presbyter-bishops and deacons with the assent of the whole Church. We may see in this an apostolic succession for both the bishops and deacons.[19] But this apostolic succession is to be conceived in terms of the continuing body of the Church, the succession of these offices, both bishop and deacon, being only a part of it.

The Shepherd of Hermas

The Shepherd of Hermas, once widely read and considered Scripture by Clement of Alexandria, Origen, and Irenaeus,[20] contains in its original section (c. 96)[21] a reference showing the importance of the deacons in the life of the Church. In his vision, Hermas sees a tower under construction as a symbol of the building of the triumphant Church. Some stones fit perfectly, others are rejected, as will be those in the Church who do not repent. Hermas writes,

> Now hear about the stones that go into the building. The stones that are square and white and fit their joints are the apostles and bishops and teachers and deacons who have lived in the holiness of God, and have been bishops and teachers and deacons for God's chosen in purity and reverence.[22]

Hermas again mentions deacons in one of the parables toward the end of his work.[23] These are men who have betrayed the trust of their office. In his concern for repentance he writes,

> The ones that are spotted are deacons who served badly and plundered the living of widows and orphans, and made profit for themselves from the ministry they

---

18. Echlin argues that since deacons were associated with the bishops "both in their ministry and in their expulsion, we may conclude that the diaconal function involved ministry of liturgy and charity." His reference is to *1 Clement* 44, but this has nothing at all to say about liturgical function.

19. Reicke, "Deacons in the New Testament and in the Early Church," 11.

20. Edgar J. Goodspeed, *A History of Early Christian Literature,* rev. and enl. Robert M. Grant (Chicago: University of Chicago Press, 1966), 32 (hereafter cited as Goodspeed, *Early Christian Literature*).

21. The first section of the *Shepherd,* Visions 1–4 (in Edgar J. Goodspeed, *The Apostolic Fathers — An American Translation* [New York: Harper & Brothers, 1950]), probably was written during the last years of the leadership of Clement of Rome, which ended in 97 (see Goodspeed, *Early Christian Literature,* 30–34). Cf. Johannes Quasten, *Patrology,* vol. 1, *Beginnings of Patristic Literature in Patrology* (Westminster, Md.: Newman Press, 1950), 92–93.

22. Hermas, *Shepherd,* Vision 3.5.1, in Goodspeed, *Apostolic Fathers,* 112.

23. The second section of Hermas, *Shepherd,* Vision 5 through the end, is to be dated in the second century a few years after the first, though parables 9 and 10 may be still later additions. Goodspeed and Grant's (*Early Christian Literature,* 30–34) argument for this dating and against the time of Pius I (140–155) is to be preferred.

had accepted to perform. So if they persist in the same desire, they are dead and have no hope of life. But if they turn and perform their service purely, they will be able to live.[24]

The care of the poor and especially of widows and orphans was a special and major concern of the Church in the ancient world, and here as elsewhere the evidence shows that the deacons had direct responsibility in this work.

The Didache

Although the date of the *Didache* is uncertain, its section on Church order, chapters 6 to 15, seems to reflect the rural churches of Syria in the sub-apostolic age. It probably was originally a separate document dating from the late first century, which was then placed with the first section and the last chapter and edited by a scribe in Alexandria, c. 150.[25]

Therefore, consideration of the *Didache* belongs in the sub-apostolic age, when the primary leadership of the Church was undergoing a transformation from that of apostles, apostolic delegates, prophets, and teachers to that of bishops, presbyters, and deacons. The author of the *Didache* first discusses teachers, apostles, and prophets in that order.[26] He then writes,

> You must, then, elect for yourselves bishops and deacons who are a credit to the Lord, men who are gentle, generous, faithful, and well tried. For their ministry to you is identical with that of the prophets and teachers. You must not, therefore, despise them, for along with the prophets and teachers they enjoy a place of honor among you.[27]

The clear implication here is that bishops and deacons are being added to the leadership of the Church for the same functions as heretofore had been rendered by the prophets and teachers alone.[28] The admonition to give them honor along with the older form of prophets and teachers suggests that they are not yet considered on a par and entirely accepted by all. Further, whereas the prophets and teachers had been primarily charismatic, the bishops and deacons are apparently elected by the Church and commissioned through the laying on of hands. They too, then, are given the charisma of the Spirit but in a more orderly fashion.[29] This commissioning through the laying on of hands is to be seen as the confirmation of the charisma given by the Spirit.[30]

It is noteworthy that in the *Didache* the term "bishops" is used in the plural, not the singular. Further, the bishops and deacons are lumped together and are

24. Hermas, *Shepherd*, Parable 9.26.2, in Goodspeed, *Apostolic Fathers*, 193.

25. Cyril C. Richardson, Introduction to "The Teaching of the Twelve Apostles, Commonly Called the Didache," in *Early Christian Fathers*, ed. Richardson, 162–65.

26. *Didache* 11–13, in *Early Christian Fathers*, ed. Richardson, 176–78.

27. *Didache* 15, ibid., 178.

28. Fuller, "Early Catholicism." Cf. Lowrie, *The Church and Its Organization*, 331–42.

29. Fuller, "Early Catholicism."

30. Lowrie, *The Church and Its Organization*, 342.

said to fulfill the same function as the prophets and teachers did. Clearly, the office of bishop was not the same office as that of deacon, just as the role of prophet was not the same as that of teacher. Rather, the mention of the two together may well have been due to their together constituting a ruling council for the local Church, although we cannot be certain.

Edward Echlin argues from the text of the *Didache* cited above that both bishops and deacons preached and taught as well as performing certain other functions.[31] Brockman maintains, on the other hand, that deacons were chosen by the community for only a "catechetical role ... to undertake the instruction of the faithful with edification."[32] He consistently avoids ascribing to deacons the role of preaching liturgically. In light of the evidence here and elsewhere it is highly probable, if not certain, that the bishops and not the deacons took over the prophets' functions of presiding at the Eucharist, preaching, and teaching. In view of the lack of other evidence, it is most unlikely that deacons preached. The deacons would, as other sources indicate, have liturgical functions at the Eucharist in addition to their other functions. But it is important to remember that functions in the Church were not then so rigidly defined and "the official *charismata* of the early church were not severally exclusive. Any individual could perform as many functions as his spiritual endowments allowed."[33]

Ignatius

In the letters that Ignatius, the martyr-bishop of Antioch, wrote as he journeyed from Syria to suffer his martyrdom in Rome in the reign of Trajan, 98–117,[34] there emerge for the first time the clearly distinguishable orders of bishops, presbyters (or elders), and deacons. This picture represents a stage of development beyond that found in the Pastoral Epistles and *1 Clement*.[35] In the latter, the local churches are governed by councils of officials, probably presbyters or presbyter-bishops, with deacons possibly being included in some places. These councils were subject to apostolic delegates such as Timothy and Titus.

But in the Ignatian letters the single bishop emerges as the leading figure in the Church. The Ignatian bishop represents the "monepiscopate," a term de-

---

31. Echlin, *The Deacon in the Church Past and Future,* 17.

32. Brockman, *Ordained to Service,* 21.

33. Shepherd, "Ignatian Letters," 154.

34. Eusebius dates the martyrdom of Ignatius at 107 in his *Chronicles, The Church History of Eusebius* 3:36, in *Eusebius: Church History, Life of Constantine the Great, and Oration in Praise of Constantine,* trans. and ed. Arthur Cushman McGiffert, in *Nicene and Post-Nicene Fathers,* 2d ser., 1:169. However, modern scholars generally agree only that he was martyred in Rome in the reign of Trajan (98–117): Kirsopp Lake, Introduction to "The Epistles of Ignatius," in Lake, *The Apostolic Fathers,* vol. 1 (Cambridge, Mass.: Harvard University Press, 1912; rpt., 1970), 166; Richardson, Introduction to "The Letters of Ignatius," 75.

35. Shepherd, "Ministry, Christian," 3:391. Cf. Richardson, *Early Christian Fathers,* 1:76.

noting rule of the local church by a council of presbyters (possibly including deacons)[36] over which one bishop presides.[37] "Monepiscopate" differentiates the episcopal office in the pre-Nicene period both from that in the churches ruled by a council of presbyters or presbyter-bishops along the Jewish synagogue model and that which arose in the fourth century with emergence of the city bishops as metropolitans. Although the Ignatian letters have often been thought to picture the monarchical episcopate in the churches of Asia Minor in the early years of the second century,[38] the Asian bishops did not possess the autocratic authority implied by that term.[39] Ascribing such a place to the Ignatian bishop is reading back into history the radical transformation of the Church's leadership in the fourth century. Lemaire thinks the language of the Ignatian letters probably indicates that "the ministerial vocabulary first became fixed at Antioch and that the word *episkopos* has designated the president of the local Christian community."[40] He quotes K. A. Strand in seeing the struggle of the Church with heresy as a major reason for the development of the monepiscopate, as it did at that time, in the East.[41] The monepiscopal Ignatian bishop did not govern or rule the Church but rather was president of the community and of the presbyteral council when it was adopted by the Pauline churches, the latter possessing the authority to rule in the local church. These bishops were comparable not to contemporary diocesan bishops but to the presbyters or pastors today who preside over local congregations.

Ignatius uses the symbolism of the bishop as the type of God the Father, the presbyters as that of the college of the apostles, and the deacons as Jesus Christ: "Correspondingly, everyone must show the deacons respect. They represent Jesus Christ, just as the bishop has the role of the Father, and the presbyters are like God's council and an apostolic band. You cannot have a Church without these."[42] Dix sees here the same ordering of the Church in its eucharistic assembly that he finds reflected in the Revelation. In his description the Church, which at this time was never thought of in terms of a building,[43] was arranged so that the bishop sat at the front in a chair covered by a white linen cloth facing the people across the table or altar. The presbyters were seated in a semicircle

---

36. Shepherd, "Ignatian Letters," 142.

37. *Early Christian Fathers,* ed. Richardson, 76. Reginald Fuller ("Early Catholicism") sees the same development and the emergence of the monepiscopate in Ignatius.

38. E.g., Schweizer, *Church Order in the New Testament,* 154; Lietzmann, *A History of the Early Church,* 2:58; John Knox, *The Early Church and the Coming Great Church* (New York: Abingdon Press, 1955), 121.

39. Shepherd, "Ignatian Letters," 141.

40. Lemaire, "The Ministries in the New Testament," 145.

41. Ibid., 145–46.

42. Ignatius, *Trallians* 3, in *Early Christian Fathers,* ed. Richardson, 99. Cf. Ignatius, *Magnesians* 6, in *Early Christian Fathers,* ed. Richardson, 95.

43. Dix points out that the word *church* means "invariably...the solemn assembly for the liturgy, and by extension those who have a right to take part in this" until the third century. (Dix, *Shape of the Liturgy,* 20). Cf. Fuller, "Church," 46.

on either side of the bishop. Two of the deacons stood beside the bishop, with the others either at the front of the congregation or scattered throughout it.[44]

The subdeacons and acolytes assisted the deacons and guarded the doors. Other members, men on one side and women on the other, faced the bishop, with the catechumens and visitors at the back. Dix believes this arrangement was adopted by the end of the first century, because it is reflected in the vision of the heavenly assembly in the Revelation, which he dates c. 93.[45] Whether or not Dix is correct in this early date (by Dix's own testimony some details such as the presence of subdeacons and acolytes do not come until later), the general arrangement pictured is that of the universal practice as it shortly came to be. It reflects both the nature of the Church and the character of its offices, which continued throughout the pre-Nicene period.

In Ignatius's letter to the Trallians we find specific references to the liturgical function of the deacons at the Eucharist:[46] "Those too who are deacons of Jesus Christ's 'mysteries' must give complete satisfaction to everyone. For they do not serve mere food and drink, but minister to God's Church."[47] In 1 Corinthians Paul speaks of being "stewards of the mysteries of God" (1 Cor. 4:1; cf. 1 Cor. 2:7; 13:2; 14:2). Although the Greek word "mystery" used here generally refers to sacred rites, and Christians later applied it to the sacraments, Paul uses it rather to mean secret knowledge of God's plan revealed in the gospel.[48] Thus, Ignatius's use of "mysteries" in connection with the deacons would not in itself be sufficient to infer liturgical function. However, his statement that the deacons "minister to God's Church," when set beside his contrast to their not merely serving food and drink, a probable reference to the Christian "agape" or "fellowship meal," does indicate their participation in the Eucharist liturgically. Ignatius uses the terms "eucharist" and "agape" to denote the same type of assembly, both describing the entire celebration of the community. Conclusive evidence for the separation of the Eucharist and the agape into independent gatherings comes, at least in the East, only at the end of the second century.[49]

It is also probable that Ignatius's exhortation to a single Eucharist implies a liturgical function for the deacons:[50] "Be careful then, to observe a single Eucharist. For there is one flesh of our Lord, Jesus Christ, and one cup of his blood that makes us one, and one altar, just as there is one bishop along with the presbytery and deacons, my fellow slaves."[51] The admonition to "a single Eucharist"

---

44. Dix, *Shape of the Liturgy,* 28.

45. Dix may have intended rather that the *general arrangement* was adopted by the end of the first century, since he states later (ibid., 35) that the "minor orders" came into existence by the end of the second century.

46. *Early Christian Fathers,* ed. Richardson, 99n.

47. Ignatius, *Trallians* 2, in ibid., 99.

48. Barrett, *1 Corinthians,* 99–100.

49. Shepherd, "Ignatian Letters," 149.

50. Echlin, *The Deacon in the Church Past and Future,* 21.

51. Ignatius, *Philadelphians* 4, in *Early Christian Fathers,* ed. Richardson, 108.

here is probably due to separate Eucharists held by a group of Judaizers.[52] But his mention of "one flesh," "one cup," "one altar," and "one bishop," all being an integral part of the Eucharist, would clearly indicate that along with the "one bishop," "the presbytery and deacons," who are his "fellow slaves," also have a prominent place in the Eucharist.

It has been asserted that deacons are said to preach in Ignatius's letters.[53] In one of the texts cited Ignatius writes, "Consequently, it would be a nice thing for you, as a church of God, to elect a deacon to go there [Antioch] on a mission, as God's representative, and at a formal service to congratulate them and glorify the Name."[54] The function of this deacon would, however, be that of a special representative or ambassador to the Church at Antioch. In the light of no other evidence it is unlikely that the phrase "glorify the Name" is a reference to preaching. Echlin refers to another passage in *Philadelphians* to support diaconal preaching in the Ignatian letters, although a fair translation of the passage will not bear this interpretation. Richardson renders the text, "Now about Philo, the deacon from Cilicia. He is well spoken of and right now he is helping me in God's cause."[55] Echlin bases his argument on a translation that runs, "Philo . . . is at present giving me his help in preaching God's word."[56] Other authorities do not support this reading.[57] It must be concluded that there is insufficient evidence in these letters to maintain that preaching was a function of the diaconate in these writings.

It is sometimes assumed that the deacon's position as seen in the writings of Ignatius was that of assistant to the bishop, as the bishop emerged a single figure in the monepiscopate.[58] It is true that at times they did act in this capacity. Philo, the Cilician deacon, was helping Ignatius at the time he wrote to the Philadelphians; but in the same sentence we are told that so was Rheus Agathopus, who is described as "a choice person" and is apparently not a deacon.[59] Ignatius asks the Church at Ephesus to let their deacon, Burrhus, whom he describes as "my fellow slave," remain with him.[60] But Burrhus is said to be a deacon of the Church at Ephesus, not of the bishop, and his position appears

---

52. *Early Christian Fathers,* ed. Richardson, 108n.
53. Holmes, *Future Shape,* 25. Echlin, *The Deacon in the Church Past and Future,* 21.
54. Ignatius, *Philadelphians* 10, in *Early Christian Fathers,* ed. Richardson, 111.
55. Ignatius, *Philadelphians* 11, in ibid.
56. Echlin, *The Deacon in the Church Past and Future,* 21.
57. See Gerald G. Walsh, "The Letters of St. Ignatius of Antioch," in *The Apostolic Fathers,* vol. 1 of *The Fathers of the Church,* trans. Francis X. Glimm, Joseph M. F. Marique, and Gerald G. Walsh (New York: Cima Publishing, 1947), 117, which reads "ministering in the word of God." A similar reading is found in *The Apostolic Fathers with Justin Martyr and Irenaeus,* in *Ante-Nicene Fathers,* ed. Roberts and Donaldson, 1:85: "who still minister to me in the word of God." Lake's translation reads, "who is at present serving me in the word of God" (Lake, *Apostolic Fathers,* 1:251). J. B. Lightfoot renders the phrase, "who now ministereth to me in the word of God" (Ignatius, *The Apostolic Fathers,* trans. J. B. Lightfoot, ed. and completed by J. R. Harmer [1891; rpt., Grand Rapids: Baker Book House, 1956], 82).
58. *Early Christian Fathers,* ed. Richardson, 76.
59. Ignatius, *Philadelphians* 11, in ibid., 111.
60. Ignatius, *Ephesus* 2, in ibid., 88.

incidental to the request. The evidence in these letters indicates that the position of the deacon was that of a servant of the Church, who naturally at times acts to assist its leading officer.

Further, as has been said, the office of the Ignatian bishop is far more analogous to the parish presbyter, priest, or pastor in the Church today than to that of a diocesan bishop. Were the place of the deacon in Ignatius translated in terms of the Church today, the deacon would be a servant of the parish, who would act at times in assisting the head of the parish.

However, the most striking aspect of Ignatius's letters regarding the place of the deacon in the Church is his reference to their symbolizing Jesus Christ. Ignatius at this point refers to the bishop as a figure of God the Father and the presbyters as symbolizing the apostolic council. He then says, "Let the deacons (my special favorites) be entrusted with the ministry of Jesus Christ who was with the Father from eternity and appeared at the end (of the world)."[61] In a similar context, as we have noted before, he writes that they are to be respected because "they represent Jesus Christ."[62] Ignatius can think in these terms and use this order with the deacons in the third place yet representing Jesus Christ because ministerial order was not conceived in terms of status or rank but rather of function. So long as we think in categories of a graded structure we cannot understand the development of these orders in the ancient Church.[63] The office of the deacon, although mentioned third, is not inferior but is in fact that of Christ himself.

It is because of the high esteem in which the deacon was held that he may have been included in the governing council and was mentioned at one point along with the bishop and presbyters as among those to whom obedience is to be given. The basic concern of Ignatius is for the unity of the Church as he writes,

> Flee from schism as the source of mischief. You should all follow the bishop as Jesus Christ did the Father. Follow, too, the presbytery as you would the apostles; and respect the deacons as you would God's law. Nobody must do anything that has to do with the Church without the bishop's approval. You should regard the Eucharist as valid which is celebrated either by the bishop or by someone he authorizes.[64]

It is also to be noted that Ignatius does not say that the "someone" authorized by the bishop to preside at the celebration of the Eucharist hold any particular office. In view of the functional nature of the offices, the respected place of the deacon, and particularly the liturgical function already possessed by the deacon, it is entirely conceivable that the bishop would have authorized a deacon to preside at the Eucharist when he was unable to be present at this early time.[65]

---

61. Ignatius, *Magnesians* 6, in ibid., 95.
62. Ignatius, *Trallians* 3, in ibid., 99.
63. Shepherd, "Ignatian Letters," 158.
64. Ignatius, *Smyrneans* 8, in *Early Christian Fathers,* ed. Richardson, 115. Cf. Ignatius, *Polycarp* 6, in *Early Christian Fathers,* ed. Richardson, 119.
65. Echlin, *The Deacon in the Church Past and Future,* 22.

Polycarp

In the letter of Polycarp to the Philippians, which comes after the martyrdom of Ignatius and is probably to be dated c. 115–120,[66] the qualifications set forth for deacons are reminiscent of those in 1 Timothy:

> Likewise the deacons should be blameless before his [God's] righteousness, as servants of God and Christ and not of men; not slanderers, or double-tongued, not lovers of money, temperate in all matters, compassionate, careful, living according to the truth of the Lord, who became "a servant of all."[67]

Here it is noteworthy that the deacons are to be "servants of God and of Christ and not of men," which in effect indicates that the deacons are not thought of as assistants to the bishop. Polycarp also speaks of the necessity of the people within the Church "being obedient to the presbyters and deacons,"[68] who together may have comprised the ruling council at Philippi.

The End of the Post-Apostolic Age

By the end of the age of the apostolic fathers the leadership of the Church is clearly passing from the charismatically appointed apostles, prophets, and teachers of the primitive Church to the threefold orders of bishops, presbyters (or elders), and deacons. While at first the bishops and deacons may have had responsibilities only for the business affairs of the Church,[69] they seem almost immediately to have begun to assume liturgical and pastoral functions. Although various factors were involved in this change, such as the decreasing number of prophets possessed with charismatic gifts, and the threat of Gnosticism, it is to be remembered also that the change did not occur "without the guidance and authority of the Holy Spirit,"[70] and in this sense "can be understood as of divine institution."[71]

To assert the guidance and authority of the Holy Spirit here is not to imply that the Holy Spirit is always the guiding force behind all that happens in the Church. Although he is always present, obviously he is not always heeded. However, in this early period, especially the pre-Nicene age, of more costly Christianity and of undeniably great zeal for and commitment to Christ within

---

66. Massey Shepherd argues convincingly for the unity of Polycarp's letter and, therefore, for the traditional dating of it (Introduction to "The Letter of Polycarp, Bishop of Smyrna, to the Philippians," in *Early Christian Fathers,* ed. Richardson, 122–23). However, some follow the theory of P. N. Harrison, in which chap. 13 and possibly 14 are considered one letter and dated at this time and chaps. 1–12 are thought to be another letter from c. 135 (in Altaner, *Patrology,* 111).

67. Polycarp, *Philippians* 5, in *Early Christian Fathers,* ed. Richardson, 133.

68. Ibid.

69. Shepherd, "Ignatian Letters," 152–53. Cf. Lietzmann, *A History of the Early Church,* 1:193, 2:58.

70. Lampe, *N.T. Ministry,* 20.

71. Karl Rahner, *Bishops: Their Status and Function,* trans. Edward Quinn (Baltimore: Helicon Press, 1964), 17.

the Church generally, the guidance of the Holy Spirit is clearer and more apparent and assuredly present in the emerging order of the offices within the Church's ministry.

The three orders, however, do not constitute the ministry of the Church at the end of the post-apostolic age. The ministry of the Church continues to be, as it had been from the first, the service rendered by all of the Church's people to God, to one another, and to others. The three orders were delegated certain functions within this ministry. At this time the monepiscopate had developed in some churches with a single bishop presiding both over a council of presbyters (and deacons?) and over the eucharistic assembly. Presbyters acted as a council for the governance of the local Church, and deacons served charitable and other needs of the Church and participated liturgically at the Eucharist.

The deacons had liturgical and administrative functions of their own. They were a full order with *leiturgia* and *diakonia,* which were distinctive. These functions were firmly bound together and were increasingly not to be interchanged with those of other orders.[72] But we must wait to learn from succeeding writers more about these functions.

Although the deacons were subject to the ruling council of the local Church, they were "servants of the Church" and "of God," not of another order or official. It is undoubtedly true that from the outset the deacon had a close relationship with the bishop. However, it is all too easy to read back into the first and second centuries what is to be found later in this connection. As the bishops of the urban centers later became metropolitans, following the monepiscopate, and assimilated the rule of the corporate presbyterate, it is probable that some of the deacons, particularly in the cities, came to be thought of as the liturgical and administrative assistants of their bishops rather than of the Church. From the time the primary leadership of the Church passed from the apostles or apostolic delegates, prophets, and teachers to the bishops (or presbyter-bishops), presbyters, and deacons, the bishop did possess a sacramental and liturgical dominance. But it is to be remembered that this was only in the context of the Church. The bishop was the "high priest" and not the "priest," because the priesthood was in this early period clearly seen to belong to the whole body of the Church.[73] The presbyter had no liturgical function, although he may have been designated by the bishop to assume liturgical functions at the Eucharist when the bishop could not be present, as reported by Ignatius.[74] It is, however, entirely possible, as we have observed, that a deacon could have been the one so authorized. But, in any event, the deacon appears from the earliest time to have had liturgical function that was not derived from the bishop.

---

72. Dix, *Shape of the Liturgy,* 112.
73. Ibid., 29–34. Cf. Dix, "Ministry in the Early Church," 282n.
74. Ignatius, *Smyrneans* 8, in *Early Christian Fathers,* ed. Richardson, 115. Cf. Dix, *Shape of the Liturgy,* 34.

Chapter 5

From the Post-Apostolic Age
to the Constantinian Era

Justin Martyr

Justin Martyr, one of the most learned Christian writers and the most volumi-
nous up to his time, describes the worship of the Church at Rome c. 150 in his
Apology.[1] In this valuable account of the Eucharist Justin records that after "the
prayers" had been concluded and the kiss of peace exchanged, bread and wine
mixed with water are brought to "the president of the brethren," who gives praise
and glory to God and offers thanks at length over them. Justin continues: "When
the president has given thanks and the whole congregation has assented, those
whom we call deacons give to each of those present a portion of the consecrated
bread and wine and water, and they take it to the absent."[2]

For the first time we have specific mention of this liturgical function of the
deacons. It is to be noted here that this earliest record makes it the function of
the deacons alone to administer both the Bread and the Wine at the Eucharist.
We see, too, the depth of their understanding of the organic nature of the Church
by the deacons' taking the eucharisticized Bread and Wine to those who were
absent, thereby asserting the unity of the body of Christ. The importance of
this is emphasized by Justin's repeating the point in reference to the weekly
Eucharist each Sunday: "They [the consecrated elements] are sent to the absent
by the deacons."[3]

Dix thinks that the administration of both the Bread and the Wine by the deacons is the authentic practice of the Church and that it continued after Justin's
time.[4] Later evidence supports this view, and John Bligh is probably correct in
maintaining that for centuries after Justin deacons continued to administer the
chalice even to presbyters and bishops, although probably not to a presiding
bishop. He reports that Durandus says this practice is still legally correct but is

---

1. Goodspeed, *Early Christian Literature,* 103; Justin, *Apology* 65–67, "The First Apology of
Justin, the Martyr," trans. Edward R. Hardy, in *Early Christian Fathers,* ed. Richardson, 285–88.
2. Justin, *Apology* 65, in *Early Christian Fathers,* ed. Richardson, 286.
3. Justin, *Apology* 67, in ibid., 287.
4. Dix, *Shape of the Liturgy,* 135–36.

no longer done in the Roman Catholic Church.[5] Bishops at this time were, as has been said, presidents of congregations, not leaders of dioceses.

It is also of interest that only the office of deacon is mentioned by name here in Justin's portrayal of Christian worship at Rome in the mid-second century. Justin's designation of the presiding officer at the Eucharist as "the president of the brethren" or "one of the brethren who was presiding," either of which are legitimate translations of the Greek, should not be taken to imply that a single bishop had not yet emerged at Rome in what we have termed the monepiscopate.[6] Justin, as an apologist, was writing for non-Christians and therefore uses "president," a term they will understand, just as he uses "Sunday" instead of "the Lord's Day."[7] Irenaeus's account of the visit of the aged Bishop Polycarp to Rome a year or two before his martyrdom in 155 or 156 calls Anicetus, whom Polycarp came to visit, its bishop.[8] Clearly the monepiscopate is present at Rome in Justin's time.

Irenaeus

Irenaeus, who saw and heard Polycarp in Smyrna in his youth and later became bishop of Lyons in Gaul, is the first to call Stephen of Acts 6 a deacon, as was previously noted. He writes (c. 185),

> And still further, Stephen who was chosen the first deacon by the apostles, and who of all men, was the first to follow the footsteps of the Lord, being the first that was slain for confessing Christ, speaking boldly among the people, and teaching them, says: "The God of glory appeared to our father Abraham."[9]

He also mentions Nicolas (or Nicolaus), whom he says "was one of the seven first ordained to the diaconate by the apostles," and credits him with founding

---

5. John Bligh, "Deacons in the Latin West Since the Fourth Century," in *Theology* 58 (1955): 425. (Citation in G. Durandus, *Rationale divinorum officiorum* [Lyons, 1574], 4, 54, 2.)

6. Justin, *Apology* 65, in *Early Christian Fathers,* ed. Richardson, 1:286; *The Apostolic Fathers with Justin Martyr and Irenaeus,* in *Ante-Nicene Fathers,* ed. Roberts and Donaldson, 1:185n.

7. Introduction by Edward R. Hardy to Justin, "The First Apology of Justin, the Martyr," in *Early Christian Fathers,* ed. Richardson, 225–31; Justin, *Apology* 67, in *Early Christian Fathers,* ed. Richardson, 287. For the same reason he refers to "those whom *we call* deacons."

8. Shepherd, Introduction to "The Letter of Polycarp," in *Early Christian Fathers,* ed. Richardson, 121–23; Irenaeus, *Against Heresies* 3.3.4 and 3.4.3, in *Early Christian Fathers,* ed. Richardson, 374, 375.

9. Irenaeus, *Against Heresies* 3.12.10, in *Ante-Nicene Fathers,* ed. Roberts and Donaldson, 1:434. Irenaeus makes an almost identical reference to Stephen in Book 4.15.1, in *Ante-Nicene Fathers,* ed. Roberts and Donaldson, 1:480. Echlin (*The Deacon in the Church Past and Future,* 30) quotes the similar passage in Irenaeus (4.15.1) as, "Luke also has recorded that Stephen, who was first elected into the assembly by the apostles" but the text of his reference, an earlier edition of the *Ante-Nicene Fathers* (*The Writings of Irenaeus,* trans. Alexander Roberts and W. H. Rambout [Edinburgh: T. & T. Clark, 1868], 5:419), in the American reprint edition reads "Stephen, who was first elected into the *diaconate* by the apostles" (italics added). (Vol. 5 cited by Echlin is almost certainly an error.)

the sect of the Nicolaitans referred to in Revelation 2:6, although his connection with this heretical group is mere conjecture.[10]

Irenaeus thus begins the tradition, which modern scholarship finds almost certainly incorrect, that the Seven of Acts 6 were the first deacons. It is probable that Irenaeus simply made the connection between "deacon," which could mean "table waiter," and the purpose of the appointment of the Seven given in Acts, "to wait on tables." In this connection it is to be noted again that in spite of the mention of Stephen preaching in Acts and of Irenaeus's reference to Stephen in order that he might quote him both here and in Book 4, there is no evidence that preaching was ever a function of deacons in the early Church, a fact that is in itself indicative that the Seven were not deacons.

The Pseudo-Clementines

The "Epistle of Clement to James" introducing the *Homilies* in the *Pseudo-Clementines* speaks of the deacons being as eyes to the bishop:

> Moreover let the deacons of the church, going about with intelligence, be as eyes to the bishops, carefully inquiring into the doings of each member of the church, ascertaining who is about to sin, in order that, being arrested with admonition by the president, he may haply not accomplish the sin. Let them check the disorderly, that they may not desist from assembling to hear the discourses, so that they may be able to counteract by the word of truth those anxieties that fall upon the heart from every side, by means of worldly casualties and evil communications; for if they long remain fallow, they become fuel for the fire. And let them learn who are suffering under bodily disease, and let them bring them to the notice of the multitude who do not know of them, that they may visit them, and supply their wants according to the judgment of the president. Yea, though they do this without his knowledge, they do nothing amiss. These things, then, and things like to these, let the deacons attend to.[11]

The duties enumerated for the deacons here are these:

1. They are to be the "eyes of the bishop" for the purpose of seeing those about to sin, so that the "president" may exhort the person to refrain.

2. They are to "check the disorderly" in Christian meetings, so that the people may hear the "discourses" and have the "word of truth" to counteract temptation.

---

10. Irenaeus, *Against Heresies* 1.26.3, in *Ante-Nicene Fathers,* ed. Roberts and Donaldson, 1:352; Rackham, *The Acts of the Apostles,* 84.

11. *Epistle of Clement to James* 12, in *Pseudo-Clementines, Homilies,* in *Ante-Nicene Fathers,* ed. Roberts and Donaldson, 8:220. This letter, ostensibly written by Clement of Rome to James of Jerusalem, along with another by Peter to James, was designed to give the *Homilies* credibility. The *Pseudo-Clementines* probably date from between 313–325 in their present form but were based on an earlier fictional work about Clement probably written c. 260, which in turn probably drew from two earlier sources: these two earlier documents are dated c. 160–220 (Goodspeed, *Early Christian Literature,* 83, 74, 78; and Altaner, *Patrology,* 105).

3. They are to learn of the sick and "bring them to the notice of the multitude," not the bishop, so that the people of the Church may visit them and supply their needs as the bishop deems necessary.

Although the bishop is to determine what may be necessary, the deacons are still primarily servants of the Church and not of the bishop. Speaking out of this tradition, the author here observes that even if they do these things without knowledge of the bishop, whom he prefers to call "the president," they do nothing amiss.

The pseudo-Clementine literature contains another mention of deacons, but it adds little to our knowledge. The author writes, "Let the deacons, going about, look after the bodies and the souls of the brethren, and report to the bishop."[12]

Tertullian

Tertullian, destined to become the first great figure of Latin Christianity, was born in Carthage, the son of a Roman centurion. Well educated, he became a lawyer. He was converted to Christianity c. 193 at Rome and was ordained a priest. He returned to his native Carthage, where in the first several years of the third century he became a Montanist, a rigorist group protesting what they considered to be the laxity of the Catholic Church. Even so, Tertullian ranks among the greatest of Western theologians and is credited in large measure with giving the Western Church the clear language of its theology.

In his work *On Baptism,* c. 200, he stated that deacons can baptize with the bishop's authority:

Of giving it [Baptism], the chief priest (who is the bishop) has the right: in the next place, the presbyters and deacons, yet not without the bishop's authority, on account of the honour of the Church, which being preserved, peace is preserved. Beside these, even laymen have the right.... But how much more is the rule of reverence and modesty incumbent on laymen — seeing that these powers belong to their superior — lest they assume to themselves the specific function of the bishop![13]

His interest in asserting the authority of the bishop seems to stem largely, like that of Ignatius, from his concern for the Church's unity, for he explains that schism can easily follow when others assume the bishop's functions. The reference here, it is to be remembered, is to the local Church, where the bishop is the primary leader of a congregation. Laymen, therefore, should baptize only in case of necessity. But by laymen he does not mean women. In this chapter he denies the right of women to assume the functions either of baptizing or teaching.

Although function still seems to be uppermost, Tertullian's use of "superiors" to designate the place of the bishop in reference to the laity connotes a growing

---

12. *Pseudo-Clementines, Homilies* 3.67, in *Ante-Nicene Fathers,* 8:250.
13. Tertullian, *On Baptism* 17, in *Latin Christianity: Its Founder, Tertullian,* in *Ante-Nicene Fathers* (1957), 3:677.

conception of rank and status attaching themselves to the offices of the Church. Of more importance, however, is his use of *summus sacerdos,* which above is translated "chief priest" but which may also be rendered "high priest."[14] The expression is not used elsewhere by Tertullian and is not known to have been used earlier.[15] Bishop Wordsworth writes in this connection of the emergence of the office of the bishop in the first half of the third century:

> The Bishop then, as a central authority in a sacrificial worship offered by the whole priestly race, became inevitably the *archiereus* or *"sacerdos,"* terms which came into use about the first quarter of the third century and were accepted generally from the middle of the same period.[16]

Cyprian, who derived many of his ideas from Tertullian, took over *summus sacerdos* and "built on it — and on the use of *ara* — his doctrine of the ministry, separating the Episcopate from the Presbyterate, and the clergy from the laity."[17]

But Tertullian himself asserts strongly the organic and functional nature of the Church and its people. In *The Exhortation to Chastity,* c. 205, one of his last works before his Montanist period, he argues that not only must those chosen for the "sacerdotal order" be men of one marriage but so also the laity. The tradition that priesthood belongs to the whole Church is here asserted when Tertullian asks, "Are not even we laics priests?" He further asserts that in cases of necessity, when no priests are present, laymen have the rights of priests. In such an event he says,

> You offer [celebrate the Eucharist], and baptize, and are priest, alone for yourself. But where three are, a church is, albeit they be laics.... Therefore, if you have the right of a priest in your own person, in cases of necessity, it behooves you to have likewise the discipline of a priest whenever it may be necessary to have the right of a priest.... Hence we are bound to contend that the command to abstain from second marriage relates first to the laic; so long as no other can be a presbyter than a laic, provided he has been once for all a husband.[18]

---

14. Ernest Evans translates the expression as "high priest" (see *Tertullian's Homily on Baptism: The Text Edited with an Introduction, Translation, and Commentary,* ed. Ernest Evans [London: SPCK, 1964], 35). It represents *archiereus* in the Vulgate (J. M. Lupton, *Q. Septimi Florentis Tertulliani — De Baptismo* [Cambridge: University Press, 1908], 46). *Archiereus* is used to mean "high priest" in Mark 2:26, 14:47, and "of Christ" in Heb. 2:17, 3:1. In the plural it is used as "chief priests" in Matt. 2:4; Mark 8:31 (G. Abbott-Smith, *A Manual Greek Lexicon of the New Testament* [Edinburgh: T. & T. Clark, 1937], 62).

15. Lupton, *Q. Septimi Florentis Tertulliani,* 46n.

16. John Wordsworth, *The Ministry of Grace: Studies in Early Church History with Reference to Present Problems* (London: Longmans, Green, 1901), 124.

17. Goodspeed, *Early Christian Literature,* 178; Lupton, *Q. Septimi Florentis Tertulliani,* 46n. Cf. Wordsworth, *The Ministry of Grace,* 133. Cf. also Audet, *Structures in Christian Priesthood,* 83. He states that Cyprian's view, exemplified in his assertion that the clergy "ought to serve only the altar and sacrifices, and to have leisure for prayers and supplication," made in reference to a Christian's having appointed a presbyter guardian in his will (Epistle LXV.1), is "still a novelty upon the third century scene, [and] undoubtedly marks a major change in the conception of the church's pastoral care."

18. Tertullian, *Exhortation to Chastity* 7, in *Ante-Nicene Fathers,* ed. Roberts and Donaldson, 4:54.

Although the purpose of his discussion is to show that digamy ("a second legal marriage after the termination of the first")[19] is not allowed, and although many would not agree that laymen might celebrate the Eucharist, his argument does reveal that his conception of the Church is soundly organic and apostolic. He can say, "Where three are, a church is, albeit they be laics." The laity are as much the Church as are the clergy. He here sets forth a profound truth about the nature of the Church which the clericalism of later centuries totally obscured.

Hippolytus

Hippolytus, who as a young man was a pupil of Irenaeus and succeeded him as the foremost figure of Greek Christianity in the West, wrote *The Apostolic Tradition,* c. 215,[20] in the last part of the episcopate of Zephyrinus, bishop of Rome from 198–217, whom he strongly opposed, considering him "an ignorant and illiterate individual and one unskilled in ecclesiastical definitions," who was "accessible to bribes and covetous."[21] In this compact manual we have the earliest text of the ordinal (ordination rites) and the first detailed information about ordination to the diaconate.[22] The tradition given here undoubtedly in some important respects represents the practice of the Church at Rome long before the third century.[23]

The Apostolic Tradition directs that deacons are to be chosen like the bishops and presbyters, which is by election of all the people. Hippolytus states clearly the place of the deacon in the Church in Rome at this time when he explains why only the bishop lays hands upon him in ordination:

> When the deacon is ordained, this is the reason why the bishop alone shall lay his hands upon him: he is not ordained to the priesthood but to serve the bishop and to carry out the bishop's commands. He does not take part in the council of the clergy; he is to attend to his own duties and to make known to the bishop such things as are needful. He does not receive that Spirit that is possessed by the presbytery, in which the presbyters share; he receives only what is confided in him under the bishop's authority.[24]

---

19. *Webster's Ninth New Collegiate Dictionary,* s.v. "Digamy."

20. Goodspeed, *Early Christian Literature,* 143, 149–50, for date.

21. Hippolytus, *Refutation of All Heresies* 9.6, in *Ante-Nicene Fathers,* ed. Roberts and Donaldson, 5:128.

22. The Standing Liturgical Commission of the Protestant Episcopal Church in the United States of America, *Prayer Book Studies VIII: The Ordinal* (New York: Church Pension Fund, 1957), 5; Vischer, "The Problem of the Diaconate," 22.

23. R. C. D. Jasper and G. J. Cuming *(Prayers of the Eucharist: Early and Reformed,* trans. and ed. Jasper and Cuming, 2d ed. [New York: Oxford University Press, 1980], 21) put the tradition represented here some fifty years earlier at Rome close to the time of Justin Martyr.

24. Hippolytus, *Apostolic Tradition* 9.1, 2–4, in *The Apostolic Tradition of Hippolytus: Translated into English with Introduction and Notes,* trans. and ed. Burton Scott Easton (Cambridge: University Press, 1934), 38, 39 (hereafter cited as *Apostolic Tradition of Hippolytus,* trans. and ed. Easton).

Here the deacon is not part of the ruling council of presbyters over which the bishop presides. Rather, the deacon has become the servant of the bishop in Rome, carrying out his orders, a position significantly different from that in Ignatius where they are "servants of the Church" and "subject to the bishop and presbytery," or in Polycarp where they are "servants of God" and may share in the rule of the Church. This change, as we shall soon note, is even to be seen in the difference between the wording of the ordination prayer in *The Apostolic Tradition,* representing the older tradition, and Hippolytus's explanation of it.

It is helpful for us to remember in understanding the place of the deacon in Hippolytus's writings that the leadership and rule of the Church at Rome was originally set in a council of presbyters or presbyter-bishops and probably remained so longer there than in most churches originally governed by such presbyteral councils. As Rome adopted the threefold offices, the deacon would not have had the prestige on this account which he had in churches where the leadership had been vested in the bishops and deacons and where he would more easily have become subject to and assistant of the bishop. In addition, Easton rightly points to the importance of the development of the monarchial bishop in deacons becoming the assistants and delegates of the bishops. As the bishop assumed rule of the local Church and controlled church activity, the deacons would in the normal course of events become his assistants. Easton is also probably right in maintaining that the emphasis placed by Hippolytus on explaining why the bishop alone lays his hands on a deacon in ordaining him shows that the custom, while of long standing in Rome, was still questioned.[25]

The prayer of ordination given at this point in *The Apostolic Tradition* refers to the part the deacon has in the Eucharistic offerings:

> O God, who hast created all things and hast ordered them by thy Word, the Father of our Lord Jesus Christ, whom thou didst send to minister thy will and to manifest to us thy desire; grant [the] Holy Spirit of grace and care and diligence to thy servant, whom thou hast chosen to serve the church and to offer in thy holy sanctuary the gifts that are offered to thee by thine appointed high priests, so that serving without blame and with a pure heart he may be counted worthy of this exalted office, by thy goodwill, praising thee continually. Through thy Servant Jesus Christ, through whom be to thee glory and honour, with [the] Holy Spirit, in the holy church, both now and always and world without end. Amen.[26]

In the prayer God is asked to give the Holy Spirit to the man being ordained deacon. The twofold nature of the office is seen in the mention of pastoral or charitable and liturgical functions: "to serve the Church" and "to offer in the holy sanctuary the gifts." Here we find the term "high priest" is used in reference

---

25. Easton, *The Pastoral Epistles,* 183.
26. Hippolytus, *Apostolic Tradition* 9.10–12, in *Apostolic Tradition of Hippolytus,* trans. and ed. Easton, 38–39.

to the president of the Eucharist.[27] We would note also that the office of the deacon is described as "exalted."

However, one of the most significant things to be seen here is that this prayer appears to represent an older stratum of tradition than Hippolytus's introduction to it. In the introduction, as we have seen, emphasis is laid on the bishop alone laying hands on the deacon with the explanation that the deacon is ordained to serve the bishop, but in the older ordination prayer embodying the original tradition, the deacon is clearly "to serve the Church," a subtle but significant departure.

Hippolytus makes one further point regarding the ordination of deacons. He tells us that a confessor, "if he has been in bonds for the name of the Lord," shall not have hands laid on him for either the diaconate or the presbyterate, "for he has the honour of the presbyterate by his confession." But to qualify, a confessor must have either been "punished with bonds" or "shut up in prison."[28] Bishops, however, must receive the laying on of hands, a requirement that may have been due to the necessity for unquestionable designation of this office since there was only one bishop in one place.[29]

The Apostolic Tradition tells us something of the liturgical function of the deacon. In describing the baptismal Eucharist at Easter, Hippolytus relates that the deacons bring the offerings of the people to the bishop, who eucharisticizes or consecrates them. The offerings of this period at the Eucharist were small loaves of bread and probably a little wine in a flask brought by each person. The deacons probably arranged the oblations on the altar, standing on the people's side. Then, Hippolytus directs, the bishop with all the presbytery lays his hand upon the offering and says the thanksgiving.[30]

However, in contrast to the practice of the deacon administering both the Bread and the Wine reported by Justin Martyr, Hippolytus says that the bishop shall distribute the Bread and the presbyters the three cups (water, milk, and the Wine) or if there were not enough presbyters, then the deacons were to "hold the cups."[31] Departure from earlier practice is even more strongly evident in the following statute, which Burton Scott Easton regards as a later addition. Here deacons are to break the Bread and the bishop is to give the Bread "with his own hand." Easton comments that section 2 is clearly added to the original. Section 2 adds that the presbyters are also to break and give the Bread. Further,

---

27. The prayer for the ordination of the bishop refers to the bishops both in terms of "priests" and "high-priesthood" (Hippolytus, *Apostolic Tradition* 3.3 and 6, in *Apostolic Tradition of Hippolytus,* trans. and ed. Easton, 34).

28. Ibid., 10.1–2, p. 39.

29. Marion J. Hatchett, "Rites of Ordination," lectures at the School of Theology, Sewanee, Tenn., Summer, 1975.

30. Hippolytus, *Apostolic Tradition* 23.1, in *Apostolic Tradition of Hippolytus,* trans. and ed. Easton, 48. Cf. 4.2, p. 35, where the deacons bring the offering to the bishop at the Eucharist for the ordination of a bishop; Dix, *Shape of the Liturgy,* 104, describes the offering.

31. Hippolytus, *Apostolic Tradition* 23.5–7, in *Apostolic Tradition of Hippolytus,* trans. and ed. Easton, 48–49.

when a deacon approaches a presbyter with the paten, the deacon is to "hold out his robe," a sign of respect.[32] Later tradition does appear to have been inserted into the text.

Trevor Jalland states that Ambrose of Milan speaks of the deacons administering only the chalice at Milan in *Duties of the Clergy*.[33] In the passage cited Ambrose relates that Lawrence, martyred c. 258, a deacon of Bishop Xystus (Sixtus II) of Rome, asks his bishop if he is not "a fitting servant" to suffer martyrdom with him. Speaking of himself, he says, "To him to whom thou hast entrusted the consecration of the Saviour's blood, to whom thou hast granted fellowship in partaking of the Sacraments, to him doest thou refuse a part in thy death?" As the translator points out, "consecration" is a strange expression for a deacon to use in reference to himself.[34] However, taken in the context of the practice of the Church, it is rightly understood to mean simply that Lawrence, as a deacon, administered the chalice. The fact that Lawrence is speaking of joining his bishop in martyrdom makes the reference to the deacon's liturgy in administering Christ's Blood especially appropriate. Although the Bread is not mentioned here, it is apparent, especially in light of *The Apostolic Tradition*, that this was administered by his bishop.

It may be, as Jalland also states, that deacons administer only the chalice in North Africa by the middle of the third century.[35] But at the point in Cyprian's *Treatise on the Lapsed* which he gives as his reference, the deacon is simply said "to offer the cup to those present" and nothing is said about the Bread.[36] It is more likely that the deacon lost the function of distributing the Bread at the Eucharist in the course of the fourth century with the transformation of the presbyterate, although the practice may have survived much later in Syria and perhaps elsewhere.[37]

It is further to be noted in Hippolytus's account that the deacons play a prominent part in the administration of Baptism. The Baptism is administered by a presbyter or, possibly, a bishop, assisted by deacons. Prior to the baptismal candidates entering the water, deacons stand on either side of the presbyter holding the oils the presbyter will use in anointing. The deacon on the left holds the oil of exorcism, so named for its purpose and because it is exorcised, not

---

32. Ibid., 24, p. 58. Dix argues statute 24 is original. "Textual Materials," in Hippolytus, *The Treatise on the Apostolic Tradition of St. Hippolytus of Rome,* ed. Dom Gregory Dix (New York: Macmillan, 1937), 82 (hereafter cited as *Hippolytus,* ed. Dix).

33. T. G. Jalland, "The Doctrine of the Parity of Ministers," in *The Apostolic Ministry,* ed. Kirk, 348.

34. Ambrose, *Duties of the Clergy* 1.41.214, in *St. Ambrose: Select Works and Letters,* trans. H. de Romestin, in *Nicene and Post-Nicene Fathers,* 2d ser., 10:35; The translator believes that the use of "consecration" here may be explained as due to either the close association of the deacon with the celebrant-bishop or to the sanctification of the faithful in receiving the sacrament. Massey Shepherd concurs with Jalland that it simply means Lawrence administered the chalice (personal communication to the author).

35. Jalland, "Parity of Ministers," 348.

36. Cyprian, *Treatise* 3.25, in *Ante-Nicene Fathers,* 5:444.

37. Jalland, "Parity of Ministers," 348.

blessed. The deacon on the right holds the oil of thanksgiving (chrism), the name derived from its blessing still being in the form of a thanksgiving. The presbyter anoints each candidate with the oil of exorcism after the renunciations, probably over the entire body, the clothing having been removed at the beginning of the baptismal rite. No impropriety was involved because all non-Jews in the Greco-Roman world were accustomed to nakedness in the public baths. A deacon, likewise naked, goes into the water with the candidates for the Baptism, the presbyter probably standing beside the water. After the Baptism, the presbyter anoints each with the oil of thanksgiving, again presumably over the whole body. They are then clothed and brought into the Church, where the bishop lays his hands upon them with prayer and then anoints them on their foreheads with the oil of thanksgiving, using a Trinitarian formula.[38]

The duty of the deacons to be alert to inform the bishop of any who are sick is repeated by Hippolytus, although now the subdeacons can do this as well.[39] The bishop at this point is referred to as the "high priest."

It would also appear that the deacons at Rome may have had the duty of teaching. *The Apostolic Tradition* directs,

> Let the deacons and the presbyters assemble daily at the place which the bishop may appoint; let the deacons (in particular) never fail to assemble unless prevented by sickness. When all have met they shall instruct those who are in the church, and then after prayer, each shall go to his appointed duties.[40]

These assemblies for instruction are apparently those discussed by Hippolytus in succeeding sections. They seem to have been held on weekdays and were frequent, although probably not every day. Instruction was intended for the people of the Church generally, who "will hear God speaking through the instructor." The only mention of a teacher in this later section is in the sense of one specially gifted, which could mean one endowed with a special charisma who might or might not have been one of the clergy.[41] However, it is probable that the ordinary instruction at these meetings was given by the deacons, since they are not only mentioned here before the presbyters but are to be present without fail.

If the bishop is not present at an *agape* (Christian fellowship meal), Hippolytus tells us that the faithful must take the "blessed bread," which is not the Eucharist, and the catechumens the "exorcised bread" only from the hand of a presbyter or deacon. The text makes it apparent that deacons can bless this non-eucharistic bread: "And even if the bishop should be absent when the faithful meet at a supper, if a presbyter or a deacon is present they shall eat in a similar orderly fashion.... But if (only) laymen meet, let them not act presumptuously, for a layman cannot bless the blessed bread."[42]

---

38. *Apostolic Tradition of Hippolytus* 21–22, trans. and ed. Easton, 45–47, and "Notes," 90, 91, 93.
39. Hippolytus, *Apostolic Tradition* 30, p. 53.
40. Ibid., 33.1, 2, p. 53.
41. Ibid., 35, 36.1, p. 54.
42. Ibid., 26.11, 12, p. 51.

The Apocalypse (Vision) of Paul

The Apocalypse (or *Vision*) *of Paul,* a document that probably originated in Egypt c. 245 and had much influence on the Middle Ages,[43] pictures presbyters, bishops, and deacons as among the ranks of the damned in that order. The author writes relative to his vision of a deacon:

> I saw another man in the fiery river up to his knees. Moreover his hands were stretched out and bloody, and worms proceeded from his mouth and nostrils and he was groaning and weeping, and crying. He said: Have pity on me! for I am hurt above the rest who are in this punishment. And I asked, Sir, who is this? And he said to me: This man whom thou seest, was a deacon who devoured the oblations and committed fornications and did not right in the sight of God, for this cause he unceasingly pays this penalty.[44]

It is interesting that the order here at this date lists the presbyter first and then the bishop and the deacon, perhaps reflecting the importance of the presbyteral council with the monepiscopate in this area in the middle of the third century. It is further to be noted that it is the deacon who is said to suffer more than any other. This is apparently due to his having "devoured the oblations," since the presbyter is also guilty of fornication. The close association of the deacons with the oblations of the people is here affirmed, and the implication is that the deacons took for themselves offerings intended for the poor, especially widows and orphans.

The Latter Half of the Third Century (and Beyond)

The poor and needy had always been a major concern of the Church and were the special responsibility of the deacons. Although this ministry of service, by the middle of the third century, was probably not stressed so much as it had been previously, it was and remained one of the Church's great concerns. At Rome in the time of Bishop Fabian, who died in the Decian persecution of 250, the deacons had been so burdened with this work that the bishop divided the city into seven regions corresponding to the number of deacons, fixed at Rome and in some other places at seven due to the influence of Acts 6. A deacon was put over each and the office of subdeacon created to assist the deacons and then to succeed them. The churches of the Roman deaconries became the titles of the cardinal deacons at a much later time.[45]

The legend of Lawrence, deacon of the Church at Rome martyred in 258, serves to illustrate the importance of the care of the poor in the work of

---

43. Quasten, *Patrology,* 1:146–48.

44. *Apocalypse (Vision) of Paul* 36, in *Documents, Remains of the First Ages: Biographical Synopsis, Index,* in *Ante-Nicene Fathers,* ed. Roberts and Donaldson, 9:160.

45. Reicke, "Deacons in the New Testament and in the Early Church," 12; Lietzmann, *A History of the Early Church,* 2:249; Leo Gillet, "Deacons in the Orthodox East," in *Theology* 58 (1955): 416n.

the diaconate. The legend relates that, when arrested and ordered to hand over the treasures of the Church, Lawrence brought the poor of the Christian community.[46]

Deacons Made Bishops

At Rome, as Hans Lietzmann affirms, "the college of deacons stood next to the bishop, and constituted his executive, and the papal throne was usually filled from one of its members." Often, in fact, throughout the Church of the second and third centuries the senior deacon was elected to succeed the bishop, whose executive assistant he had been.[47] And the practice continued long after. Joseph Bingham observes in this connection that it was not necessary to be ordained presbyter to be made bishop and adds, "Deacons were as commonly made bishops as any other."[48] The selection of deacons rather than presbyters oftentimes to fill vacancies in the bishop's office was logical, since many of the bishop's duties were administrative, as were the deacon's, following the emergence of the monepiscopate and later the monarchial episcopate.

Various examples of deacons being made bishops may be cited.[49] Eusebius as a deacon represented Dionysius, bishop of Alexandria, at the Council of Antioch called in 264 to deal with Paul of Samosota. The Laodiceans came to know him there and elected him their bishop. Caecilian was archdeacon when ordained bishop of Carthage in 311 at the beginning of the Donatist schism. Athanasius was the principal deacon of Alexandria when he succeeded Alexander as its bishop in 328. Felix, a deacon of the Roman Church, was appointed to succeed Liberius, bishop of Rome, when the latter was sentenced to exile by Emperor Constantius, c. 355, for resisting Arianism, although Liberius afterwards accepted the Arian formula and was allowed to reoccupy his see.[50] John

---

46. R. P. Symonds, "Deacons in the Early Church," *Theology* 58 (1955): 408.

47. Lietzmann, *A History of the Early Church,* 2:249; Dix, "Ministry in the Early Church," 283.

48. Joseph Bingham, *The Antiquities of the Christian Church: The Works of Joseph Bingham,* Books I–III, ed. R. Bingham, new ed. (London: Oxford University Press, 1855), 2.10.5, 1:109. The concept of the clerical offices as a hierarchical structure through which one must move to attain the higher rank develops later and is discussed in chap. 6.

49. It has sometimes been said that Heron, the successor of Ignatius of Antioch, was a deacon when elected bishop: e.g., John Mason Neale, *The Patriarchate of Alexandria,* vol. 2 of *A History of the Holy Eastern Church* (London: Joseph Masters, 1847), 21 (hereafter cited as Neale, *Alexandria*), cites Eusebius (*Hist. Eccl.* 3.36), but Eusebius does not say that Heron was a deacon in the citation. *The Epistle of Ignatius to Hero* does say so, but it is spurious, dating from the fourth century (*Ante-Nicene Fathers,* ed. Roberts and Donaldson, 1:113–15).

50. John Mason Neale, *A History of the Holy Eastern Church,* vol. 3, *The Patriarchate of Antioch,* ed. George Williams (London: Rivingtons, 1873), 54–55 (hereafter cited as Neale, *Antioch*); Eusebius, *Ecclesiastical History* 7.11.26, 32.5, in *Nicene and Post-Nicene Fathers,* 2d ser., 1:302, 318, and 318n; Optatus 1.16, in *The Work of St. Optatus, Bishop of Milevis, Against the Donatists,* trans. O. R. Vassal-Phillips (London: Longmans, Green, 1917), 31; Theodoret, *The Ecclesiastical History of Theodoret* 1.25, in *Theodoret, Jerome and Grennadius, Rufinius Historical Writings etc.* (1953), in *Nicene and Post-Nicene Fathers,* 2d ser., 3:60–61, 79. Cf. Socrates Scholasticus, *The Ecclesiastical History* 2.37, in *Socrates, Sozomenus: Church Histories* (1952), in *Nicene and Post-Nicene Fathers,* 2d ser., 2:65; *Oxford Dictionary of the Christian*

Chrysostom, who became bishop of Constantinople in 398, made one of his own deacons, Hercalides, bishop of Ephesus.[51]

Beyond the fourth century we continue to find examples of deacons being elected bishop. In the fifth century, c. 446, Leo the Great, bishop of Rome, wrote that metropolitans are to be chosen from "the presbyters of that same church or from the deacons."[52] The most famous of these deacons was Gregory the Great, who as a deacon had been sent by Pelagius II of Rome as his *apocrisiarius* to the imperial court in Constantinople and after returning to his monastery in Rome was elected bishop of that city while still a deacon in 590 to succeed Pelagius.[53] Andronicus, a deacon of the Church of Angelium when chosen, succeeded Anastacius as Jacobite Patriarch of Alexandria in 614. As late as the twelfth century we find that upon the death of Chail IV, Jacobite Patriarch of Alexandria, in 1102, one of the two candidates for his successor was John, a deacon, although his rival, Macarius, was elected by the synod.[54]

The election of deacons to the episcopate serves to illustrate the importance of the office and the esteem in which it was held. In the third century the deacons seem often to have overshadowed the presbyters in their importance and influence. Although this was soon to change, at least as a common occurrence, the office did retain much of its former respect and honor for many centuries before it declined into relative insignificance.

Didascalia

In the Syrian *Didascalia,* dating probably from c. 220–250, the number of deacons is to be in proportion to the size of the local Church, unlike Rome and some other places where it was fixed at seven. The author sees a close relationship between the bishop and the deacons. They are to "be of one mind," a point made even stronger later in the work when the bishop and the deacon are to be "of one counsel, and of one purpose, and one soul dwelling in two bodies." As in the Ignatian letters, the deacon is to "make all things known to the bishop, even as Christ to His Father."[55] But the deacon is now, a century after Ignatius, first to take care of all the work that he can, reflecting the increase in numbers in the churches. With the added responsibilities thrust upon the bishop as leader of the local Church, the office has become somewhat more remote than previously. The deacons are to act as intermediaries for the bishop, and the people are to have

---

Church, ed. F. L. Cross and E. A. Livingstone, 2d ed. (London: Oxford University Press, 1974), 821 (s.v. "Liberius").

51. Altaner, *Patrology,* 374, for date; Socrates, *The Ecclesiastical History* 6:11, in *Nicene and Post-Nicene Fathers,* 2d ser., 2:146.

52. Leo the Great, *Letter* 14.7, in *The Letters and Sermons of Leo the Great,* trans. Charles Lett Feltoe: *The Book of Pastoral Rule and Selected Epistles of Gregory the Great,* trans. James Barmby (1956), in *Nicene and Post-Nicene Fathers,* 2d ser., 12:18.

53. Altaner, *Patrology,* 557.

54. Neale, *Alexandria,* 2:55, 237.

55. *Didascalia Apostolorum: The Syriac Version* 2.44, 3.13, trans. R. Hugh Connolly (Oxford: Clarendon Press, 1929), 109, 148. For document date, Altaner, *Patrology,* 56.

very free access to the deacons, and let them not be troubling the head at all times. For neither can any man approach the Lord God almighty except through Christ. All things therefore that they desire to do, let them make known to the bishop through the deacons.[56]

The *Didascalia* is also dependent upon Ignatius's writings in likening the bishop to God the Father, the deacons to Jesus Christ, and the presbyters to the apostles.[57] It is to be noted here that the deacons are mentioned just after the bishops, due undoubtedly both to their close association with the bishop and to their importance in the Church. But it is important to remember that the bishop at this time was in reality comparable to the leader of a congregation today, not the leader of a diocese.

The *Didascalia*, unlike Ignatius, adds two other classes of offices. Between the deacons and the presbyters in the section just referred to, the document directs that "the deaconess shall be honoured by you in the place of the Holy Spirit," the expression originating as a result of "spirit" being feminine in Semitic languages such as Hebrew, Aramaic, and Syriac. Then, following the presbyters, the church order states that "the orphans and widows shall be reckoned by you in the likeness of the altar." Such symbolism is repeated elsewhere in the document, especially in connection with the widows. Their association with "the altar" derives from the fact that they offer prayers for the Church and receive gifts from the Church for their support.[58] They are not, of course, to be considered with the major orders, but both classes do represent a development in the century since Ignatius.

These deaconesses have many but not all of the functions of the male deacons. The *Didascalia* says that they are required for the ministry to women. They are needed to go to visit some women in places where sending a deacon might cause scandal, especially among the heathen, as to visit women who are sick and others who are in need, and to bathe those recovering from sickness. The liturgical function of the deaconess is that of anointing women in Baptism, since this anointing normally covered the whole body but was restricted to the head when no woman was present to do it. The document prefers that the anointing be done by a deaconess but allows another women to do it when a deaconess is not present. The deaconess is also to instruct the women following their Baptism in how to keep the seal of Baptism unbroken by purity and holiness of life. The invocation of the divine names, however, is to be pronounced by a man. The emphasis is on letting "a woman rather be devoted to the ministry of women, and a male deacon the ministry of men."[59]

Some have seen in the *Didascalia* a role for the deaconess comparable, or virtually so, to that of the deacon. Their duties, such as visiting women in pagan

---

56. *Didascalia Apostolorum* 2.28, p. 90.
57. Ibid., 2.26, p. 88.
58. Ibid., 88n. Cf. 3.6, pp. 133–34; 3.10, p. 143; 4.5, p. 156.
59. Ibid., 3.12, 3.13, pp. 146–48.

households where a deacon would not be allowed, caring for other women who are sick, and instructing women after Baptism, are similar, and so also is their attending and anointing women in Baptism. However, deaconesses are mentioned in only two places in the document in contrast to many references to deacons, and their presence is not required in the one liturgical function recorded, that of anointing in Baptism. They have no liturgical function apart from other women at the Eucharist.

Aimé Georges Martimort in her scholarly historical study of deaconesses affirms that deaconesses were not female deacons. She writes in reference to this document, which gives deaconesses a greater role than other documents,

> The ministry performed by deaconesses was thus an important one. In chapter 16 of the *Didascalia,* it is presented as parallel with that of the deacon, so much so that Fr. Cipriano Vagaggini was moved to describe it as one of the two branches of the Church's total ministry subsumed under the diaconate: "The diaconal ministry of the Church had two branches: a masculine ministry and a feminine one for ministering to women specifically." This is to forget, however, as we saw earlier in chapter 9 of the *Didascalia,* that deaconesses were placed in a separate category from deacons....The roles were...not exactly parallel. Deaconesses took no part in the liturgy. Indeed, their part in the rite of baptism itself was very restricted; they simply completed the anointing begun by the celebrant. Nor did they pronounce the invocation, or epiclesis. In no way could they be considered on the same level as deacons: they were their auxiliaries.[60]

Martimort explains that social conditions in the eastern region of the Roman Empire brought about the creation of deaconesses, the greatest of which had to do with the Church's requirement of total nudity in Baptism and the inappropriateness in that culture of men viewing or anointing the bodies of women in that state. In the conclusion to her study Martimort finds no justification for considering deaconesses female deacons. She observes that "during all the time when the institution of deaconesses was a living institution, both the discipline and the liturgy of the churches insisted upon a very clear distinction between deacons and deaconesses."[61]

The author of the *Didascalia,* in contrast to *The Apostolic Tradition,* which directs that deacons, bishops, and presbyters alike are to be chosen by the people, states that the presbyters and deacons are appointed by the bishop. In reference to the deacons he writes, "O bishop...those that please thee out of all the people thou shalt choose and appoint as deacons: a man for the performance of the most things that are required, but a woman for the ministry of women."[62]

The same practice seems to have been followed in North Africa at this time, although the North African bishops ordinarily acted with the advice of the clergy and people. Cyprian says that deacons are appointed by the bishop. But he also

---

60. Aimé Georges Martimort, *Deaconesses: An Historical Study,* trans. K. D. Whitehead (San Francisco: Ignatius Press, 1986), 42–43.

61. Ibid., 43–44, 247.

62. *Didascalia Apostolorum* 3.12, p. 146.

teaches that bishops, presbyters, and deacons are to be appointed in the presence
of all the people according to the example of the apostles given in Acts 4. In a
letter to the clergy and people of Carthage from his retreat he also explains that
he has ordained Aurelius a reader without consulting them because the young
man was "already approved by the Lord." But his custom was otherwise, for he
states, "in ordinations of the clergy, beloved brethren, we usually consult you
beforehand, and weigh the character and deserts of individuals, with the general advice."[63] Influences of the monepiscopate would seem to have persevered
longer in North Africa than in Syria.

Throughout this Syrian Church order the presbyters appear secondary
"though senior" to the deacons, who are the bishop's "close and constant" com-
panions. The presbyters are to be counselors of the bishop and councilors of the
Church. The presbyters and the deacons together are to form a council with the
bishop for rendering judgments in disputes between members of the Church.[64]

The *Didascalia* also sees a close connection between the priests and the
levites of the Old Testament and the clergy of the Church.[65] The comparison
is to be found in many writings of the Church fathers, but it is clearest here. It
makes possible the application of the rules regarding the first-fruits, tithes, and
other offerings to the Church and so providing for the clergy's support as well
as for the orphans, widows, and others in need. Instructions are given for the
distribution of income among the clergy, although provision for the presbyters
seems to be optional, indicating that the office of deacon developed into a full-
time occupation before that of the presbyters. In North Africa, Cyprian mentions
the "monthly divisions" in connection with ordaining presbyters.[66]

In the *Didascalia* we find the first recorded liturgical formula for the deacon.
After the dismissal of the catechumens and before the beginning of the prayers,
when the bishop stands in the church to pray, the author directs, "Wherefore,
O bishops, that your oblations and your prayers may be acceptable, when you
stand in the Church to pray let the deacon say with a loud voice: Is there any
man that keepeth aught against his fellow?"[67] Here we see the organic nature of
the Church as well as the liturgical formula. Peace and love among all members
of the Christian community are needed if the oblations and prayers of the Church
at the Eucharist are to be acceptable to God.

In another reference to the liturgical function of the deacon, two deacons with
specific duties at the Eucharist are mentioned: "But of the deacons let one stand
always by the oblations of the Eucharist; and let another stand without by the

63. Cyprian, *Epistle* 32.1, 64.3, and 67.4, 5, in *Ante-Nicene Fathers,* ed. Roberts and
Donaldson, 5:311–12, 336, 370–31.
64. Symonds, "Deacons in the Early Church," 409; *Didascalia Apostolorum* 2.28, 2.47,
pp. 90, 111.
65. Ibid., 2.26, p. 86.
66. Vischer, "The Problem of the Diaconate," 23; *Didascalia Apostolorum* 2.26, 2.28, pp. 86,
90; Cyprian, *Epistle* 33.5, in *Ante-Nicene Fathers,* 5:314.
67. Connolly, Introduction to *Didascalia Apostolorum,* xii; *Didascalia Apostolorum,* 2.54,
p. 117.

door and observe them that come in; and afterwards, when you offer, let them minister together in the Church."[68] The oblations are the offerings of the people, which may well have been put on a table near the entrance as the people arrived. It is almost certainly correct to assume that later in the third century, if not at this time, deacons did bring the oblations of bread and wine to the bishop at the altar following the liturgy of the word and just prior to the beginning of the Eucharist itself. However, there is no evidence to indicate, as has been asserted, that the deacons at this date spread a linen cloth over the altar before placing the oblations upon it. Although such a covering may well have been used, there is nothing to indicate that it was placed there in the course of the Eucharist or by the deacons.[69]

The author continues to discuss the arrangement of the assembly and instructs the deacon "who is within" to keep order and insure that "decency and decorum" prevail. It is an additional duty of the deacon to inquire of those coming from another congregation whether that person belongs to the Church. And the *Didascalia* tells us the bishop may delegate either deacons or presbyters, mentioned in that order, to baptize.[70]

The third century was a period in which the dignity and importance of the deacon increased at the expense of the presbyter. Perhaps the climax is recorded in the *Didascalia,* where the deacon usually takes precedence over the presbyter. The churches of the pre-Constantinian era were relatively small. In most places a single bishop presided over the Church and could administer its needs with the assistance of the deacons and the direction of the presbyterial council. However, the situation was soon to change with the rapid growth of the Church in the next century, following the adoption of the Constantinian policy of toleration, with the resultant delegation of more and more duties to the presbyters.[71]

Cyprian

Cyprian is the "most clear and comprehensive" of all the fathers "in his conception of the body of Christ as an organic whole, in which every member has an honourable function."[72] Ignatius taught "Do nothing without the bishop," but Cyprian emphasizes the equally primitive concept, "Let bishops do nothing without the presbytery and people." Cyprian, in writing to the presbyters and

---

68. *Didascalia Apostolorum,* 2.57, p. 120.

69. In describing the pre-Nicene Eucharist Dix says that it was the function of the deacon to cover the altar with a linen cloth after the exchange of the kiss of peace, just prior to the Eucharist itself (*Shape of the Liturgy,* 104). However, his reference is from Optatus of Milevis, which he dates c. 360. Optatus states simply that the altar is covered and says nothing about the deacons: "which of the faithful is there who is unaware that during the celebration of the Mysteries, the wood of the altar is itself covered with linen?" (*Optatus* 6.1, p. 251, though Dix's reference is to 6.2, in which the cloth is not mentioned).

70. *Didascalia Apostolorum* 2.58, 3.12, pp. 120, 146–47.

71. Easton, *Pastoral Epistles,* 183; Marion J. Hatchett, "Seven Pre-Reformation Eucharistic Liturgies," in *St. Luke's Journal of Theology* 16, no. 3 (June 1973): 17 (hereafter cited as Hatchett, "Seven Liturgies").

72. A. Cleveland Coxe, "Introductory Notice to Cyprian," in *Ante-Nicene Fathers,* 5:263.

deacons from his retirement during the Decian persecution in 250, clearly expressed his concept of the interdependence of all orders and between the laity and the ordained within the Church. He declared it his principle that "from the first commencement of my episcopacy, I made up my mind to do nothing on my own private opinion, without your advice and without the consent of the people."[73]

One cannot help but note the freedom and flexibility shown by the early Church. Much of this stemmed from the profound understanding of its organic nature. Cyprian could say that under extreme circumstances a deacon could convey sacramental absolution because it was the Church that possessed the ministry and the sacraments and administered the means of God's grace. He mentions this unusual function of the deacons when he directs that they may hear confessions of the lapsed who have certificates from the martyrs and are in imminent danger of death when a presbyter cannot be found. Then, "the imposition of hands upon them for repentance" will bring them forgiveness. Some modern Roman Catholic theologians have maintained that this was sacramental confession.[74] There was order but not the sterile narrowness that has permeated so much of the Church's thinking with the rampant clericalism of later centuries.

Apostolic Constitutions

Although the deacons would acquire the right to read the Gospel lesson in the Eucharist, it does not appear that they possessed this privilege in the third century as R. P. Symonds thinks probable. Cyprian, in writing to the Church at Carthage during his temporary retirement from the city, regarding the ordination of Celerinus as a reader, speaks of this function as belonging to the readers.[75] It is in the *Apostolic Constitutions,* c. 380, that a deacon or a presbyter *in that order* is directed to read the Gospel.[76] Jerome (d. c. 420) refers to deacons reading the Gospel, the context implying that it was a customary function at that time. Sozomen says that at Alexandria the Gospel lesson was read by the archdeacon, "whereas in many places it is read by the deacons, and in many churches only by the priests; while on noted days it is read by the bishops, as for instance at Constantinople, on the first day of the festival of the resurrection."[77]

73. Cyprian, *Elucidations* 2 and *Epistle* 5.4, in *Ante-Nicene Fathers,* 5:283, 410.

74. Ibid., 12.1, 5:293; Herbert Thurston, "Deacons," in *The Catholic Encyclopedia,* ed. Charles G. Herbermann et al. (New York: Encyclopedia Press, 1908), 4:649.

75. Symonds, "Deacons in the Early Church," 412; Cyprian, *Epistle* 33.5, in *Ante-Nicene Fathers,* 5:313.

76. Altaner, *Patrology,* 59, for date; *Apostolic Constitutions* 11.57, in *Lactantius, Venantius, Asterius, Victorinus, Dionysius, Apostolic Teaching and Constitutions, Homily, and Liturgies* (1951), in *Ante-Nicene Fathers,* 7:421.

77. Jerome, *Letter 147.6,* in *St. Jerome: Letters and Select Works,* trans. W. H. Fremantle, assisted by G. Lewis and W. H. Martley (1954), in *Nicene and Post-Nicene Fathers,* 2d ser., 6:292; Sozomen, *Ecclesiastical History* VII.19, in *Nicene and Post-Nicene Fathers,* 2d ser., 2:390.

Apparently, it was in the fourth century that the deacon acquired the prerogative of reading the Gospel at the Eucharist, although it was not exclusive. There seems to be no evidence that deacons were allowed to preach at this time. The sermon was given by the presiding officer, usually a bishop, seated in his chair.[78]

One of the liturgical functions sometimes ascribed to deacons of the third century is that of bidding the intercessory prayers of the faithful at the Eucharist. While it is possible that the deacons began this practice in the third century, it is not mentioned in the Egyptian sacramentary of Serapion, dating from c. 350. Bishop Wordsworth says that in this sacramentary all prayers are said by the bishop, except one for the bishop and the Church, which may have been said by another bishop or a presbyter. He specifically remarks that there is nothing for the deacons to say.[79] The earliest reference to the deacons bidding the prayers of the people is in the Syrian *Apostolic Constitutions,* c. 380.

There the deacons do have a most prominent part. In addition to reading the Gospel, as we noted above, they announce various stages of the liturgy, such as dismissing the hearers: "Let none of the hearers, let none of the unbelievers stay." They bid the various intercessory prayers of the Church. They announce the kiss of peace, keep order, and with the subdeacons guard the doors. They bring the oblations to the altar and two of them stand beside the altar with fans to insure that insects do not get into the chalices. At the conclusion a deacon says, "Depart in peace." Dix rightly states that only the bishop spoke directly to God on behalf of the Church, while the deacon spoke *to* the Church.[80]

We have already seen that the *Didascalia* in the first half of the third century says that the deacons in Syria at that time called out, "Is there any man that keepeth aught against his fellow?" just after the catechumens had been dismissed and before the bishop began the prayers of the faithful. What we see a century and a half later in the *Apostolic Constitutions* regarding the deacon announcing phases of the service and bidding the prayers of the people is a logical development and is fully in accord with the pre-Nicene concept of the organic nature of the Church. Therefore, we may well assume that these functions of the deacon did grow, perhaps in the Syrian Church, spreading elsewhere between the time of the *Didascalia* and the *Apostolic Constitutions.*

Theodore Klauser observes that it is noteworthy that Hippolytus does not mention the deacon's call summoning the attention of the people with the words, "Listen, attend," or with his announcement, "The holy Things for the holy

78. Marion J. Hatchett, *Sanctifying Life, Time, and Space: An Introduction to Liturgical Study* (New York: Seabury Press, 1976), 45.

79. Dix, *Shape of the Liturgy,* 31 (cf. Hatchett, *Sanctifying Life,* 49); Quasten, *Patrology,* vol. 3, *The Golden Age of Greek Patristic Literature from the Council of Nicaea to the Council of Chalcedon* (Westminster, Md.: Newman Press, 1950), 82; *Bishop Serapion's Prayer Book — An Egyptian Sacramentary Dated Probably about A.D. 350–356,* 2d ed., trans. John Wordsworth (London: SPCK, 1923), Introduction, 24, 86n. Serapion is also spelled Sarapion.

80. *Apostolic Constitutions* 8.1.14 and 8.2.5, 6, 11, 12, in *Ante-Nicene Fathers,* 7:483, 485ff; Dix, *Shape of the Liturgy,* 35.

people!" However, he says, "It is possible, nevertheless, that both of these (or something similar) were in use at this time."[81]

Certainly, the position of the deacon shown in the *Didascalia* was of such prominence that it would be natural for him to assume added functions at the Eucharist in the third century in Syria. And in light of these factors we are probably justified in assigning to him the bidding of the prayers of the Church in this region by the end of the century. However, conditions following the Constantinian policy of toleration, particularly the marked increase in numbers in the Church and the acquisition of more permanent and suitable buildings for the Eucharist, were more conducive to the rather elaborate liturgical development in the deacon's office found in the *Apostolic Constitutions* and care should be exercised in ascribing them to the third century.

Baptism by Deacons

At the beginning of the third century we find evidence that the deacon was on a par with the presbyter in the administration of Baptism. Tertullian's treatise *On Baptism* is extremely important not only as the earliest work on this subject but as the only pre-Nicene treatise on any of the sacraments.[82] He writes, "The supreme right of giving (Baptism) belongs to the high priest, which is the bishop: after him, to the presbyters and deacons, yet not without commission from the bishop, on account of the Church's dignity: for when this is safe, peace is safe."[83]

Tertullian, writing c. 198–200, in his early, orthodox period, adds that in emergencies even laymen baptize, but emphasizes that presbyters and deacons may ordinarily do so with the consent of the bishop. We have already noted that the *Didascalia* not only affirms that the bishop may delegate to either deacons or presbyters the right to baptize but mentions them in that order.[84] Canon 77 of the Council of Elvira, c. 306, provides, "If a deacon, that takes care of a people without either bishop or presbyter, baptizes any, the bishop shall consummate them by his benediction." Bingham sees this to mean that the canon "plainly supposes that deacons had the ordinary right of baptizing in such churches over which they presided" and is certainly correct.[85]

Jerome verifies this function of the deacon in his work *Against Luciferians,* c. 379:

> I do not deny that it is the practice of the Churches in the case of those who living far from the greater towns have been baptized by presbyters and deacons, for the bishop to visit them, and by the laying on of hands to invoke the Holy

81. Theodore Klauser, *A Short History of the Western Liturgy: An Account and Some Reflections,* trans. John Halliburton (London: Oxford University Press, 1969), 15.

82. Quasten, *Patrology,* 2:278.

83. *Tertullian's Homily on Baptism,* ed. Evans, 35.

84. *Didascalia Apostolorum* 3.12, pp. 146–47. Quasten, *Patrology,* 2:280, for date.

85. Bingham, *The Antiquities of the Christian Church,* 2:20.9, 1:258.

Ghost upon them. . . . It is that without ordination and the bishop's license neither presbyter nor deacon has the power to baptize.[86]

He also adds that of necessity laymen may and often do baptize. Cyril of Jerusalem, d. 386, strongly implies that both deacons and presbyters baptize regularly, at least in the smaller towns, as a matter of their office.[87]

It is to be remembered that, in the pre-Nicene Church when the organic principle prevailed and the functions of the various offices were not so sharply defined, the deacon was not an "inferior" order, and the Church was in the process of delegating liturgical functions to meet the needs of growing numbers. In this period even the Eucharist was at times presided over by a deacon. We recall Ignatius's instruction, "You should regard the Eucharist as valid which is celebrated either by the bishop or by *someone* he authorizes."[88] In the late third century, probably during the Diocletian persecution, some deacons offered (presided over) the Eucharist, a practice forbidden by the Council of Arles, 314,[89] but one the council did not declare invalid. The fact that deacons and congregations could easily accept the deacon offering the Eucharist, probably in the absence of both the bishop and presbyters, a practice that Edward Landon says "in many places had been allowed," shows the importance of the deacon and his prominence in the practice of the Church's liturgies.[90] We may rightly include Baptism as a function of the deacon by virtue of his office, although with authorization by the bishop, at this time.

Deacons Put Over Churches

Many of the same factors that led to the deacon being authorized to baptize along with the presbyter also apparently gave rise to deacons being given the charge of small congregations, at least on occasion. Canon 77 of the Council of Elvira, c. 306, which we have noted, is unambiguous in this regard when it refers to a deacon who "takes care" of a congregation without either a bishop or presbyter (*"Si quis diaconus regens plebem sine episcopo vel presbytero"*). In his commentary on the Council of Elvira and fourth-century Christianity, Alfred

---

86. Jerome, *The Dialogue Against the Luciferians* 9, in *Nicene and Post-Nicene Fathers,* 2d ser., 6:324. Altaner, *Patrology,* 470, for date.

87. Cyril of Jerusalem, *Catech.* 17.35: "For, at the season of baptism, when thou art come before the Bishops, or Presbyters, or Deacons (for its [the Holy Spirit's] grace is everywhere, in villages and in cities, on them of low as on them of high degree, on bondsmen and on freemen, for this grace is not of men, but the gift is from God through men), approach the Minister of Baptism but approaching, think not of the face of him thou seest, but remember this Holy Ghost of whom we are now speaking" (in *St. Cyril of Jerusalem. St. Gregory Nazianzen* [1955], in *Nicene and Post-Nicene Fathers,* 2d ser., 7:132).

88. Ignatius, *Smyrneans* 8, in *Early Christian Fathers,* ed. Richardson, 115 (italics added).

89. Canon 15, Arles, in Charles Joseph Hefele, *A History of the Christian Councils, from the Original Documents to the Close of the Council of Nicaea, A.D. 325,* in Hefele, *History of the Councils,* 1:193. Bingham, *The Antiquities of the Christian Church,* 2.20.8, 1:255.

90. Edward Landon, *A Manual of Councils of the Holy Catholic Church* (London: Griffith Farrar & Co., n.d.), 1:45. Early in chap. 6 consideration is again given to this and certain other evidence of the deacon presiding at the Eucharist.

Dale states that new churches were not directed by bishops of their own but were under the charge of a presbyter or deacon. Charles Joseph Hefele probably rightly applies this to the expansion of the Church from larger towns into the countryside, a presbyter or deacon being sent from the larger place to the rural assembly, which remained under the bishop of the town.[91]

Bingham says that "country-presbyters and deacons" were put over churches, citing Canon 77 of Elvira, and with Hefele sees this in reference to country congregations. However, Bingham in the same chapter goes on to speak several times about "country-presbyters" being "fixed upon" country churches without including deacons,[92] indicating that although the practice existed presbyters were more frequently put in charge of rural congregations.

The *Testament* of the forty martyrs of Sebaste, who died c. 320, may be interpreted as indicating by implication that deacons in Armenia led rural congregations: "We also salute the faithful in the district of Sarein, the priest with his people, the deacons with their people; Maximus with his people, Haesychius with his people, Cyriacus with his people."[93]

The writings of Jerome, *Against Luciferians,* and Cyril of Jerusalem, *Catechetical Lectures,* which have just been cited in connection with Baptism, also lend some weight to deacons having oversight of rural churches in the late fourth century. The fact that they apparently baptize would lead to this conclusion. Also in connection with Baptism, the Council of Toledo, 400, directs that "before Easter deacons or sub-deacons shall fetch the chrism from (the bishop)," who alone may consecrate it.[94] Canon 3 of the First Council of Vaison, 442, is quite similar.[95] Gregory of Tours writes that Cautinus, who was later made bishop of Auvergne, was, "in his diaconate, in charge of the church of that village."[96] Wilhelm Schamoni sees in these references to Toledo, Vaison, and Gregory of Tours evidence that deacons as a normal practice were placed over parishes.[97] However, with the probable exception of Gregory's reference, it is

---

91. Hefele, *History of the Councils,* 1:169, 170; Alfred W. W. Dale, *The Synod of Elvira and Christian Life in the Fourth Century* (London: Macmillan, 1882), 70. Hefele includes the *chorepiscopoi* along with the presbyters and deacons as being put over these rural congregations.

92. Bingham, *The Antiquities of the Christian Church,* 9.8.4–5, in 3:413–18. Canon 13 of Neocaesarea is also cited but only presbyters are mentioned in it in this connection.

93. *Testament,* trans. Wilhelm Schamoni, in Schamoni, *Married Men as Ordained Deacons,* trans. Otto Eisner (London: Burns & Oates, 1955), 72. The *Testament* of the martyrs of Sebaste, in contrast to their *Acts,* is authentic. Altaner, *Patrology,* 250.

94. Charles Joseph Hefele, *A History of the Councils of the Church, from the Original Documents, A.D. 326 to A.D. 429,* trans. Henry N. Oxenham, in Hefele, *History of the Councils,* 2:421 (Canon 20 of Toledo).

95. Charles Joseph Hefele, *A History of the Councils of the Church, from the Original Documents, A.D. 431 to A.D. 451,* trans. editor of Hagenbach's *History of Doctrines,* in Hefele, *History of the Councils,* 3:165.

96. Gregory, Bishop of Tours, *De Gloria Confessorum.* Cap. 30, in *Patrologiae Latinorum,* ed. J. P. Migne (Paris: n.p., 1879), 71:851.

97. Schamoni, *Married Men as Ordained Deacons,* 74. He also cites Canon 49 of Agde, 506, but Hefele, *History of the Councils,* 4:84, does not regard this canon as genuine. Further, the pertinent part may be otherwise interpreted: "Deacons and priests who are appointed to a

certainly possible that there were both presbyters and deacons in these country churches, who together constituted the leadership.

A careful analysis of the evidence leads to the conclusion that deacons did exercise leadership in at least some rural congregations in the third and fourth centuries. However, this assertion must be a guarded one. As we have seen, the Church gradually delegated most of the liturgical functions of the bishop to the presbyter and not, at least generally speaking, to the deacon. Deacons did not preach or "offer" (preside at) the Eucharist by virtue of their office, although exceptions have been noted to the latter function. Therefore, they could not ordinarily have functioned as heads of congregations in the same way that bishops and later presbyters did. It is too much to claim, as Schamoni does, that

> in the transitional period between antiquity and the early middle ages, when the Church expanded into the country areas, the deacon did great work as precursor and pioneer of the priest in the filial churches; by virtue of his ordination, he acted as leader of the community.[98]

The deacon's office did give him the prestige but not the requisite liturgical function to have the place as head of the eucharistic assembly. And in light of the existence of the *chorepiscopi,* there would seem to be no compelling reason that the Church at that time would have been hesitant to have ordained presbyters to preside at the Eucharist even in small rural churches. It is probable that in most places there were both presbyters and deacons in the country churches. Since deacons had the right to baptize with the same authorization needed by the presbyter, they may well have baptized with a presbyter present, a possibility that would avoid the inference drawn from references that deacons headed congregations because they baptized, as cited in the passages from Jerome, *Against Luciferians,* and Cyril of Jerusalem, *Catechetical Lectures.*

Although contrary to the thinking of later centuries, the organic conception of the early Church along with the importance of the deacon and the permanency of his office would have made it possible for small places under a nearby bishop to have been put under the charge of a deacon, even though there was also a presbyter there, but one who might have been much younger and less experienced. However, whatever the circumstances were when these small churches were put under the care of deacons, the practice does not appear to have been general.

The Blessing of the Paschal Candle

As we have seen, in Hippolytus deacons did have the authority to bless the non-eucharistic "blessed bread" at an *agape,* at least in the absence of the bishop. Another blessing, one that belonged to the deacon then and is still the dea-

---

parish may not alienate anything of the ecclesiastical property entrusted to them" which does not necessarily imply that deacons were placed over parishes in the absence of priests. Schamoni appears to press the evidence further than it will bear in light of the lack of other testimony.

98. Schamoni, *Married Men as Ordained Deacons,* 32.

con's prerogative in the Roman and Anglican Churches today, is that of the paschal candle at the Great Vigil of Easter. The lighting and blessing of the paschal candle, symbolizing the return of light to the spiritual world in the risen Christ, remains one of the Church's most impressive sacramentals. Its origin is, however, shrouded in antiquity.[99]

We do know from Eusebius that the deacons were closely associated with the lights used during the night of the Easter Vigil at Jerusalem, at least in the third century. In relating the report of a miracle by Narcissus, bishop of Jerusalem c. 200, in which water was reputed to have been changed into oil through his prayer, Eusebius writes, "They say that the oil once failed while the deacons were watching through the night at the great paschal vigil."[100] Although the miracle is not to be thought genuine, the report does indicate the existence of the vigil as a long-established custom by the time of Eusebius in Jerusalem.

Elsewhere Eusebius also tells us that Constantine the Great "changed the holy night vigil into a brightness like that of day, by causing waxen tapers of great length to be lighted throughout the city: besides which, torches everywhere diffused their light, so as to impart to this mystic vigil a brilliant splendor beyond that of day."[101] The Great Vigil of Easter appears to have been well established in the fourth century in the East.

The most important of the ceremonies relating to the lights of the Easter Vigil as they have come down to us is the lighting and blessing of the paschal candle by the deacon. Dix sees its origin in the ceremony at the beginning of the vigil service on Holy Saturday, which he believes was in use at Jerusalem in the fourth century, in which the deacon blessed the lamp put beside the lectern to provide light for the lector. On the other hand, W. J. O'Shea argues that the paschal candle is not derived from the custom of symbolizing the resurrection of Christ with lights at the Easter Vigil, although this symbolism may subsequently have influenced it. Rather, he thinks the probable origin is in the daily ceremony of the deacon lighting and blessing a lamp in the evening to provide needed illumination for the evening services, which in time became an elaborate ceremony accompanied by psalms, chants, and prayers called the Lucernarium.[102]

The truth probably encompasses both customs. The daily ceremony of lighting and blessing a lamp to provide light for the evening services would naturally take on greater significance at the Easter Vigil and be influenced by the use of the lighted lamps and candles symbolizing the risen Christ. It is almost inevitable that the lights of the Easter Vigil would have suggested the special paschal candle symbolizing the risen Lord at the daily ceremony of lighting and blessing a lamp when it was done at the Easter Vigil and is probably implied in Dix's discussion.

99. W. J. O'Shea, "Easter Vigil," in *New Catholic Encyclopedia*, 5:10.
100. Eusebius, *Church History* 6.9.2, 3, in *Nicene and Post-Nicene Fathers*, 2d ser., 1:255.
101. Eusebius, *Life of Constantine* 4.22, in *Nicene and Post-Nicene Fathers*, 2d ser., 1:545.
102. Dix, *Shape of the Liturgy*, 23, 24n; O'Shea, "Easter Vigil," 5:10.

The lack of citations referring to the earliest mention of this is due in part to a letter from Jerome to a deacon named Praesidius mentioning it, but which was thought to have been spurious from the sixteenth to the present century because of additions to it. However, critical studies increasingly attest to its authenticity, and we may consider it to be genuine.[103] Another citation from Augustine is doubtful, since the crucial phrase, which Augustine uses to introduce several lines of praise, is literally "verses in praise of a (the) candle," although Bettenson translates the sentence in the text, "This is how I put the same thought in some verses in praise of the paschal candle." But Bettenson sees the reference as being to perhaps "a votive candle offered as a prayer or a thanksgiving," not a reference to the paschal candle blessed by a deacon on Holy Saturday.[104] Marcus Dods gives the first reading as, "It is this which some one has briefly said in these verses in praise of the Creator," with the alternate, "Which I briefly said in these verses in praise of the taper."[105] The three verses of praise that follow end with a direct address to the Creator.

Jerome's letter to Praesidius, written no later than 384, is the first clear reference to the blessing of the paschal candle.[106] The deacon Praesidius, who served the Church at Piacenza in northern Italy, had asked Jerome to write the hymn of blessing, called the Exultet, which he was to sing over the paschal candle at the Easter Vigil. Although Jerome declines to do so primarily because, he said, the Scriptures offer a dearth of material about wax and candles, he does positively attest to the existence of the ceremony at that time.

It is in Ennodius, bishop of Pavia, 514 to 521, that we find the oldest forms for this blessing.[107] His extant works include two blessings for the paschal candle.[108] Ennodius became deacon at Pavia c. 493 but moved to Milan c. 496.

103. J. N. D. Kelly, *Jerome: His Life, Writings, and Controversies* (New York: Harper & Row, 1975), 111 and n.

104. Augustine, *The City of God* 15.22, trans. Henry Bettenson (Harmondsworth, Middlesex, England: Penguin Books, 1971), 636 and n. Bettenson here also says that the chant of the Easter Vigil called the *Exultet* has sometimes been attributed to Augustine "without good reason."

105. Augustine, *City of God,* in *Nicene and Post-Nicene Fathers,* 1st ser., 2:303. John Healy's translation reads "Creator" with no alternative (Augustine, *The City of God,* ed. R. V. G. Tasker [London: J. M. Dent & Sons, 1945], 2:89). J. W. C. Wand's reads "Paschal Candle" but gives "Creator" as alternate (*St. Augustine's City of God,* abridg. and trans. Wand [London: Oxford University Press, 1963], 258).

106. Kelly, *Jerome,* 111, for date. Jerome, *Epistle* 28, *Ad Praesidium, De Cereo paschali,* ed. Jacques Paul Migne, *Patrologia cursus completus,* Series latina, Tomus 30, *S. Hieronymi, Tomus undecimus* (Paris: n.p., 1846), 182–88, published on microcards, 1960, Fo-60, M359-2, vol. 30, card 1 (of 6), pp. 1–88. Duchesne mentions this letter in a footnote and dates it in 384, but in accord with the assumption that it was apocryphal he says that it is "attributed" to Jerome (L. Duchesne, *Christian Worship, Its Origins and Evolution: A Study of the Latin Liturgy Up to the Time of Charlemagne,* 5th ed. [London: SPCK, 1923], 253n).

107. Altaner, *Patrology,* 572, for date. Tyrer says that the oldest witness to the blessing of the paschal candle is the two blessings in Ennodius, but as we have seen the earliest reference is in Jerome. Tyrer probably still assumes this work of Jerome to be spurious (*Historical Survey of Holy Week: Its Services and Ceremonial* [London: Oxford University Press, 1932], 150).

108. Ennodius, *Opuscula miscella* 9 and 10, "Benedictio Cerei," in *Magni Felicis Ennodii: Opera Omnia,* vol. 6 of *Corpus Scriptorum Ecclesiasticorum,* recensuit et commentario, Guilelmus Hartel (Vindobonae: Apud C. Geroldi Filium Bibliopolam Academiae, 1882), 415–22.

Duchesne believes the two blessings are formularies drawn up for Ennodius's own use as a deacon of Pavia before he became its bishop. It is of passing interest to note that Ennodius was the first to restrict the title of *papa* almost entirely to the bishop of Rome.[109]

Did Deacons Preach?

It has frequently been asserted that preaching was a function of the diaconate in the early Church.[110] An examination of the evidence, however, does not support this conclusion.

Since the time of Irenaeus, as we have noted, the Seven of Acts 6 were considered by some to have been deacons, although modern scholarship has come down overwhelmingly on the side of John Chrysostom and other early writers who said the Seven were not deacons. Stephen and Philip, the only two of the Seven mentioned later in the New Testament, have been thought of as evangelists, Philip being so described in Acts 21:8. Although Brockman argues that the thing Stephen and Philip are doing in Acts "represents an essentially catechetical instruction" and that they are simply doing what any committed Christian would,[111] the picture there strongly suggests more than that. Their role, as we have seen, appears to be one of leadership, and preaching is distinctly implied. Yet, in spite of this, there is a dearth of evidence to support preaching as a diaconal function anywhere or at any time in the early Church.

Canon 2 of the Council of Ancyra, c. 314 C.E., has been interpreted to indicate that the deacon did preach at that time. The canon refers to lapsed deacons who had returned to the Church. It provides that they shall keep their office but specifies in this connection that they "shall abstain from making proclamations (*kerussein*)."[112] Hefele here translates this term as "preach," apparently on the assumption that deacons did preach, but adds in his commentary that other proclaiming functions of the deacon are also intended under the prohibition of this canon.[113] The fact is that these other proclaiming functions are well authenticated; preaching is not. Bingham argues convincingly that "preaching" here is not correct but rather the term is to be understood to refer to the deacon as "the sacred crier of the congregation," citing others maintaining this view. Henry Percival in his commentary on the canon supports Bingham and sees this as a

---

109. Altaner, *Patrology,* 572, 574; Duchesne, *Christian Worship,* 253n.

110. Echlin, *The Deacon in the Church Past and Future,* 17, 21, 76. Cf. Schamoni, *Married Men as Ordained Deacons,* 15, and Holmes, *Future Shape,* 25. Bingham, *The Antiquities of the Christian Church,* 2.20.11, 1:260–61, says that deacons preached but only with the license of the bishop.

111. Brockman, *Ordained to Service,* 8.

112. The Council of Ancyra, in *The Seven Ecumenical Councils,* ed. Percival, in *Nicene and Post-Nicene Fathers,* 2d ser., 14:63.

113. Hefele, *History of the Councils,* 1:202–3.

reference to the reading of the Gospel and the numerous proclamations of the deacons at the Eucharist.[114]

Echlin quotes the *Didache* to support his assertion that deacons preached:[115]

Elect therefore for yourselves bishops and deacons worthy of the Lord, humble men and not covetous, and faithful and well tested; for they also serve you in the ministry of the prophets and teachers. Do not, therefore, despise them, for they are the honored men among you along with the prophets and teachers.[116]

Echlin rightly sees, as we have noted previously, that the bishops and deacons took over the function of the prophets and teachers. However, he argues that deacons as well as bishops assumed the functions of both the prophets and teachers, and therefore of preaching:

Deacons did by reason of their office what prophets and teachers did by reason of their charism which was itself becoming institutionalized. The task of prophets and teachers, therefore of *episcopoi* and deacons, was to preach.[117]

Other evidence from the period indicates that the bishop was the one who assumed the function of presiding at the eucharistic assembly and preaching from the prophets, and the deacons assumed other functions in the leadership and ministry of the local Church. Brockman interprets the *Didache* to mean that the deacon's ministry of the word at this time was of a catechetical nature.[118] In light of the evidence, it is more logical to interpret this passage to mean simply that the leadership of the Church was transferred in this period from the prophets and teachers to the bishops and deacons, the bishops assuming some of the functions and the deacons others. Evidence from other sources clearly makes preaching along with presiding at the Eucharist a function of the bishop, not the deacon.

The letter of Ignatius of Antioch *To the Philadelphians* is also seen by Echlin to contain evidence that deacons preached at this early date. He translates the pertinent passage, "Philo, the deacon from Cilicia who has been so well spoken of, is at present giving me his help in preaching God's word." However, Gerald Walsh in *The Fathers of the Church* translates the phrase in question, "who is now ministering to me in the word of God," and the translator of this letter in the *Ante-Nicene Fathers* renders it "who still ministers to me in the word of God." Richardson translates the phrase "he is helping me in God's cause."[119] Again, the weight of evidence clearly favors an understanding other than preaching.

---

114. Bingham, *The Antiquities of the Christian Church*, 2.20.10, 1:260. See Percival's commentary on Canon 2, in *The Council of Ancyra*, in *Nicene and Post-Nicene Fathers*, 2d ser., 14:64.

115. Echlin, *The Deacon in the Church Past and Future*, 16.

116. *The Didache or Teaching of the Twelve Apostles* 15.1, 2, trans. Francis X. Glimm, in *The Apostolic Fathers*, vol. 1 of *The Fathers of the Church*, trans. Glimm et al., 183.

117. Echlin, *The Deacon in the Church Past and Future*, 17.

118. Fuller, "Early Catholicism"; Brockman, *Ordained to Service*, 21.

119. Echlin, *The Deacon in the Church Past and Future*, 21 (the citation is *To the Philadelphians* 11); Ignatius, *To the Philadelphians* 11, in "The Letters of St. Ignatius of Antioch," trans. Gerald G. Walsh, in *The Apostolic Fathers*, vol. 1 of *The Fathers of the Church*, trans. Glimm et

In the fifth century there is one clear reference to a deacon preaching. The historian Philostorgius reports, c. 430, that Aetius, a deacon of Antioch, was allowed to preach publicly in the church by his bishop, the Arian Leontius. Echlin cites this as evidence not only that the deacons "still preached" but also that the deacon Aetius "contributed to the demise of diaconal preaching" by preaching Arianism.[120] But it is more probable that preaching by deacons is not to be found later because it was never a function of the order itself.

The great classic writer of the Syrian Church, Ephraem Syrus, d. 373, who remained a deacon throughout his life, is described by Altaner as "a brilliant exegete, controversialist, preacher, and poet." His reputation as a preacher, however, may well be due to the excellence of his written compositions, which Jerome records were read in many churches immediately after the Scriptures, presumably as the sermon at the Eucharist.[121] The reading of such homilies by deacons is in accord with the legislation of the Second Council of Vaison (529). Canon 2 provides, "Not only in the cities, but also in all rural churches the priests may preach. If the priest is hindered through sickness, a deacon should *read a homily by a Father of the Church*."[122] The clear implication here is that deacons did not preach. However, even were it true that Ephraem preached, he apparently did so more due to his special charisma than to his office as a deacon.

In writing of the diaconate in the medieval Church, Brockman says that it is clear that deacons were "ordained to the ministry of the word" and that this ministry remains a major diaconal function in both the East and the West. However, he sees it in a missionary context, envisioning the deacon in his ancient role as a kind of messenger of the bishop who sought out "those in need, prospective converts, and the poor" and brought word back to the bishop.[123] He does not mention liturgical preaching.

The assertion that deacons preached as a matter of their office in the early Church is clearly contrary to the evidence. The function belonged normally to the president of the eucharistic assembly, and except when deacons functioned in that capacity as an extraordinary act, there is very little, if any, reason to believe that they preached before the Church. It is probable that preaching came to be thought of as a diaconal function in the Medieval period, when the diaconate

---

al., 117; Ignatius, *To the Philadelphians* 11, in *Ante-Nicene Fathers,* 1:85, and in *Early Christian Fathers,* ed. Richardson, 111.

120. Philostorgius, *Ecclesiastical History* 3.17, in *Patrologiae Cursus Completus Omnium SS. Patrum, Doctorum Scriptorumque Ecclesiasticorum Sive Latinorum, Sive Graecorum,* ed. J. P. Migne (Turnholt, Belgium: Brepols, n.d.), 65:508–9; Echlin, *The Deacon in the Church Past and Future,* 76.

121. Altaner, *Patrology,* 401; Jerome, *De Scriptor. Eccles.* 115, in Bingham, *The Antiquities of the Christian Church,* 1:262n. The Greek text, in which Photius says that Ephraem composed several excellent sermons that were translated into other languages after his death, is also given in Bingham, *The Antiquities of the Christian Church,* 1:262n.

122. Hefele, *History of the Councils,* 4:170. Italics added.

123. Brockman, *Ordained to Service,* 28.

had become largely an interim or transitional office on one's journey to the priesthood.[124]

A Permanent Vocation

There is one other major aspect of the diaconate that should be noted before we turn to the fourth century. In the pre-Nicene Church the diaconate was conceived of as a permanent vocation. Deacons could become presbyters but usually did not. The clerical offices were not yet regarded as grades through which one moved from the inferior to the superior. However, considerable development did take place after the emergence of the monepiscopate in the second century and its adoption throughout the Church.[125]

It was natural that the bishop came to be considered the highest official because he was president of the local Church, presiding over both the presbyteral council and the eucharistic assembly. Next would come the presbyters. They were normally older, and at least in those churches that had originally been governed by a council of presbyters, one of their number had presided. Their position and honored place is shown by their forming a semicircle on either side of the bishop at the Eucharist. The deacons, normally being younger and actively serving the Church in their distinctive functions both pastorally and liturgically, as time went on naturally came to be thought of as ranking after the bishops and presbyters. However, it would be a mistake to overemphasize the importance of the presbyters in relation to the deacons in this period, as we shall shortly see.

Certainly, by the middle of the third century a developed conception of gradation with respect to the clerical offices is clearly in evidence. Cyprian can write at that time that Pope Cornelius

> was not one who on a sudden attained to the episcopate; but, promoted through all the ecclesiastical offices, and having often deserved well of the Lord in divine administrations, he ascended by all the grades of religious service to the lofty summit of the Priesthood.[126]

Cyprian, however, did not view the various offices of the Church as "steps" up a ladder in the sense that was to develop. This idea was not present except perhaps in embryonic form, as has been affirmed by Walter H. Frere: "It is noticeable that the idea that 'the Christian clergy consisted of a hierarchy of grades, through each of which it was *necessary* to pass in order to reach the higher offices,' was not yet current."[127] Such a concept of hierarchical structure was only to develop later, as we shall see when we turn to the fourth century. The various orders

---

124. Cf. Hardy, "Deacons," 29.

125. Symonds, "Deacons in the Early Church," 412; Cyprian, *Epistle* 5.4, in *Ante-Nicene Fathers,* 5:283.

126. Cyprian, *Epistle* 51.8, in *Ante-Nicene Fathers,* 5:329.

127. Walter Howard Frere, "Early Forms of Ordination," in *Essays on the Early History of the Church and the Ministry by Various Writers,* 2d ed., ed. H. B. Swete (London: Macmillan, 1921), 263–312 and 226n.

were still regarded as permanent vocations, Baptism being the only sacramental prerequisite.

Whether or not presbyters ever later became deacons is an interesting subject and important only because the possibility of asking the question is indicative of the pre-Nicene conception of the Church's offices. There seems to be no recorded instance of this having happened, although that could be due to the sparsity of records in the very early period. If such transitions did occur, they were rare. Presbyters were usually older and probably would have been allowed to function as deacons when necessity demanded from an early time, although it is perhaps more likely that someone from among the younger men of the local Church would have been pressed into service under such circumstances. There was certainly no concept of a "higher" order containing within itself the "lower." By the time of the *Apostolic Constitutions,* c. 380, it was clearly stated that "it is not lawful for any one of the other clergy to do the work of a deacon."[128] Each order was viewed as a lifelong vocation long after the transition in the fourth-century Church set the stage for the radical theological change involved in a hierarchical structure with graded ranks.

In the eighth century, the noted Alcuin provides an example of continuing lifelong diaconal vocations. Born c. 730 of a noble family near York in England, he was ordained deacon in 770. A man of vast learning, Alcuin was persuaded by Charlemagne to join his court in 781, where he served as the emperor's most distinguished advisor and rekindled the light of classical and biblical learning in the Frankish kingdom. He was made abbot of Tours, to which he retired in 796. He died there on May 19, 804, still a deacon.[129]

In the eleventh century the archdeacon of Rome continued to be in deacon's orders. Archdeacon Hildebrand would undoubtedly have remained a deacon had he not been elected to fill the papal throne in 1073.

Thomas of Celano, a contemporary of Francis of Assisi, who joined the Franciscan friars c. 1214, wrote the earliest biography of Francis (d. 1226) at the command of Pope Gregory IX in 1228. In describing the Eucharist on Christmas Eve c. 1223 at Greccio, when Francis had a creche prepared and thus inaugurated the custom of putting nativity scenes in the churches at Christmas, Celano says that Francis was a deacon. He writes, "The saint of God was clothed with the vestments of a deacon, for he was a deacon, and he sang the holy Gospel in a sonorous voice.... Then he preached to the people standing about."[130] Francis was never ordained a presbyter.

In the late fifteenth century Cardinal Piccolomini administered the diocese of Siena as a deacon for forty years until his election to the papacy in 1503.

---

128. *Apostolic Constitutions* 8.28, in *Ante-Nicene Fathers,* 7:494.

129. *The Proper for the Lesser Feasts and Fasts. 1991 together with the Fixed Holy Days* (New York: Church Hymnal Corp., 1991), 226; L. Wallach, "Alcuin," in *New Catholic Encyclopedia,* 1:279.

130. *The Oxford Dictionary of the Christian Church,* 1373; John R. Moorman, *Saint Francis of Assisi* (London: SPCK, 1963), 101; Thomas of Celano, *The First Life of St. Francis* 30.86, trans.

At the Council of Trent, 1545–63, Cardinal Reginald Pole was one of its three presidents. He was in deacon's orders at that time and remained so until being made a bishop later.[131]

In the Church of England in the early seventeenth century Nicholas Ferrar's life demonstrates that there could still be a place for a lifelong vocation as a deacon. Coming from a family prominent in the affairs of the Virginia Company, he was ordained a deacon when that company was dissolved in order to establish a unique religious community in 1626 at Little Gidding. There in a manor house he, his mother, his brother and sister with their spouses and nineteen children, and a number of servants formed a community for prayer, study, and service. Their discipline of prayer was rigorous. Their works included education of the children of the district and care of the poor and the sick. Ferrar died in 1637 as a deacon, but the community continued until Little Gidding was sacked by the Puritans in 1646. Inspired by this community, T. S. Eliot named the last of his *Four Quartets,* considered to be one of the great religious poems of the twentieth century, "Little Gidding."[132]

The story of David Pendleton Oakerhater is not only that of a genuine deacon in the nineteenth and early twentieth century in the American Episcopal Church but one that brings great credit to Native Americans. This splendid man was a Cheyenne warrior who distinguished himself for bravery and leadership as an officer in an elite corps of the Cheyenne in their conflict with the U.S. government. He was among twenty-seven warrior leaders taken captive, charged with inciting rebellion, and imprisoned in Florida in 1875 by the Army of the United States. There, due to the interest and concern of an Army captain, they learned English and encountered Christianity. He and three other prisoners went north to study for ordination, helped financially by a Mrs. Pendleton. In 1878 he was baptized in Syracuse, New York, taking the name David Pendleton Oakerhater in honor of his benefactress.

He was ordained deacon in 1881 in the Episcopal Church and returned to Oklahoma. He told his people, "You all know me. You remember, when I led you out to war, I went first, and what I told you was true. Now I have been away to the East and I have learned about another captain, the Lord Jesus Christ, and he is my leader. He goes first, and all he tells me is true. I come back to my

---

in Marion A. Habig, *St. Francis of Assisi: Writings and Early Biographies: English Omnibus of the Sources for the Life of St. Francis* (Chicago: Franciscan Herald Press, 1972), 301. Although it is possible to interpret this text and later references, which are dependent upon it, to mean that Francis was deacon at the Eucharist without having been ordained to the office, the interpretation given by the translator is more probable. Conrad L. Harkins, Director of the Franciscan Institute, St. Bonaventure University, St. Bonaventure, N.Y., and an expert on the life of Francis, states that in his opinion "it is morally certain that Francis was a deacon" (personal communication to the author). Cf. André Callebaut, "Saint François lévite," *Archivum Franciscanum Historicum* 20 (1927): 193–96.

131. Brockman, *Ordained to Service,* 30.

132. *The Proper for the Lesser Feasts and Fasts. 1991,* 80; John R. H. Moorman, *A History of the Church in England,* 2d ed. (New York: Morehouse-Barlow, 1967), 236.

people to tell you to go with me now in this new road, a war that makes all for peace."

For half a century he worked among his people, often at great personal sacrifice, to found and operate schools and missions and to serve them with pastoral care as well until his death on August 31, 1931. He is known among the Cheyenne Indians of Oklahoma as "God's Warrior." His feast day on the Episcopal calendar is September 1.[133]

Brockman says that the diaconate as a permanent vocation remained at Rome in a curious form until nearly the turn of the twentieth century. There, certain members of the papal diplomatic corps were in deacons' orders until the dissolution of the Papal States in 1870, the last of them dying before the end of the century.[134]

The Subdiaconate and Minor Orders

Cyprian's reference to "all the grades of religious service" would include the minor orders in existence at the time.[135] The development of these orders was basically a true expression of the Church's ministry in that it exhibited and expressed the breath and variety of that ministry much more than the three major orders alone do.

In the mid-second century Pope Cornelius wrote that there were then seven subdeacons, forty-two acolytes, and fifty-two exorcists, readers, and janitors or doorkeepers at Rome. From Tertullian we know that the office of reader had come into existence a half century earlier.[136] Hippolytus mentions readers and subdeacons and specifies that hands shall not be laid upon them, since they are not ordained. However, by c. 380 the *Apostolic Constitutions* direct that subdeacons and readers are to be ordained.[137] But as Bishop Wordsworth says in his translation of the collection of prayers of Serapion, bishop of Thmuis in the Nile delta, dating probably from before 350, the absence of ordination forms for the subdeacons, readers, and interpreters mentioned there indicates that only the bishops, presbyters, and deacons were ordained at that time in Egypt.[138] Cyprian himself mentions both subdeacons and acolytes in his letters. Acolytes assisted at the Eucharist and appear to be found only in the West, where they became numerous.[139]

---

133. Ibid., 320.

134. Brockman, *Ordained to Service,* 30, 31.

135. Cyprian, *Epistle* 51.8, in *Ante-Nicene Fathers,* 5:329.

136. Eusebius, *Church History* 6.43.11, in *Nicene and Post-Nicene Fathers,* 2d ser., 1:228; Tertullian, *On Prescription Against Heretics* 41, in *Ante-Nicene Fathers,* 3:263.

137. Hippolytus, *Apostolic Tradition* 12, 14, in *Apostolic Tradition of Hippolytus,* trans. and ed. Easton, 40–41; *Apostolic Constitution* 8.3.21, 22, 26, in *Ante-Nicene Fathers,* 7:492–93.

138. Wordsworth, in *Serapion's Prayer Book,* 87n. The attribution to Serapion of this collection of prayers, preserved in an eleventh-century manuscript on Mount Athos, has been questioned, but the Egyptian origin and date appear to be the same. Dix, *Shape of the Liturgy,* 162. Cf. Jasper and Cuming, trans. and eds., *Prayers of the Eucharist,* 38.

139. Cyprian, *Epistle* 27.3, in *Ante-Nicene Fathers,* 5:306; A. J. Maclean, "Ministry (Early

The existence of the subdiaconate is in itself evidence of the growing importance of the office of deacon in the late second and early third centuries. The office of subdeacon arose due to the need to release deacons from some of their duties. The subdeacon's primary work was to aid the deacons at the Eucharist and in their other functions. Mention of the office in the Syrian *Didascalia,* which probably dates from the first half of the third century, perhaps even its earlier decades, is evidence that the subdiaconate had become widespread if not universal by the middle of the third century.[140] In the fourth century the office is mentioned in the legislation of councils such as Elvira (c. 305), Canon 30; Antioch (c. 341), Canon 10; and Laodicea (343–381), Canons 20–22 and 25.[141]

Christian)," in *Encyclopedia of Religion and Ethics,* ed. James Hastings (New York: Scribner's, 1916), 8:668.

140. Frere, "Early Forms of Ordination," 305; Maclean, "Ministry (Early Christian)," 8:668; *Didascalia Apostolorum* 2:34, p. 96; Altaner, *Patrology,* 56.

141. Hefele, *History of the Councils,* 1:149; *Nicene and Post-Nicene Fathers,* 2d ser., 14:113, 144.

Chapter 6

The Radical Transition
of the Fourth Century

The Importance of the Deacon

The deacon entered the fourth century as a person of considerable importance and prestige in the Church. We have already noted that frequently a deacon was elected bishop. Deacons served not only as executive assistants of the bishops but represented them on occasion at councils. Pope Sylvester sent two presbyters and two deacons to represent him at the Council of Arles, c. 314, where the British Church was represented by three bishops and a deacon.[1]

The deacon Athanasius was perhaps the most notable example of the period. He played a leading role in the first ecumenical council in 325. Theodoret tells us that while "a very young man, although he was the principal deacon" of Alexandria, Athanasius attended the Council of Nicaea in the retinue of its bishop, Alexander. There, he "so defended the doctrines of the apostles, that . . . he won the approbation of all the champions of the truth." Although no minutes of Nicaea have survived, it is likely that the influence of Athanasius was exercised from the sidelines, since the records of all later ecumenical councils and ancient synods of bishops indicate that advisors brought by bishops could exercise great influence but did not sit, speak, or vote in formal council sessions. Shortly after the council adjourned, Alexander died and Athanasius succeeded him as bishop of that great city.[2]

Other testimony to the importance of the deacon at this time, particularly in relation to the presbyter, is seen in the repeated reminders to the deacons regarding the limits of their functions and their "inferiority" to the presbyters.

Canon 18 of Arles, 314, is directed against "city deacons," who have apparently assumed prerogatives or authority belonging to the ruling presbyteral council, although the exact application is uncertain: "Concerning the city dea-

---

1. Landon, *A Manual of Councils of the Holy Catholic Church*, 1:44.
2. Theodoret, *Ecclesiastical History* 1.25, in *Nicene and Post-Nicene Fathers*, 2d ser., 3:60–61.

cons, that they take not so much upon themselves but preserve to the presbyters their order, that they do nothing without the presbyters' knowledge."[3]

As noted in the previous chapter, Canon 15 of Arles forbids deacons "to offer" (preside at) the Eucharist, which in many places seems to have been allowed, probably during the Diocletian persecution when no bishop and perhaps no presbyters were available.[4] This practice may not have been so much a presumption as a reflection of the importance of the diaconate and the old "organic" theology wherein the priesthood belonged to the whole people of God and distinctions between orders were not so clearly drawn. It was in fact in the third century that "the line between clergy and laity was only beginning to be defined."[5]

The matter of deacons presiding as chief eucharistic celebrants was definitely settled in 325 by Canon 18 of Nicaea, which states that according to neither canon nor custom do the deacons have any right "to offer" the Eucharist and should not, therefore, administer to presbyters, who do "offer," or touch the Eucharist before the bishop. Further, the canon provides, the deacons are not to sit among the presbyters whose "inferiors" they are, the legislation itself attesting by its protest to the high esteem in which the diaconate was held. As we have seen already, the practice of deacons administering the Eucharist to the presbyters, now condemned and forbidden at Nicaea, was the practice of the earlier period. It is the reflection of the more organic concept of the Church in the pre-Nicene age, where office was not so much a matter of rank and status but rather of function. It was only natural that the deacons administer the Eucharist to the "liturgically non-participant but revered and seated" presbyters of the congregation.[6] However, since the role of the presbyter was changing from one of membership in the governing presbyterial council to one of the pre-Nicene bishop as president of the local Church and the eucharistic assembly with the right by virtue of the office "to offer" or preside at the Eucharist, it seemed to the Council inappropriate for deacons to administer the Eucharist to them.

Terminology here can be confusing and misleading. In our time we have been accustomed to speak of the eucharistic president as *"the celebrant"* of the

3. Stevenson, ed., *New Eusebius*, 324. Cf. Hefele, *History of the Councils*, 1:194.

4. Hefele, *History of the Councils*, 1:193. Stevenson (*New Eusebius*, 324) numbers this Canon 16. Symonds, "Deacons in the Early Church," 412, supports deacons so offering by stating that Tertullian in *De exhort. Cast.* 7 taught that laymen could offer the Eucharist under exceptional circumstances: "Accordingly, where there is no joint session of the ecclesiastical Order, you offer and baptize, and are priest, alone for yourself. But where three are, a Church is, albeit they be laics.... Therefore, if you have the *right* of a priest in your own person, in cases of necessity, it behooves you to have likewise the discipline of a priest wherever it may be necessary to have the right of a priest." (*On Exhortation to Chastity*, in *Ante-Nicene Fathers*, ed. Roberts and Donaldson, 4:54.) However, *On Exhortation to Chastity* was probably written shortly before Tertullian's conversion to Montanism. Earlier, in his pre-Montanist *The Prescription against Heretics* 41, he forcibly rejects the idea.

5. Frere, "Early Forms of Ordination," 304.

6. George H. Williams, "The Ministry of the Ante-Nicene Church (c. 125–325)," in *The Ministry in Historical Perspective*, ed. H. Richard Niebuhr and Daniel D. Williams (New York: Harper & Brothers, 1956), 58 (hereafter cited as Williams, "Ante-Nicene").

Eucharist; and sometimes when presbyters or bishops act as co-eucharistic presidents, they are called "concelebrants." But are not all the baptized celebrants and concelebrants of the Eucharist? This expression significantly diminishes the status of all the baptized, by implication suggesting that others who have no right to the presiding function are somehow not celebrants, or at best celebrants of much lower degree. Does not such terminology in effect deny the priesthood bestowed on all the faithful in Baptism? There was good reason for the Church in its pristine period to refuse to call any of its leaders "priest." If we take seriously the New Testament view that Christ is the one, true priest of his priestly people and all the baptized share in his royal priesthood, then it is clear that the person who presides at the Eucharist is only *a celebrant,* although perhaps in some sense the "chief celebrant" or the presiding celebrant.

The importance of the diaconate in this early period is to be seen as much in its lingering eminence as anywhere else, even as it slowly declined. Ambrosiaster, in the time of Pope Damasus (366–384), was moved to write "On the Boastfulness of the Roman Deacons," because the deacons there attempted to take precedence over the presbyters. Jerome tells us that at Rome a presbyter is only ordained on the recommendation of a deacon and that "their paucity makes deacons persons of consequence, while presbyters are less thought of owing to their great numbers."[7] The "paucity" here is a reference to the number of deacons at Rome having been fixed at seven, reflecting the belief among some at that time that the Seven of Acts 6 were deacons. The position of the deacons, especially at Rome, was enhanced by their close association with the bishop and their responsibility in administering large funds and great estates.[8] Jerome wrote his letter to Evangelus in reference to the latter's inquiry regarding Ambrosiaster's observations about the deacons at Rome. Jerome is more interested in showing that presbyters and bishops are the same than that the deacons there are arrogant. However, Jerome continues regarding deacons:

> But even in the Church of Rome the deacons stand while the presbyters seat themselves, although bad habits have by degrees so far crept in that I have seen a deacon, in the absence of the bishop, seat himself among the presbyters, and at social gatherings give his blessing to them.[9]

The history of the diaconate prior to Jerome's time indicates that what Jerome supposes to be newly acquired "bad habits" are but a reflection of the traditional prestige and place of the deacon in the early Church, especially before Nicaea. It was the presbyters who were increasing in importance as they became less numerous and assumed the place and functions of the pre-Nicene bishops.

---

7. Ambrosiaster (Pseudo-Augustine), *Quaestiones Veteris et Novi Testamenti CXXVII 101,* trans. Alexander Souter, in *Corpus Scriptorum Ecclesiasticorum Latinorum* (1908; rpt., New York: Johnson Reprint Corp., 1963), 50:193–98; Jerome, *Letter 146.2,* p. 388.

8. Bligh, "Deacons in the Latin West Since the Fourth Century," 423. Cf. Greenslade, Introduction, to Jerome, *Letter 146,* p. 384.

9. Jerome, *Letter 146,* p. 384.

It is interesting to note that in 495 a Bishop Victor wrote to Pope Gelasius complaining that some of his deacons were refusing to be ordained presbyters. In September of that year the pope wrote advising the bishop not to try to coerce the deacons into becoming presbyters but that certainly he had subdeacons or acolytes of sufficient maturity whom he could ordain directly to the presbyterate.[10]

We see the importance the deacons still retained in the seventh century when the Council of Toledo, 633, directs that deacons "are not to raise themselves above the presbyters, and stand in the first choir whilst the priests are in the second."[11]

Dix remarks that

> no deacon ever played again quite the sort of part which Athanasius seems to have played at Nicaea as the righthand man of Bishop Alexander, though at Rome the archdeacon (who was still a man in deacon's orders) could still be a most important functionary as late as the eleventh century, as the Archdeacon Hildebrand was to show.[12]

Hildebrand was appointed archdeacon of Rome in 1059. It is an interesting historical anomaly that he sat on the papal throne for more than two months prior to his becoming a bishop, for a month as a deacon and then as a priest. He was elected pope and enthroned still in deacon's orders on April 22, 1073, being ordained priest on May 22 and bishop on June 29 of that year.[13]

Ariald, another deacon of the eleventh century, demonstrates that Hildebrand was not simply an isolated case. He achieved prominence as leader of a reform party in the Church at Milan, protesting against what had been termed the dissolute life of the clergy there, many of the clergy including the archbishop being married at that time.[14]

A Constitutional Change?

One of the decisive events of history occurred on October 28, 312, when Constantine the Great defeated Maxentius, attributing his victory to the help of the Christian God. From that time onward Constantine was for practical purposes a Christian, although he delayed Baptism until shortly before his death in 337, a practice not uncommon at the time due to the belief that one would then die

---

10. Michel Andrieu, *Les Ordines Romani du haut moyen âge* (Louvain: *Spicilegium Sacrum Lovaniense*, 1956), 3:564–65. Cited in J. Neil Alexander, "A Call to Adventure: Seven Propositions on Ministry," in *This Sacred History: Anglican Reflections for John Booty*, ed. Donald S. Armentrout (Cambridge, Mass.: Cowley Publications, 1990), 29.

11. Hefele, *History of the Councils*, 4:454.

12. Dix, "Ministry in the Early Church," 283–84.

13. A. J. MacDonald, *Hildebrand: A Life of Gregory VII* (London: Methuen, 1932), 58, 89, 92, 95.

14. John William Bowden, *The Life and Pontificate of Gregory the Seventh* (New York: J. R. Dunham, 1845), 89. It is of interest to note that the controversy centered on marriage of the clergy and money, the Archbishop Guido and many of the clergy of Milan being married.

cleansed from all sin.[15] The story of Constantine's forethought regarding his burial place is an interesting footnote to history related by Eusebius. The emperor built the magnificent Church of the Apostles in his capital, which was modestly named Constantinople. He had twelve tombs "to be set up in this Church, like sacred pillars in honor and memory of the apostolic number, in the center of which his own was placed, having six of theirs on either side of it." Eusebius, a great admirer of Constantine, reports that the emperor became sick shortly after celebrating the first Easter services in the new church. He was baptized "in the usual manner" by the bishops he had assembled in Nicomedia when his recovery seemed unlikely and died there on Pentecost, which Eusebius adds, "one might justly call the feast of feasts."[16] His body was returned to the capital for burial in the midst of the tombs created for the Twelve.

Constantine's victory made him ruler of the West, and in 323 he became sole emperor with his final defeat of his co-emperor, Licinius. The Church had experienced rapid growth during the peace of the last half of the third century following the edict of Gallienus in 260, but it now increased by "leaps and bounds" under the imperial favor and patronage of Constantine. Williston Walker points out that, due to factors such as the rejection of Montanism and the lessening belief in the immediate return of Christ, the century before Constantine had already seen "the spread of worldliness in the church — a tendency much increased by its rapid growth from heathen converts between 202 and 250." The tendency toward a double standard, one for serious Christians and another for others who were "Christians in little more than in name," was increasing and was accelerated by the teaching of Tertullian and Origen that there is a distinction between the "advice" given in the gospel for those who strive toward greater holiness and "requirements" which are binding on all.[17] This double standard not only laid the groundwork for monasticism but prepared the way for other major changes in the next century.

Following the adoption of the Constantinian policy of toleration for Christianity and equality for all religions by the co-emperors at Milan in 313, radical

---

15. Williston Walker, *A History of the Christian Church* (New York: Scribner's, 1947), 95, 110–11. Walker mentions the notable example of Constantine's Baptism in connection with infant Baptism. He says that infant Baptism did not become universal until the sixth century (96). He believes it probable that infants were not baptized until the latter half of the second century, citing Irenaeus (*Heresies* 2:22) as the first, though obscure, mention of infant Baptism, c. 185. Tertullian writes of it in *Baptism* 18, but discouraged it until after "character was formed." Walker adds, "Less earnest men than Tertullian felt that it was unwise to use so great an agency of pardon till one's record of sins was practically made up. Origen considered infant baptism to be an apostolic custom" (*Commentary on Romans* 5). Cyprian taught that Baptism should be administered as early as possible due to original sin (*Letters* 58–64).

16. Eusebius, *The Life of Constantine*, in *Nicene and Post-Nicene Fathers*, 2d ser., 1:60–64.

17. Walker, *A History of the Christian Church*, 103–5, 111, 112. Montanism is not unlike some contemporary expressions of Christianity claiming special dispensations of the Holy Spirit characterized by prophetic enthusiasm and belief that the return of Christ is near. "About 156 Montanus proclaimed himself the passive instrument through whom the Holy Spirit spoke. In this new revelation Montanus declared the promise of Christ fulfilled, and the dispensation of the Holy Spirit begun" (58).

changes took place in the Church's ministry in the course of the century.[18] The transition in the diaconate can only be understood in relation to the episcopate and presbyterate as the three orders together underwent a marked transformation. Dix argues that the change was "administrative" and not "constitutional" and is possibly correct in the way he defines these terms.[19] However, the transition of the fourth century is one so profound and far-reaching that it may rightly be called constitutional.

Canon 18 of Nicaea seems to sum up in many ways the developments within the ministry in the second and third centuries that made the transformation of the fourth century possible.[20] Canon 18 decrees:

> It has come to the knowledge of the holy Synod that in certain places and cities, the deacons give the Eucharist to the presbyters, whereas neither canon nor custom allows that they who have no authority to offer should give the Body of Christ to those who do offer. It has also been made known that now some of the deacons receive the Eucharist even before the bishops. Let all such practices be done away, and let the deacons keep within their proper bounds, knowing that they are the ministers of the bishop and inferior to the presbyters. Let them, therefore, receive the Eucharist, according to their order, after the presbyters, either the bishop or presbyter administering it to them. Further, the deacons are not to be allowed to sit among the presbyters; for this is done contrary to the canon and due order. But if any one even after this decision will not obey, let him be put out of the diaconate.[21]

This canon of Nicaea does demonstrate that the Church is in the process of assimilating the social order's pretensions of rank and status. It is emerging as a major religion with considerable prestige in the fabric of the Roman Empire. The emperor, Constantine the Great, had embraced Christianity and had contributed large sums to enable the Church to erect fine buildings. The number of Christians had rapidly increased following the adoption of the policy of toleration in 313 at Milan by Constantine and his co-emperor, Licinius, which gave Christianity legal equality with other religions of the Empire and restored all church property confiscated from Christians during recent persecutions. This influx had forced organizational changes upon the Church, which increasingly looked to the imperial state as its model.

Not long after Nicaea, the Council of Antioch in 341 ordered that the bishop in the chief city or metropolis of each province would have precedence over the

---

18. Dix, *Shape of the Liturgy*, 34. Cf. Dix, "Ministry in the Early Church," 283–85, and George H. Williams, "The Ministry in the Later Patristic Period (314–451)," in *The Ministry in Historical Perspective*, ed. Niebuhr and Williams, 60 (hereafter cited as Williams, "Later Patristic"). Also, Massey H. Shepherd, "The Church in the Fourth Century," lectures at the Graduate School of Theology, Sewanee, Tenn., 1970.

19. Dix, "Ministry in the Early Church," 187–90, 291–95. Cf. A. G. Hebert, *Apostle and Bishop: A Study of the Gospel, the Ministry, and the Church-Community* (New York: Seabury Press, 1963), 66.

20. Williams, "Ante-Nicene," 58.

21. Stevenson, *New Eusebius*, 363. It might also be noted that there is no concept of the indelibility of orders here, the offending deacon to be "put out of the diaconate."

other bishops of the province. The council said it was acting in accord with traditional practice of long standing,[22] but instead it was confirming this relatively recent development. Creation of metropolitans or archbishops was one phase in the erection of a hierarchy of graded ranks as the Church restructured its offices along the lines of the Roman Empire in the fourth century.

The use of candles or lights and incense in processions is symbolic of the change involving the pretensions of worldly status that occurred at this time. The custom was originally an honor given to higher civil officials of imperial Rome and, since the time of Constantine, was utilized by the Church to honor the bishop and other church officials.[23] Other symbols of status were also adopted in the Church. In the late fourth century the bishops assumed the title "pontiff," which came from the title given to members of the Pontifical College, the council of priests who presided over the imperial pagan religion of ancient Rome with the Pontifex Maximus at its head. The pope was given the latter title, "Pontifex Maximus" (Supreme Pontiff), a title the emperors had retained for themselves since the creation of the Empire.[24] Even the stole, which was once thought to have come from the ancient handkerchief or neckcloth and modified to become part of the ceremonial dress of the clergy, probably derives from a scarf worn over the tunic and chasuble in ancient Rome by senators and consuls as an insignia of their status.[25] This latter view could indicate a common origin with the pallium worn by the bishops.[26]

The custom of carrying lights before the gospel procession is of interest in a study of the diaconate. It is in accord with the practice reported by Jerome: "Throughout the whole Eastern Church, even when there are no relics of the martyrs, whenever the Gospel is read the candles are lighted, although the dawn may be reddening the sky, not of course to scatter darkness, but by way of evidencing joy."[27] Joseph Jungmann believes this use to have been common to all the liturgies and was done to honor the gospel book. Its origin appears to have come from the use of the Roman state in setting two burning candles on either side of a book setting forth the powers granted to an official by the emperor. Jungmann says that the carrying of lights and incense in the gospel procession before the book containing Christ's word is to honor Christ himself and solem-

22. Kenneth Scott Latourette, *A History of Christianity*, vol. 1, *To A.D. 1500* (New York: Harper & Row, 1975), 185.

23. Joseph A. Jungmann, *The Mass of the Roman Rite: Its Origins and Development*, trans. Francis A. Brunner, 2 vols. (Dublin: Four Courts Press Ltd., replica ed., 1986) 1:446.

24. S. E. Donlon, "Pontiff," *New Catholic Encyclopedia;* "Pontifex," *Encyclopedia Americana*, International ed. (Danbury, Conn.: Grolier, 1992).

25. Both Duchesne (*Christian Worship*, 390–91) and Percy Dearmer (*The Ornaments of the Ministers*, new ed. [London: A. R. Mowbray & Co., 1920], 62) maintain this origin for the stole. Cyril E. Pocknee, *Liturgical Vesture: Its Origins and Development* (London: A. R. Mowbray, 1960), 21–22. Cf. Gilbert Cope, "Vestments," in *A Dictionary of Liturgy and Worship*, ed. J. G. Davis (New York: Macmillan, 1972), 368.

26. Pocknee, *Liturgical Vesture*, 21. Cf. Duchesne, *Christian Worship*, 391.

27. Jerome, *Against Vigilantius*, in *St. Jerome: Letters and Select Works*, trans. Fremantle, assisted by Lewis and Martley, in *Nicene and Post-Nicene Fathers*, 2d ser., c. 7, 6:420.

nize his entry, seeing a direct parallel to the "personal honor paid to the bishop" in the same way.[28]

Some thought, however, should be given to the desirability of a separate gospel book. The noted Anglican liturgical scholar Marion Hatchett recently told me that he had come to question the use of a separate gospel book because it diminishes the symbol of the unity of the Scriptures. Such fragmentation of scriptural unity does contradict in some degree the unity created by the restoration of the ambo as the one place from which the Scriptures are read and preached. Certainly lights carried before the deacon in the gospel procession and held on either side of the ambo during the reading of the Gospel in the Eucharist singularly honor Christ and do not divide the symbol.

Even though in places there may have been deacons whose conduct was presumptuous, the legislation of Nicaea in this respect was primarily due to the transition occurring in the Church. Time-honored customs, such as deacons administering the Eucharist to presbyters and even nonpresiding bishops, are mistakenly assumed by Nicaea to be prideful innovations and condemned. Prideful innovations were, in fact, those pretensions to worldliness being incorporated into the warp and woof of the Church's life. The declaration that deacons are "inferior" not only reflected the change taking place but served to further it.

One further point needs to be made regarding the place of deacons in Canon 18. The canon directs, "let the deacons keep within their proper bounds, knowing that they are the ministers of the bishop." At this time the diocese with a single bishop was only beginning to emerge. Although the city of Rome did have a single bishop and a number of churches apparently presided over by presbyters by 325, the bishop's office was still generally that of the leader of a local congregation. Translated into terms of today, the deacons referred to as "ministers of the bishop" at Nicaea generally would be ministers of the presbyter or pastor of a parish church or congregation, not of the bishop, in the contemporary Church. As dioceses emerged and bishops became metropolitans, some deacons were indeed ministers of these bishops, and these deacons were the more prominent in dioceses like Rome, which limited the number of deacons to seven. It is a misreading of history to suppose that deacons of this period were normally ministers of the diocesan bishop. The original meaning of the title "archdeacon" actually supports this point. Although it is ordinarily assumed today that the title "archdeacon" was created to designate the chief deacon, such was not the case. It originally was used to designate the "bishop's deacon."[29] This point is the more significant when it is remembered that the first mention of the archdeacon comes c. 365 after the emergence of the diocese. It is clear that, although the bishop in many places did have a deacon to minister as his assistant, most deacons did not serve under a diocesan bishop after the emergence of the diocese

---

28. Jungmann, *Mass of the Roman Rite*, 1:445–46.
29. Hardy, "Deacons in History and Practice," 21. Cf. Bligh, "Deacons in the Latin West Since the Fourth Century," 426.

in this period. This appears to be a much later development associated with the transitional diaconate.

The Presbyter Gains Liturgical Function

The primary though by no means the only development to be noted in Canon 18 of Nicaea has to do with the exchange of function between the bishop and the presbyters. As we have noted, the bishop of the later New Testament period and the sub-apostolic age had or came to have the liturgical monopoly emphasized by Dix.[30] The "special place" of the presbyters was simply to sit in a semicircle beside the bishop at the Eucharist, denoting their honored place as elders of the Church and members of the ruling presbyteral council, but without liturgical function. However, by Nicaea the presbyter had acquired as a prerogative of his office the right "to offer" (preside at the celebration of) the Eucharist in the place of the bishop. The council now confirmed this right. Following the adoption of the policy of toleration for the Church by the co-emperors at Milan in 313 and the ensuing growth in numbers of Christians and of congregations and church buildings, a single bishop in a city of any considerable size could no longer function as the pastor and normal president of the eucharistic assemblies in all the churches of the city. Authorization for presbyters "to offer" (preside at) the Eucharist was made possible by the departure from the pre-Nicene practice of having a bishop as the leader of every local church. The Church, particularly in metropolitan areas, began to take on some characteristics of the later diocese. The bishop remained the pastor of his own church but most of his liturgical functions were delegated to presbyters for the surrounding churches.[31] Dix writes,

> The history of the episcopate is in one sense the history of the steady breaking down of its primitive liturgical monopoly. It was inevitable that as the Church grew this should be so by the mere necessity of numbers. By the fourth century only the power of ordaining remains a strictly episcopal preserve.[32]

Although Dix sees the change as inevitable due to increasing numbers, size alone did not necessitate the change, at least in the form it took. Bishops could well have continued as the overseers of every congregation with the presbyters forming the governing council and the deacons assisting the Church's life and work in widely varied ways. The change came about because the Church's structure changed as it reshaped its life in reflection of imperial Rome.

The transformation of the fourth century was gradual. Between Clement (c. 96) and Hippolytus (c. 215), presbyters began to participate liturgically by joining the bishop in laying hands on the oblations, which were probably held

---

30. Dix, *Shape of the Liturgy*, 33.
31. Ibid., 33–34.
32. Dix, "Textual Materials," lxxx.

in front of them by deacons, as the bishop said the thanksgiving, thus beginning to share with the bishop his role in "offering" the Eucharist or acting as "chief celebrant." We must not forget that in this early period consecration in the Eucharist was not viewed in terms of a personal possession or even that of any office. The priesthood belonged to the Church, and the Church as a body, Christ's body, offered the Eucharist, led by its officers.[33] Therefore, it was a natural development for the presbyter to join the bishop in this way, a development that visibly symbolized the corporate, organic nature of the Church. But the presbyter could only "offer" the Eucharist with the bishop and join in the laying on of hands in the ordination of a presbyter, this being due to the original nature of the presbyterate as a corporate body that ruled the local Church.[34] However, even the distinctiveness of this liturgical participation in "offering" the Eucharist is somewhat blurred by the fact that the deacons, who probably held the bread on patens before the presbyters during the thanksgiving, themselves broke eucharisticized Bread which was on the altar before the bishop, joined in the administration of the Bread, if needed, and administered the chalice.

Although the date when presbyters first "offered" the Eucharist apart from the bishop is uncertain, the practice apparently had come about by the latter part of the third century. The Council of Ancyra, held in the capital of Galatia, c. 314, gives clear testimony to the transformation that had taken place in the office of presbyter, attested to by the acceptance of these canons at Nicaea. Canon 1 of Ancyra is concerned with the restoration of lapsed presbyters. It provides, "Nevertheless it is not lawful for them to make the oblation, nor to preach, nor in short to perform any sacerdotal function."[35] The fact that these presbyters are now inhibited from "offering" the Eucharist (oblation) and preaching and performing any priestly function demonstrates that these functions had now not only been delegated to the presbyterate but were considered theirs as a matter of course, at least in this region. Canon 18 of Nicaea demonstrates that by 325 the prerogative was considered to be inherent in the office throughout the Church, indicating that it had become universal.

It may well have first come about as a result of the bishop's absence in the persecutions. Dix sees the first reference to the practice in a letter of Cyprian. But Cyprian is here addressing both his presbyters and deacons from his retirement in the Decian persecution of 250 and directs only that they "should in my stead discharge my duty, in respect of doing those things which are required for

---

33. Dix, *Hippolytus*, 24.2, p. 44; Cf. Dix, "Textual Materials," 82; Dix, *Shape of the Liturgy*, 29.

34. Dix, "Textual Materials," lxxx. Dix states that the *only* difference in liturgical function between the presbyters and deacons in this document that he can see is in the presbyters' joining in the laying on of hands at ordination. This seems an overstatement in view of his maintaining that in Hippolytus the presbyters did come to participate liturgically as stated, which deacons are not allowed to do. See also in his edition of *Hippolytus*, "Textual Materials," 82, and in *Shape of the Liturgy*, 34, where the same point is made.

35. In *Nicene and Post-Nicene Fathers*, 2d ser., 14:63.

the religious administration."[36] This certainly is not a clear reference. He believes that at least by the third century the number of Christians in a few of the great cities had resulted in the delegation of the presidency of the Eucharist to presbyters.[37] This, however, may well be too early, since the conception of a diocese with a single bishop had not yet developed. Although it has frequently been said that the delegation of liturgical function to the presbyters was made by the bishop, it is probable that it was originally the decision of the presbyteral council, presided over by the bishop, and only later, in retrospect as the monarchial episcopate flourished, came to be thought of as the delegation of the bishop.

Perhaps the most ironic aspect of the delegation of functions is to be seen in the fact that it was only possible because of the old organic concept of the Church. While it was logical to delegate the function of presiding at the Eucharist to the presbyters, who had come to participate liturgically with the bishop and were senior in the sense of their standing in the community, the delegation was theologically possible only because of the earlier concept of the Church as an organic society that as a whole possessed the priesthood of Christ and that could delegate and authorize those whom it chose to exercise these functions. (It could as well have selected deacons as presbyters to preside at the Eucharist.) Thus, the irony is that with the transition that came about partially as a result of this delegation, the organic understanding that had made the delegation possible was largely lost.

The principle, which is clearly evident here, has the most profound and fundamental implications for us today. The Church, ever seeking the guidance of the Holy Spirit, has the plenitude of authority from its Lord to structure its life and order as it sees fit in striving to fulfill its task in the world. Understanding of this principle gives Catholicism — broadly defined — far greater breadth than it has had in centuries and brings it to a new vision of its internal life and a new charity in its appreciation of other Christians.

The Presbyter Becomes a "Priest"

Tertullian and Hippolytus were the first to use the words "priests" and "high priest" in reference to officers of the Church.[38] Although the term "priest" was originally applied to presbyters as well as bishops in the middle of the third century, Dix says that the change of language regarding the office of the presbyter did not become general until the latter half of the fourth century.[39]

---

36. Dix, *Shape of the Liturgy*, 34, finds the first reference to the practice in Cyprian, *Epistle* 5.2.

37. Dix, "Ministry in the Early Church," 281.

38. Massey H. Shepherd Jr., "Priests in the NT," in *The Interpreter's Dictionary of the Bible*, ed. Buttrick, 3:891; Tertullian, *On Baptism* 17, in *Ante-Nicene Fathers*, 3:677; Hippolytus, *Refutation of All Heresies* 1. Preface, in *Fathers of the Third Century: Hippolytus, Cyprian, Caius, Novatian, Appendix* (1951), in *Ante-Nicene Fathers*, 5:10.

39. Dix, "Ministry in the Early Church," 282. Cf. Williams, "Ante-Nicene," 29, and Dix, *Shape of the Liturgy*, 34.

The priesthood, which had originally belonged to the whole Church with the bishop in time coming to be called only "high priest," now increasingly came to be thought of as associated with the bishops and presbyters.[40] The presbyter was termed a "priest," a *sacerdos* or *hiereus,* designations the apostolic Church clearly refused to use, instead of "presbyter" or "elder." It is to be noted, however, that in spite of the increasing use of the term "priest" for "presbyter," the councils continued to use the term "presbyter" for many centuries. It is also instructive to note that the English word "priest" is derived from the Greek term *presbyteros,* meaning "elder," and not from the Latin *sacerdos* or Greek *hiereus,* which are translated "priest."[41]

Dix says that Optatus, Bishop of Milevis, was the first in the West to apply the term *sacerdos* and then with qualification (*sacerdos secundi ordinis*) to presbyters. He reports that c. 360 *hiereus* was found on gravestones of presbyters in Asia Minor. Optatus, writing c. 365, even terms deacons a third degree of the priesthood (*sacerdotium*), although this seems to be the only reference of its kind in antiquity and perhaps reflects the older idea of priesthood in the Church. The presbyter is not called "high priest" (*archiereus* or *sacerdos* without qualification) due to the long association of that term with the bishop, who had been "the 'high-priest' in the midst of the whole 'priestly' People of God." "Priesthood" now is thought of as belonging to the presbyterate instead of being "the function of all members of the church with the bishop as 'high-priest,' " an important impoverishment.[42]

The Diocese Emerges

With the delegation of the bishop's liturgical functions to the presbyter and the latter's assumption of the bishop's pastoral role, the city "parish" was acquiring characteristics of what later was to be called a diocese. Although the bishop continued his role in his own church, he was also head of the churches of the city and the surrounding communities, which were becoming "parishes" as the word later came to be used. The country churches were still under rural bishops, who were called *chorepiscopoi* in the fourth century.[43]

The first reference to the *chorepiscopoi* by this name is in the canons of the councils of Ancyra and Neocaesarea, c. 314.[44] Already they were being suppressed and becoming almost a separate class between the bishops of the cities

---

40. Dix, *Shape of the Liturgy,* 29–34.

41. See *Webster's New Collegiate Dictionary* (Springfield, Mass.: G. & C. Merriam, 1979), s.v. "Priest."

42. Dix, "Ministry in the Early Church," 282n; Optatus, *Against the Donatists* 1.13, in *The Work of Optatus,* trans. Vassall-Phillips, 26; Dix, *Shape of the Liturgy,* 34.

43. Williams, "Later Patristic," 60; Hefele, *History of the Councils,* 1:17–18.

44. Arthur W. Haddan, "Chorepiscopus," in *A Dictionary of Christian Antiquities,* ed. William Smith and Samuel Cheetham (Hartford: J. B. Burr, 1880), 1:354. In the West they are not mentioned until the next century at the Council of Riez.

and the presbyters.[45] Canon 13 of Ancyra declares it to be unlawful for them to ordain presbyters and deacons without the consent of the (city) bishop, and Canon 8 of Nicaea provides for the demotion of Novatian bishops who "come over" to the Catholic Church in a place where there is a Catholic bishop, to the position of a "Chorepiscopus, or presbyter," indicating that the council saw little, if any, difference between these rural bishops and the presbyters.[46] Arthur Haddan believes the office of *chorepiscopus* continued until the ninth century in the East and the tenth in the West.[47] George Williams says that the first mention of rural presbyters is in Dionysius of Alexandria (d. c. 265) but that, though probable, it is not certain that they had only *ad hoc* sacerdotal powers. As the number of *chorepiscopoi* diminished, presbyters were for the first time put in charge of local communities, except perhaps in Egypt.[48]

The peculiar situation we find in Egypt until the middle of the third century is reminiscent of the time of presbyter-bishops in the post-apostolic age as seen in 1 Clement. Jerome says that down to the episcopates of Heraclas (233–249) and Dionysius (249–265), the presbyters of Alexandria elected the bishop and implies that they also ordained him:

> For even at Alexandria from the time of Mark the Evangelist until the episcopates of Heraclas and Dionysius the presbyters always named as bishop one of their own number chosen by themselves and set in a more exalted position, just as an army elects a general, or as deacons appoint one of themselves whom they know to be diligent and call him archdeacon.[49]

Lightfoot maintains that the inference may be made that the presbyters themselves ordained the Alexandrian bishops up to this time, citing Ambrosiaster[50] and the testimony of Eutychicus, Patriarch of Alexandria, 933–940, who says the custom continued until the time of Alexander, patriarch from 313–326. Eutychicus also states that the only bishop in Egypt up to the time of Demetrius (190–233), who appointed three others, was at Alexandria. Demetrius's successor, Heraclas (233–249), added twenty more. In this case presbyteral ordination would have been a virtual necessity.[51] With this increase in the number of bishops in Egypt, what appears to have been the last vestige of the presbyter-bishop

---

45. Williams, "Ante-Nicene," 57, 59.

46. *Council of Ancyra*, in *Nicene and Post-Nicene Fathers*, 2d ser., 14:68. See also Canon 14 of Neocaesarea, and *Council of Nicaea*, in *Nicene and Post-Nicene Fathers*, 2d ser., 14:85, 19–20.

47. J. W. C. Wand, *A History of the Early Church to A.D. 500*, 3d ed. (London: Methuen, 1949), 119. Hefele (*History of the Councils*, 1:18) says the office of *chorepiscopus* had been abolished by the Council of Chalcedon in 451 but was reestablished in the Middle Ages in the form of bishops without dioceses. Haddan ("Chorepiscopus," 1:354) is almost certainly correct in seeing the continuation of the office until it disappears in the East and the West.

48. Williams, "Ante-Nicene," 57. He reports that this evidence is preserved in Eusebius's *Church History* 7.24.6 (in *Nicene and Post-Nicene Fathers*, 2d ser., 1:309).

49. Jerome, *Epistle 146, To Evangelus*, in *Nicene and Post-Nicene Fathers*, 2d ser., 6:288.

50. See in this chapter, "The Presbyter Becomes a Bishop (Almost)."

51. Lightfoot, *St. Paul's Epistle to the Philippians*, 231, 232. Massey Shepherd wrote in a personal communication to the author, "To my knowledge the only bishop in Egypt until the second half of the third century was that of Alexandria. The Bishop of Alexandria was a peculiarly

disappeared. The presbyter-bishop of the late first century, who had functioned as a bishop, lost these functions finally, but by Nicaea presbyters generally had acquired the functions of bishops, with the probable exception of ordination.

The Presbyter Becomes a Bishop:
The Bishops Assume Rule from the Presbyters

As the presbyter assumed the role of the bishop in the local congregation, the presbyterate lost its corporate character and function. The bishop at the same time assumed much of the rule of the Church that had formerly been exercised by the corporate presbyterate acting as a council of the Church with the bishop as its president. We remember that in Hippolytus the bishop is not called the "ruler" of the Church. The presbyter, not the bishop, is ordained "that he may sustain and govern thy people."[52] The bishop has given up his liturgical and sacramental monopoly to the presbyters but in the process has assumed the government of the Church in large measure. Collegiality of the bishops begins to develop with these changes.

In the pre-Nicene Church the clergy, including the bishops, were thought of primarily as belonging to the local Church. This is seen in various canons of the fourth century. Canon 2 of Arles provides that "ordained clerics," which probably refers to minor orders, are to stay in the places of their ordination. Canon 21 provides that presbyters and deacons who leave the places of their ordination and wish to be transferred are to be deposed. Canon 15 of Nicaea, 325, repeated at Antioch in 341, prohibits any bishop, presbyter, or deacon from moving from one city to another, decreeing that any such act would be "totally annulled."[53] However, the focus was moving away from the local Church. Later in the century, as the organic character of the Church eroded, the idea of clergy belonging first to the Church at large and, therefore, being free to move, was fostered theologically by Augustine's development of a theology of order during the Donatist controversy, which conceived of the validity of the sacraments and the ministerial orders virtually apart from the context of the Church.[54]

The bishop, who in the period before Nicaea had to get the consent of the presbyteral council for all that he did regarding policy, now increasingly took over the rule of the Church both as an individual and, meeting with his fellow bishops, as a corporate body in synods and councils. Synods become frequent: Canon 5 of Nicaea provides that there be two in every province each year to

---

'pope-patriarch' who ruled as a monarch over his domain of Egypt and Libya, ordaining bishops for churches as he willed."

52. Hippolytus, *Apostolic Tradition* 8, in *Apostolic Tradition of Hippolytus*, trans. and ed. Easton, 37.

53. Hefele, *History of the Councils*, 1:185, 195, 422–23. Although this canon was adopted as Canon 21 of Antioch in 341, Hefele observes that it was frequently broken.

54. Augustine, *On Baptism, Against the Donatists* 1.1.2, in *Nicene and Post-Nicene Fathers*, 1st ser., 4:411–12.

deal with disciplinary matters. Even though the Syrian *Apostolic Constitutions,* c. 380, still speaks of presbyters as constituting "the sanhedrin and senate of the Church," the presbyteral council is now replaced by a council of bishops as the decision-making body of the Church. A. G. Hebert well observes that one important result of this process was that "the check upon episcopal autocracy which had previously existed had now largely disappeared."[55]

In the exchange of function between the bishop and the presbyter, the bishop retained exclusively but a single liturgical and sacramental right — control over ordination of the clergy.[56] However, the distinction between the two offices was sufficiently blurred in the late fourth century that some of the fathers asserted that the two are essentially the same. The presbyter Jerome says in a letter to Evangelus:

> I am told that someone has been mad enough to put deacons before presbyters, that is, before bishops. For when the apostle clearly teaches that presbyters are the same as bishops, must not a mere server of tables and widows be insane to set himself up arrogantly over men through whose prayers the body and blood of Christ are produced?

He cites Titus 1:5–7 as a "passage which clearly proves a bishop and a presbyter to be the same," although he asks rhetorically, "For what function excepting ordination, belongs to a bishop that does not belong to a presbyter?"[57] Chrysostom in his homily on 1 Timothy 3:8–10 says that Paul discussed the character and qualities bishops should have and then passed over presbyters to deacons because

> between Presbyters and Bishops there was no great difference. Both had undertaken the office of Teachers and Presidents in the Church, and what he [Paul] has said concerning Bishops is applicable to Presbyters. For they are only superior in having the power of ordination, and seem to have no other advantage over Presbyters.[58]

Although the equating of presbyters with bishops is not generally to be found in the writers of this period, Lightfoot says that Pelagius, Theodore of Mopsuestia, and Theodoret also acknowledge it.[59] The emergence of such an equation does illustrate the extent to which presbyters have assumed the functions of bishops

---

55. *Council of Nicaea,* in *Nicene and Post-Nicene Fathers,* 2d ser., 14:13; *Apostolic Constitutions* 2.28, in *Ante-Nicene Fathers,* 7:411; Hebert, *Apostle and Bishop,* 67. Cf. Dix, *Shape of the Liturgy,* 34.

56. *Apostolic Constitutions* 8.46, in *Ante-Nicene Fathers,* 7:499; Jerome, *Epistle to Evangelus* 146.1, in *Nicene and Post-Nicene Fathers,* 2d ser., 6:289; John Chrysostom, *Homily* 11, 1 Tim. 3:8–10, in *Saint Chrysostom: Homilies on Galatians, Ephesians, Philippians, Colossians, Thessalonians, Timothy, Titus, and Philemon,* in *Nicene and Post-Nicene Fathers,* 1st ser., 13:441.

57. Jerome, *Epistle to Evangelus* 146.1, in *Nicene and Post-Nicene Fathers,* 2d ser., 6:288–89.

58. Chrysostom, *Homily* 11, 1 Tim. 3:8–10, in *Nicene and Post-Nicene Fathers,* 1st ser., 13:441.

59. Williams, "Later Patristic," 62; Lightfoot, *St. Paul's Epistle to the Philippians,* 99. References are to Pelagius on Phil. 1:1, 1 Tim. 3:12, Tit. 1:7; Theodore of Mopsuestia on Phil. 1:1, Tit. 1:7, and especially 1 Tim. 3; and Theodoret on Phil. 1:1, 1 Tim. 3:1–2, and Tit. 1:7.

and the importance they have gained during the course of the century. It further indicates the radical transformation that occurred as the old organic conception and structure of the Church broke down.

In Ambrosiaster we find further evidence of the breakdown of the idea of a functional ministry and new teaching which facilitated the transformation to a "vertical" structure of hierarchy. Like Jerome and Chrysostom, the bishop and the presbyter are one:

> The Apostle Paul proves that a presbyter is a bishop when he instructs Timothy, whom he had ordained as a presbyter, what sort of person he is to create a bishop. For what is a bishop but the first presbyter, that is, the highest priest? Finally, he calls these men none other than fellow presbyters and fellow priests. Does a bishop call his minister fellow deacons? No, for they are much inferior, and it is a disgrace to mix them up with a judge (?). For in Alexandria and throughout Egypt, if a bishop is lacking a presbyter confirms (ordains?-*consignat*).[60]

Not only do we see here the fact that in the author's eyes the presbyter is a bishop, probably even ordaining in Egypt, but also that the diaconate has become "much inferior." However, of more importance is Ambrosiaster's assertion that "the greater order contains within itself the lesser."[61] It is at this point that we see the extent of the change that has taken place, for now there not only are "greater" and "lesser" offices but the "greatest" contains them all.

The view that the presbyter and bishop are essentially the same office is not simply one of the distant past. Prior to Vatican II the standard dogmatic manuals of the Roman Catholic Church set forth the three major orders as subdeacon, deacon, and priest, a view current but not universally held since the eleventh century. Peter Lombard, bishop of Paris, d. 1160, who was largely responsible for fixing the number of the sacraments at seven and whose work, *Libri IV Sententiarum,* became the theological textbook of the medieval period, taught that the highest order of the ministry was the "presbyterate," to use the word he used, although he believed that the episcopate alone possessed the plenitude of the presbyterate. Pope Paul VI in 1972 abolished the subdiaconate, leaving the diaconate, the presbyterate, and the episcopate as the three major orders.[62]

The Diaconate Declines: A Third Order

With the steady transformation of the presbyterate and the increasing importance of the presbyter as an individual apart from the corporate presbyterate, the di-

---

60. Ambrosiaster, 101.5, in *Pseudo-Augustine, Quaestiones Veteris et Novi Testamenti CXXVII*, trans. Souter, in *Corpus Scriptorum Ecclesiasticorum* 50, 196.

61. Ibid., 101.4, in 50:195–96.

62. Peter S. Moore and Herman Hausheer, "Peter Lombard," in *An Encyclopedia of Religion*, ed. Ferm; Thomas Tally, "The Liturgy of the Bishop," a lecture taped by the author, delivered at the conference of the Association of Diocesan Liturgy and Music Commissions in Chicago, November 8–11, 1982 (later printed in *Open*, the newsletter of Associated Parishes, Alexandria, Va.).

aconate began to decline, although deacons continued, as we have noted, for a long time as men of importance.

By the latter part of the fourth century the deacons ceased to form the bishop's personal staff. As the presbyters took the place of the bishop in the churches of the "diocese," the deacons became their assistants as well, although this is not documented until about 500. However, the relationship of the deacons with the presbyters was never clearly defined. Vischer observes that this lack of definition caused repeated difficulties and rightly sees it as one of the major reasons for the decline of the diaconate in the Middle Ages.[63] With their increase in numbers and subordination to the presbyterate, deacons became a third order.

Cursus Honorum: From "Horizontal" Organic to "Vertical" Hierarchical Structure

By the end of the fourth century there was an extension of the clerical ministry above the level of diocesan bishop, together with an increase of the "minor orders." The earliest use of the term "metropolitan" is found in the fourth century. Canons 4 and 6 of the Council of Nicaea mention them.[64] The suppression of the *chorepiscopoi,* mentioned earlier, is indicative of the developing status of the urban bishops. Canon 10 of Antioch, 341, provides that the *chorepiscopoi,* once on a par with other bishops, may ordain presbyters and deacons only with the consent of the bishop of the city to which he and his district are subject. Bishops of provincial capitals developed status as metropolitans with the right of presiding in provincial councils and increasingly disassociated themselves from the local presbyteries, developing a sense of collegiality. Canon 24 of Laodicea, 343–381, lists subdeacons, readers, singers, exorcists, and doorkeepers as belonging to the "minor orders."[65] Such a structure easily gives rise to the idea of a succession of grades onto which one moves from lower to higher, traditionally called *cursus honorum.*

The decline of the diaconate springs more from the development of the idea of *cursus honorum* than from any other single factor. The model used by the Church was that of the organization of the Roman Empire.[66] The transformation here stands in marked contrast to the old organic structure of the Church and its ministry of the pre-Nicene period. Prior to the fourth century, as we have seen, the Church's ministry was one in which every person had a part and each functioned for the benefit of the whole. Offices were not thought of in terms of orders but in terms of functions, each related to the other. But by the end of the

63. Williams, "Later Patristic," 63. Cf. Jalland, "The Parity of Ministers," 347; Vischer, "The Problem of the Diaconate," 25.

64. Maclean, "Ministry (Early Christian)," 666; *Council of Nicaea,* in *Nicene and Post-Nicene Fathers,* 2d ser., 14:11, 15.

65. In *Nicene and Post-Nicene Fathers,* 2d ser., 14:113; Williams, "Ante-Nicene," 59; *Council of Laodicea,* in *Nicene and Post-Nicene Fathers,* 2d ser., 14:144.

66. Dix, "Ministry in the Early Church," 284; Frere, "Early Forms of Ordination," 306.

fourth century a radical transformation had taken place in the structure of the Church's ministry, which affected the basic character of the Church itself. The old "horizontal" concept and structure were replaced by one that was "vertical" and hierarchical. This structure has continued to the present time essentially unchanged, at least in Catholic Christendom.

It has been widely maintained that from the late fourth century onward ordination to each of the successive offices was required. Bligh says that popes Siricius, Innocent I, and Zosimus "insisted on adherence to this orderly progressing through the lesser orders to the higher." C. H. Turner states that a serious development of the fourth century was the idea "that the Christian clergy consisted of a hierarchy of grades through each of which it was *necessary* to pass in order to reach the higher offices."[67] However, the evidence does not support these views. It is true that the idea of *cursus honorum* grew up in the fourth century, and many, perhaps most, probably did go through the succession of grades. But it appears to have been a long time before the rule became binding.

Among the earliest references to holding the various offices in succession is that given by Cyprian. He writes regarding the character of Pope Cornelius, 251–253, that he "was not one who on a sudden attained to the episcopate; but, promoted through all the ecclesiastical offices, . . . he ascended by all the grades of religious service to the lofty summit of the Priesthood."[68] He then records that the episcopal office was forced upon him, refuting the detractors of Cornelius. Cyprian's point here is clearly to show that Cornelius had demonstrated his ability and his fitness for the office. Cyprian speaks of "grades of religious service," but the context gives an entirely different perspective than that of rank, in which each grade was required in succession to reach the top, although the idea of a succession of grades is now present. We would recall that Cyprian himself had not so moved through each office.

Turner points to an inscription of Pope Damasus referring either to himself or his father as the earliest known case in point of *cursus honorum*.[69] However, the inscription simply reads, "Exceptor, lector, levite, sacerdos," which indicates no more than that he did hold these various offices. There is no evidence to support the theory that he held these offices in succession because that was required.

Pope Siricius, Damasus's successor, does state in a letter to Himerius, bishop of Tarragona, c. 385, that those ordained are to go through the offices in succession. However, it is clearly not because there was any necessity for one to hold the various offices in themselves but rather "that through these periods the integrity of his life and of his faith has gained approbation."[70] The point is even

---

67. Bligh, "Deacons in the Latin West Since the Fourth Century," 421–22; C. H. Turner, "The Organization of the Church," in *The Cambridge Medieval History*, ed. H. M. Gwatkin (Cambridge: University Press, 1936), 1:150 (italics added).

68. Cyprian, *Epistle* 51.8, in *Ante-Nicene Fathers*, 5:329.

69. Turner, "The Organization of the Church," 151.

70. Siricius, *Epistle 1 to Himerius* 13, 14 (Cap. 9 and 10), in *Patrologiae Latinorum*, ed. Migne, 13:1142–43.

clearer in Zosimus's letter to Hesychius, bishop of Salonae, c. 418. Speaking of the widespread practice in Gaul, Africa, and Spain of admitting laymen to the priesthood in ways "contrary to the precepts of the Fathers," without spending sufficient time and undergoing discipline in the lower orders, he continues:

> For if secular offices bestow high position not on those who have just entered the vestibule of action but on the one who through time has been tested on very many levels, who can be found so arrogant, so impudent as, in the service of heaven (which should be given greater weight and, like gold, should be tested repeatedly in the fire), to desire to be a leader immediately when he has not previously been a recruit and to wish to teach before he learns?[71]

Pope Innocent I writes in a similar vein to Felix, first bishop of Nuceria, c. 402:

> Let no one become lector, acolyte, deacon, or priest rapidly, for if they perform for a long time in the minor offices and their lives and their obedience are equally approved, thereafter let them come to the priesthood when the merits of their duties have been measured, and let them not carry off prematurely what an upright life deserves to receive.[72]

The evidence from these sources does not then indicate that a new sacramental requirement had been added. Baptism was still the only sacramental prerequisite for ordination to any office in the Church. The principle involved in the advice of these popes writing to their fellow bishops was not that of *cursus honorum* proper but rather that of fitness for office as set forth by Cyprian and stated in the conciliar decrees of the fourth century.

The first clearly explicit conciliar legislation on this point, fitness for office, was that of the Council of Sardica, 343 or 344. Canon 2 of Nicaea legislates against recent converts who with little instruction are "straightway brought to the spiritual laver, and as soon as they have been baptized, are advanced to the episcopate or the presbyterate."[73] Canon 10 of Sardica develops this idea:

> If some rich man or professional advocate be desired for bishop, he be not ordained until he have fulfilled the ministry of reader, deacon, and presbyter, in order that, passing by promotion through the several grades, he may advance (if, that is, he be found worthy) to the height of the episcopate. And he shall remain in each order assuredly for no brief time, that so his faith, his reputable life, his steadfastness of character and considerateness of demeanour may be well-known, and that he, being deemed worthy of the divine sacerdotal office (sacerdotium, i.e., the episcopate) may enjoy the highest honour.[74]

---

71. Zosimus, *Epistle 9 to Hesychius* 2 (Cap. 1), in *Patrologiae Latinorum*, ed. Migne, 20:671.

72. Innocent I, *Epistle 37 to Felix* 6 (Cap. 5), in *Patrologiae Latinorum*, 20:604–5.

73. *Council of Nicaea*, in *Nicene and Post-Nicene Fathers*, 2d ser., 14:10. It may be noted that Canon 80 of the *Apostolic Canons*, probably c. 550, is similar to this canon of Nicaea (*Ante-Nicene Fathers*, 7:505).

74. *Council of Sardica*, in *Nicene and Post-Nicene Fathers*, 2d ser., 14:424–25. Canon 20 of the disciplinary canons of the Council of Braga, 563, also described the rule of going through successive offices (Hefele, *History of the Councils*, 4:386).

The canon is directed against an abuse that had arisen and attempts to insure that only men whose qualifications have been verified by service in the Church are ordained to positions of leadership. Wealth and success in other fields are inadequate qualifications for offices in the Church.

Ordination to the episcopate without passing through the "successive grades" apparently continued for a long time. Frequently, deacons were ordained bishops without ever having been made presbyters, and the rule of Nicaea against ordaining recently baptized converts to the episcopate seems to have been frequently broken. Joseph Bingham observes that in the time of Gregory of Nazianzus, made bishop of Constantinople in 381 (d. c. 390), "this rule was frequently transgressed, without any reason or necessity."[75] Gregory, in his oration on Basil the Great, bishop of Caesarea, d. 379, says that when Basil was made a bishop

> it was not by suddenly advancing him, nor by cleansing [baptizing] and instructing him in wisdom at the same time, as is true of the majority of those today who aspire to the episcopate. He received the honour according to the law and order of spiritual advancement. [He explains that] the same holds true in military affairs: one is soldier, captain, general. This order is the best and most advantageous for subordinates. If the same system were in force in our case, it would be of great value.[76]

It is apparent that the system of *cursus honorum* was not yet in effect.

In 381 Nectarius was named successor to Gregory of Nazianzus as patriarch of Constantinople.[77] Sozomen records that he was nominated by the emperor when still unbaptized, although this fact seems to have been generally unknown until after the nomination. Nectarius was then baptized and apparently ordained bishop without intermediate orders: "When at last consent had been given to the imperial mandate, Nectarius was baptized, and while yet clad in his white robes was proclaimed bishop of Constantinople by the unanimous voice of the synod." By being "proclaimed bishop" Sozomen apparently means that he was ordained, since he had just referred to the bishops' consent and he afterwards speaks of "the ordination of Nectarius."[78] Further, Socrates records that Nectarius was "seized upon by the people, and elected to the episcopate, and was ordained accordingly by one hundred and fifty bishops then present" at Constantinople.[79] It is worth noting that the Church of the third century or before would hardly have elected an unbaptized person bishop.

---

75. Bingham, *The Antiquities of the Christian Church*, 2.10.4, 1:127.

76. Gregory Nazianzen, *Oration on St. Basil the Great* 25, 26, in *Funeral Orations by St. Gregory Nazianzen and St. Ambrose*, trans. Leo P. McCauley, vol. 22 of *Fathers of the Church* (New York: Fathers of the Church, 1953), 50.

77. The manner of his election is uncertain. Theodoret says he was selected by the members of the Council of Constantinople meeting in 381 (*Ecclesiastical History* 5.8, in *Nicene and Post-Nicene Fathers*, 2d ser., 3:136). Socrates refers to his having been elected by the people themselves (*Ecclesiastical History* 5.8, in *Nicene and Post-Nicene Fathers*, 2d ser., 2:121).

78. Sozomen, *Ecclesiastical History: A History of the Church in Nine Books from A.D. 324 to A.D. 440*, in *The Greek Ecclesiastical Historians of the First Six Centuries of the Christian Era* (London: Samuel Bagster & Sons, 1846), 333.

79. Socrates, *Ecclesiastical History* 5.8, in *Nicene and Post-Nicene Fathers*, 2d ser., 2:121.

The fact that Ambrose, who was governor of Milan, was unbaptized when elected bishop of that city in 374 is well known. His former secretary and biographer, the deacon Paulinus,[80] tells us that when Ambrose finally agreed to the election he demanded Baptism by a Catholic bishop and records, "Thus, when he was baptized, he is said to have fulfilled all the ecclesiastical offices, so that he was consecrated bishop on the eighth day with the greatest favor and joy on the part of all."[81] Ambrose himself says that his ordination to the office of bishop was not according to the prescribed rule prohibiting a new convert being ordained to the episcopate:

> How I fought against being ordained! And, finally, when I was compelled, I tried at least to have the ordination deferred! But the prescribed rule did not avail, pressure prevailed. Yet the Western bishops approved my ordination by their decision, and the Eastern bishops, too, by their examples. Yet the ordination of a new convert is prohibited lest he be lifted up by pride. If the ordination was not postponed it was because of constraint, and if humility which is becoming to the priesthood is not wanting, where there is no cause, blame will not be imputed.[82]

Nowhere from the period does there seem to be any record of Ambrose having passed through each office on succeeding days, or at all.

The most probable interpretation of this record in light of the evidence generally from the period is that Baptism was still considered to be the only requisite for ordination to the episcopal office. Socrates says that the bishops present at Ambrose's election baptized him "for he was then but a catechumen" and were about to ordain him but he refused. The matter was referred to Emperor Valentinian who sent word that they should "do the will of God by ordaining him.... Ambrose was therefore ordained." Similar evidence is found in Theodoret's *Ecclesiastical History.*[83] To deduce from the evidence that after Ambrose was baptized he was ordained bishop after "passing through various stages of the ecclesiastical hierarchy," as his recent biographer Angelo Paredi and others do,[84] is reading back into the fourth century what was to become the custom and requirement much later. Neither Socrates nor Theodoret seems to be aware that intermediate steps are necessary in this case or others. Elsewhere, for

---

80. Altaner dates Paulinus' biography c. 422 (in Altaner, *Patrology*, 445). Cf. John A. Lacy, Introduction to Paulinus, *Life of St. Ambrose*, trans. Lacy, *Early Christian Biographies*, in vol. 15 of *Fathers of the Church*, ed. Deferrari, 27, 28.

81. Paulinus, *Life of St. Ambrose* 3.9, in *Early Christian Biographies*, 38.

82. Ambrose, *Epistle 59, To the Church at Vercelli*, in *Saint Ambrose, Letters*, trans. Mary Melchior Beyenka, in vol. 26 of *Fathers of the Church*, ed. Deferrari, 345. The translator indicates that Ambrose probably has Nectarius's ordination as bishop of Constantinople in mind by his reference to the examples of the Eastern bishops, Ambrose having mentioned this in his *Epistle 42, To Theodosius*, given on 26:220.

83. Socrates, *Ecclesiastical History* 4.30, and Theodoret, *Ecclesiastical History* 4.6, in *Nicene and Post-Nicene Fathers*, 2d ser., 2:113–14, 3:111.

84. Angelo Paredi, *Saint Ambrose: His Life and Times*, trans. M. Joseph Costelloe (Notre Dame: University of Notre Dame Press, 1964), 124. Others maintaining this are: Frederic W. Farrar, *Lives of the Fathers* (Edinburgh: Adam and Charles Black, 1884), 2:120; Dix, "Ministry in the Early Church," 284.

example, Theodoret makes a special point of commending Athanasius for having done an admirable job in offices he had filled before election as a deacon to the see of Alexandria, again asserting the principle of fitness for office.[85]

John Chrysostom reports that Philogonius, bishop of Antioch, 324, was "taken from the court of judicature and carried from the judge's bench to the bishop's throne." Augustine in a letter, 423, describes how a young man, Antonius, who was only a reader and without experience in the "labours pertaining to the various degrees of rank in the clerical office," was accepted on his suggestion by the people of Fussala and apparently made bishop immediately without any other prior office.[86]

In a letter to the bishop of Thessalonica, c. 444, Pope Leo continues to teach the desirability, though not the necessity, of men proving themselves by serving in the various offices: "After a lapse of time he who is to be ordained a priest or deacon may be advanced through all the ranks of the clerical office, and thus a man may have time to learn that of which he himself also is one day to be a teacher."[87] Leo himself was apparently ordained bishop of Rome directly from the diaconate. Prosper of Aquitaine records that after the death of Bishop Sixtus IV the Church of Rome awaited the return of the "Deacon Leo" from a diplomatic mission to reconcile Aetius and Albinus in Gaul. "Then," he writes, "the Deacon Leo having performed his public commission, being presented with praise by his countrymen, was ordained 43rd Bishop of the Church of Rome."[88] Trevor Jalland in his biography of Leo is apparently unable to find any evidence for Leo's ever having been ordained presbyter. He described his election while still in deacon's orders and then says he "was consecrated Bishop of Rome on September 29th, A.D. 440."[89]

This custom apparently continued at Rome until at least the time of Gregory the Great, who succeeded Pelagius II in 590. Gregory, a deacon, was chosen by "all the people" to succeed Pelagius. But Gregory strove to avoid the high office. Gregory of Tours recounts the ordination of the deacon Gregory like this:

> And when Gregory was making ready to go to a hiding place he was seized and brought by force to the church of the blessed apostle Peter and there he was consecrated to the duties of bishop and made pope of the city. Our deacon did

---

85. Theodoret, *Ecclesiastical History* 1.25, in *Nicene and Post-Nicene Fathers*, 2d ser., 3:61.

86. John Chrysostom, "De Beato Philogonio" 6, *Contra Anomoeos*, in *Patrologia sive Latinorum sive Graecorum*, ed. J. P. Migne (Turnholt, Belgium: Brepols, n.d.), 48:752; Augustine, *Epistle* 209.3, in *St. Augustin: Prolegomena, Confessions, Letters*, in *Nicene and Post-Nicene Fathers*, 1st ser., 1:560.

87. Leo, *Epistle* 6.6, *To Anastasius*, in *Nicene and Post-Nicene Fathers*, 2d ser., 12:6.

88. Prosper of Aquitaine, *Chronicon*, A.D. 440, in *Monumenta Germaniae Historica*, ed. Georgius H. Pertz et al. (Berlin and Hanover: n.p., 1826), 1:478.

89. Trevor Jalland, *The Life and Times of St. Leo the Great* (London: SPCK, 1941), 37–38. Charles Feltoe in his Introduction (in *Nicene and Post-Nicene Fathers*, 2d ser., 12:vi) says that Leo was ordained both priest and bishop of Rome on September 29, 440. However, no reference is given, and this appears to be only a supposition.

not leave until Gregory returned from the port to become bishop; and he saw his ordination with his own eyes.[90]

James Barmby in the "Prolegomena" to his translation of Gregory's works also says that, after the emperor's confirmation of Gregory's election had arrived in Rome and Gregory had been found, he was brought "to the church of St. Peter, and there at once ordained, on the 3rd of September, A.D. 590."[91]

In his study of Roman ordination Michel Andrieu says that, according to the *Liber Pontificalis,*[92] which contains biographies of the popes to the end of the ninth century, subdeacons who became presbyters in the eight and ninth centuries were ordained directly to that order without ever having been deacons. He notes also that many deacons in these centuries were ordained bishops of Rome without ever having been presbyters and presbyters became popes without ever having been deacons. None were ordained to both the diaconate and the presbyterate. The first of the many Roman deacons called to the papal throne to be ordained presbyter prior to the episcopate was the archdeacon of Rome in 1073.[93]

Sixth-century inscriptions on towers and some literary references record that deacons died in Gaul at sixty, seventy, or eighty years.[94] Alcuin, who was ordained deacon when about 35 years old and who died in the year 804 at about 75, was never ordained priest.[95] But such men increasingly become the exception. Orders gradually came to be regarded by and large as "rungs" in the clerical ladder through which one had to go to attain the "full ministry" of the priesthood, with some few being "advanced" to the episcopate. It is to be noted that even this terminology of "full ministry" and "advanced," which we take for granted today, was foreign to the spirit of the pre-Nicene Church, although the idea of "advancing" began to develop in the latter part of this period.

Joseph Bingham appears to be correct in asserting that the practice of going through the several orders on successive days was a practice virtually unknown until the time of Photius, who became patriarch of Constantinople in 858. David Nicetas in his *Life of Ignatius* records that Photius was made a monk the first day, a reader the second, a subdeacon the third, a deacon on the fourth, a presbyter the fifth, and patriarch on the sixth. A century later at Rome we find a

90. Gregory, Bishop of Tours, *History of the Franks*, trans. Ernest Brehaut (New York: Columbia University Press, 1916), 227–28.

91. James Barmby, "Prolegomena," in *Nicene and Post-Nicene Fathers*, 2d ser., 12:xvi, xvii.

92. The *Liber Pontificalis*, begun in the sixth century, contains biographies of the popes down to Stephen V (885–891). An edition by Louis Duchesne adds the lives of the popes up to 1431. Christopher Rengers, "Liber Pontificalis," in *An Encyclopedia of Religion*, ed. Ferm.

93. Andrieu, *Les Ordines Romani du haut moyen âge*, 564–65. Cited in Alexander, "A Call to Adventure," 28–29; Tally, "The Liturgy of the Bishop."

94. Bligh, "Deacons in the Latin West Since the Fourth Century," 422. Bligh says (421) that "at the beginning of the fourth century the diaconate had already become a step in the ecclesiastical *cursus honorum*," but this appears to be almost a century too early as a widespread practice and even much more than that as a sacramental requisite.

95. Eleanor Shipley Duckett, *Alcuin, Friend of Charlemagne* (New York: Macmillan, 1951), 26, 304.

layman appointed to the papal throne by Otto I going through successive offices from the least to the greatest. In 963 Leo VIII was made successively doorkeeper, reader, acolyte, subdeacon, deacon, presbyter, and finally bishop. Bingham rightly points out that this practice was contrary to the true intent and meaning of the ancient canons "that men should continue some years in every order, to give some proof of their behaviour to the Church."[96] Since the original publication of *The Diaconate: A Full and Equal Order* in 1981, the evidence for *cursus honorum* as a requirement in the ordination process has been widely recognized as coming many centuries later than had been generally thought.

Even though the requirement of passing through the various offices as a succession of grades came long after the fourth century, its basis was established in that century. The older tradition requiring only Baptism prior to ordination to any office simply seems to have lingered on. In the pre-Nicene Church the organic idea of the Church determined the procedure. The bishop was not conceived to be one who had all the powers and functions of the Church's ministry, "the full ministry." This ministry with all of its powers and functions belonged to the Church and its Lord. The bishop had his function in the body of the Church and was ordained to it, just as presbyters and deacons had theirs. In that age, although less so in the late third century, it would have seemed as much a violation of the principle of "order" for the deacon to fulfill the function of a presbyter as for the presbyter to act as a deacon, although as we have seen the lines were not so clearly drawn and in urgent necessity deacons or presbyters sometimes assumed the function of the bishops. Even in the late fourth century the *Apostolic Constitutions* declares, "It is not lawful for any one of the other clergy to do the work of a deacon."[97]

The Profound Consequences

The shaping of the Church through a hierarchical structure in its clerical ministry from the plenitude of the greatest to the paucity of the least on the basis not of *diakonia* or service but of office has obscured the essential nature of the Church, so much so that we hardly comprehend the admonition that "other clergy" are not permitted to do the work of a deacon. The fundamental change was from the principle of organism to that of hierarchy, which ultimately led to a theology in which the greatest was the sum of all its parts, much like the Russian or Chinese dolls that fit into one another until all are contained in the largest. The organic character of the Church's ministry was destroyed.[98] Paul's great analogy of the Church as the body of Christ became as an empty shell.

---

96. Bingham, *The Antiquities of the Christian Church*, 1:131, 132; Nicetas David of Paphlago, *Vita s. Ignatii*, in *Patrologiae sive Latinorum, sive Graecorum*, ed. J. P. Migne (Turnholt, Belgium: Brepols, n.d.), 105:511–12; Tally, "The Liturgy of the Bishop."

97. Dix, "Ministry in the Early Church," 284; *Apostolic Constitutions* 8.28, in *Ante-Nicene Fathers*, 7:494.

98. Williams, "Ante-Nicene," 29.

Clericalism developed, bringing about the very kind of distinction between the clergy and the laity that the apostolic Church had refused to make. The theology of a ministry in which *all* were commissioned and empowered in Baptism for their particular and varied ministries with the Church through ordination authorizing its leaders for their several functions, howbeit with divine grace, was abandoned. Over time the Church's ministry came to be seen as the possession and/or obligation of the clergy and perhaps also of those set apart in "religious" orders with what little ministry the ordinary laity were to do derived from the clergy. Even the terminology designating those living in communities under vows of poverty, chastity, and obedience as belonging to "religious" orders (although they were not necessarily ordained), and members often referred to as "religious" is indicative of the clericalism that permeated the Church for many centuries. These great Christian institutions undoubtedly contributed much to the cause of Christ, but the implication in their members being termed "religious" reflects and implies the sense that they were somehow more religious than others not so committed. But the New Testament makes clear that there is no distinction in the commitment expected, indeed demanded, by Christ among his followers. In the gospel, undivided loyalty is a primary requisite for discipleship (Luke 9:57–62; cf. Matt. 8:19–22). It is just this kind of false distinction that led the apostolic Church to reject religious titles such as *sacerdos* or *heireus*.

Marion Hatchett observes that in the late Middle Ages ordination was in effect replacing Baptism as initiation into the Church:

> In the late middle ages several more elements were added: prayers and blessings and imperative formulae (including an additional laying on of hands with the formula "Receive the Holy Spirit, whose sins you remit they are remitted, and whose sins you retain they are retained," at the ordination of presbyters), the hymn Veni Creator Spiritus, a delivery of instruments of office (a Gospel book for deacons, chalice and paten for presbyters, and a staff, ring, and mitre for bishops), and anointings. The precedent for many of these additional ceremonies, especially the anointings, can be found in the early baptismal rites; ordination was in effect replacing baptism as initiation into the Church.[99]

The subtle but insidious nature of the transition is to be seen in the use of the adjective *laikos*. Originally in the New Testament, as we saw earlier, it meant "one of the people of God" and included all members of the Church. As a general term, it had come by the third century to mean "one of the people of God" who was not a clergyman. But by the fifth century it meant "profane."[100]

The Church that had affirmed the goodness of all creation and chosen words without sacred connotations to designate its officers in its apostolic period now created a dichotomy. Illustrative of the distinction that arose between the sacred and the profane are the decrees of the Council of Laodicea, 343–381. Canon 24 provides, "No one of the priesthood, from presbyters to deacons, and so on in

---

99. Hatchett, *Commentary on the American Prayer Book*, 504.
100. Dix, "Ministry in the Early Church," 285.

the ecclesiastical order to subdeacons, readers, singers, exorcists, doorkeepers, or any of the class of Ascetics, ought to enter a tavern." Canon 54 of the same council directs that "members of the priesthood and of the clergy must not witness the plays at weddings or banquets; but, before the players enter, they must rise and depart."[101]

The sacralization of the clergy in contrast to the laity is clearly in evidence by the middle of the fourth century. The clergy and those termed "ascetics" (those "practicing self-denial as a measure of personal and esp. spiritual discipline")[102] were set apart from the *laos* as "sacred" persons for whom the ordinary amusements of society were not appropriate. Lay persons apparently could freely enjoy such activities, but the clergy had become "holy" people in a world that was no longer seen to be unified by the immanence of God's presence permeating all things.

Celibacy

Celibacy and continence of the clergy is another manifestation and contributing cause of this distinction with its implied dualism. It is important not only due to its implication regarding the distinction between the sacred and the profane but also because it was a major cause of the decline of the diaconate as celibacy became obligatory, particularly in the West.

When we look for Jewish antecedents in the Old Testament we find no instance of anyone voluntarily embracing a life of celibacy. Celibacy is virtually unknown among the Jews. Marriage was a sacred duty in obedience to the command "increase and multiply." The rabbis taught that men should marry by the age of about 18, and the Hebrew language does not even contain a word for "bachelor." Indeed, continence is permitted by the rabbinical schools for periods of only one to two weeks unless it is necessitated by a particular occupation. J. Massingberd Ford reports that the Mishnah and Gemara direct that coitus shall be "every day for them that are unoccupied; twice a week for labourers; once a week for ass drivers; once every thirty days for camel drivers; and once every six months for sailors."[103] When continence is practiced during military campaigns or by the Essenes, there is no suggestion that coitus was intrinsically evil.[104]

---

101. *Council of Laodicea*, in *Nicene and Post-Nicene Fathers*, 2d ser., 14:144, 157. Canon 21 of Laodicea (ibid., 14:140) states that "the subdeacons have no right to a place in the Diaconicum, nor to touch the Lord's vessels." Hefele (Hefele, *History of the Councils*, 2:313) believes *diaconicum* refers to the place where the sacred vessels and vestments were kept and the prohibition against touching the sacred vessels refers to the deacon's duties, the meaning of the canon being that the subdeacons are not to assume the functions of the deacons.

102. *Webster's Ninth New Collegiate Dictionary*, s.v. "ascetic."

103. J. Massingberd Ford, *A Trilogy on Wisdom and Celibacy*, The Cardinal O'Hara Series: Studies and Research in Christian Theology at Notre Dame (Notre Dame: University of Notre Dame Press, 1967), 23–24, 43, 49; Joseph Blenkinsopp, *Celibacy, Ministry, Church* (New York: Herder & Herder, 1968), 27.

104. Ford, *A Trilogy on Wisdom and Celibacy*, 52–58. Cf. 1 Sam. 21:5.

The author of the Pastoral Epistles expressly puts the prohibition against marriage in the class of "subversive doctrines inspired by devils" and describes it as a denial of the goodness of creation (1 Tim. 4:1–5). Nevertheless, there was a growing though not unanimous tendency in the early centuries of Christianity in favor of continence or celibacy.

Clement of Alexandria, writing c. 200, sees the ideal of the Christian Gnostic as one who marries and has children, because he conquers more temptation and so comes to a higher excellence. Although probably apocryphal, Clement also records Peter's last words to his wife as she was being led to martyrdom:

> They say, accordingly, that the blessed Peter, on seeing his wife led to death, rejoiced on account of her call and conveyance home, and called very encouragingly and comfortingly, addressing her by name, "Remember thou the Lord." Such was the marriage of the blessed, and their perfect disposition toward those dearest to them.[105]

Eusebius says that Clement wrote regarding the marriage of the apostles "on account of those who rejected marriage." He quotes Clement: "Or will they reject even the apostles? For Peter and Philip begat children; and Philip also gave his daughters in marriage."[106]

Tertullian agrees that marriage is good but maintains that celibacy is better. In an apparent reference to 1 Timothy 2:2 and Titus 1:6 he says that Paul does not permit men "twice married" to preside over the Church.[107] In his work *On Monogamy* after his break with the Church, c. 207, he protests against Catholic clergy who are digamists, indicating that many clergy have been married a second time: "Why, how many digamists, too, preside in your churches; insulting the apostle [Paul], of course; at all events, not blushing when these passages are read under their presidency."[108]

Hippolytus gives other evidence that digamy was not uncommon at that time but indicates it was contrary to the tradition. He writes unfavorably of Pope Callistus, 217–222:

> About the time of this man, bishops, priests, and deacons, who had been twice married, and thrice married, began [to be allowed] to retain their place among the clergy. If also, however, any one who is in holy orders should become married, [Callistus permitted] such a one to continue in holy orders as if he had not sinned.[109]

---

105. Clement of Alexandria, *Miscellanies* 7.11, 7.12, in *Fathers of the Second Century: Hermas, Tatian, Athenagoras, Theophisbus, and Clement of Alexandria (entire)* (1956), in *Ante-Nicene Fathers*, 2:541, 543. Cf. Philip Schaff, *Ante-Nicene Christianity A.D. 100–325*, in *History of the Christian Church* (New York: Scribner's, 1924), 2:406–7.

106. Eusebius, *Church History* 3.30, in *Nicene and Post-Nicene Fathers*, 2d ser., 1:161–62. The thing illustrated here is the tradition of the Church, not the historicity of the statement. The quotation is from *Miscellanies* 3.6.

107. Tertullian, *To His Wife* 1.2, 3, 7, in *Ante-Nicene Fathers*, 4:39–40, 43.

108. Tertullian, *On Monogamy* 12, *Ante-Nicene Fathers*, 4:69.

109. Hippolytus, *The Refutations of All Heresies* 9.8, in *Ante-Nicene Fathers*, 5:131.

Clearly, Hippolytus believed that such marriages were sinful. But Hippolytus was dissenting from Callistus's teaching that a bishop who is guilty even of "[a sin] unto death" is not to be deposed. While Hippolytus does say that Callistus allowed those in orders to marry and retain their places "as if they had not sinned," it is not clear whether this is a reference to digamy or to the later requirement that men ordained before marriage must remain celibate.[110]

The Council of Elvira, c. 305, decreed the most ancient command of celibacy or, technically, continence for the clergy.[111] Its thirty-third canon declared: "Bishops, presbyters and deacons — indeed, all clerics who have a place in the ministry [of the altar] — shall abstain from their wives and shall not beget children — this is a total prohibition: whoever does so, let him forfeit his rank among the clergy."[112]

Edward Schillebeeckx affirms that the question for many centuries was actually that of continence. He observes that the law of celibacy dates only from the twelfth century. The requirement of Elvira is that the clergy are to "abstain from their wives" and "not beget children." The motivation lying behind the legislation not only of Elvira but of succeeding councils was "the unsuitability of sexuality for someone who stands at the altar, that is, the ancient motive of 'cultic purity'; the sacred and the 'impure' are mutually exclusive." This is also the reason increasingly given in the writings of the fathers of the fourth century relating to continence of the clergy in contrast to that of monks, virgins, and widows.[113]

The implications here set the clergy apart as those who are distinct from and superior to others in the Church, those ordained being closest to God. Further, "cultic purity" brought about by continence ultimately carries with it the implication that sexual intercourse is in some way tainted. These ideas stand in marked contrast to those of the New Testament and generally of the pre-Nicene Church.

Conciliar decrees continue to legislate in a similar vein. Canon 10 of the Council of Ancyra, 314, provides that deacons who are unmarried at the time of their ordination but who state that they must marry "because they are not able to abide so" shall continue in their office after marrying, because the bishop had conceded it to them. But if one was silent on this and later marries, he shall "cease from the diaconate."[114]

A proposal was made at the Council of Nicaea, 325, forbidding bishops, presbyters, deacons, and possibly subdeacons who had been married at the time of their ordination from having intercourse with their wives.[115] The similarity of

---

110. Schaff seems to believe Hippolytus opposed the marriage of clergy after ordination (2:409).

111. Hefele, *History of the Councils*, 1:150.

112. Council of Elvira, in Stevenson, *New Eusebius*, 307.

113. Edward Schillebeeckx, *Celibacy*, trans. C. A. L. Jarrott (New York: Sheed and Ward, 1968), 40, 58.

114. *Council of Ancyra*, in *Nicene and Post-Nicene Fathers*, 2d ser., 14:67.

115. Socrates, *Ecclesiastical History* 1.11, in *Nicene and Post-Nicene Fathers*, 2d ser., 2:18;

this proposal with Canon 33 of Elvira would lead to the conclusion that it was made by the Spanish bishop Hosius. However, Bishop Paphnutius of a city in Upper Thebes, a confessor who had lost an eye in one of the persecutions and who had never been married, argued that marriage is honorable and that intercourse of a man with his wife is chaste. He thought it would be sufficient for those who had been unmarried when ordained to remain so according to what both Socrates and Sozomen report was said "to be the ancient tradition of the Church." The counsel of Bishop Paphnutius prevailed, and no law prescribing continence for the clergy was enacted at Nicaea.[116]

The anathema of the Council of Gangra, variously dated from 340 to 376, upon those maintaining that it is not lawful to partake of the Eucharist when the presbyter is married indicates the growing tendency toward clerical celibacy. In this period Athanasius also defends the married state or at least optional celibacy when he writes to Dracontius, c. 355, contrasting first of all many bishops who have not married with monks who are the fathers of children, and conversely bishops who are fathers of children and monks who are apparently celibate ("of the completest kind").[117]

Digamy is prohibited for bishops, priests, and deacons in the *Apostolic Constitutions* and the *Apostolic Canons,* both c. 375, and later at the Council of Orleans, c. 537. Each of these also provides that one unmarried at the time of ordination must remain celibate.[118] However, the *Apostolic Canons* do not allow a bishop, priest, or deacon to "cast off his wife under pretense of piety."[119] A few years later, c. 413, Augustine teaches that second marriages are lawful for any, terming Tertullian and others heretical for teaching otherwise.[120]

Married bishops, priests, and deacons are required to refrain from intercourse with their wives under the penalty of deposition by the councils of Carthage (401), Orange (441), and Orleans (c. 537).[121] However, although the historian

---

Sozomen, *Ecclesiastical History* 1.23, in *Nicene and Post-Nicene Fathers*, 2d ser., 2:256. Sozomen adds subdeacons to the list of orders included.

116. Hefele, *History of the Councils*, 1:436; Socrates, *Ecclesiastical History* 1.11, in *Nicene and Post-Nicene Fathers*, 2d ser., 2:18; Sozomen, *Ecclesiastical History* 1.23, in *Nicene and Post-Nicene Fathers*, 2d ser., 2:256. 138. Canon 4, Council of Gangra, in J. Stevenson, ed., *Creeds, Councils, and Controversies: Documents Illustrative of the History of the Church A.D. 337–461* (London: SPCK, 1966), 4.

117. Canon 4, Council of Gangra, in Stevenson, ed., *Creeds, Councils and Controversies*, 4; Athanasius, *To Dracontius* 9, in *St. Athanasius: Select Works and Letters*, trans. Archibald Robertson (1953), in *Nicene and Post-Nicene Fathers*, 2d ser., 4:560.

118. *Apostolic Constitutions* 6.17, in *Ante-Nicene Fathers*, 7:457. *Apostolic Canons*, Canon 17, which also includes "any one of the sacerdotal catalogue," and Canon 27, which permits only readers and singers among the clergy to marry after ordination; *Ante-Nicene Fathers*, 7:501. Council of Orleans, canons 6 and 7, in Hefele, *History of the Councils*, 4:205–6.

119. *Apostolic Canons*, Canon 6, in *Ante-Nicene Fathers*, 7:500.

120. Augustine, *On the Good of Widowhood* 6, in *St. Augustin: On the Holy Trinity, Doctrinal Treatises, Moral Treatises*, in *Nicene and Post-Nicene Fathers*, 1st ser., 3:443. Cf. Augustine, *De haeresibus ad Quodvultdeum*, 86.

121. *Council of Carthage*, Canon 4, in Hefele, *History of the Councils*, 2:424. *Council of Orange*, Canon 22 and 23, in Hefele, *History of the Councils of the Church*, 3:4. Although only deacons are named, the bishops and priests are implied. Canon 24 of Orange excepts those

Socrates is an Easterner, he does mention among the unusual customs of which he has heard that in Thessaly "if a clergyman in that country, after taking orders, should sleep with his wife, whom he had legally married before his ordination, he would be degraded." In the East he tells us that all clergy abstain from their wives, but they "do so of their own accord." He adds that there are many bishops among the clergy who have had children by their legal wives during their episcopates.[122]

The Eastern Church retained the fourth-century practice regarding clerical celibacy. Celibacy there was gradually limited to bishops, who were usually chosen from among the monks. The rule of a single marriage for the other clergy was adhered to, the marriage taking place before ordination. The final legislation in the Eastern Church on this subject was that of the Council of Trullo, 692. Canon 13 of that Council explicitly states that presbyters, deacons, and subdeacons are not to be deprived of cohabitation and intercourse with their lawful wives and that no presbyter or deacon may dismiss his wife on the pretense of piety. It also refers to the rule of the Western Church regarding continence of married clergy, saying that lawful marriage by men in holy orders is "the ancient rule and apostolic perfection and order."[123]

Raymond Lawrence argues convincingly in his historical study of the conflict of sexual values in the West, *The Poisoning of Eros,* that the Church abandoned its original Jewish-Christian anthropology, which affirmed both the unity of persons and the inherent goodness of all creation, including the flesh, and adopted a syncretistic standard of sexual purity from pagan philosophy and religion supported by the adoption of a dualistic "platonist anthropology" of body and soul. He sees this transition to have occurred by the time Christianity became the imperial religion in the fourth century. After discussing dissenting voices within the Church, he concludes: "Ambrose, Jerome, and Augustine together established unambiguously the ideal of virginity or sexual purity as the highest forms of the Christian life and established a corresponding platonic anthropology of body/soul dualism." However, he gives Augustine, as the preeminent theologian of the early Church, the dubious credit of being the primary influence in creating the negativism that has characterized the Western Church's attitude toward sex from that time.[124]

In his treatise *On the Good of Marriage* Augustine teaches that the only proper purpose of marital sexual intercourse is procreation: "For necessary sexual intercourse for begetting is free from blame, and is itself alone worthy of

---

previously ordained but prohibits such deacons from being made priests or bishops. The *Council of Arles* (c. 450) permits the wife of a cleric to live in the house of her husband only if she also has taken a vow of chastity (Canon 3: Hefele, *History of the Councils of the Church,* 3:168).

122. Socrates, *Ecclesiastical History* 5.22, in *Nicene and Post-Nicene Fathers,* 2d ser., 2:132.

123. Schaff, *Ante-Nicene Christianity A.D. 100–325,* 412; P. Delhaye, "History of Celibacy," in *New Catholic Encyclopedia,* 3:371; *Council of Trullo,* Canon 13, in *Nicene and Post-Nicene Fathers,* 2d ser., 14:371.

124. Raymond J. Lawrence Jr., *The Poisoning of Eros: Sexual Values in Conflict* (New York: Augustine Moore Press, 1989), 6–7, 24, 103, 122, 131.

marriage. But that which goes beyond this necessity, no longer follows reason, but lust." He goes on to say that in marriage, if intercourse is for procreation, it is allowed by Paul "as a matter of pardon" and he calls it a "fault." And intercourse beyond the "necessity of begetting" is "pardonable" in marriage. Intercourse even in marriage for procreating is tainted by the lust of concupiscence. Marriage is said to be good but "not to seek offspring after the flesh . . . is assuredly better and holier," provided the freedom gained is used to please God. Continence is termed the "root-virtue." It is better even than intercourse for the purpose of procreation within a marriage.[125]

Gregory the Great's influential *Pastoral Care* went a step beyond Augustine, who had refused to say that pleasure itself was sinful. Gregory writes:

> The married must be admonished to bear in mind that they are united in wedlock for the purpose of procreation, and when they abandon themselves to immoderate intercourse, they transfer the occasion of procreation to the service of pleasure. Let them realize that though they do not then pass beyond the bounds of wedlock, yet in wedlock they exceed its rights. Wherefore, it is necessary that they should efface by frequent prayer what they befoul in the fair form of intercourse by the admixture of pleasure.[126]

Pleasure itself in marital intercourse is seen to befoul the human spirit with sin.

Gregory's teaching was reinforced in eighth-century England by the Venerable Bede including in his *The Ecclesiastical History of the English People* a portion of a letter from Gregory to Augustine of Canterbury stating that "lawful intercourse cannot take place without fleshly desire" and "the desire itself can by no means be without sin."[127] In light of such thought, it is more understandable that Gregory also affirmed the law of Leviticus directing that a man should not enter a church after sexual intercourse with his wife until after he has washed, and even then not immediately, and a woman after childbirth is not to enter a church for 33 days in the case of a son and 66 days in that of a daughter. The admonition is perhaps softened with the explanation that this is to be understood figuratively.[128] One wonders how the birth of a son could be construed as mitigating the uncleanness here attached to childbirth and how, if these acts are tainted, staying out of a church works to make one purer and more acceptable to God.

In the thirteenth century, Thomas Aquinas essentially followed the tradition so firmly established by Augustine and Gregory, although he attempted to lessen the condemnation of sexual pleasure that was part of that tradition by a theoretical affirmation of its essential goodness. But in envisioning conception as

---

125. Augustine, *On the Good of Marriage*, trans. C. L. Cornish, in *Nicene and Post-Nicene Fathers*, 1st ser., c. 11, 3:404; Augustine, *On the Good of Marriage*, c. 6 and 32, 3:402, 412.

126. Gregory the Great, *Pastoral Care*, trans. and ann. Henry Davis (Westminster, Md.: Newman Press, 1950), pt. 3, chap. 27, 188–89.

127. Bede, *Bede's Ecclesiastical History of the English People*, ed. Bertram Colgrave and R. A. B. Mynors (Oxford: Clarendon Press, 1969), 1.27.8, pp. 95–97.

128. Gregory the Great, *Pastoral Care*, 3.27, pp. 188–89; and Bede, *Bede's Ecclesiastical History* 1.27, p. 91. The number of days is directed by Leviticus 12:4, 5.

taking place in the Garden of Eden without penetration, the semen accomplishing its purpose in the same way menstruation flows without compromise of the woman's virginity, Thomas fails to transcend and, in fact, perpetuates the sex-negative tradition.[129] Such teaching certainly played a major role in the development of celibacy and its exaltation along with that of virginity, and the relegation of the married state to low degree. The teaching of Ambrose, Augustine, Gregory, Bede, and Thomas Aquinas concerning sexual intercourse even within marriage was highly successful in negating both Jewish and early Christian anthropology and Jesus' own affirmation of the goodness of the whole person, physical and spiritual, including sexuality. The effects have been far-reaching and devastating in Western society. Certainly this betrayal of Christian values has been responsible for a great many marital problems and divorces and may be even the primary cause of Western society's reaction to the negative valuation of human sexuality in what is often called the "sexual revolution." With all of its excesses it does assert the goodness and joy of God's creation of the sexuality of human beings.

But it should not be assumed that the enforcement of celibacy was due solely to theological or ascetic reasons. In the sixth century, a decree by Emperor Justinian prohibiting a man who had children from becoming a bishop and directing that a married cleric who became a bishop must live in continence gives evidence of a sociological reason: the problem of the Church's property being inherited by a cleric's children. We see this again in the refusal of Pope Pelagius I, 557, to consent to the ordination of a bishop because the man was married and had children who might inherit church property. His consent was granted only with the provision that adequate security be provided for the Church's property.[130]

By the tenth century the problem had become far more acute. Henry C. Lea, in his detailed history of celibacy, tells us that at this time "all possessions previously held by laymen on precarious tenure were rapidly becoming hereditary." Society was in a chaotic transition period in which there was virtually universal disorder. As centralized power eroded, property and offices became the property of those who held them, even though they may have been given to the Church. Under the feudal benefice system, married clergy were succeeded in the benefice by their sons, who may have had no interest in the welfare of the parish. In addition, property formerly belonging to the Church also may have been appropriated under the system by the clergy for such purposes as providing dowries for their daughters.[131]

---

129. Thomas Aquinas, *Summa Theologiae* 13: *Man Made to God's Image*, ed. and trans. Edmund Hill (Blackfriars in conjunction with McGraw-Hill, 1964), Ia.98.1 and 2, pp. 150–59.

130. Schillebeeckx, *Celibacy*, 35–36, 65. Cf. Henry C. Lea, *The History of Sacerdotal Celibacy in the Christian Church* (New York: Russell & Russell, 1957 (first published under the title *An Historical Sketch of Sacerdotal Celibacy in the Christian Church* [Philadelphia: Lippincott, 1867]), 40, 57.

131. Lea, *History of Sacerdotal Celibacy*, 114–16; Latourette, *A History of Christianity*, 365–66. Cf. Schillebeeckx, *Celibacy*, 60–61.

The problem was far from theoretical. In 925 the Council of Tours decided in favor of two priests, Ronald and Raymond, father and son, in reference to their complaint against another priest for certain tithes. The council awarded these tithes to them and their successors forever. In the same century a bishop of Verona, Rathenius, implies that his clergy were all married and objects to successive priest-fathers making their sons priests, begging them to rear their sons as laymen in order to protect the Church's property. We see the extent of the laxity in society generally when the bishop says that were the canon on repeated marriages enforced only boys would remain in the Church.[132]

Pope Benedict VIII attempted to bring about reform c. 1018 through legislation aimed at preventing the alienation of church property by the families of priests. Under these canons, marriage was forbidden to priests, deacons, and subdeacons, and they were not to cohabit with a woman. Children born to offenders were "declared to be forever serfs of the Church and could not be freed or granted rights of property inheritance." However, in spite of this attempt at reform, Desidenius, abbot of Monte Cassino who became Pope Victor III, reports that under Benedict IX, who was made pope in 1032 when reportedly only ten or twelve years old and brought the papacy to its lowest depths of degradation, all clerical orders lived openly in marriage throughout Italy.[133] Conditions elsewhere in the West appear to have been similar so far as clerical marriage was concerned.

The papacy, especially under Hildebrand, became determined to free the Church from the feudal benefice system as well as to enforce the law of celibacy for ascetic or theological reasons.

Following the marked success of Hildebrand as Pope Gregory VII, 1073–1085, in enforcing celibacy among the clergy, the final stage in the struggle for celibacy in the West came when the First and Second Lateran councils of 1123 and 1139 declared clerical marriage invalid instead of only illicit.[134] The Reformation of the sixteenth century ended celibacy in the West in those churches not adhering to Rome. But only in our own time has the Roman Catholic Church begun to relax the rule. The Second Vatican Council provides:

> With the consent of the Roman Pontiff, this diaconate will be able to be conferred on men of more mature age, even upon those living in the married state. It may also be conferred upon suitable young men. For them, however, the law of celibacy must remain intact.[135]

Celibacy, then, began as a voluntary act for the sake of the Kingdom of God. Gradually, it was reinterpreted to be a superior state. In the fourth century, re-

---

132. Lea, *History of Sacerdotal Celibacy*, 116, 118.

133. Delhaye, "History of Celibacy," 3:372; J. J. Fox, "Papacy," *Encyclopedia Americana* (New York: Americana Corp., 1938), 21:253; Lea, *History of Sacerdotal Celibacy*, 145–46.

134. Delhaye, "History of Celibacy," 3:373.

135. Constitution of the Church 3.29, in *Documents of Vatican II — All Sixteen Official Texts Promulgated by the Ecumenical Council, 1963–65*, ed. Walter M. Abbott (New York: Guild Press, 1966), 56.

strictions began to be placed on clerical marriage, which eventually in the West developed into compulsory celibacy and were an important factor contributing to the decline of the diaconate in the Middle Ages. In writing of the change in the diaconate from an office he sees to have been more important than the priesthood in many respects in the early centuries to one that was "merely a step on the way to the priesthood," Vischer states, "One essential feature of the transformation of the office of deacon was that celibacy became a binding rule for deacons — at any rate in the Western Church."[136]

With the development of a hierarchical structure in which the "higher" order contained within itself the "lower," what point was there for men who had to commit themselves in either case to abstain from one of the strongest and most fundamental of all human desires, that of sex and procreation, to aspire only to the "lower" order? Celibacy was undoubtedly not the only cause for the diaconate to wane and probably not so important as the change in the theology of the nature of the Church, but certainly it was a major factor. Without this rule married men would have continued to offer themselves to the Church for this office and would almost certainly have enabled it to retain at least many of the distinctive functions that are essential to its integrity and vitality. Even today, the Roman Catholic Church has tacitly recognized the importance of celibacy as a deterrent to the diaconate by relaxing the rule of celibacy in the restoration of the office of deacon as a "permanent" vocation. It could do so because celibacy has always been a matter of discipline and not of doctrine in the Church. Pope Paul VI in his encyclical on celibacy, *Sacerdotalis caelibatus,* June 24, 1967, reaffirmed the traditional position regarding the celibate state but conceded that celibacy is not demanded by the nature of the priesthood.[137]

Theological Implications of Celibacy

The development of compulsory celibacy for the clergy was inseparably related to the breakdown of the old organic concept and structure of the Church. It appears to be in part a result but also a facilitating factor in this breakdown. So long as all the people of God were seen to possess and together constitute the Church's ministry, the kind of distinctions we have discussed between members of the Church (clergy and laity) were unlikely to occur. However, as the ministry came increasingly to be conceived in terms of the clergy, it became far easier to draw lines and set some people, places, and things aside as being more sacred. Compulsory clerical celibacy is one of the major ways in which such distinctions were made. In light of this, it is not difficult to see why the old functional idea of the Church's ministry being shared by all the people of God would give way to one in which it is summed up in, if not possessed by, the clergy, who to some

---

136. Vischer, "The Problem of the Diaconate," 25.
137. Bernardino M. Bonansea, "Celibacy," in *Encyclopedia Americana*, International ed. (New York: Americana Corp., 1977), 6:131.

extent shared this ministry particularly with others in "religious" communities who had taken a similar vow of celibacy.

But the implications are much broader for the Church and its ministry today. The Church, which had at the outset affirmed the inherent goodness and unity of all creation, gradually adopted a dualistic distinction between the sacred and the profane. The clergy, who were once laity like any others although with distinct functions, became sacred persons apart from the laity. The inherent goodness of at least parts of the material world was denied. By implication, spiritual things were the things that were good and not simply of a higher order and of prime importance. Much of the material world and many of the concerns of daily life were relegated to the realm of the profane.

The implications of this dualistic position gradually came to fruition as the centuries passed. The effect of the clergy and those called the "religious" being considered to belong to the sacred, marked off particularly by celibacy, and the laity to the "secular" or "profane" was to degrade the laity and implied for them a lower standard of morality, particularly one that allowed marriage. The counsels of perfection seemed to apply essentially to the clergy and the "religious." Still today in the minds of many Christians full commitment to Christ means joining the ranks of the clergy or the "religious." Even the use (or misuse?) of the word "religious" in this way implies this kind of attitude.

In American Christianity in general, the ultimate conclusion of the subtle change that took place in the early Church is perhaps to be seen in the puritanism of the Victorian era. The modern concept of God as one who is concerned with "spiritual things" is perhaps the most tragic result of this course, because God is left out of most of real life. This divorce of God from "nonspiritual" things is directly related to the abandonment of a Jewish and early Christian anthropology and the resulting negative attitudes toward human sexuality, marriage, and intimacy.

In the Christian West the best and highest kind of life came to be seen as that of the priest or those belonging to monastic or "religious" orders. Such vocations were to "sacred" callings, which were set in contrast to "secular" vocations. And it is noteworthy that the primary way in which these vocations were different from those of others came to be that they did involve a commitment to celibacy. Celibacy seems to be the primary thing symbolizing an inherent or implicit denial of the goodness of the physical world.

Celibacy thus became a great symbol of the ideal regarding human sexuality. "Symbol" is used here as defined by Urban Holmes, as a powerful representation that has many meanings and evokes many feelings.[138] Gibson Winter emphasizes the importance of symbols:

> Man is the symbolic being who is shaped by symbol and, in turn, reshapes symbols and thus remakes his world. The power of symbol rests, however, on the power of sociality, which it expresses, extends, and serves to renew. Participating

---

138. Urban T. Holmes III, *Ministry and Imagination* (New York: Seabury Press, 1976), 46.

in symbols, sharing a world through them, means participating in the relational character of man's being which has been expressed, enriched, and empowered through these symbols.[139]

Sexuality itself can be classified as an archetypal symbol and is among the most powerful for humanity.[140]

In a very real sense celibacy became the symbol of sexuality in the concept of the "fully committed," which was looked upon as the "ideal" Christian life in Western civilization. Although the reformers of the sixteenth century abolished compulsory celibacy and Martin Luther forcefully asserted the inherent goodness of human sexuality, the influence of tradition and the continuing practice of the Roman Catholic Church rendered their efforts only partially successful. An important strain of Anglican spirituality in the nineteenth century, and up into the 1950s at least, tended to regard the monastic or "religious" life as in some sense an ideal. The existence of its married clergy and Article 32 of its Thirty-nine Articles of Religion, which declared that "Bishops, Priests, and Deacons, are not by God's Law, either to vow the estate of single life, or to abstain from marriage" but shall at their own discretion "judge the same to serve better to godliness,"[141] served to mute overt teaching exalting celibacy as the preferred way. But Protestantism along with Anglicanism did do away with the symbol of celibacy, which was important and in the long run has worked toward correcting the problem.

However, the sixteenth-century reformers failed to recognize and correct the underlying dualistic attitudes separating the "sacred" and the "secular," the "spiritual" and the "material," which we saw emerging in the early Church. Calvinism, which heavily influenced all of Western Christianity and especially American Christianity, in fact broadened this cleavage. The puritanical attitudes that came to prevail in American Christianity and culture and reached their zenith in the nineteenth and early twentieth centuries by implication denied the goodness of much that was beautiful or pleasurable. Although the symbol of celibacy was abandoned, the content was retained.

A Vestigial Remnant: The Transitional Diaconate

As the diaconate lost its importance, it was increasingly restricted to liturgical functions.[142] A detailed history of its decline over the centuries to become a

---

139. Gibson Winter, *Elements for a Social Ethic: Scientific Perspectives on Social Process* (New York: Macmillan, 1966), 227.

140. Holmes, *Ministry and Imagination*, 48, with references to its power and importance at numerous other points in this book.

141. Lawrence, *The Poisoning of Eros*, 166–81; *The Book of Common Prayer and Administration of the Sacraments and Other Rites and Ceremonies of the Church* (New York: Church Hymnal Corp. and Seabury Press, 1979), 874.

142. Vischer, "The Problem of the Diaconate," 25.

vestigial remnant in modern times of the great diaconate of the early Church is of slight interest and has little relevance for today.

Although there were vestigial remnants of the ancient office for centuries, the diaconate was gradually, if unintentionally, transformed into another office, much as the presbyterate was transformed in the fourth century when presbyters assumed the functions of the pre-Nicene bishop, save that of ordination. With few exceptions, candidates for ordination to the diaconate believed themselves called to be presbyters or priests, not deacons. They were trained to be priests, not deacons. And after ordination to the diaconate, they served as apprentice priests, not deacons, except for having liturgical function largely restricted to that of the ancient diaconate. A notable exception regarding liturgical function was permission for deacons to preach liturgically. The Church had in effect created a different office, the transitional diaconate, even if it masqueraded under the same name.

After a brief summary of diaconal functions in the early Church, we will turn to consider the restoration of the diaconate in the Church of the late twentieth century as the separate and equal order it was originally. The implications of such a restoration are broad and important for the total life of the Church, far more extensive than would appear initially.

A Summary of Diaconal Functions with Date and Source

The functions of the diaconate as that office developed in the Church, along with the date and source of the earliest reference, are listed below. It is to be remembered that generally the function was exercised by the deacon prior to the reference, sometimes probably considerably earlier.

Pre-Nicene

> *Symbolize the servant-ministry of the Church.*

c. 95   Possibly constitute with the bishops the ruling council in some churches. (*Didache,* also Ignatius and Polycarp)

c. 96   Administer the distribution of alms to the poor and needy. (*Shepherd of Hermas*)

c. 115   Symbolize Jesus Christ. (Ignatius)

c. 115   Be the Servant of the Church. (Ignatius, also Polycarp)

c. 115   Act as an agent or ambassador of the Church. (Ignatius)

c. 115   Function liturgically at the Eucharist. (Clear in Ignatius, although probable in the *Didache,* c. 95)

c. 150   Administer the eucharistic Bread and Wine to all present. (Justin Martyr)

c. 150   Take eucharistic Bread and Wine to absent. (Justin Martyr)

c. 200 Be the "eye" of the bishop in all matters but especially in discovering the pastoral needs of the people. (*Pseudo-Clementines*)

c. 200 Keep order in the Christian meetings. (*Pseudo-Clementines*)

c. 200 Report the sick to the congregation for their visits and help. (*Pseudo-Clementines*)

c. 200 Baptize on a par with presbyters with the bishop's authorization. (Tertullian)

c. 215 Instruct the people at weekday noneucharistic assemblies. (Hippolytus)

c. 215 Assist with the oils of exorcism and thanksgiving at Baptism. (Hippolytus)

c. 215 Bring the people's oblations to the bishop and probably arrange them at the Eucharist. (Hippolytus)

c. 215 Bless noneucharistic bread at Christian fellowship meals in the bishop's absence. (Hippolytus)

c. 215 Administer the chalice only in Hippolytus, but probably in most places also continue to administer the Bread until sometime in the fourth century. (Hippolytus)

c. 215 Be the servant of the bishop. (Hippolytus)

c. 235 Guard the doors and keep order among the people at the Eucharist. (*Didascalia*)

c. 235 Announce a bidding to the people at the Eucharist. (*Didascalia*)

c. 235 Judge disputes with the presbyters between members of the Church. (*Didascalia*)

c. 235 Function as full-time paid servants of the Church. (*Didascalia*)

c. 306 On occasion, head small, rural congregations. (Elvira)

c. 314 On occasion, preside at the Eucharist, probably under extraordinary circumstances and in the absence of a bishop (or presbyter?). (Forbidden at Arles)

Post-Nicene

c. 380 Announce various stages of the Eucharist. (*Apostolic Constitutions*)

c. 380 Read the Gospel at the Eucharist. (*Apostolic Constitutions*)

c. 380 Bid the prayers of the people at the Eucharist. (*Apostolic Constitutions*)

c. 380 Announce the kiss of peace. (*Apostolic Constitutions*)

c. 384 Bless the paschal candle. (Jerome)

These functions are pastoral, charitable, and liturgical, connecting and illustrating the interrelation of these activities of the Church in its ongoing life. The deacon is par excellence the embodiment of the ministry of Christ in the world.

Part Two

The Renewal of the Diaconate Today with Reflections for the Twenty-first Century

Chapter 7

Organism as the Principle
of Renewal

The stage was set in the Renaissance with its new insights into the Scriptures and the life of the early Church for the recovery of a pre-Nicene concept of the Church's organic character and total ministry. Even with the extremes and errors of the Reformation period, we may see the first stages of the fruition of this renewal in the developments of the sixteenth century. However, the reformers of the sixteenth century, whether of the Reformation or of the counter-Reformation, were men of their own times and subject to the limitations imposed by the tradition and culture of the age, as are we. It is too much to expect that they would have been able at that point to see and augment the full implications of their insights. Such a radical change as would then have occurred might have proven to be a disaster for the Church.

But now in the late twentieth century as the Constantinian establishment of the Church in the West disintegrates and the Church disengages itself from an identification with society, it is again examining its life in the light of scriptural truths, particularly as they are illuminated by the practice of the early period and the writings of the leaders of that period, that the Holy Spirit may guide it to renewed life and vigor.

On the most fundamental level, it is apparent that there are two basic ways to think of the Church's nature and function. First, the Church can be seen as an institution governed and directed by the clergy, who "shape the policy and make the plans for implementing it, and then *enlist recruits,* the laity, to assist them in carrying out these plans." Or second, the Church can be viewed as the people of God in which "every member has a share in a common, though differentiated, responsibility."[1] The analogy in the first instance is that of employers and employees. In the second it is that of a team. Football and soccer provide good examples of the team analogy. The captain is not only the leader but also a player, using his particular abilities along with the others, who together play the game.

---

1. F. A. Cockin, "Ministers of the Priestly People," *Theology* 65 (January 1962): 7.

A. T. Hanson says that, although Church traditions have maintained in theory that the clergy are only part of a corporate ministry, in the Protestant traditions it is not true in practice and in Catholic traditions even the theory has been discarded. In the latter, the bishop in theory and in practice is not head of a team but superintendent over an area. A presbyter or priest has similar oversight in a town where there is but one parish of that tradition. In larger places there may be many presbyters but they do not usually work as a group.[2] Those in charge of parishes customarily function largely as superintendents over congregations if not over a geographical area. Today, however, a consensus appears to be emerging, at least in the West among the major churches, that the New Testament picture is of a corporate ministry of the whole people, each of whom has an important function and who together constitute the ministry of Christ and his Church.

It is most encouraging to note that a report prepared by Richard L. Rashke under the sponsorship of Pro Mundi Vita, the international research and information center in Brussels, states, "[American Roman] Catholics are beginning to realize that the full impact of Vatican II lies . . . in a shift in the very understanding of the Church itself from a hierarchical institutional model to a community people-of-God model." In writing about the growing interest in the Roman Catholic Church in team ministry in the United States, the report records that "team ministry is a logical application of a theological principle: ministry belongs to all Christians, not just to the ordained."[3]

The Church needs the functions of rule; of preaching; of healing; of teaching; of visiting the sick; of caring for the poor, the lonely, the troubled, and the depressed; of praying; of administering the sacraments; and of ministering in other ways to the lives of people in a broken world. The other side of the coin is that the Church's people need to do these things — all *need* to minister. The need of *all the baptized* to minister is often overlooked as the focus is placed on the tasks of ministry at hand. But there is no real substitute for active ministry in deepening and enriching the lives of God's people. This truth is well illustrated, even dramatically, in Twelve Step programs, which are in fact the steps of the Christian life applied to the lives of persons with addictive behavior problems. The experience of Alcoholics Anonymous, the greatest of these programs, is that the success of recovering alcoholics is largely dependent upon their doing what the Church calls ministry: helping others with similar problems to find what they have found and so also to live not only with sobriety but with serenity. The essence of these Twelve Step programs is spiritual. Through helping others recovering persons learn to love themselves, others, and God.

---

2. Hanson, "Shepherd, Teacher and Celebrant," 31.
3. Richard L. Rashke, *The Deacon in Search of Identity* (New York: Paulist Press, 1975), 5, 13. The report records that in 1972 team ministries had been created or their feasibility studied in half of the dioceses in America. In 1974 one diocese had 30 teams (13). There were at least four team pastoral training centers being operated in the United States at that time along with a national placement agency for those in the field (15).

So great is the task of ministry and so great is our need to minister that it can only be accomplished by recovering the fullness of an organic ministry constituted by no less than all the people of God. Obviously the primary meaning of a corporate conception of the ministry has to do with the local church. This is where it must be recovered if it is to have reality.[4]

In our complex world it is widely recognized that the priest or pastor of a local church can do only a very limited part of what is needed, even in relatively small parishes. But there exist within these Christian communities ample numbers of people capable of meeting the challenges to ministry, just as there were in the early Church. Each congregation should be able to raise up from its own membership those whom it needs. But how is this to be done?

The Organic Principle

In recent years much emphasis has been placed on lay ministry, and rightly so. However, because the organic principle of the pre-Nicene Church has not been properly understood or implemented, there has been a "confusion of orders." Laity have been delegated functions traditionally belonging to another order.[5] Pope Paul VI pointed this out in his apostolic letter, *General Norms for Restoring the Permanent Diaconate in the Latin Church,* issued *motu proprio,* saying that some functions of deacons have been given to lay persons but suggesting that these lay persons performing a diaconal ministry would benefit by the grace of ordination to the office.[6] There is no question of authority here. As we noted in a previous chapter, the Church has broad authority to structure and change its forms of ministry. This position is supported by a committee of the Catholic Theological Society of America in "A Report on the Restoration of the Office of Deacon as a Lifetime State" made at the request of the Bishops' Committee on the Permanent Diaconate in the United States. In speaking of the members of this committee the report states,

> Their studies, discussions, and reflections have led them to the conviction that the Church is free — much freer than is often recognized — to shape the structures of its various ministries, including the traditional triadic structure of episcopate, presbyterate, and diaconate, for the good of men.

In the process of discerning which are the most apt structures and functions, tradition must be reverenced. But tradition itself has no clearer and stronger word

---

4. Hanson, "Shepherd, Teacher and Celebrant," 31.

5. Massey H. Shepherd Jr., "Prayer Book Revision," lectures at the Graduate School of Theology, Sewanee, Tenn., Summer, 1970. Dr. Shepherd specifically termed the Episcopal Church's authorizing lay administration of the chalice a "confusion of orders," stating that the function properly belongs to the diaconate.

6. Pope Paul VI, *General Norms for Restoring the Permanent Diaconate in the Latin Church (Motu Proprio),* U.S. Catholic Conference, Washington, D.C., June 18, 1967 (hereafter cited as Paul VI, *Permanent Diaconate*).

to say to us than that, as a matter of fact, the Church has frequently exercised great freedom in adapting form to purpose, structure to mission.[7]

The question then becomes not so much what the Church can do but rather what the Church should do to accomplish the mission given by Christ and to meet the needs of people in our world.

The problem with "confusion of orders" is that the organic nature of the Church is in some sense negated. In a physical body a particular organ, such as the eye, has been created to fulfill a certain function. It is true that the hands can fulfill some of the functions of the eyes, but never so well as the eyes themselves. Although a lay person may assume functions of a clerical office, such as that of the deacon, it does make a significant difference that such a person has neither the authorization nor the grace of the office itself. And we see another aspect of the problem of "confusion of orders" in the attempt, for whatever reason, of one order to assume almost the totality of ministry. Many of the problems of the Church today in relationship to ministry are due to the presbyters or pastors assuming, or trying to assume, all the functions of the ministry. The term sometimes used to describe this aspect of the presbyterate is aptly the "omnivorous priesthood." The terminology here is that of Catholic traditions, but it is equally applicable to pastors in Protestant churches.

The "General Instructions of the Roman Missal" today attempt to restore the ancient practice of the Church by directing that each take only his or her rightful part in the eucharistic Liturgy. The instruction states,

> Everyone in the eucharistic assembly has the right and duty to take his own part according to the diversity of orders and functions. In exercising his function, everyone, whether minister [sic] or layman, should do that and only that which belongs to him, so that in the liturgy the Church may be seen in its variety of orders and ministries.[8]

This provision has ended the abuse of priests serving as deacons at the Eucharist according to a study prepared by the American Roman Catholic Bishops' Committee on the Liturgy.[9] It has also served to encourage broad lay participation.

It is worth observing only because it is so common across denominational lines that the word "minister" in this statement is used in differentiation from "layman." The same usage is even more unfortunate in liturgical formularies, since they are used by the people, as in the Episcopal Church's 1979 *Book of Common Prayer*. One example (others could be cited) is in one of forms of intercessory prayers for the Eucharist. After praying for certain bishops by name, prayer is added "for all bishops and other ministers [presumably priests

---

7. "A Report on the Restoration of the Office of Deacon," par. 8, p. 192.

8. "General Instructions of the Roman Missal," no. 58, in *The Roman Missal, the Sacramentary* (New York: Catholic Book Publishing, 1974), 28.

9. In Bishops' Committee on the Liturgy, *The Deacon, Minister of Word and Sacrament*, Study Text VI (Washington, D.C.: U.S. Catholic Conference, 1979), 14.

and deacons], and for all the holy people of God [presumably the baptized who have not had the grace of ordination bestowed upon them, which by implication would have made them ministers]."[10] Such usage, although understandable in light of history, is regrettable, the more because it is apparently done unconsciously. Lay people are the baptized, and the New Testament understanding of Baptism clearly sees ministry given to all at Baptism. The purpose of language is to communicate, and most do understand what is meant when "minister" is used to indicate the ordained. But so long as "minister" is so used, it is unlikely that the baptized generally will think of themselves as being the primary ministers of the Church called to undertake most of its ministry.

The Episcopal Church has also moved toward restoration of the reality and integrity of the several orders within the Church. Its 1979 *Book of Common Prayer* directs,

> In all services, the entire Christian assembly participates in such a way that the members of each order within the Church, lay persons, bishops, priests, and deacons, fulfill the functions proper to their respective orders, as set forth in the rubrical directions for each service.[11]

The proper liturgical role of the deacon is set forth in the several liturgies. Although extensive lay participation has become the rule in Episcopal parishes in recent years, as is also true in the Roman Catholic Church (and others that have not restored the historic diaconate), many have not as yet been enriched by the presence of deacons.

The lack of in-depth comprehension of the nature of the Church and its several orders is illustrated much too frequently on parish and diocesan levels when genuine deacons are present, yet their special functions are assigned to lay people, priests, or even bishops. I have witnessed this anomaly all too often as have others knowledgeable about and sensitive to this problem. No doubt, the motivation to involve the laity is good, but there are ample opportunities for lay people to function in nondiaconal roles. Authorization for the laity to perform functions historically belonging to the deacon has been given only because there is a real need for the function and deacons have not been and are not usually available. A notable example of this practice is lay administration of the eucharistic elements when deacons are present in sufficient numbers. Another is that of a priest or bishop reading the Gospel at the Eucharist with a deacon standing by.

In an age such as ours, which values and utilizes specialization of function far beyond any society of the past, the Church should be all the more attuned to the need and advantage of differentiation of function provided by many participants of varied offices. This is true especially in light of the New Testament

---

10. *Book of Common Prayer and Administration of the Sacraments and Other Rites and Ceremonies of the Church*, 390.

11. Ibid., 13.

emphasis on differing gifts of the Spirit. Some fall into the category of the ordained ministry, some lay ministry, when we see in these terms differentiation of function and also of the manner and nature of authorization for ministry. Donald Tytler well observes,

> What is needed is nothing less than a revolution of thought and feeling on the part of laity and clergy towards one another. It is not just a matter of straightening out the theology of ministry, if by that phrase is meant chiefly the intellectual acceptance of certain right (i.e., biblical) ideas of ministry. There is required a radical change of ideas between the body of the clergy and the mass of laity and between individual clergy and laymen.[12]

The crux of the radical change required is to see again the fact that all are *laos,* all are ministers of Christ, sharing in his ministry and priesthood, although in different ways.

In our time the apostolic and New Testament concept that all are laity is difficult for clergy and laity alike to grasp. It is even more difficult to comprehend the extensive implications involved and to implement them. But the importance of doing so can hardly be overestimated. The present archbishop of Canterbury, George Carey, and John Hind included a profound statement by Bishop Geoffrey Paul in their contribution to a recent book. The bishop said,

> The Church of God is not divided into two groups, two unequal elements, clergy and laity, but the people of God is what it says it is. It is all and only laity, and it needs to be glad of it and remember it all the time. Clergy are laity, with a special calling, a special anointing, a special function and they are a special sign that God means redemption for all the world, but they remain laity, and woe betide them if they ever forget it.[13]

There is no evidence from the early Church that there is any ontological change (a change of being) brought about by ordination. In all fairness it should be stated that the question was not raised in the early Church, so there is only silence regarding it. However, the idea seems to me to vary from the baptismal theology of the pre-Nicene Church. The theory that ordination creates an ontological change is apparently a Medieval development coming about at least in part due to the transference of theological content from Baptism to ordination. The great mystery of Baptism does create an ontological change in every person baptized. It is the second birth, giving the Holy Spirit, uniting that person to Christ in his death and resurrection, ingrafting the person into the body of Christ, and making the person an adopted child of God. The sacraments do cause the grace they signify.[14] Ordination certainly confers grace, the grace needed for the

---

12. Donald Tytler, "Each in His Own Order," in *New Ways with the Ministry*, ed. John Morris (London: Faith Press, 1960), 25.

13. Geoffrey Paul, quoted in George Carey and John Hind, "Ministry, Ministries, and the Ministry," in *Stepping Stones: Joint Essays on Anglican Catholic and Evangelical Unity*, ed. Christina Baxter, John Stott, and Roger Greenacre (London: Hodder & Stoughton, 1987), 55.

14. Aidan Kavanagh, *The Shape of Baptism: The Rite of Christian Initiation* (New York: Pueblo Publishing, 1978), 146.

particular office, but grace is constantly flowing from God to his people through the sacraments, in response to prayer, and simply from the love and graciousness of God. Relative to the grace of the various ministries of the Church, Neil Alexander writes, "Baptismal grace empowers all ministry, lay and ordained. When one is ordained to the diaconate, one does not receive an additional injection of grace, but the grace given in baptism is called forth — kindled for the public work of *diakonia* in the Church."[15]

What may be said of the diaconate is equally applicable to other ordination rites. There is no indication in the New Testament that Christ needed or received any further gift than the gift of the Holy Spirit bestowed upon him in his Baptism. To assert that Christ did not need further gifts because he was God incarnate is to beg the question. As Paul wrote, probably quoting from an early Christian hymn, the preexistent, divine Christ "emptied himself [of his divine attributes] ... being born in human likeness" (Phil. 2:7). Irenaeus said, "He became what we are that we might become what he is." He lived a human life, truly human. His Baptism in the Jordan River, not his incarnation, empowered him for his messianic role. In Baptism we "put on" Christ, share in his life, and receive the Holy Spirit. It is in Baptism alone that the essential being of a person is transformed.

Baptism makes all Christians equally members of the *laos,* the people of God. Office and ordination do give the Church's authority for the exercise of certain functions in and for the whole body of Christ and call forth the grace needed for the office, but neither office nor ordination changes the status of any or make some "more equal" than others.

From a New Testament viewpoint, except for its profound doctrine of human pride, it is difficult to understand the Church's rapid and seemingly unconscious adoption of pretensions to rank and status, particularly on the part of its bishops, presbyters, and deacons as the Church moved in the fourth century from a persecuted, illegal community with a horizontal, organic structure in which all were *laos* to a privileged, established religion with a vertical, hierarchical superstructure adorned with the trappings of the imperial Roman state.

The archbishop of Canterbury, George Carey, and John Hind describe the gift of the Spirit in Baptism and the gifts given to all thereby as "the central nervous system of the New Testament doctrine of ministry" and therefore assert, "Ministry belongs to the people of God as a gift." They elucidate,

> This concept of ministry belonging essentially to the "laos" of God sharply divided the New Testament Church from its Jewish background or, indeed, pagan religions of its day. No room is found in it for a separate caste which alone is a channel of salvation for others or which alone has the right "to minister." On the contrary, the revolution of Christianity is centered in its understanding of the

---

15. Alexander, "A Call to Adventure," 27.

entire body as being a "royal priesthood" with a variegated diversity and richness about the ministries given by the Holy Spirit which are offered to its Lord.[16]

What is at issue here is not the orders, which came into being in the New Testament period and have endured to the present, but the perception of these offices and the way they are exercised in the Church in relationship to the whole body of the *laos*. All the baptized are equally God's people. All have equally been given the gift of the Holy Spirit, and the Spirit has bestowed upon each unique gifts for the welfare and benefit of the whole. As in the human body, the work of each member is vital to the welfare of the whole, one not necessarily greater than another. It is this principle, the organic principle, that should again inform the Church's perception of itself and its ministry.

---

16. Carey and Hind, "Ministry, Ministries, and the Ministry," 55.

Chapter 8

The Deacon as Symbol

Perhaps the most misunderstood idea relating to the diaconate is the fact that its primary significance does not lie in any of its functions, whether pastoral, charitable/societal, or liturgical. The origin of the diaconate and its development in the first centuries reveals above all the deacon as symbol par excellence of the Church's ministry. The deacon illuminates the indelible character of *service* Christ put on his ministry and of *servant* on those who minister. He is the embodiment of the first principle of this ministry: *sent* to *serve.*

As we have already noted in another connection, a symbol, in the sense we are using the word, is a powerful representation that has many meanings and evokes many feelings. We would recall that humankind are symbolic beings who are formed and molded by symbol and who themselves reshape symbols and thereby shape their world.[1] Although it would be perhaps simplistic to see in the decline of the diaconate the cause of the Church's losing *diakonia* as the primary thrust of its ministry, it is true that as this primary symbol of the early Church was degraded and essentially lost over the centuries service to others became less and less central in Christian ministry. It is reasonable to conclude that the loss of the deacon as symbol was at least a highly significant factor in the reshaping or refocusing of the Church's ministry.

This development would seem almost inevitable as a result of the Church restructuring its ordained ministry hierarchically from greater to lesser and adopting the civil trappings of rank. The character and focus of the ministry changed, with the integrity of the diaconate mortally compromised as it was recreated into a transitional office in the ecclesial ladder to reach the pinnacle of the priesthood and, for a few, the episcopate. These offices became symbols of power and authority, reshaping the character and focus of ministry. The seven deacons of Rome became cardinal "deacons" of the Church of Rome. Certain continental bishops were electors of the Holy Roman Empire. English bishops sat in the House of Lords, as some continue to do, and certain priests were members of the House of Commons.[2] Prior to the American Revolution, the

---

1. Winter, *Elements for a Social Ethic*, 227.

2. Theoretically, I have been told, certain presbyters of the Church of England could still sit in the Commons, but it has been so long since this right has been exercised that an attempt to do so would probably create a constitutional crisis, or possibly today the British would simply laugh.

Church of England had no bishops in the American colonies, due essentially to the objection many colonists had to these lordly symbols of status and power. Priesthood and ministry became virtually synonymous terms. The priests were those who ministered, the laity were those ministered to. Remembrance of the servant nature Christ had given to the ministry of all his people continued in noble ascriptions relating to the hierarchy, such as "a servant of the servants of God," and in ceremonies, such as the washing of feet on Maundy or Holy Thursday by popes, other bishops, and monarchs. But these were forms largely devoid of the reality of humble service expressed in Christ's washing the feet of his disciples and exemplified by the deacons of the early Church. Even so, there have always been both clergy and laity who have lived out this ministry in lives of humble service. The deacon, Francis of Assisi, is perhaps the most notable example, but here the observation that Francis is "the most admired but the least emulated of all the saints" is noteworthy.

The deacon above all epitomizes within his or her office the ministry Christ has given to his Church, the servant ministry to which we are all called and commissioned in our Baptism. The particular functions are, of course, important. They give meaning and content to the symbol of deacon. However, as Article 16 of the original guidelines of the Roman Catholic Bishops' Committee on the Permanent Diaconate stated, the deacon's "overall symbolizing of the service is more meaningful than his specific functions."[3] The current guidelines speak of ordination as choosing a person "to fulfill a role representative of both Christ and the Church," making the deacon a sacrament of Christ to the Church. Following ordination,

> The believing community then receives the man as one who, in his sacramental consecration, permanent commitment, and specific ministry, is a sacrament to it of Jesus Christ himself.[4]
>
> As it would be a distortion and betrayal of the ministries of bishops and priests to think that only they have responsibility for the upbuilding of the Church in faith or for the praise of God in worship, so also ordination to the diaconate does not set a man apart in order for him to have a monopoly on the Church's service. The deacon's distinctiveness is, rather, *sacramental*: what *all* in the Church are to be and to do is made visible and effective by the liturgical consecration and empowerment of *some* members among them. Within the one great sacrament of Jesus Christ which is the Church, the sacrament of orders symbolizes at once the unity and diversity of Christian service.[5]

---

3. Bishops' Committee on the Permanent Diaconate, *Permanent Deacons in the United States: Guidelines on Their Formation and Ministry* (Washington: U.S. Catholic Conference, 1971), 8 (hereafter cited as Bishops' Committee, *Permanent Deacons*).

4. Bishops' Committee on the Permanent Diaconate, *Permanent Deacons in the United States: Guidelines on Their Formation and Ministry*, 1984 Revision (Washington, D.C.: U.S. Catholic Conference, Inc., 1985): 22, p. 13 (hereafter cited as Bishops' Committee, *Permanent Deacons*, 1984 rev.).

5. Ibid., 27, pp. 14, 15.

The need for a powerful symbol to proclaim that the ministry of the Church is *diakonia* is indeed great. It is all too apparent that Christian congregations generally tend to be self-centered and self-serving, although not so much as a matter of deliberate intent as of inheriting a form of Christianity which conceives of ministry essentially in spiritual terms of bringing personal salvation to individual souls. The social unrest, demonstrations, and strife of the 1960s in the United States was certainly in part at least due to the failure of the Church in recent generations to be concerned about and to serve the poor and powerless in the face of gross economic and social injustice in the midst of an affluent and professedly democratic society. The Church needs to heed the advice of a Lutheran leader, Thure-Gengt Molander, who urges the recovery of the fundamental nature of Christian ministry. "The Church," he said, "must become a diaconal Church in the deepest and most forward-looking sense, or it will not be the Church."[6]

Other Ministries Enhanced

Although we shall deal separately with the relationship between the deacon and other orders of the clergy, it is appropriate that we consider here briefly the idea that the diaconate is not needed on the one hand because lay people today can do virtually all that the deacon can do and on the other that priests can do all the deacons can do and much more.

The crux of this problem lies, first of all, in a failure to understand the organic nature of the Church as it was founded by Christ and developed in the pre-Nicene period: it is a community in which its many members have been given differing gifts by the Spirit for the upbuilding and welfare of the whole. On the one hand, as we have seen, the omnivorous priesthood subsumed unto itself virtually all categories of ministry in the Medieval period, as is symbolically seen in liturgy by priests routinely assuming the functions of the deacon and the laity in the Eucharist. The result has been a fundamental "confusion of orders." On the other, in recent years as the need for renewal in the Church has become painfully evident, particularly in a recovery of lay ministry, lay people have been authorized to perform liturgical functions that historically belong to the diaconate. They have been authorized to lead the prayers of the people, administer the eucharistic elements, and in some traditions to read the Gospel at the Eucharist. No small part of the reason for lay authorization has been the absence of deacons, along with the need to expand the conception that ministry belongs to all the people of God and to symbolize this essential truth liturgically in the Church's rites, especially the Eucharist. Lay authorization for primary diaconal functions also blurs the organic concept of the Church as Christ's body and contributes to this fundamental "confusion of orders."

---

6. Lutheran Church in America, *Minutes, Fifth Biennial Convention*, Minneapolis, June 25–July 2, 1970 (Philadelphia: Board of Publication of the Lutheran Church in America, 1970), 449.

Beyond this is the underlying idea that the primary function of the deacon is to do something. But as we have seen, his or her first reason for being is *to be* something. H. Boone Porter Jr. has astutely observed that bishops are not ordained primarily in order to do the few distinctive things that are unique to their order. Rather he says, bishops are ordained "primarily to preach the Gospel and to unify, lead, and oversee the church." Most of their time is spent in doing such things as reading the daily office, answering mail, seeing visitors, and attending meetings, which lay people can also do. The special functions of a bishop, notably ordaining, "belong to the bishop because he is the authoritative spokesman of the church, not *vice versa*. "[7] The primary function of the bishop, like the deacon, is to be something, not to do something. He is a symbol of the unity of the Church in faith and fellowship not only throughout the world today but throughout the ages and, as such, a spokesman for the Church to the world.

In turning to the question of why deacons are ordained, Porter sees their role to be uniquely Christian with no real counterpart in secular organizations:

> Their mandate, some of us believe, is to give sacramental embodiment to our Lord's teaching that the greatest shall be servant of all, and to lead the church as a whole in implementing this teaching. To the secular world, this does not, and cannot make sense. Even for us Christians, it is not easily understood.[8]

Patrick McCaslin and Michael G. Lawler rightly observe "that any parish without the sacramental presence of a deacon to symbolize the call of the local church to diakonia is sacramentally incomplete.... Any church with a pastor but no deacon is declaring in symbol the absence of diakonia from its mission." After pointing out that ordination does not make deacons out of nondeacons but recognizes in the ministry of a lay person true diaconal ministry, "the very ministry the Church is called and sent to perform," and the deacon as "an incarnation of the Church," they say,

> In ordination [the Church] *publicizes* this recognition, that is, it proclaims in public that this person being ordained is the kind of person it itself is called and sent to be, and it designates him now to be its officially sanctioned representative symbol of diakonia.[9]

McCaslin and Lawler see diaconal ordination making a difference both in the Church and in the deacon. Regarding the Church, they say,

> By ordaining this person [the Church] has acknowledged something that it had never acknowledged before, namely, that this man is a deacon and, in his diaconate, an outstanding symbol of the Church itself, and therefore of the Christ

---

7. H. Boone Porter Jr., "Ordained Ministers in Liturgy and in Life," in *The Living Church* (Milwaukee, Wis.: Living Church Foundation, January 9, 1977), 13.

8. Ibid., 14.

9. Patrick McCaslin and Michael G. Lawler, *Sacrament of Service: A Vision of the Permanent Diaconate Today* (New York: Paulist Press, 1986), 42, 54, 55. Father McCaslin was founding president of the Association of Permanent Diaconate Directors in the United States (Roman Catholic) (italics in original).

whose sacrament it is, and therefore of God whose sacrament Christ is. Its ordination of him affirms in him the talent-charism for the diaconate, and affirms in
itself the ongoing commitment to be a deacon-Church. This affirmation ordains
this deacon to be an exemplar of diakonia to the whole Church.[10]

The "talent-charism" referred to is defined as "poverty" or "evangelical poverty understood as total availability to others," which is explained by the words
one deacon spoke as he was leaving the church after his ordination: "Now I
no longer live on my time." McCaslin and Lawler see ordination as affirming
and reinforcing this charism and talent for being available to others and publicly
placing it at the disposal of the Church and of Christ. This "poverty" is part
at least of the other difference made by ordination, that in the deacon himself.
Further, the deacon becomes a symbol:

> Now [the deacon] receives an affirmation from the Church that the ministry he
> does is the Church's ministry, and he receives an ordination to continue to do that
> ministry, now not only as a private member, but also as a publicly and solemnly
> designated representative, of the Church. As an ordained deacon he performs not
> only the diakonia he always performed, but also a new and solemn one. Now he
> symbols for the Church and all its members what it and they are, and calls them
> to be what he and they are, namely, deacons in the Church of the presence of
> Christ, of grace, and of God.[11]

Deacons then are not ordained essentially in order that they may perform the
distinctive functions of their order but to hold up *diakonia* as central to all
Christian ministry.

Restoration of a true diaconal ministry will enhance the other ministries of
the Church. In relationship to lay ministry, "A Report on the Restoration of the
Office of Deacon as a Lifetime State" by a committee of theologians of the
Catholic Theological Society of America to the Bishops' Committee on the Permanent Diaconate states that "far from rivaling or inhibiting the ministry of
laymen, the ministry of deacons, when it is judiciously exercised, will power-
fully promote that ministry."[12] The deacons envisioned here are a reality today
in many places. They live like lay people with jobs, families, and social responsibilities as before but yet are ordained deacons and minister in their special
ways liturgically, pastorally, and charitably. Their ministries have, as the report
foresaw, brought new dimensions to the ministry of the laity. Some deacons, as
Ormonde Plater points out in his recent book, have come to see their ministries
primarily in terms of enabling lay ministry.[13]

---

10. Ibid.
11. Ibid., 42, 43.
12. "A Report on the Restoration of the Office of Deacon," par. 23, p. 198.
13. Ormonde Plater, *Many Servants: An Introduction to Deacons* (Cambridge, Mass.: Cowley
Publications, 1991), 65, 197–98. Ormonde Plater is a prominent deacon of the Episcopal Church
living in New Orleans. He is editor of *Diakoneo*, a publication of the (Anglican) North American
Association for the Diaconate.

Neil Alexander describes the order in this way: "The diaconate, therefore, is an order within the church, whose members have been blessed with special charisms and authorized to publicly perform certain functions that enable them to embody and model on behalf of all an intensified *diakonia*."[14] This diaconal ministry has served and continues to serve to complement and enlarge the ministry and effectiveness not only of the laity but also of bishops and more especially of parish priests and pastors, with whom they generally serve. The enhancement of the other orders by a restored diaconate will be more apparent as we go on to consider its renewal.

---

14. Alexander, "A Call to Adventure," 24.

Chapter 9

A Full and Equal Order
RESTORING THE DIACONATE

In our consideration of the development of the Church's ordained ministry we found that the greatest single cause of the decline of the diaconate was the development of *cursus honorum.* There is, of course, nothing inherently detrimental in one person holding various offices requiring differing and, in some instances, increasing responsibility in the Church. As the ancient councils and many of the fathers of the early Church saw, it was good for one to demonstrate by service in the Church proper qualifications for positions of leadership entailing greater responsibility, particularly in reference to the episcopate. However, to see the ministry of the Church essentially as a graded succession of offices not only contradicts the organic character with which the Church was originally endowed by Christ and his Spirit but also affirms the very worldliness denied by Christ. Such a view sees the ministry largely in terms of authority, power, and honor, not of service. The ministry is properly *diakonia,* service, a truth needing reiteration just because it has been so neglected, if not forgotten. Lampe affirms that "the study of the New Testament gives us the assurance that, so long as a commissioning and *diakonia* are its keynotes, the essentials of the apostolic ministry of the first century are present and operative in our totally different world."[1]

The first step in the restoration of the essential character of the ministry of the pre-Nicene Church is the reassertion of the principle that each order and office is a distinct and distinctive vocation to which the Holy Spirit calls the various members of the Church as he wills. As this principle comes alive, increasingly the ministry will include and utilize all the people of God.

A necessary part of any profound renewal of the ministry must include abandoning all requirements of passing through successive orders or offices. Baptism must be restored as the only sacramental prerequisite for ordination and/or commissioning to any office in the Church. Of course, the ancient concern that those chosen for positions of leadership will have first demonstrated their fitness for the office by their service *in the Church* is still valid. Social status or "success" in other fields fits one no better today than in ancient times for stepping directly

---

1. Lampe, *N.T. Ministry*, 20.

into positions of leadership and responsibility in the Church, a fact to be especially noted at a time when secularism has made considerable inroads into the thinking of large numbers of Christians. There have been exceptions like Ambrose of Milan and Thomas Becket of England, but they are notable just because they are rare. However, it is one thing to test people with the criteria of committed service in the Church and another to require a succession of offices, which is no guarantee in itself of genuine *diakonia*.

Karl Rahner in his *Theological Investigations* relating to the restored diaconate regarded the requirement for ordination of "absolute" (life-long) deacons to the minor orders as "superfluous."[2] The principle Rahner objected to was unchanged by Paul VI's continuing the requirement that diaconal candidates be "installed" into the "offices" of lector and acolyte instead of "ordained" into the "minor order." *A Plan of Union for the Church of Christ Uniting,* published in 1970, sets forth a most enlightened proposal for a diaconate under this scheme. The diaconate is to be a "distinctive vocation" with the emphasis on service restored to the ministry of the deacon. It is not to be a stage of preparation of presbyters.[3] Since the plan was not accepted by the participating churches, the proposal was not put into practice.

In the Roman Catholic Church the Council of Trent, 1545–63, directed the restoration of the diaconate, including it in a decree relating to the minor orders. On July 15, 1563, the council decreed:

> That the function of holy orders from the deacon to the porter, which have been laudably received in the Church from the times of the Apostles, and which have been for some time discontinued in many localities, may again be restored to use in accordance with the canons, and may not be derided by the heretics as useless, the holy council burning with desire to restore the ancient usage, decrees that in the future such functions shall not be exercised except by those constituted in these orders, and it exhorts in the Lord each and all prelates of the churches and commands them that they make it their care to restore these functions, so far as it can be conveniently done, in cathedral, collegiate and parochial churches of their diocese, if the number of people and the revenues of the church are able to bear it.[4]

The decree apparently contemplates principally liturgical functions. The council had rejected a proposal on July 6 of that year setting forth a diaconate specifically mandating a ministry to the poor. However, the decree approved

---

2. Karl Rahner, *Later Writings,* trans. Karl H. Kruger, vol. 5 of *Theological Investigations* (Baltimore: Helicon Press, 1966), 314.

3. Consultation on Church Union, *A Plan of Union for the Church of Christ Uniting* (Princeton, N.J.: n.p., 1970), 53.

4. Session 23, "Decree Concerning Reform," in chap. 17, "In What Name the Exercise of the Minor Orders Is to Be Restored," in *Canons and Decrees of the Council of Trent,* trans. H. J. Schroeder (St. Louis: B. Herder Book Co., 1941), 174.

did show some appreciation for the Church as a corporate body whose members had distinctive functions. Unfortunately, it was never implemented.[5]

Roman Catholicism

The renewal in the Roman Catholic Church, begun in the pontificate of John XXIII, has moved it noticeably in the direction of recovering the Church's organic character. A part of this at least has been steps taken to restore the diaconate as a distinctive order, a process begun by the Second Vatican Council in its Constitution on the Church (*Lumen Gentium*) promulgated by Pope Paul VI in 1964. The council spoke of the need for the diaconate in the future to be "restored as a proper and permanent rank of the hierarchy."[6] The Roman pontiff implemented this decree in 1967 by publication of *General Norms for Restoring the Permanent Diaconate in the Latin Church*. We may consider his declaration that the diaconate "is not to be considered as a mere step towards the priesthood, but it is so adorned with its own indelible character and its own special grace" that it is to be considered a "permanent" vocation[7] as not only providing for the restoration of a true diaconate but also as taking the first step towards abolishing its interim character.

The National Conference of Catholic Bishops in the United States approved the restoration of the diaconate for this country in 1968[8] and requested permission for this restoration from the Vatican "both to complete the hierarchy of sacred orders and to enrich and strengthen the various diaconal ministries at work in the United States with the sacramental grace of the diaconate."[9]

The request was approved the same year, marking the beginning of a program that has flourished. At the end of 1976 there were 1,875 permanent deacons in the Roman Catholic Church in North America out of 3,125 in the world.[10] In January of 1993 the International Center for the Diaconate, Freiburg, Germany, reported 11,067 Roman Catholic deacons in North America, more than half of the 18,834 in 115 countries in the world.[11]

---

5. Bishops' Committee on the Liturgy, *The Deacon, Minister of Word and Sacrament*, 13; Echlin, *The Deacon in the Church Past and Future*, 105.

6. *De Ecclesia, The Constitution on the Church of Vatican Council II Proclaimed by Pope Paul VI, November 21, 1964*, ed. Edward H. Peters (Glen Rock, N.J.: Paulist Press, Deus Book, 1965), par. 29, pp. 122–23.

7. Pope Paul VI, *Permanent Diaconate*, 2.

8. Rashke, *The Deacon in Search of Identity*, 23.

9. Bishops' Committee, *Permanent Deacons*, par. 1, p. 1.

10. *Diaconal Quarterly* 2, no. 1 (Winter 1977): 8. In December 1976, deacons in Europe totaled 722 and in Central and South American 389. By October 31, 1980, the diaconate in the United States alone numbered 4,656 with 2,514 diaconal candidates. See also *Diaconal Quarterly* 7, no. 1 (Winter 1981): 35.

11. Statistics distributed by the Bishop's Committee on the Permanent Diaconate, Deacon Sam Taub, Executive Director. At this time Europe had 4,989, Central and South America 2,302, Africa 276, Australia and Oceana 102, and Asia 98.

However, a graded hierarchical structure is very much in evidence in the Roman Church. Paul VI in his Apostolic Constitution on *Approval of a New Rite for the Ordination of Deacons, Priests, and Bishops* calls special attention to this graded structure by first stating that priests do not possess the "highest degree" of the ministry and then reiterating the statement of Vatican II:

> In the lower grade of the hierarchy are deacons on whom hands are imposed "not for the priesthood, but for the ministry" (Constitutions of the Church of Egypt, III, 2). Strengthened by sacramental grace, they serve the People of God in the *diaconia* of liturgy, word, and charity, in communion with the bishop and his presbytery.[12]

Direction was also given by Paul VI in the *General Norms* issued June 18, 1967, that "present discipline be observed until it is revised by the Holy See" in conferring "those orders which precede the diaconate" as well as the diaconate itself.[13] On August 15, 1972, Paul VI promulgated apostolic letters requiring all diaconal candidates to receive the "offices" of lector (reader) and acolyte, which are now referred to as "ministries" and "should no longer be called minor orders." Admission to these ministries is by "installation," not "ordination," and is reserved to men.[14] A publication of the Archdiocese of Omaha, current in 1992, stated that directives from Rome set the interval between lector and acolyte at six months, although "the order of reception does not seem to matter."[15] The guidelines for *Permanent Deacons in the United States* simply state as a requirement for ordination that there must be a declaration that the ministries of lector and acolyte have been "received and exercised" and that "interstices have been observed" without a time period being mentioned. Ordination to the diaconate now constitutes "entrance into the clerical state."[16]

"Sacred" Ministers

It is encouraging that Echlin refers to the mention by Vatican II of deacons being of "lower grade" but says that this "does not imply an ascending theology of ministry," since they are servants of Christ and the Church. In his conclusion he writes, "The deacon's role is not 'lower than' nor 'inferior to' the priest's, he is not a potential rival; his charism is *different* than any other

---

12. Pope Paul VI, *Approval of a New Rite for the Ordination of Deacons, Priests and Bishops*, Apostolic Constitution, June 18, 1968, U.S. Catholic Conference, Washington, D.C., 5. He quotes here the Constitution on the Church, par. 29.

13. Pope Paul VI, *Permanent Diaconate*, 10.

14. Pope Paul VI, *An Apostolic Letter in Motu Proprio Form Laying Down Certain Norms Regarding the Sacred Order of the Diaconate, An Apostolic Letter in Motu Proprio Form By Which the Discipline of First Tonsure, Minor Orders and Subdiaconate in the Latin Church Is Reformed*, issued August 15, 1972 (Washington, D.C.: U.S. Catholic Conference, 1972), 5–7, 11–12, 13.

15. "The Basic Philosophy of the Permanent Diaconate Program for the Archdiocese of Omaha" (Photocopied, n.d.), 4.

16. Bishops' Committee, *Permanent Deacons*, 1984 rev., 12, 39.

charism in the Church including that of the priest."[17] Here we see asserted the pre-Nicene organic conception of the Church and its ministry. However, the documents themselves do very definitely envision a vertical, hierarchical structure of ministry and tend to perpetuate the false dichotomy between clergy and laity. By implication the laity is not a "sacred order." While technically the laity is not ordained and therefore, it is argued, not an order, the terminology conveys the impression that the laity is at most less sacred than the clergy. The new rite for admission for candidates to the diaconate and priesthood specifically states the candidate is to declare publicly his "will to offer himself to God and the Church, so that he may exercise a sacred order."[18] By ordination they enter "the clerical state" with the implication of becoming "sacred persons." Can one be more sacred than one is made in Baptism?

In Anglicanism the same problems prevail. The canons of the Episcopal Church in America until recently frequently implied that the clergy constitute the totality of the Church's ministers,[19] and its forms of intercessory prayer for the Eucharist reinforce this concept by the use of such phrases in some of them as those bidding prayer "for all bishops and other ministers, and for all the holy people of God."[20] Common terminology used to designate all three of its clerical offices at once is the "Sacred Ministry," implying that lay ministries are at least less sacred, if at all. A hierarchical structure remains with laity, deacons, priests, and bishops following in ascending order. The three orders continue to constitute a class of "sacred persons."

However, the Episcopal Church has also moved in the direction of recovering the New Testament concept of ministry as belonging to all the people. This is expressed in various ways in its revised Prayer Book of 1979, and the catechism of that book specifically asserts that "the ministers of the Church are lay persons, bishops, priests, and deacons" and includes a description of "the ministry of the laity" along with and equal to those of the clerical orders.[21]

Although there are differences, the situation in the Lutheran, Presbyterian, United Methodist, United Church of Christ, Baptist, Christian, and other churches seems to be fundamentally parallel. The clergy generally are sacralized as against or apart from the laity. Theologically the "full ministry" is only in the office of the presbyter, priest, pastor, or "minister." The diaconate, where it

---

17. Echlin, *The Deacon in the Church Past and Future*, 116, 130–31. Echlin translated the term "lower grade" as "lesser rank."

18. Bishops' Committee on the Liturgy, *The Deacon, Minister of Word and Sacrament*, 6.

19. *Constitutions and Canons for the Government of the Protestant Episcopal Church in the United States of America Otherwise Known as The Episcopal Church Adopted in General Conventions, 1789–1979, Together with the Rules of Order* (New York: Seabury Professional Services, 1979), Title 3, Canons 21–25, pp. 92–100. Canon 21, for example, is entitled "Of Ministers and Their Duties," the reference being to the three clerical orders. *Constitutions and Canons (1991)*, Title 3, Canon 14, the comparable section, is now entitled "Of Clergy and Their Duties," 80.

20. *Book of Common Prayer and Administration of the Sacraments and Other Rites and Ceremonies of the Church According to the Use of the Episcopal Church*, 390.

21. Ibid., 855.

exists, ranks second best and the laity a poor third. Sociologically, the "real" clergy, the priests and pastors, and their wives, if any, are isolated from full social involvement even with their parishioners.

Deacons and Transitional Deacons

Although too much can be made of terminology, the particular words we use are often of considerable importance due to the subtle implications they convey, even unconsciously. This is certainly true of designations that have come into use for vocational deacons in order to distinguish them from those ordained to serve a brief transitional "diaconate" before ordination to the priesthood. In the Episcopal Church the term *"perpetual* deacon" has been used for vocational deacons. Roman Catholics generally prefer *"permanent* deacon." Elsewhere we noted Karl Rahner uses *"absolute* deacon." One seems little better than the other. The words "perpetual" and "permanent" have to do with the nature of the vocation itself. They are not comparable to the use of "nonstipendiary" or "worker" priest, since such terms have to do with the source of compensation and/or the way in which such priests function.

Realistically the "diaconate" of those on their way to the priesthood or, in the terminology of other traditions, presbyterate or eldership, is another office. Such deacons are not called to the diaconate, are not trained for the diaconate, and do not serve diaconal ministries, except in the broader sense. They are, in fact, called to be priests, trained to be priests, and usually serve essentially priestly ministries after being ordained deacons. Such terms compromise the integrity of the diaconate and degrade the office. The term "deacon" should stand alone, without any modifying term, when the reference is to a real deacon, one called to that office, trained for that office, and ordained to serve in that office as a permanent vocation. If any adjective is used, it should be "transitional" and used to designate the transitional diaconate. This usage serves to recover the integrity of the office as the separate and equal order it was in the early Church.

Anglicanism

In the Anglican Communion the Lambeth Conference, the worldwide council of its bishops, adopted an important resolution regarding the diaconate at its 1958 meeting. Resolution 88, "The Office of the Deacon," states, "The Conference recommends that each province of the Anglican Communion shall consider whether the office of Deacon shall be restored to its primitive place as a distinct order of the Church, instead of being regarded as a probationary period for the priesthood."[22] This statement serves to call the attention of Anglicanism to the office of deacon with the implication that restoration is in order. Although

---

22. *The Lambeth Conference 1958, The Encyclical Letter from the Bishops together with the Resolutions and Reports* (Greenwich, Conn.: Seabury Press, 1958), 50.

the conference has no legal authority, it carries great moral weight throughout Anglicanism.

The statement of Lambeth 1958 is further to be interpreted in light of the report of its committee, which stated that in recent years the offices of reader and catechist have grown in the Anglican Communion and have largely taken over the traditional functions of the deacon. The report said that part of the problem stems from the fact that the Anglican diaconate requires the dedication of the whole of the deacon's life to this vocation. But of prime importance, the committee concluded that the Anglican Church needs to decide either to restore the diaconate or to give it up.[23]

The problem referred to by the Lambeth committee, that the Anglican deacon was required to dedicate the whole of life to this vocation, was and probably still is the case in some provinces of the Anglican Communion but not in the Episcopal Church in the United States. The canons of the Episcopal Church had been changed previously to allow for a diaconate that would be regarded as a permanent vocation and in which those entering it could continue to support themselves in their previous occupations. Such deacons were ordained in a number of dioceses, but attendant problems led rather quickly to the disuse of this form of the diaconate in most dioceses.

The experience of the Episcopal Church from its failed experiment with the "perpetual diaconate" of the post–World War II era provides a valuable lesson. The problems seemed to manifest themselves particularly in two areas. Many who were ordained deacon under this program soon were dissatisfied with the diaconate and sought to go on and be ordained priest. This was perhaps made easier in the 1950s by the Episcopal Church's need for priests in considerably greater numbers than were then available to meet its rapid growth. A considerable number of these deacons were ordained to the priesthood without adequate training, going in through what was termed "the back door." In addition, the relationship between the deacon and the priest was not sufficiently clear, so that at times a priest moving to a new parish with a "perpetual" deacon felt threatened,[24] although the number of cases where this was an actual problem has undoubtedly been highly overestimated.

Akin to this is another problem, which had a part in the reluctance of some Episcopal bishops to ordain these nonstipendiary (nonsalaried) deacons, who earn their own living in other work. In our highly mobile society deacons may often be transferred or move due to their non-Church employment to other parishes or dioceses, where there may not be a place or even a welcome for their ministries. Although this sociological problem will be considered in the next chapter, might we not ask at this point if there is any inherent reason why

_____

23. Ibid., 106.

24. *A Self-Supporting Ministry and the Mission of the Church*, by A Group of Sixty Bishops, Other Clergy, and Lay People of the Episcopal Church (New York: The Division of Christian Ministries of the National Council of the Episcopal Church, and the Overseas Missionary Society, 1964), 8.

a deacon moving to another place should create a greater problem than a lay person? Does not the lay person also have a ministry that will be available and might not be accepted in another place?

The underlying problems appear to be more fundamental, however. At that time the Episcopal Church still considered the office of deacon an "inferior" order both in theory and in practice. The ordinal of the 1928 *Book of Common Prayer* concluded with a prayer that the newly ordained deacons "may so well behave themselves in this *inferior* Office, that they may be found worthy to be called unto the higher Ministries."[25] The ministry was still conceived of largely in terms of graded ranks, not in terms of members of an organic society. The diaconate was the first step up the major ladder to the top, so that it seemed to be only logical that one would go on to the priesthood.[26] This thinking was also strengthened by training that tended to imply that these deacons would be semiprofessional in the priestly model. Preparation was somewhat modified for such a deacon from that required of the "transitional" deacon but was essentially a lesser version of the training needed for the priesthood.[27]

These deacons were seen largely in terms of unpaid assistants to the priests in parish churches. The Church's canon provided that the deacon "shall exercise his Ministry as *assistant* in any parish or parishes" to which he is assigned.[28] The deacon was not viewed as a servant of the Church whose ministry was service to the Church or to others for the Church, but as an assistant to the priest. The underlying model for the office was clearly the priesthood. Further, and of great importance, the ministry of these deacons was usually primarily liturgical. Typically, pastoral and charitable functions which give liturgical functions meaning and purpose were all but nonexistent. The result was that they often felt a sense of frustration in the office and aspired to the priesthood for fulfillment.

The experience of the Episcopal Church with this type of diaconate has resulted in its making major changes both in its liturgical forms and canon law. In writing of the Church's 1979 *Book of Common Prayer,* Marion Hatchett states,

---

25. *The Book of Common Prayer and Administration of the Sacraments and Other Rites and Ceremonies of the Church According to the Use of the Protestant Episcopal Church in the United States of America* (New York: Church Pension Fund, 1945), 535 (commonly called the 1928 *Book of Common Prayer*).

26. Essentially this is the position taken by J. Robert Wright in a report prepared for the Ministries' Commission and the bishop of New York regarding the "permanent diaconate," where he argues for proliferation of a nonstipendiary priesthood as against a permanent diaconate, as though they are mutually exclusive. See J. Robert Wright, "Ministry in New York: The Non-Stipendiary Priesthood and the Permanent Diaconate," in *St. Luke's Journal of Theology 19* (December 1975): 40–41. However, in an address entitled "The Distinctive Diaconate in Historical Perspective," delivered at the National Conference on the Diaconate at Notre Dame University in June 1979, Wright concludes with the implication that the diaconate should be restored as a distinctive order (Boston, National Center for the Diaconate, n.d.).

27. See Canon 34, Sec. 10 (b) (1), p. 83 and Canon 29, Sec. 2, pp. 68–69, *Constitutions and Canons (1958)*.

28. Ibid., Canon 34, sec. 10, p. 83.

The rites recover for us the traditional liturgical and pastoral functions of the various orders of ministers. The bishop takes his place as chief pastor and minister of Word and Sacraments. The ministry of the deacon is set forth as a distinctive servant-ministry rather than as an internship or stepping stone. The ministry of the presbyter is depicted as a collegial ministry. The participation of the laity is broadened and increased.[29]

The canons on the ministry adopted at the Church's General Convention in 1973 provided for the implementation of such a recovery. These canons envisioned a "diaconate with new expectations of how this order of ministry might be utilized in evangelism, pastoral care, and liturgy."[30]

Other important canonical changes have been made as a clearer understanding of the nature of the diaconate has emerged, such as a modification of training requirements moving away from the seminary model for "local deacons." Another significant change rescinded a 1964 authorization allowing deacons to be put in charge of congregations, recognizing that presiding over congregations is properly a presbyteral and not a diaconal function, although an appropriate exception was made for transitional deacons.[31]

There has been renewed and widespread interest in the restoration of the diaconate in the Episcopal Church since the adoption of these canons. At the request of the Episcopal House of Bishops, the Church's Council for the Development of Ministry prepared a report in 1979 describing, analyzing, and interpreting the Episcopal diaconate. At that time there were more than 500 deacons in the Episcopal diaconate in the United States, about 420 to 450 of whom were classified as active. The study reports that 94 percent of Episcopal bishops believed the Church should have a vital diaconate, but the need to clarify the role and duties of the diaconate and its effect on other ministries, especially lay ministries, before expanding diaconal programs was expressed. The report also called for new models for the selection, training, and examination of diaconal candidates to equip them to carry out a servant ministry.[32]

Organizations such as the North American Association for the Diaconate, a voluntary association primarily of Episcopal deacons in the United States but including deacons of the Anglican Church of Canada and the Evangelical Lu-

---

29. Marion J. Hatchett, "The New Book: A Continuation of or a Departure from the Tradition?" in *Open*, the newsletter of Associated Parishes (June 1977): 7.

30. H. Boone Porter, Jr., *Canons on New Forms of Ministry* 1973 (Kansas City: Roanridge, n.d.), 1.

31. Canon 34, Sec. 10 (c), p. 77, *Constitution and Canons (1964)* deleted the prohibition against deacons being placed in charge of congregations and explicitly authorized this practice for congregations "unable to receive the services of a resident Priest." Title III, Canon 13, Sec. 2 (a), p. 79, *Constitution and Canons (1991)* prohibits a deacon from being in charge of a congregation, an exception being made for transitional deacons. Sec. 1 (a) and (b), p. 79, direct that all deacons are to serve under the "direction and supervision" of the bishop, although the bishop may appoint someone to supervise the deacons.

32. *The Church, The Diaconate, The Future, The Report of the Diaconate*, 2.3, 2.5, submitted by the Council for the Development of Ministry to the House of Bishops, the General Convention, September 1979, Denver.

theran Church in America and others interested in the diaconate; the Associated Parishes, Inc.; and the Association of Diocesan Liturgy and Music Commissions have actively supported and encouraged renewal of the diaconate in the Episcopal Church.

By January of 1994 the diaconate in the Episcopal Church in the United States had more than tripled during the previous fifteen years, numbering 1,524 deacons, 865 being men and 659 women. The Anglican Church of Canada reported 61 deacons.[33]

"Direct" (Per Saltum) Ordination

In April 1977, at Wewoka, Oklahoma, the Council of Associated Parishes, an Episcopal organization dedicated to liturgical renewal, boldly advocated abandonment of the transitional or interim diaconate in favor of direct ordination to the diaconate or priesthood, a major step toward returning to the practice of the early and undivided Church in which Baptism was the only sacramental prerequisite for ordination to the diaconate, presbyterate, or episcopate. "The Wewoka Statement," as it is called, received widespread publicity in the Episcopal Church. The statement declares,

> The Associated Parishes Council is committed to the renewal of the order of deacon as a full, normal ministry in the Church, alongside the priesthood. The diaconate is not properly a stepping-stone or a back door to the priesthood. It is not an auxiliary ministry. Deacons and priests have equal but different ministries whose functions are clearly outlined in the new ordinal of the Proposed Book of Common Prayer.
>
> In an effort to clarify the distinctive character and importance of each order, as well as the ministry of the laity, we feel that candidates for the priesthood should be ordained directly to that order. Deacons should be eligible to be elected bishop and ordained directly to that order.
>
> The ministry of lay persons, bishops, priests, and deacons is one in the Body of Christ our great high priest who came as one who serves.[34]

Since that time other voices have been raised in the Episcopal Church for this cause, among them the North American Association for the Diaconate, the national Conference of the Association of Diocesan Liturgy and Music Commissions, and several of its diocesan conventions. Voices advocating direct ordination have now logically moved to include the episcopate as well. Ambrose, who was ordained bishop "directly" from Baptism but raised the prestige of the see of Milan to rival Rome in his time, provides an outstanding example

---

33. *Diakoneo* 16, no. 1 (Epiphany 1994): 2.

34. *Open*, the newsletter of Associated Parishes (June 1977): 1. *The Proposed Book of Common Prayer* became the official book in 1979.

of the value of this practice from the early Church. In a historic decision the 1991 General Convention of the Episcopal Church adopted a resolution directing a study of direct ordination, sometimes called *per saltum* ordination, a term literally translated as "by a leap."

Abandoning the transitional diaconate is the logical conclusion of steps taken in both the Anglican Communion and the Roman Catholic Church to recover the diaconate and the wholeness of the organic ministry of the early Church. As we have seen, the practice of requiring candidates for ordination to move, as up a ladder, from deacon to priest to bishop, called *cursus honorum,* came many centuries later than was thought. The justification for the practice, although not as a requirement, repeatedly asserted by the fathers of the early Church and the ancient councils was simply to insure that a man had proven himself suitable for an office involving more responsibility, particularly the episcopate, before assuming it.

Clearly it cannot be maintained that the continuation of the medieval requirement of *cursus honorum* is in any way necessary for the ordained ministry to be fully catholic and apostolic. In fact, the opposite might convincingly be argued: *cursus honorum* is less than fully catholic, denigrating as it does the apostolic theology of the Church.

The use of the diaconate as a transitional office on the way to the presbyterate was in all probability the single most important factor in bringing about its decline, and even then it took centuries to reduce the order to one of "inferior" status. The importance of the diaconate as a distinct and equal order is forcefully demonstrated by such men as Pope Gregory the Great, remaining a deacon until his ordination to the episcopate in 590, never having been a presbyter.

The importance to the Church of restoring the integrity of the diaconate as the distinct ministry different from but equal to any other ministry can hardly be overestimated. Its integrity requires the Church's return to direct ordination. A graded structure of ordained ministry denigrates not only the diaconate but, more important, the whole of the ministry of the laity, implying as it does that the laity are not commissioned and empowered as full ministers of the Church through Baptism. The Church must again restore Baptism as the primary sacrament of ministry and the only sacramental prerequisite for ordination.

The Omnivorous Priesthood

Many of the major problems relating to the renewal of the diaconate today can only be understood, or probably even perceived, against the background of the ordained ministry prior to the restoration of the order in our time. The single model of ministry, the ordained priesthood or presbyterate, is like a persistent virus that infects our thinking and acting in subtle but insidious ways.

For example, diaconal training programs more often than not have used a reductionist seminary model, although significant progress has been made in many places and efforts continue to create a model appropriate to the real diaconate. Preaching is frequently thought to be a normal diaconal function by virtue of ordination, clearly a function only of bishops and presbyters in the early Church. Deacons are routinely assigned to officiate at services equally appropriate to trained lay persons when presbyters are not available. Many believe that when a priest is away on vacation or a parish having a deacon is in between presbyters the deacon is temporarily in charge. In places where they are not prohibited, many deacons use the outward symbols of the ordained priesthood, round collars and "the Reverend" before their names, some even adopting black suits. Deacons are frequently seen by clergy and laity alike to be a kind of (usually) unpaid substitute curate or assistant to the priest instead of having distinct ministries of widely varied kinds.

The presbyterate of the past has aptly been called the "omnivorous priesthood," having become all-encompassing, although not so much by intention as by an unintentional evolution over the centuries. Its tendency to be perpetuated both by the ordained and the laity is certainly natural in an institution that rightly holds its tradition in high esteem. However, the renewal and vitality of the Church in our time requires that its subtle encroachments on other ministries be recognized and abandoned.

The Eastern Orthodox

The Eastern Orthodox Church has retained the diaconate to a greater degree than either the Roman Catholic or Anglican churches, although it has ceased to have any charitable functions.[35] Interestingly, among the Orthodox, only one person may be ordained at a single liturgy, and each ordination requires the consent, at least in theory, of the whole people of God given by the acclamation *"Axios!"* ("He is worthy!") at one point in the service. In mentioning this, Timothy Ware notes that during the present century congregations in Constantinople and Greece have on several occasions shouted their disapproval with *"Anaxios!,"* but to no avail.[36]

Among the Orthodox churches the diaconate is largely restricted to liturgical functions in the Eucharist.[37] The deacon is the leader of the choir and directs the movements of the Liturgy. The Orthodox deacon offers certain prayers himself and calls on the priest to utter his prayers. In the Byzantine liturgies he is called "concelebrant" twice by the priest. After the entrance the priest returns the censer to the deacon and addresses him, "Remember me, O my brother and concelebrant." The Byzantine ordination rite does not present the office as tran-

---

35. George Khodr, "The Diaconate in the Orthodox Church," in *The Ministry of Deacons*, ed. Department of Faith and Order, 40.

36. Timothy Ware, *The Orthodox Church* (Baltimore: Penguin Books, 1964), 297.

37. George Florovsky, "The Problem of Diaconate in the Orthodox Church," in *The Diaconate Now*, ed. Richard T. Nolan (Washington, D.C.: Corpus Books, 1968), 85, 95.

sitional, although the Armenian and Coptic rites do.[38] Many Orthodox deacons regard their vocation today as life-long.[39]

From time to time Orthodox deacons share in the pastoral and administrative work of the Church, but this appears to be inconsequential generally. In Russia in the 1880s the diaconate was reinstituted in parishes of over 700 members and given responsibility for education, both religious and general.[40] However, when I visited the Russian Orthodox Cathedral of the Holy Trinity in San Francisco for its beautiful Sunday Liturgy in the fall of 1988, the priest, Fr. George Sondergaard then serving as dean, told me that Russian Orthodox deacons serve essentially as liturgical ministers and are chosen on the basis of their ability to sing the Liturgy. Their Liturgy is sung throughout and deacons have a prominent role in it. The surpassing beauty of that liturgy brought to mind the story of the pre-Christian Russian court sending emissaries to Constantinople to investigate Christianity and, after witnessing the Divine Liturgy there, returning with the report that it was as if they had been in heaven itself.

In April of 1993 while on a study program in St. Petersburg Theological Academy and Seminary, one of the two major theological institutions of the Russian Orthodox Church, I met a number of deacons of the Russian church and saw many of them participating in their splendid liturgies during Holy Week and Easter. I also had a personal interview regarding the Russian Orthodox diaconate with Archpriest Vladimir Sorokin. He expressed great interest in the renewal of the diaconate in the Anglican and Roman Catholic churches and indicated the desirability of the Russian church considering a renewal of its diaconate in the years ahead. For them the tradition of the "holy fathers" is central. Father Sorokin hopes that pastoral and social functions will be added to their diaconate. In view of the tremendous energy the Russian church is expending, demonstrating great vitality, in order to rebuild its life and recover its identity after 70 years of persecution, it may be some years before they consider a diaconate with pastoral and charitable/societal as well as liturgical functions.

The archdeaconry of the Ecumenical Patriarchate of Constantinople is of considerable importance. The archdeacon arranges the services and sends out preachers, including bishops. It is said that the only liturgies attended by the great archdeacon are those celebrated by the Ecumenical Patriarch. Both Coptic ordination rite and canon law retain the pastoral and social admonitions to the deacon from the ancient Church: To visit widows, orphans, and the afflicted; to bring the afflicted to the attention of the bishop or priest; and to minister to the poor. But charitable concern has disappeared from their ministries.[41]

---

38. Khodr, "The Diaconate in the Orthodox Church," 41, 42.
39. Ware, *The Orthodox Church*, 297. Florovsky, "The Problem of Diaconate in the Orthodox Church," 95.
40. Khodr, "The Diaconate in the Orthodox Church," 43.
41. Ibid., 42–43.

Other Traditions

Although some Protestant churches do have the office of deacon, Protestantism in general does not have the diaconate as a separate order of the ordained ministry.[42] This is not to say that these traditions cannot enrich a recovery of the diaconate. At a conference in Chicago sponsored primarily by the Roman Catholic Archdiocese of Chicago in 1984, James Notebaart, Vice-president of the Liturgical Conference and a priest, then of St. Paul, Minnesota, gave a memorable presentation on Baptism and baptismal fonts in which he generally recommended placing major fonts capable of immersing adults near the main entrance to the church. However, his response to a question regarding placing fonts in the front of the church still rings loud and clear. We cannot, he said, ignore several centuries of some Protestant traditions placing their fonts in the front of the church.[43] Similarly, we cannot ignore the experience of these traditions relating to the diaconate and diaconal ministry.

The office of deacon historically has not been a part of either Lutheranism or Methodism. The Presbyterians, Reformed, Congregationalists, Baptists, and Disciples have a diaconate that generally would appear to be a lay ministry.[44] However, important diaconal ministry has certainly been a part of these traditions and there is considerable interest in these churches in renewal or recovery of the office. The widespread interest is well illustrated by representation at the Ecumenical Consultation on the Diaconate and Diaconal Ministry sponsored by the Faith and Order Commission of the National Council of Churches in the U.S.A. held in Dallas in December of 1988 with the Roman Catholic bishop of Fort Worth, Joseph P. Delaney, and the director of the Permanent Deacon Formation Program of that diocese, Ann Healey, as hosts. Denominations sending diaconal representation were the American Baptist Church, Episcopal, Christian Church-Disciples of Christ, Roman Catholic, Evangelical Lutheran Church in America, United Methodist, Presbyterian Church U.S.A., Reformed Church of America, and United Church of Canada.

The Lutherans

Martin Luther envisioned a nonordained diaconate apparently shaped by his understanding of Acts, a view that has undoubtedly created a reluctance within Lutheranism to ordain those whom Lutherans today call deacons. Luther declared:

> The diaconate is a ministry, not for reading the Gospel or the Epistle, as the practice is nowadays, but for distributing the wealth of the Church among the

---

42. Robert S. Paul, "The Deacon in Protestantism," in *The Diaconate Now*, ed. Nolan, 40.

43. James Notebaart, "Initiation: Sign and Action of the Assembly," Forum on Worship, Environment, and the Visual Arts, September 23–26, 1984, Bismarck Hotel, Chicago. Father Notebaart was then Director of Worship, Archdiocese of St. Paul/Minneapolis and Vice-President of the Liturgical Conference.

44. Paul, "The Deacon in Protestantism," 41, 45.

poor, that the priests may be relieved of the burden of temporal things, and may give themselves more freely to prayer and to the word. It was for this purpose, as we read in the Acts of the Apostles, that deacons were appointed.[45]

The diaconate in European Lutheranism is such a nonordained ministry, one without liturgical function but with extensive pastoral and charitable ministries.

Johann Hinrich Wickern is considered to have founded this diaconate in 1840 in Hamburg by forming a community with true pastoral and charitable ministries, which worked with youth "in moral danger" as "home missioners" in Prussian prisons and as wartime military medical orderlies or assistants to army chaplains. Other communities were founded for varied purposes, such as nursing, social welfare, education, and parish work. In the 1960s there were fifteen *Brudenhäuser* communities in Germany, numbering some 4,550 deacons with several hundred more in Scandinavia.[46] They are not ordained and have no liturgical function.

The Evangelical Lutheran Church in America has a relatively small number of deacons in seven of its synods, but most of them are in two: the Metropolitan Synod of New York and the Delaware-Maryland Synod. At the beginning of 1994 there were forty-three deacons, twenty-seven men and sixteen women.[47] In addition to pastoral and societal functions, these deacons report liturgical ministry generally in the traditional model and preaching as well. Although some of them consider themselves to be ordained, officially they are "set apart" for this ministry.[48] The Church also has the Deaconess Community of about 115 members with ministries from social service to church music and administration.[49]

Prior to the Lutheran Church in America's merger with two similar churches to form the Evangelical Lutheran Church in America in 1988, a plan for establishing the diaconate in the LCA was presented to its 1976 convention, but due to the press of business was made a "document for study" until its next meeting.[50] The plan was dropped at its 1978 convention. However, there is apparent continued interest in the diaconate. The "concordat of agreement" emerging from the Lutheran-Episcopal Dialogue in the United States in mid-January 1991, an agreement to establish full communion between the two Churches, states, "the threefold ministry of bishops, presbyters, and deacons in historic succession will be the future pattern of the one ordained ministry of Word and Sacrament

---

45. Ibid., 42.

46. Herbert Krimm, "The Diaconate in the Lutheran Church," in *The Ministry of Deacons*, ed. Department of Faith and Order, 54, 55.

47. *The Directory of Deacons: Episcopal Church, Anglican Church of Canada, Evangelical Lutheran Church in America* (Providence, R.I.: North American Association for the Diaconate, 1991), 33–34. *Diakoneo* 16, no. 1 (Epiphany 1994): 2.

48. James Moser, an Evangelical Lutheran deacon of Baltimore, reported this information to me.

49. "The Deaconess Community of the Evangelical Lutheran Church in America" (Gladwyne, Pa.: The Deaconess Community, the Evangelical Lutheran Church in America, n.d.).

50. Lutheran Church in America, "Report on the Ministry of Deacons," mimeographed, n.d.

in both churches as they begin to live in full communion." Regarding the diaconate specifically, the concordat notes, "both churches acknowledge that the diaconate, including its place within the threefold ministerial office, is in need of continued study and reform, which they pledge themselves to undertake in consultation with one another." The concordat is proposed for consideration of the General Convention of the Episcopal Church, possibly at its triennial meeting in 1994, and the Churchwide Assembly of the Evangelical Lutheran Church in America, possibly in 1995.[51]

The Reformed Tradition

It is interesting that John Calvin in the fourth book of his *Institutes of the Christian Religion* includes the deacon as a permanent and necessary office in the Reformed Church. Calvin distinguished between two diaconal functions and two types of deacons to accomplish them.

> The care of the poor was entrusted to the deacons. However, two kinds are mentioned in the letter to the Romans: "He that gives, let him do it with simplicity; ...he that shows mercy, with cheerfulness" (Rom. 12:8). Since it is certain that Paul is speaking of the public office of the church, there must have been two distinct grades. Unless my judgment deceive me, in the first clause he designates the deacons who distribute the alms. But the second refers to those who had devoted themselves to the care of the poor and sick. Of this sort were the widows whom Paul mentions to Timothy (1 Tim. 5:9–10).... If we accept this (and it must be accepted), there are two kinds of deacons: one to serve the church in administering the affairs of the poor; the other, in caring for the poor themselves.[52]

Following Acts 6, the Seven of which Calvin considered to be administrative deacons, and 1 Timothy, deacons are to be ordained by the laying on of hands, and in light of this and other New Testament evidence are to be a permanent and necessary order in the Church.[53]

Elsie Anne McKee says that two passages taken together provide the grounds for Calvin's inclusion of women in the diaconate:

> Calvin understands Romans 12:8 as a bridge between the administrative deacons of Acts and the servant/nurse he saw elsewhere in the New Testament church. This last, the second sort of charitable deacon, is the "deaconess" found in the 1 Timothy 5:3–10 organization of widows, of whom Phoebe in Rom. 16:1–2 is an outstanding example.[54]

---

51. Tom Dorris, "Lutheran-Episcopal Pact Includes Deacons," in *Diakoneo* (March 1991): 1. Tom Dorris, a deacon of the Evangelical Lutheran Church of America, the Synod of Metropolitan New York, was at that time editor of the Ecumenical Press Service of the World Council of Churches, Geneva, Switzerland.

52. John Calvin, *Institutes of the Christian Religion*, ed. John T. McNeill, trans. Ford Lewis Battles Library of Christian Classics 21 (Philadelphia: Westminster, 1960), 4.3.9, p. 1061.

53. John Calvin, Joannis Calvini, *Opera quae supersunt omnia*, ed. G. Baum, E. Cunitz, E. Reuss, and continuators. Quoted in Elsie Anne McKee, *John Calvin on the Diaconate and Liturgical Almsgiving* (Geneva: Librairie Droz, 1984), 146. Cf. Calvin, sermon on Acts 6:1–3, f 185 r–v, quoted on p. 156.

54. McKee, *Calvin on the Diaconate*, 267.

There was basic agreement among Presbyterians, Congregationalists, and Baptists in seventeenth-century England that church offices should be those of pastor (whom they saw as the presiding elder or bishop of the New Testament), teaching elder, ruling elder, and deacon. In essence there were several kinds of elders and deacons. Whatever else may be said of the structure of these offices in Puritan thought, it resembled that of the early Church in the important respect that it was conceived of as being essentially horizontal. The offices were distinct because it was believed that Christ instituted these offices with their own designated functions. Thus, the deacon was not thought of as an inferior office, even if it was a lay office.

The statement of Jeremiah Burroughes, one of the Dissenting Brethren at the Westminster Assembly, shows the high regard the Puritans had for all church offices: "Once a man be chosen as an officer in the Church, all that power that ever any in that office had since Christ's time, in any church in all the Christian world, or ever can have to the coming of Christ again, falls upon him."[55] This high understanding of church offices was perhaps a reflection of the dedicated regard of the Puritans for their Christianity, although seemingly lacking in an understanding of the key character of all ministry as *diakonia*.

The Reformed tradition today embodies a large number of deacons and deaconesses, although they are not ordained and do not hold an official office in their churches. The ministry performed by the men and women in these diaconal communities is that of parish workers, missionaries, social and medical workers, educators and teachers, and other similar types of service.[56]

The Presbyterians

The practice of American Presbyterian congregations has varied regarding the diaconate for historical reasons. A "collegiate" diaconate existed in some of their churches early in American history but many churches had none. Their General Assembly repeatedly urged the adoption of the diaconate in the early and mid-nineteenth century. The term "board" came into use in connection with the Presbyterian diaconate before the Civil War and has largely replaced the use of "diaconate."[57]

Following the schism occurring due to the Civil War, the Southern Church (the Presbyterian Church in the U.S.) increasingly entrusted to the deacons the management of the congregations' temporal affairs, the delegation becoming statutory after 1922. In the Northern branch (the Presbyterian Church in the U.S.A.), the temporalities were committed to trustees, and the Board of Deacons continued to minister pastorally and charitably to various human needs. This diaconate is corporate in nature, although members are elected by the congregation

---

55. Quoted in Paul, "The Deacon in Protestantism," 48.

56. Claude Bridel, "Note on the Diaconal Ministry in the Reformed Churches," in *The Ministry of the Deacon*, 58–59, 61.

57. Robert W. Henderson, "Notes on the Diaconate in American Presbyterianism," in *The Ministry of Deacons*, ed. Department of Faith and Order, 65.

and are ordained deacons. It is also optional. Some congregations formerly having Boards of Deacons have instead instituted "deacons' committees" appointed from the ordained ruling elders of their governing councils, called sessions. Ordination to either the office of deacon or ruling elder is for life, although deacons when elected to the session are ordained ruling elders. It has been said that the Northern churches have "few deacons but rather many Boards of Deacons." Since the uniting of the Northern and Southern churches in 1958, efforts have been made to "recognize" those in some specialized ministries as deacons.[58]

A report on *The Nature of Ministry* presented to the 176th General Convention of the United Presbyterian Church in the U.S.A. first set forth Calvin's teaching on the diaconate but then added a significant concession to contemporary practice: "To them also may be properly committed the management of the temporal affairs of the church."

The Baptists

Although the Baptists have no authoritative formularies to which one may appeal for either doctrine or practice, they do have in their early tradition declarations on the ministry that advocate an ordained diaconate of servant ministry. John Smyth, who organized the first English Baptist Church in Amsterdam early in the seventeenth century, stated in his last confession:

> We believe . . . That Christ hath set in His outward church two sorts of ministers: viz. some who are called pastors, teachers or elders, who administer in the word and sacraments, and others who are called Deacons, men and women: whose ministry is to serve tables and wash the saints' feet.[59]

Thomas Helwigs, founder of the first Baptist Church in England in 1612, affirmed this twofold ministry. It is interesting that, unlike any other Baptist confession, the Orthodox Creed of the General Baptists, adopted in 1678, lists the officers of the Church as "Bishop, or Messengers; and Elders, or Pastors; and Deacons, or Overseers of the Poor."[60] This creed also provides for the ordination of deacons as well as bishops and elders.

However, this tradition has not been followed in modern Baptist churches generally. Although there is considerable variation, the most common structure today is that of a single elder and a number of deacons who together form a kind of executive committee, the German Baptists using the term *Vorstand,* meaning "executive committee." However, there are some Baptist churches, especially in Germany, that have a threefold structure of a pastor with a single elder and a board of deacons. Baptist deacons at one time were customarily elected by their congregations for life but now serve for a limited period, such as three years. In

---

58. Ibid., 65–66, 67.

59. George R. Beasley-Murray, "The Diaconate in Baptist Churches," in *The Ministry of Deacons,* ed. Department of Faith and Order, 72. Quotation cited from W. J. McGlothlin, *Baptist Confessions of Faith* (London: n.p., 1910), 80.

60. Beasley-Murray, "The Diaconate in Baptist Churches," 73–74.

Great Britain they are no longer ordained, but there are Baptist churches else-where in which the custom has survived. John McBain, writing in the Southern Baptist magazine, *The Deacon,* speaks of Southern Baptist deacons as being or-dained and also calls them "ordained laymen," using quotation marks. Baptist "lay-preachers" usually are deacons and are allowed to officiate at Baptism and the Eucharist.[61]

In America the diaconate of Baptist churches in the nineteenth and earlier part of the twentieth century was primarily concerned with the business af-fairs of the congregations, although in a number of places their responsibility was larger, functioning more as a board of directors.[62] In recent years strong emphasis has been placed on encouraging a fuller diaconate with pastoral and charitable concerns in both the Southern and American Baptist churches.[63]

The Christian Church (Disciples of Christ)

The Christian Church (Disciples of Christ) does provide for the office of deacon/ deaconess as set forth in its "provisional Design for the Christian Church (Disci-ples of Christ)," adopted in 1968.[64] Their duties may include pastoral, charitable, liturgical, and administrative functions, such as visiting the sick, serving as ush-ers, caring for the poor, administering the Lord's Supper, and looking after parish property and finance. Deacons may be ordained by the laying on of hands with prayer, and ordination may be repeated as often as an individual is elected to the office.[65]

The United Methodists

The office of deaconess, created by the General Conference of 1888 of the Methodist Episcopal Church, flourished for many years and foreshadowed the creation of the "diaconal minister" by the General Conference of 1976. Of the 2,000 Protestant deaconesses in America at the turn of the century, 1,200 were Methodists. The United Brethren and the Evangelical Association, also antecedents of the United Methodist Church, provided for the office of dea-coness in 1901 and 1903 respectively. These deaconesses were responsible for the founding of many hospitals, orphanages, homes for the elderly, and other philanthropic institutions. They were trained for widely varied ministries, par-ticularly in the inner cities of America and in foreign missions. Their work

61. Ibid., 76–78; John M. McBain, "What on Earth Are Deacons For?" in *The Deacon* 7, no. 3 (April–June 1977): 37.

62. Howard Foshee, *The Ministry of Deacons* (Nashville: Convention Press, 1968, rev. 1974), 32–35.

63. See Donald F. Thomas, *The Deacons in a Changing Church* (Valley Forge, Pa.: Judson Press, 1969), for a discussion of deacons in the churches of the American Baptist Convention and Foshee, in reference to the Southern Baptist churches. The Southern Baptists also publish *The Deacon* magazine, as has been mentioned, and make a number of other materials available.

64. Kenneth L. Teegarden, *We Call Ourselves Disciples* (St. Louis: Bethany Press, 1975), 74–76.

65. *Elders'-Deacons' Manual*, compiled by P. A. Willis (Cincinnati: Christian Restoration Association, 1968), 27, 29.

provides a proud and noble chapter in the story of true diaconal service to Christ in the "least of these" and may be seen as a forerunner of the "diaconal minister" of today.[66]

The United Methodist Church in the United States has an unusual form of diaconate. They have maintained a "transitional" diaconate for those seeking to be ordained elder. But, in addition, *The Book of Discipline of the United Methodist Church* provides for the office of "diaconal minister" exemplifying the servanthood of all Christians for those who wish to enter the diaconate as a life-long vocation. Those holding the office, however, are not referred to as deacons. Educational requirements are extensive, including graduate-level training. This "diaconal ministry" was regarded as a "called-out" and "set-apart" ministry including pastoral, charitable, and liturgical functions, although these are not specifically enumerated.[67] However, the "consecration" of a deacon is now described in terms that include both "authorization" by the Church and "invocation of the Holy Spirit to empower the diaconal minister"[68] and may be considered ordination. It establishes the relationship of the diaconal minister with the United Methodist Church.[69] Service may be either part-time or full-time, and they may be employed outside the institutional Church.[70]

A Commission for Study of Ministry, formed by the 1988 General Conference of the Methodist Church and calling specifically for consideration of "a permanent order of deacon," presented its proposal at the 1992 conference. This proposal provided for "deacons" to be "consecrated" for traditional pastoral, social, and liturgical functions, but these deacons were to be "lay members" of their annual conferences.[71] E. Dale Dunlap, former academic dean of St. Paul School of Theology in Kansas City, Missouri, and Chairman of the Ministry Study Committee in 1980–84, commended the commission for proposing permanent deacons but ably objected to the confusion inherent in "consecrating" them as against ordaining them. He writes that "to do other than ordain a deacon is at best a theological incongruity and at any rate basically contradictory." He also objected to the elders being called "clergy" and the deacons "laity" in the proposal, seeing a "consecrated lay deacon" as being "a semantic misnomer."[72]

66. Rosemary Skinner Keller, Gerald F. Moede, and Mary Elizabeth Moore, *Called to Serve: The United Methodist Diaconate*, ed. Rosalie Bentzinger, assisted by Joyce King, Martha Wagner, and Margaret Gregory (Nashville: Division of Diaconal Ministry of the General Board of Higher Education and Ministry, 1987), 25–27, 56–57.

67. *The Book of Discipline of the United Methodist Church* (Nashville: Abingdon Press, 1980), pars. 302–3, pp. 169–70.

68. "Steps into Diaconal Ministry" (Nashville: Division of Diaconal Ministry, General Board of Higher Education and Ministry, The United Methodist Church, n.d.)

69. *The Book of Discipline of the United Methodist Church* (1980), par. 307, p. 174.

70. "Varieties of Diaconal Ministry" (Nashville: Division of Diaconal Ministry, The United Methodist Church, n.d.)

71. Ruth A. Daugherty, "Changes in Our Ministry: What's Being Proposed in '92," in Keith Pohl, ed., "Circuit Rider," brochure (Nashville: United Methodist Publishing House, November 1991), 4, 5.

72. E. Dale Dunlap, "Consecration or Ordination: A Critical Look at the Proposal," in ibid., 8.

The proposal also provided for "direct ordination" of elders, abolishing the requirement that elders be first ordained deacons.[73] The commission's proposal provides for the office of deaconess but incorporates it into the order of deacon.[74] The proposal failed on a 51% to 49% vote. However, every annual conference of the United Methodist Church is to study the proposal, so that it may again be considered with possible modifications. The next meeting of the General Conference will be held in 1996.[75]

The United Church of Christ

British Congregationalists originally had pastors, teaching elders, ruling elders, and deacons as officers, but the structure was modified as time passed.[76] The pastor assumed the office of teaching elder and the ruling elder disappeared. As a result, deacons became more prominent. However, if this were ever true of American Congregationalists, the deacon has long since disappeared.

The practice of the Congregationalists in the United States today, now the United Church of Christ following a merger, with its congregational polity varies regarding diaconal ministries. Some congregations have boards of deacons and deaconesses, which may meet as one group. Where such groups exist, their duties range from responsibility for worship and membership in some churches to care of benevolence in others. This diaconate is more corporate than individual, and individuals involved in it are not regarded as holding the office of deacon in the historic sense.

A Diaconate with Full Integrity

There is, then, wide variation among the churches of the late twentieth century in their understanding of and commitment to the historic diaconate. However, the Church generally has moved a long way toward the restoration of the office. It needs now to complete the task.

As the development of *cursus honorum,* the graded, hierarchical structure of the Church's ministry, was the greatest single factor in bringing about the erosion and finally the destruction of the integrity of the diaconate and ultimately with it that of the ministry of the laity, nothing would help more to restore the integrity of the diaconate, and probably that of lay ministry also, than a return to the original practice of the pre-Nicene Church by ordaining only those to the diaconate who intend to make it a permanent vocation. Others, notably those seeking the priesthood or selected for the episcopate, would be ordained directly to those orders. Baptism would become again the essential *sacramental* prereq-

---

73. Pohl, ed., "Circuit Rider," 11.
74. Daugherty, "Changes in Our Ministry," 5.
75. Reported by Ruth Kruse, head of the Diaconal Board of the Nebraska Methodist Conference and herself a "diaconal minister."
76. Paul, "The Deacon in Protestantism," 44.

uisite for ordination to any office in the Church. Baptism would be restored as the great sacrament of ministry.

Such a return to the original concept of order in the Church would help each of the orders and ministries within the Church regain its own distinctive character. The ministry would be immeasurably enriched particularly by recognizing the diaconate as the specific form of ministry that embodies and exemplifies the work Christ sent his Church into the world to do. Then, it can rightly be described as a vocation symbolizing Christ himself in a unique way. The ministry of the Church will more readily be seen for what it is truly meant to be — *diakonia,* service.

Chapter 10

The Character and Place
of the Diaconate

Clericalism

Jeffrey D. Lee, a priest from Indiana, began his address entitled "A View from the Omnivorous Presbyterate" to the 1991 meeting of the North American Association for the Diaconate with a story to illustrate one of the profound obstacles to the recovery of the diaconate and, in his words, "the even greater task of recovering a full realization of the awesome dignity of baptismal vocation and ministry of which the diaconate is the principal sign." He had taken advantage of an opportunity to participate from the pew of a parish in its Sunday Eucharist, which he described as a "lively celebration." The sermon was thoughtful and informed by solid baptismal theology about the importance of all members discovering and using their gifts for ministry. But when he presented himself to receive communion, the priest paused upon reaching him, rummaged around in the ciborium until he found a piece of the "priest's host," and gave it to him. By so doing, Lee said, the priest

> unintentionally turned the Eucharist into a betrayal of itself. The Eucharist is a sign of our common baptismal identity and solidarity. There is one Lord, one faith, one baptism — one bread and cup. There is not one food for the merely baptized and another, special food for the somewhat more-than-baptized.[1]

The problem illustrated by this seemingly innocuous and certainly well-intentioned incident is clericalism, and the story serves to show how subtle it can be. Clericalism may be defined as "a policy of maintaining or increasing the power of a religious hierarchy"[2] and has been systemic in the Church for centuries, like a great blight that infects the whole body of the faithful. It is pervasive, nurtured (often unconsciously) by clergy and laity alike, although with different motivations. Due to fallen human nature being what it is, clergy enjoy

---

1. Jeffrey D. Lee, "A View from the Omnivorous Presbyterate," an address delivered at the Biennial Conference of the North American Association for the Diaconate, Spokane, Wash., June 13, 1991 (Providence, R.I.: North American Association for the Diaconate, 1991). Fr. Lee is an Episcopal priest.
2. *Webster's Ninth New Collegiate Dictionary*, s.v. "Clericalism."

the status and authority accruing to them and laity are relieved of responsibility for ministry. Clericalism makes the priest or pastor "*the* minister" and demotes those who are "only" baptized to a poor second class status. As Lee pointed out, in the terminology of the late twentieth century, it is religious "consumerism." The clergy are the professionals who "dispense religious goods to the more or less passive consumers of the same — otherwise known as the laity."

It was the gradual rise of clericalism in the Medieval Church that resulted in the ministry coming to be considered the possession of the clergy. The inevitable consequence is the Church's impoverishment of the gifts the Spirit has given to all the baptized. Ministry is sorely limited by the relatively small number of clergy and is usually exercised largely in terms of serving the internal needs of the institution. The attitude of clericalism was succinctly expressed in my seminary back around 1950. It was jokingly said that the best Christian education program could be summed up in two words: "Yes, Father." (Some jokes contain more truth than fiction.)

Although the problems of clericalism are not equally applicable to the restored diaconate, since these deacons normally continue to live an essentially lay lifestyle, it is one of the major problems relating to the restored diaconate in the Anglican and Roman Catholic churches at the present time. In both communions the diaconate is an integral part of holy orders, and holy orders in the tradition of both is highly clericalized. The primary visible marks of clericalism are clerical collars and honorific titles. Although in the Evangelical Lutheran Church of America the diaconate is not officially an ordained office, it functions much like that of the Roman Catholics and Anglicans and appears to suffer from clericalism as well.

The philosophy that underlies clericalism exalts the clergy as somehow above and superior to those "merely" baptized. Although revised in 1984, the original guidelines laid down by the U.S. Bishops' Committee of the Roman Catholic Church for the restoration of the diaconate identified the deacon in terms of several relationships, the most notable being that "of the threefold scope of service that he shares with bishops and priests." Later, in speaking specifically of the difference between clergy and laity, the guidelines drew a sharp and clear line: "From the point of view of sacred orders, the difference is between bishops and priests on the one hand and lay people — including religious — on the other."[3]

The extensive revision of the guidelines in 1984 continued to emphasize the clerical ministry, which indeed is important to the Church and its work, but the line was not so sharply drawn between clergy and laity. The idea of a distinction not essentially of function but of lifestyle and perhaps infused character is foreign to the primitive Church and the consensus of the pre-Nicene age. It is true that the question of an ontological difference (a difference in being created by ordination) was not raised in the early Church but the implication of conciliar legislation and theological writings from the period do not support this

---

3. Bishops' Committee, *Permanent Deacons*, par. 7, p. 4, and par. 149, p. 48.

concept. Donald Tytler states that in the medieval view there were two kinds of Christians:

> The first is the clergy who live the authentic Christian life of entire devotion to God, manifested by their concentration on acts of worship and of theological reflection and also by the smallness of their income, which enables them to abstain from worldly things; the second is the laity, who practice a second-best type of Christianity, marred by compromise with the world, in which they are thought to live in some way quite different from the clergy.[4]

Certainly this view is widely held today. An ontological change in the ordained is not necessary to the medieval view of two kinds of Christians, but it goes hand in hand with such a theory. Richard Rashke reports that 80 percent of American Roman Catholic priests believe there is an ontological difference between clergy and laity.[5] Although the idea of any ontological difference runs counter to the whole tenor of Vatican II and the principles of renewal held in the historic Western churches today, it would nevertheless all too often seem to underlie and subvert our thinking in subtle ways.

In the Episcopal Church a great deal has been made over a particular phrase in the ordination service for deacons. In the address to the ordinand, the bishop admonishes, "You are to interpret to the Church the needs, concerns, and hopes of the world." This is high-sounding and is certainly a legitimate work of deacons, particularly in areas involving the poor and powerless, but broadly speaking is this not, or should it not be, primarily lay ministry? The clergy are often untrained both academically and experientially in many of the concerns of society: economics, diplomatic affairs, military matters, the physical sciences, the social sciences, and so on. Christian lay men and women are. But the Church is so clericalized that this is assumed to be a function of the clergy. What the laity often lack is Christian formation. Christian formation is a primary function of presbyters and deacons, although the laity should have a vital role in this also. Adequately formed lay men and women who are authorities in these concerns of the world can and should speak to and for the Church in such matters. Would not the world listen more attentively to pronouncements of the Church made by such lay people?

Clericalism with its expression in the "omnivorous priesthood" is the root cause of the threat felt by some priests and even bishops from a restored diaconate. It is the source of the assertion, "Once a deacon, always a deacon." It is the origin of opposition to abolishing the transitional diaconate. It creates the mold of "mini-priest" for real deacons. It denigrates the diaconate. Even worse, it is the primary force that stifles lay ministry.

The diaconate challenges our constructs of ministry and calls us to new ways of thinking and acting shaped and molded in the image of Christ.

---

4. Tytler, "Each in His Own Order," 23.
5. Rashke, *The Deacon in Search of Identity*, 14.

Ministry in the Church or in the World

Much has been said in recent years relating to the proper sphere of the deacon's ministry. *Permanent Deacons in the United States: Guidelines on Their Formation and Ministry* sets forth a balanced view, particularly because it takes into account the wide diversity of diaconal ministries. Diaconal ministries are said to fall under three broad categories: love and justice, the Word, and the Liturgy.[6] Regarding the ministry of love and justice, Pope Paul VI is quoted:

> [The deacon is to be not only] the interpreter of the needs and desires of the Christian communities [but] the animator and promoter of the Church's service or *diaconia* in local Christian communities, and as a sign or sacrament of the Lord Christ himself, "who came not to be served but to serve."[7]

A partial list of ministries from a 1981 survey names seventeen of these — from serving abused children and battered women to refugees, street people, and victims of racial and ethnic discrimination. But deacons are not simply to do these things. They are to "inspire, promote and help coordinate the service that the whole Church" is to do, the reference here being to deacons acting to involve increasing numbers of laity in service ministries. The ministries listed are societal in nature, flowing from Christian love, and are directed both toward those within and without the Church. The guidelines further state that deacons have "a special responsibility to identify *to* the Church those who are in need and particularly those who are without power or voice at the margins of our society."[8]

In the pre-Nicene Church the evidence indicates that diaconal ministries of this nature were normally in and to the Church: administering the distribution of alms to the poor and needy of the community, being the servant of the Church, discovering the pastoral needs of the people for the bishop, and reporting the sick to the community for their visits and help. However, it must be remembered that the Church was not only small in numbers but an illegal body and often suffering from persecution during this period.

It is not a question of either "in the Church" or "in the world." Deacons should be everywhere.

Dress, Title, Liturgical Vestments

Deacons in a restored diaconate should continue to dress as they always have and as the baptized customarily do in their time and place. Honorific titles have no place in reference to deacons. Proper address is simply "Deacon" before the name. The motivation for using these symbols of dress and title is almost always a desire for status, status above the laity. Such motivation may be either

---

6. Bishop's Committee, *Permanent Deacons*, 1984 rev., 16–22.
7. Ibid. The document quoted is *Ad Pascendum*, Introduction.
8. Ibid., 18.

on the part of ecclesiastical authority to convey status or on the part of the person ordained to acquire it, or both. However, round collars and "the Reverend" are actually countersymbols of the new diaconate, implying as they do a false distinction between the deacon and the laity, implying that the ordained person is somehow more sacred or holy than others. Does our theology really teach us that ordination conveys either status or holiness above the baptized? Is it not Baptism that makes us God's own sons and daughters, incorporates each of us into membership in Christ's body, and gives us his Holy Spirit?

It is interesting to note that in 428, when the clergy at Rome dressed in the manner of the laymen at that time, Pope Celestine wrote to the bishops of the province condemning the use of special dress for the clergy.[9] There is certainly precedent for clergy wearing the same attire as the laity generally, and deacons should not be set apart from others in their daily lives by this or other external means. An important part of their role is to symbolize the unity of the "sacred" and the "secular."

It is important, however, that the deacons wear customary vestments for their liturgical functions. Such attire serves to bring together in the office and person of the deacon the "sacred" and the "secular." Deacons who live as lay people, earning their living in the business world and bearing all customary social and family responsibilities, are at the same time those who, like priests, are ordained for the service of the altar. Symbolically the "secular" is caught up in the "sacred" and proclaimed holy.

The primary vestments of the deacon are the dalmatic and stole worn over the alb. The stole was originally the ancient handkerchief or neckcloth and appears to have become a distinctive mark of the clergy in the fourth century.[10] It has been worn by the deacon over the left shoulder since the seventh century, as directed by the Council of Toledo, c. 633. The council explains, "The right side of the body he must have free, in order that he may without hindrance, do his service." Canon 28 of this council refers to the stole and alb as the special marks of the deacon, in contrast to the stole and chasuble of the priest.[11]

The deacon's most distinctive vestment, however, is the dalmatic, which has a long and distinguished history in the Church. It was worn by the pope and the deacons of Rome in the fourth century, but then apparently only as customary daily dress along with the laity. During the sixth century it was apparently worn by bishops and deacons as a distinguishing mark of their attire.[12] By the ninth century the dalmatic was worn universally in the West by deacons.[13]

Although the dalmatic has never passed out of use in the West, its importance declined over the centuries as the diaconate became largely a transitional stage

---

9. Dearmer, *The Ornaments of the Ministers*, 26. Cf. Duchesne, *Christian Worship*, 381

10. A brief history of the diaconal vestments is given in the Appendix.

11. Council of Toledo, Canons 28 and 40, in Hefele, *History of the Councils*, 4:453, 454.

12. Dearmer, *The Ornaments of the Ministers*, 24, 28. Cf. Pocknee, *Liturgical Vesture*, 37.

13. Walter Phillips, "Dalmatic," in *Encyclopedia Britannica* (Chicago: William Benton, 1961), 6:994. Cf. Cope, "Vestments," 376.

on the way to priesthood. It is the proper liturgical vestment for the deacon corresponding to the chasuble for the priest and, as such, should be restored as a major vestment of the Church. Its use symbolically asserts the importance of the office and its work to the Church.

One Lifestyle

As we noted previously, the implications of different lifestyles for clergy and laity are dualistic. Celibacy, which in itself and voluntarily chosen as a special calling can be meritorious, in the medieval period came to be a prime symbol of the fundamental difference in lifestyle between the clergy and the laity. Held up as the Christian ideal, it denied by implication the essential unity and goodness of all creation so absolutely affirmed in Christ by his incarnation and in his incarnate life.

We are reminded of the inherent goodness and value of marriage as well as the strong dualistic tendency in the Church by Karl Rahner in his discussion of celibacy in relation to the restored diaconate:

> It must always be borne in mind in this connection that in a true theology of marriage, marriage must really and truly not be regarded as a mere concession to human weakness (a conception attempted over and over again by an almost manichaean intellectual undercurrent in the Church) but must be seen to have an absolutely positive and essential function, not only in the private Christian life of certain individuals but also in the Church.[14]

Marriage, he sees, fills an "absolutely necessary function in the Church and for the Church" by being the "representation and living example of the mystery of Christ's union with the Church."[15]

While the abolition of compulsory celibacy in the Roman Catholic Church has been advocated by many as a matter of practicality in order to supply the number of priests needed regardless of other considerations (and may come about out of this necessity), it is far more important in its implications regarding the Christian life and ministry. Abolishing compulsory celibacy would go a long way to enable Christians, both clerical and lay, to see that the fully committed Christian lifestyle is the same for all and that all are called to particular functions in the Church's ministry. Clerical celibacy has never been and is not now a matter of doctrine but of discipline in the Roman Church.

Bishop John A. T. Robinson is right when he suggests that the kind of distinction that creates two kinds of Christians should be abandoned altogether:

> I would put the question in all seriousness, whether, with the final disintegration of medieval Christendom, the distinction between *clergy and laity,* in contrast

---

14. Rahner, *Later Writings*, 294.
15. Ibid.

with the proper distinction between the various orders of the Body, should have any further validity.[16]

The bishop thinks that abolishing this line of distinction between the clergy and the laity is primary in the restoration of the ministry to all Christians.[17] And in this connection he rightly objects to "the ministry" being used as a term in reference to the clergy, as it often is today.

In writing about the diaconate as a life-long vocation Rahner maintains that the Church has shown by its practice that it does not see "any very close and necessary connection" between the diaconate and celibacy, since it does ordain men who are married. He strongly argues that celibacy should not be required for the restored diaconate: "Marriage has a greater inner affinity with the office of deacon than has celibacy, since the deacon in his specific, official function is quite clearly the link between the clergy and the altar, on the one hand, and the world with its Christian task, on the other."[18]

Professionalism in the Various Ministries

To do away with clericalism and restore the original kinds of distinction between the various ministries of the Church is not, however, to deny the need for professionalism in the ranks of the Church's leadership. In the modern world of highly trained professionals and specialists in every field the Church more than ever needs those of high caliber and superior training as its leaders and official representatives. Its requirements should attempt to insure such professional quality, and these characteristics should be kept in mind in the selection of leaders. Essentially, this is the concern shown in the early Church in legislation and other pronouncements commending those who had proven their ability and commitment to the Church by serving in other offices prior to being made bishops.

Subject to the Parish under the Leadership of the Priest (Pastor)

The place of the deacon in the parish church today is of primary importance both for the restoration and effective functioning of the diaconate. Priests and pastors of parishes have sometimes felt threatened by proposals for the renewal of the diaconate. It is certainly true that those who have worked hard both to be ordained and to serve as priests and pastors deserve assurance that this office of deacon will support rather than undermine them.[19] The principles

---

16. John A. T. Robinson, "Taking the Lid Off the Church's Ministry," in *New Ways with the Ministry*, ed. John Morris (London: Faith Press, 1960), 14.

17. Ibid., 17.

18. Rahner, *Later Writings*, 293.

19. H. Boone Porter Jr., "Modern Experience in Practice," in Patton, ed., *New Forms of Ministry*, 95.

needed for such assurance are to be found in the position of the deacon in the pre-Nicene Church.

The deacon in that period served the local church and was subject to its authority, which was expressed through the presbyteral council presided over by a bishop, although in the latter part of this period the bishops of urban centers began to acquire the ruling authority of the presbyteral council in exchange for the presbyters acquiring the bishop's liturgical functions and assuming his role as president or primary leader of the local church. The key factor in this connection is that there was ultimately an important change in the place of the bishop in relationship to the local church. Much confusion has emanated from failure to recognize that the priest or pastor of a parish today is far more comparable to the bishop of the early period than is the bishop himself. Bishops were pastors of the local churches, not leaders or rulers of dioceses. Dioceses had not yet emerged.

The idea, then, that deacons should serve under the bishop because they were originally the bishop's assistants is a misreading of history. The diaconate was conceived as an office to serve the Church as it is expressed in the local congregation, not the bishop. Originally deacons were, as has been shown, servants of the Church working with the bishop, the presbyters, and others, all of whom were *laos,* laity. For a long time they remained essentially servants of the Church. They came to work largely under the presbyter when he replaced the bishop as president of the local church, although some were indeed assistants to the bishop as he emerged as head of a diocese. However, the primary ministry of the Church has always been and will always be on the level of the local congregation.

Increasingly today, the leadership and governing functions of the local church are being broadened to include representatives of the laity as well as the clergy. In the Episcopal Church primary responsibility has long been exercised by the parish vestry in the "temporalities," the parish rector being its president. Today in some Episcopal and many Roman Catholic congregations, parish councils have been given broad responsibilities and have proven of great value. In these parishes the priest does not surrender the role of parish leader but exercises it in a collaborative style, involving the body of the church in problems and decisions, reflecting indeed the governing presbyteral council of the first centuries with the bishop at its head. Of great importance, this type of structure provides the broad leadership base that in many ways helps provide the harmonious working together of all ministries.

Theologically, if the laity as well as the clergy are the Church, they should share responsibility with the leaders of a parish for decisions relating to the spiritual as well as the material concerns of the Church. Pragmatically, in a society involved in an authority crisis, such as ours, shared responsibility is more acceptable and more productive. In parishes using this type of structure today the clergy usually find broader support for their ministries and more effectiveness in their leadership. Within the structure of such parishes deacons would normally play a vital role. Clearly they would not only be participants in but would be subject to its governing council. They would serve to support and strengthen the pastors or rectors both by gaining a new empathy with them in their work and by extending their ministries far beyond what they themselves can do.

However, for the sake of all concerned and the welfare of congregations, it should be clearly established that deacons exercising their ministries in a parish are directly subject to the parish pastor or priest. The deacon should be one whose support may be counted on, actively, ordinarily, but by silence at times if necessary. As we have previously noted, failure to have this relationship clearly defined after the transition of the fourth century was an important contributing factor in the problems relating to the diaconate and its decline and in modern times hinders its restoration. And even when authority is shared, as with the presbyteral councils of the pre-Nicene age, it needs be remembered that the president of the congregation is its primary leader and structures are needed that foster support for the president's leadership by all members of the congregation. Other structures tend to be counterproductive. For the welfare and upbuilding of the local church and for the prosperity of the diaconate as well, the relationship between the president of the congregation and the deacons needs to be well defined as in the pre-Nicene Church. Further, the primary parish leader and the deacons need to keep uppermost in their hearts as well as their minds the admonition of the Syrian *Didascalia,* dating from c. 220–250, that they are to "be of one mind" and "of one counsel, and of one purpose, and one soul dwelling in two bodies."[20] No wiser or stronger advice can be given.

Major Significance
of Diaconal Numbers in Parishes

The restoration of the diaconate as a full and equal order envisions a number of deacons in the average parish. Even relatively small churches would normally have two or three deacons, and the larger the church the more deacons there would be. We often forget that Christian congregations tended to be very small until the fourth century. The Church at Ephesus, c. 60, probably numbered about fifty people. And the situation did not change substantially as the Church moved into the second century. The house-church of Doura-Europa in the first half of the third century could hold few more than sixty people in its largest room, which measured 40 feet by 16 feet. Similar numbers are confirmed elsewhere. Yet the plural "deacons" is ordinarily used in reference to the churches.[21]

---

20. *Didascalia Apostolorum,* 2.44, p. 109; 3.13, p. 148.
21. Audet, *Structures in Christian Priesthood,* 96, 97–98. Some conciliar legislation, as that of Nicaea, Canon 15 (in *Nicene and Post-Nicene Fathers,* 2d ser., 14:86), provided that "the deacons ought to be seven in number...even if the city be great." However, other documents state that the number should be in accord with the size of the church (see *Ante-Nicene Fathers,* ed. Roberts and Donaldson, 7:432).

It is important in restoring the diaconate that we avoid the implication that truly committed discipleship involves ordination. Those ordained to the diaconate should be *representative* of the various Christian ministries of service. There should be equally committed lay people who are not ordained. One major factor in determining how many are to be ordained in a congregation is the need for liturgical functions that historically belong to the diaconate.

A group of deacons in contrast to a single deacon in a local church gives the diaconate a considerably different character. The office is not then identified with the personality of one particular individual. Any personality difference between a priest or pastor and a deacon becomes less significance. But of more importance, such a body of deacons is symbolic of the extensiveness of the Christian ministry of service as they function liturgically, pastorally, and charitably. The functioning of such deacons might do more than anything else to "declericalize" the Church's ministry, to bring Christians to believe that ministry belongs to every baptized member of the Church, providing, of course, that the deacons have not been clericalized.

Diocesan Deacons

Although we have been considering deacons on the parish level, this does not rule out the possibility of "diocesan" deacons, subject directly to the bishop. An archdeacon could well assist the bishop as he originally did in administering the affairs of the diocese. And there are various other ministries suitable to the deacon but not necessarily related to the local parish which appropriately could be put directly under the bishop's oversight. These include not only some of the more numerous nonstipendiary diaconal ministries but also some of those done by full-time paid employees of the Church in such capacities as diocesan administrators, stewardship facilitators, or institutional workers.

Full Participation in Governing Structures

The status of the restored diaconate should be such as to allow deacons to participate fully in the governing structures of the Church. As members of a distinct order, they should be represented on parish councils, vestries, or boards, in diocesan conventions or councils, and in other regional and national bodies. Deacons living in society with the lifestyle of laity but at the same time being clergy are in a position to make a unique contribution to these various legislative and policy-making bodies. However, there is no compelling reason even in a parish that all resident deacons be incorporated into the governing structures. As their numbers increase, the inclusion of all deacons could be impractical and unadvisable. The principle of elected representation logically applies here, the deacons electing from among their number those who are to represent them in the respective bodies.

On Deacons Voting

The question of deacons having voice and vote in diocesan conventions of the Episcopal Church in the United States has been receiving increasing attention over the last several years and is relevant to other democratically structured churches. The controversy is symptomatic of the subtle but pervasive clericalism that plagues Christianity today as it has for centuries. Clericalism ever seeks to protect the turf of the clergy, although in this instance it is the turf only of the highly clericalized and powerful presbyterate.

The traditional Episcopal diocesan structure creates a convention composed of all diocesan clergy and also of lay delegates elected by their respective congregations. Clergy and laity sit and debate together with the bishop presiding. On most issues clergy and laity also vote as one house. However, on matters judged to be of greater consequence, clergy and laity vote separately, a concurrent majority of each group being required for the passage of a resolution or for an election to take place. Clergy and laity voting separately is frequently called a "vote by orders," although the term is probably incorrect in that "laity" rightly applies to all the baptized while those in "orders" are the ordained. Deacons, who until recently have been transitional,[22] have voted as a matter of course with the presbyters.

In this debate four principal proposals have been advanced:

1. All deacons would continue, as in the present structure, to have both voice and vote, voting along with the priests when clergy and laity vote separately. The argument here is that voting would be less time-consuming, particularly in elections where there may be several candidates for the same office, such as those of bishops or delegates to the national convention, and the voting may continue for many ballots. Although the vote of more numerous deacons could prevail over a majority of the presbyters, this would rarely happen. Therefore, there is not sufficient reason for presbyters and deacons to vote separately, complicating the process by having three sets of ballots to count instead of two.

2. All deacons would be clerical members of the convention with voice but no vote. It is maintained that since deacons are ordained to a servant ministry it is inappropriate for them to vote. But is not the ministry of all the baptized servant ministry? The diaconate exists in part at least to remind all of us that as Christians we are servants, and indeed no less so than the deacons. If true humility means that deacons should not vote, then logically should any of us vote? Voting may rightly be seen as no less a form of service than is speaking. Further, the effect of deacons having no vote would certainly significantly decrease their interest in attending the conventions. Few would argue that a voice without a vote does not diminish the importance of membership in a body.

---

22. In addition to the transitional deacons there were a relatively small number of deacons ordained under the old canon for the "perpetual diaconate." They also voted with the priests but their numbers were such that they were not seen as posing any problem.

It has been suggested that the diaconal office is such that they should voluntarily abstain from voting. Deacons are certainly free to abstain from voting, as are any others. But canonical legislation denying any group the vote immediately removes its voluntary character, even if the proposal comes originally from members of the group, as in this case the deacons themselves.

3. All deacons would be clerical members of the convention with both voice and vote but would vote as a separate group from both the presbyters and the laity on major issues. The reasoning here is that the presbyters are then protected from their vote being overwhelmed by more numerous deacons on a matter of importance. However, as the number of deacons increases, a convention could easily become unwieldy were all the deacons of a diocese to attend.

4. Deacons from each parish, or those not serving in a parish from their group, would elect deacons to represent them from among their number. Deacon delegates would have both voice and vote in the convention and would vote either with the presbyters or separately. This proposal would provide for diaconal representation but prevent the number of deacons at conventions from becoming so large that numbers would be unwieldy or that the number of deacons would be disproportional. Those who are concerned that the vote of the priests could be defeated by a preponderance of deacons would be protected, of course, in greater degree were the deacons and priests to vote separately.

In our culture great importance is attached to the right to vote. If the diaconate is truly an equal order, why should deacons not vote? Deacons certainly know more than many lay delegates, care as much as either presbyters or laity, and are as attuned to the guidance of the Holy Spirit as either. The desire to vote is not in and of itself the desire for power. Decision making in the life of the Church is, or should be, a form of service.

At issue here is the wholeness of the Church. As we noted earlier, Ignatius, bishop of Antioch, wrote a letter on his way from Antioch to his martyrdom at Rome c. 117 C.E., "Everyone must show the deacons respect. They represent Jesus Christ, just as the bishop has the role of the Father and the presbyters are like God's council and an apostolic band. You cannot have a Church without these." In the mind of the early Church deacons are necessary to have the Church — at least in its wholeness. Certainly the office that specially represents Christ should vote.

Another serious issue involved in disenfranchising deacons is that it denigrates the order. What the Church does speaks louder than what the Church says. Denying the vote to deacons does say that deacons are inferior to priests, and perhaps even to laity. It serves to perpetuate the graded structure in which rank is paramount. It may even encourage deacons, being human, to seek to rise to the "higher order." The problem here is not that the desire for and the right to vote gives deacons power inappropriate to the diaconate. The diaconate is essentially new, at least in the sense that a real diaconate has not existed generally in the Church for centuries. Its place and function are uncertain in the minds of many. The prospect of deacons, who have not had the same theological training as the presbyterate and who do not have the same kind of responsibility, becoming more numerous than presbyters does make some presbyters uncomfortable. The issue that can be focused upon is the right of deacons to vote. If ways are not found to allay such fears, real or imagined, the collective presbyterate may well suppress the diaconate again to the great impoverishment of the Church. For these reasons a structure providing for deacon delegates with voice and vote is to be recommended.

A Formal Agreement with Each Deacon

The guidelines of the Roman Catholic Bishops' Committee on the Permanent Diaconate wisely urge the drawing up of a written document setting forth the ministry of each deacon, observing that clear job descriptions prevent problems later due to misunderstandings on the part of those involved. The guidelines state that this document should always contain a clear statement of responsibilities, specifying "the expectations of the diocese, of the particular community in and for which the deacon serves, and of the deacon himself."[23]

In both the Roman Catholic and Episcopal churches at the present time the deacon serves under the authority of the bishop of a diocese and is assigned by the bishop to particular ministries.[24] In circumstances where the deacon serves in a diocesan capacity, as in diocesan administration or an institutional chaplaincy, the document would appropriately be drawn up by the bishop and might well be signed by both the bishop and the deacon. Where deacons are assigned to parishes, both from the theoretical and practical viewpoints, the agreement delineating the deacon's responsibilities in that ministry should be made between the parish and the deacon, signed by the pastor or rector and the deacon.

Experience will undoubtedly provide better insight into the specific content of such agreements. However, inclusion of the following points seems advisable both to inform the deacon and the parish regarding the particular ministry involved and to insure that authority conflicts be kept minimal:

1. The parish church is a body with many members, each sent by Christ with special gifts to minister first to one another and then to others.

2. All ministries of the parish are exercised under the leadership of and coordinated by the pastor or rector.

3. The fundamental ministry of the deacon is to hold before the Church the character of the whole ministry of the Church as that of service and of its ministers as servants.

4. The deacon is to strive for harmonious relationships within the parish church, lending enthusiastic support, if possible, to parish policy, the pastor or rector, and other leaders, seeking always to *build up* the Body of Christ.

---

23. Bishops' Committee, *Permanent Deacons*, 1984 rev., par. 117, pp. 43–44.
24. Ibid., par. 115–17, p. 43. *Constitution and Canons (1991)*, III.13.1(a), p. 79.

5. The special area(s) or type(s) of ministry to be exercised by the deacon should be set forth.

6. Problems arising that affect the welfare of the parish known to the deacon are to be brought to the pastor or rector and the pastor's counsel and advice are to be followed. If the deacon is unable or unwilling to follow such advice, the problem is to be taken to the appropriate ecclesiastical authority whose advice the deacon is to follow.

7. The deacon will participate in any ongoing program for the diaconate that is applicable in which participation might reasonably be expected.

8. Reports are to be made at stated intervals to the pastor or someone designated by the pastor on the special ministry of the deacon.

9. The agreement automatically terminates when a deacon moves to another community and automatically expires every three years. It may be terminated at any time either by the deacon or the pastor or rector, provided that written notice be given to the other party first of the intention to terminate the agreement, giving opportunity for discussion of any problems that may exist. Notice is to be given to the bishop or ecclesiastical authority. In no less than ten days a second notice may be given terminating the agreement. Upon termination or expiration it must be formally renewed by both the parish and the deacon in order for the deacon to continue to minister as a deacon in that parish.

Two sample letters are included in the appendix.

The ninth point above relating to termination of the agreement may seem to imply that the deacon, although ordained, is treated like a lay person licensed for a time for a particular ministry. However, in parish life the practice of what is outlined above would generally work otherwise. The dignity and permanence of ordination acts as a formidable counterbalance to the temporary nature of the agreement. In most cases renewal of the agreement would be a matter of course, a mere formality.

However, at this juncture in the restoration of the diaconate in its integrity and wholeness it is well advised to insure that the relationship between parish priests or pastors and deacons is well defined. As we have seen, historically the lack of definition was a major reason for the decline of the office. Most would agree that there would normally be no problem in a parish so long as the pastor or rector in charge when the deacons are ordained remains. A problem could arise under a new parish head were a deacon, especially one who had been there many years, to forget the nature of the diaconate and become like what some have termed in the past a "lay pope." It is important that bishops, parish priests or pastors, and the Church generally have adequate assurance that parochial deacons will not be allowed to become a burden but will be the enormous asset they should be and normally are. At this juncture, if we err, we should err on the side of too much rather than too little assurance.

It is envisioned that deacons operating within such a structure as outlined here would in all but a rare instance strengthen the work and ministry of the full-time priests and pastors. Even a new pastor or rector moving into a parish would have no reason to be threatened by the deacons already serving within that congregation. The deacons' responsibility to support the parish's primary leader would be clearly agreed to by them in their agreement with the parish, and their tenure would ultimately rest upon the consent of the pastor or rector. An additional safeguard to the peace of congregations could be provided in the form of authority given to the bishop to reassign a deacon with the consent of either the pastor or rector or the deacon. Deacons should always keep uppermost in their minds that pastors or rectors will have no cause to feel threatened by deacons who remember that their ministry is one of *diakonia*. Parish controversies are virtually always more destructive to the Body of Christ than whatever good those responsible for them seek to accomplish.

Deacons Moving to Another Place

It is apparent from conciliar legislation of the early Church cited previously that the movement of clergy from one place to another has always been a problem in the Church, so much so that it was forbidden by the canons of more than one council. This problem has again come to the fore in connection with the kind of nonstipendiary (unpaid) office created in the restored diaconate, as was mentioned in the preceding chapter in connection with the Episcopal Church's experience. In our highly mobile society, deacons, earning their livelihood from non-Church sources, will certainly move to other communities and parishes with some frequency.

It is true that deacons transferring to another location may not be welcomed in some instances by the parish priests or pastors of their new churches. It is too much to expect that clergy, who have been trained to think of the Church's ministry largely in terms of their own and who know little about the nature of the historic diaconate, would know what to do with a deacon suddenly in the midst of the parish. In a time of transition this kind of problem is bound to arise.

In this situation the deacon should remember, first of all, that ordination did not confer an absolute right for the continuation of a deacon's ministry even in the place of ordination. To think in such terms is in a profound sense a contradiction of the nature of the diaconate. Holding the office of deacon and being licensed to exercise that office in a given situation are not the same thing. This distinction is true for priests and bishops as well. The deacon rightly would want to serve in a diaconal ministry. But moving into a situation in which this diaconal ministry is not welcome, probably not understood, the deacon should see the opportunity for ministry by showing willingness to serve in some other needed way without insisting upon the kind of ministry formerly exercised either in liturgical or other terms. By the deacon demonstrating that diaconal ministry is truly *diakonia,* the priest or pastor may well come to want the full expression of the diaconate.

The fundamental difficulty here lies in what the Church is conceived to be. When the Church is conceived in organic as against hierarchic terms and ministry is seen as belonging equally to all members of the Church, the problem of deacons moving to other places is seen to be essentially the same as that of lay persons. Most parishes and their clergy are delighted to have committed lay people transferring into their midst. These lay people may have ministries and exercise them no less than deacons in the pastoral, charitable, and often the liturgical areas of the Church's life. There may be no place in the new parish for the particular ministry that the lay person has done in the former church, either liturgically or otherwise, although this is probably not often the case. But when it is, committed lay people habitually find new ways to serve. With the broad spectrum of ministries in the restored diaconate, certainly a deacon could as easily adjust.

Should not the problem be the opposite? Should not the clergy be concerned if there are no deacons to do the diaconal functions? Clergy who have lived for any length of time in most parishes today know that the diaconal functions of a pastoral, charitable/societal, or liturgical nature, but especially the former two, are not adequately being done. The attempts in the various churches to compensate for the lack of real deacons by delegating their functions, especially liturgical, to lay people is less than satisfactory, although better than having them all concentrated in the parish priest or pastor.

It is true, as has been previously stated, that ordination confers special grace and the authorization of the Church giving representative form to ministries, and it is desirable for these reasons. But there is in addition the matter of vocation. Vocation brings with it a different and enhanced sense of responsibility for the ministry and work involved, far more than do such things as a license to be a chalice administrator or lay reader or enrollment as a lector. Delegating such tasks tends to make them jobs to be done and leaves them unconnected to the pastoral and charitable concerns of the Christian community. On the other hand, a vocation to the diaconate brings the pastoral and/or charitable/societal and liturgical functions of this ministry together and adds a sense of God's calling for a life-long and many-sided work.

Ordination to a life-long vocation in the diaconate does not exclude the possibility, as is pointed out in the report on "The Restoration of the Office of Deacon as a Lifetime State," that the deacon may at some later time be called to serve outside the office of deacon for good reason. The report specifically lists a change in secular employment as one of the reasons envisioned by the committee. Others enumerated in the report are limitation of physical health, preservation of psychic health, and a change in family situation.[25]

Certainly there is no reason why a deacon, or a priest for that matter, cannot live and work effectively as a Christian in a parish without exercising the functions conveyed through ordination. Since my retirement as rector of a parish

---

25. "A Report on the Restoration of the Office of Deacon," par. 25, p. 198.

church two years ago, I have moved to a metropolitan area and become happily involved in a new congregation, functioning as a layperson. In a natural family functions change as the family situation changes. The role of parents changes radically as children grow from childhood to adulthood. As we saw earlier, the role of the presbyter changed radically between the middle of the third century and the end of the fourth century. A deacon's role may also be very different from one parish to another, even to the point that at times diaconal functions will no longer be exercised.

The mobility need not, then, create unwanted problems in a new location. It creates new opportunities. However, some safeguards can facilitate the transition. A period of residence in another parish could be required before a formal agreement might be entered into by the parish and the deacon. Meanwhile, liturgical or other service as a deacon would be on an informal basis, if at all, and then only upon written request of the parish and its priest or pastor to the appropriate ecclesiastical authority. Such a requirement would go a long way to allow the Holy Spirit time to work in the situation and to insure both that the deacon wishes to minister as such in this new congregation and that the parish will find the ministry being offered an effective instrument to enhance its total ministry.

Chapter 11

Some Considerations Regarding Qualifications

Age

The first and simplest qualification of a deacon has to do with age. The legislation of the ancient councils is still sound. The Council of Carthage, 397, set the minimum age for ordination to the diaconate at 25 years. Later councils such as Agde (506), Orleans (c. 537), and Trullo (692) affirmed this action.[1] This age allows time for individuals to gain sufficient maturity and Christian formation to make responsible decisions in so weighty a matter and yet at the same time to be young enough for their patterns of living to be shaped more readily in this ministry. Much is to be said for maintaining 25 years as the minimum age.

Pope Paul VI in his *General Norms for Restoring the Diaconate in the Latin Church* set the minimum age at 25 years, but the guidelines of the Bishop's Committee on the Permanent Diaconate set the age at 35 years in the United States with bishops able to dispense for one year.[2] The American Episcopal Church requires a person to be at least 21 years at ordination unless ordained under the canon relating to "local deacons," in which case the minimum age is 32 years.[3] One would hope that the wisdom of the ancient councils will prevail in America and elsewhere.

Gender Factors

It is beyond the scope of this study to present the arguments for and against the ordination of women to the clerical ministries of the Church. And such seems unnecessary.

---

1. Council of Carthage, Canon 4, in Landon, *A Manual of Councils of the Holy Catholic Church*, 1:121; Council of Agde, Canon 16, in Hefele, *History of the Councils of the Church*, 4:79. Council of Orleans, Canon 6, Hefele, *History of the Councils of the Church*, 4:205, Council of Trullo, Canon 14, in *Nicene and Post-Nicene Fathers*, 2d ser., 14:372.
2. Paul VI, *Permanent Diaconate*, 3; Bishop's Committee, *Permanent Deacons*, par. 135, p. 44.
3. *Constitutions and Canons (1991)*, III.6.1, p. 65, and III.9.1(b)(1), p. 72.

As has previously been observed in another connection, a study of the history and development of the Church's ordained ministry shows clearly that the Church has the authority to ordain women. The question then becomes one of whether or not such a course is that directed by the Holy Spirit to meet the needs of the Church and its mission in the contemporary world. The fact that deaconesses were not female deacons in the early Church is not of great significance, since this appears to have been due to cultural, not theological, considerations.

The nature of the diaconate, the diverse forms of diaconal ministry, contemporary sociological recognition of the inherent equality of the sexes, and the implications of biblical thought support the ordination of women as well as men to the office. Women enhance the office in both function and symbol. Nothing in this study is intended to imply that the diaconate today should be open only to males. When masculine gender is used, it is used to refer to historical fact or reference or in the generic sense.

In recent years the Episcopal Church authorized the ordination of women to its diaconate. In 1971 the Catholic Theological Society of America in a study commissioned by the U.S. Bishops' Committee on the Permanent Diaconate recommended the ordination of women to the diaconate of that church. The report of a Task Force of the Catholic Theological Society of America published in 1978 concluded that the negative arguments do not "present any serious grounds to justify the exclusion of women from ordination to pastoral office in the Catholic Church." The Bishops' Committee's own report states that among their candidates for the diaconate and the directors of diaconal programs "there is a growing conviction that women would strengthen the diaconal ministry immeasurably."[4]

High Standards

The qualifications for the diaconate listed in 1 Timothy 3, as we saw earlier, are not of Christian origin but rather those standards in general use in antiquity simply applied to this office in the Church. The principle here is applicable today. Individuals officially representing and serving the Church in the diaconate are to be those of high standards and good reputation. They are to be reliable and respected members of the communities in which they live. Married candidates should have stable, sound family life and the approval and support of their spouses for their diaconal ministries as well.

---

4. Rashke, *The Deacon in Search of Identity*, 50–51; *Research Report, Women in Church and Society*, ed. Sara Butler (Bronx, N.Y.: Catholic Theological Society of America, 1978), 47; Bishops' Committee, *Permanent Deacons*, par. 168, p. 54.

Diversity of Diaconal Ministries

Of prime importance, the candidates need depth of commitment to Christ evident in their style and manner of life which has been tested by a minimum of several years within the Christian community. Prior to becoming diaconal candidates they should be involved in some form or forms of pastoral, charitable, or societal ministry within or without their Christian communities. The nature of such ministries may be widely varied. Many of those involved in the renewal of the diaconate or assessing the qualifications of candidates see the nonliturgical functions of the office in very narrow terms of pastoral and charitable works to the virtual exclusion of a broad range of activities. Some see these ministries almost solely in terms of ministry "outside the Church." This is to forget that historically diaconal ministries included such activities as instructing the people at noneucharistic assemblies, joining presbyters in judging disputes between members of their communities, administering parishes and dioceses, and acting as theological advisors to bishops and councils, as well as those things that are normally called charitable and pastoral activities. *Diakonia,* as we saw earlier, was defined much more broadly in the early Church and should be in its renewal today. It is not an "either/or" but a "both/and" proposition.

Increasingly varied forms of ministry characterize the diaconate today. The ministry of Tom Dorris, a deacon of the Evangelical Lutheran Church of America of the Synod of Metropolitan New York, until his untimely death in an automobile accident in Sweden in 1994, illustrates a societal rather than a charitable function proper to the diaconate. He was communications director of the Life and Peace Institute in Uppsala, Sweden. Prior to this, his primary societal ministry for over a decade was that of serving as editor of the Ecumenical Press Service of the World Council of Churches in Geneva. While there, he served as a deacon in the English-speaking congregation of the Evangelical Lutheran Church. He contributed regularly to various diaconal publications. Constantino J. Ferriola Jr., a Roman Catholic deacon, had as the focus of his ministry service as executive director of the Secretariat for the Permanent Diaconate of the National Conference of Catholic Bishops in Washington, D.C., for the past several years, a ministry to which he brought outstanding gifts of grace. Among many activities, he participated in and conducted conferences in and out of the Roman Catholic Church, showing forth God's love and giving light to enlighten diaconal renewal. Now that his term is over, he has returned to his work and ministry of counseling.

The ministry of Ormonde Plater, an Episcopal deacon of New Orleans, includes charitable work in the surgical wards of Charity Hospital, where many victims of "urban warfare" are treated, pastoral work with his parish's sick and shut-ins, and institutional work for the diocese as secretary for its commission on ministry and as coordinator of lay hospital visiting in New Orleans. For the larger Church, Deacon Plater has an extensive ministry in editing, writing, and speaking about the diaconate. He exercises his liturgical ministry both in serving as a deacon at St. Anna's Church in New Orleans and in writing and speaking on the deacon's role in liturgy. In addition to other types of ministry, liturgical and pastoral, Lutheran deacon James E. Moser of Baltimore serves as a Sunday School teacher, and Episcopal deacon Sarah Tracey is the director of the School of Faith and Ministry of the Episcopal Diocese of Northern Indiana with the title of archdeacon.

The Church needs widely varied forms of ministry, and a major function of the diaconate, in addition to ministering in diverse areas, is to provide models with breath and imagination of ministries for the laity to see and emulate.

Selection: Called by the Community

The traditional concept that the ordained should have some internal sense of being called for this ministry by the Holy Spirit prior to selection or approval by the Christian community is problematic. No small part of this concept comes from the widely accepted notion that full commitment to God in Christ means seeking ordination, and basic Christian commitment has often been confused with "a call" to ordination. Such confusion is not surprising due to the long-prevalent belief that ministry per se is the possession of the ordained. But, in effect, Baptism and ordination are being confused. Baptism is the basic sacrament of ministry, and all are called to this ministry. Theologically, commitment is associated with Baptism and there is no difference between the commitment God expects among the baptized, ordained or lay.

There are certainly some compelling theological reasons to recommend the procedure of the Christian community selecting qualified laity for the diaconate, as they did in the early Church.[5] The community may often discern better than its individual members how the gifts of the Spirit bestowed in Baptism may be employed for the various ministries it needs for its life as church and for the work God calls it to undertake. Parish councils or other responsible groups might well take the initiative in discerning the gifts of its members and urging qualified lay persons to seek ordination and engage in other ministries. Certainly the community would give greater acceptance to those whom it calls, such acceptance being vital to the unity and harmony of the community, to effective ministry, and to the well-being of those who minister. This procedure assumes that the community is informed about the nature of the diaconate and is still small enough for the people generally to know each other. In some small congregations there might simply be a consensus of the community. But even in larger communities it is feasible to use this process. Certainly the Holy Spirit could work as well, or better, through this process as through any other. A person so selected would always be free, after reflection and prayer, to accept or reject such a selection. Further, the Church's screening process would be operative to forestall a misguided selection, should this occur.

---

5. Porter, "Modern Experience in Practice," 96.

Professional Screening Programs

A number of Roman Catholic programs have found an interview process helpful in the screening and development of diaconal candidates. Selection Research, Inc. (SRI), of Lincoln, Nebraska, developed the interview at the request of the Executive Committee of the National Association of Permanent Diaconate Directors in 1979. The interview is based on a model produced by analyzing ordained deacons who were regarded as best exemplifying the office. It centers around nine personality traits previously identified as important for deacons, such as "relator," "spirituality," "purpose," "family," "helping," and "teaming." Interviewers are trained by Selection Research's Deacon Perceiver Academy.[6]

The priest-director of the Omaha Permanent Diaconate Program at its inception and for some years afterwards, Patrick McCaslin, reported that the interviews gave him the tools he needed to facilitate the screening of diaconal candidates. He said that by identifying the strengths of candidates, even those who do not belong in the program feel affirmed.[7] He recommends the screening process highly.

It is certainly appropriate that the Church use such a tool, essentially borrowed from the corporate and professional world. However, the Church must do so with the realization that such standardized tests have definite limitations. There is increasing evidence that these tests may fall short of being the reliable indicators of future excellence they have been widely thought to be. Bowdoin College in Maine has abandoned use of the Scholastic Aptitude Test (SAT) for college entrance due to what it believes to be deficiencies, notably in the test's inability to measure the student's level of development, personality traits, or growth pattern in high school. An article in the New York Times Magazine regarding tests for screening premedical students notes that they do predict reasonably well student grades in the first two years of medical school, when the courses are science-oriented. However, the article reports, "they have zero — yes zero — correlation with how well students do in the third and fourth years," when the students are involved with patients in clinical situations.[8]

The human personality is so intricate and complex that it is difficult to develop standardized tests that are a true measure of the potential of individuals. A built-in limitation stems from the model used. In the case of the diaconate, the model in the SRI interview is that of men who tend to excel at accommodation and work as team members but are not strong leaders. Individuals of the type selected through this interview process are needed in the diaconate, but so are

---

6. Information sheet describing the services of the Deacon Perceiver Academy of SRI. Information is available from SRI Perceiver Academies, Lincoln, Neb.

7. Personal communication.

8. Benjamin Fine, *The Stranglehold of the I.Q.* (Garden City, N.Y.: Doubleday, 1975), 167; E. B. Fiske, "Finding Fault with the Testers," in *New York Times Magazine*, November 18, 1979, 152.

those with leadership ability. The history of the diaconate suggests that a broader model is needed to allow room for deacons who will be able leaders. Athanasius and Gregory the Great come immediately to mind. The Church today needs deacons with leadership potential for various sorts of ministries, one example being that of organizing programs of lay ministry. Further, it must always be remembered that Christians look to the guidance of the Spirit through prayer along with intelligent methods and approaches to be directed in their decisions, including the selection of their clergy.

Extensive Educational Requirements a Barrier

The qualifications for the diaconate are quite different from those for the transitional diaconate and the priesthood. The tendency to create qualifications for deacons in the same general pattern except in lesser degree as those for priests has been and remains a significant problem, stemming as it does from the centuries-old single model of ministry, that of the priest or pastor. Those concerned with the diaconate need to make a conscious effort to understand the nature and function of the diaconate and of the presbyterate and then to establish qualifications and training programs or processes suitable to the respective offices. A major consideration relative to the diaconate is its diversity, both in respect to the wide variety of diaconal ministries and to the particular situations from which deacons come and in which deacons exercise their ministries.

One of the major differences between the diaconate and the presbyterate arises from the fact that, historically, preaching is not a function of the diaconate. It is a function of the presbyterate and, therefore, became a function of the transitional diaconate. Although deacons did teach in instructing catechumens and other nonliturgical assemblies and some could well participate in instruction of various kinds today, teaching is primarily also a presbyteral function. But teaching and preaching are two different, if related, activities. Preaching at the liturgies requires extensive education, both general and theological. Many deacons may beneficially speak on their experience and work from time to time at the Sunday liturgy, but that is not the same thing as preaching. One of the most inspiring sermons I have ever heard was one preached by Marc A. Rivera, a deacon whose remarkable story is one of being raised by the hand of God from living on the streets with gangs and drugs to running Anchor House in Florida for boys like he once was. He told his own faith-filled story to a hushed congregation.[9] Some deacons may have gifts for preaching, in which event more extensive theological and homiletical training would be appropriate along with a special license to preach. But to impose a burden of

---

9. Deacon Marc Rivera has written his story, *Touched by the Father's Hand*, published by Stonecrest (1992), available from the Centre for the Diaconate, 271 N. Main St., Providence, RI 02903.

the kind of education and training appropriate for preaching on the diaconate generally is not only unnecessary but a serious barrier to the development of a vital and effective diaconal ministry. Further, such training is rarely given where deacons are authorized to preach today. The laity know only too well that ordination does not automatically transform its recipients into knowledgeable and gifted speakers.

Extensive educational requirements will exclude both those who may be intelligent and capable, devout and committed, with or capable of wonderful diaconal ministries but who lack the general educational background needed. Also excluded will be those who have the broad educational requirements and other qualifications but whose other legitimate responsibilities in such areas as their work and family life prevent them from committing the time required for additional training in the theological disciplines.

Deacons should be carefully chosen and well trained. For most, the kind of theological training the Church would like its adult laity to have is sufficient. The problem here is with the Christian formation of the baptized, or more accurately the lack of it. The catechumenate of the early Church was a process usually lasting three years. Although it involved other aspects of formation, such as the development of a Christian lifestyle and ministry, extensive catechesis of both "notional instruction on the subjective level" and "active formation on the objective level as well, involving prayer, hand-laying, exorcism, fasting, and tasting salt," was given.[10] Daily assemblies for the instruction of the catechumens during Lent are mentioned. Such formation was adequate for ordination. Since Christian formation is usually inadequate in most places today, diaconal training programs are needed to qualify candidates by remedying this deficit. But the model of such programs should be good lay formation programs, not seminary curricula.

Beyond this, more should be required for those whose ministries would be significantly enhanced by special theological study, such as those who have a gift for preaching or who might exercise their ministries in Christian education. There is a place in the diaconate for those who have seminary degrees, as is illustrated by the effective ministries of seminary-trained deacons in both the Roman Catholic and Episcopal churches. The Church might also require higher educational levels for diaconal candidates in congregations of highly educated laity. Certainly in this age of specialization deacons should be well qualified in professional areas of their ministries, such as psychological training for counselors or accounting knowledge for those with ministries helping the elderly with income tax returns.

But unquestionably, there are many basically qualified, mature Christians today in our congregations who could serve the Church well in the diaconate — some with no additional training, others with only a minimum of special training. Some indeed know God better and are already highly trained and skilled,

10. Kavanagh, *The Shape of Baptism*, 56, 60.

much more so in fact than most of the clergy, in the *diakonia* of their special ministries.

The aim of the Church in the restoration of the diaconate is to make deacons, not quasi-priests or quasi-pastors, with authentic servant ministries within the Church and without the Church in the world.

Chapter 12

The Functions and Training
of the Deacon

Functions of the New Diaconate

As we have already seen, the first and truly great function of the deacon is to be the symbol par excellence of the Church's ministry. Deacons are the embodiment of the servant ministry Christ has sent and empowered all the baptized to share. The particular functions of the deacon are therefore of signal importance, defining as they do the office. These are the things that give meaning, content, and symbolic power to what the deacon is.

Our study of the diaconate reveals that in the early Church deacons exercised their ministry in three primary areas: liturgy, pastoral care, and charitable or societal concerns. These three areas, also enumerated by Paul VI in his apostolic letter, Laying Down Certain Norms Regarding the Sacred Order of the Diaconate, provide a more useful form of classification than those customarily used.[1] Pastoral and charitable/societal functions are better delineated from one another. Although they are often similar in character, "pastoral" refers to ministries directed toward the flock of Christ while "charitable" or "societal" ministries are more to others who live outside the Church. The Church today needs to be especially intentional about charitable/societal ministries.

For centuries in the West, church and state were two names for a single society. Christianity was the established religion of western culture, even as in the United States when it was not legally established, so that pastoral ministry included virtually all people in the society. It was the Christian Era in the West. However, with the breaking-down of this establishment or the end of the Constantinian era, as this has been called, notably since World War II, the Church is no longer virtually coextensive with Western society and is again called to serve those outside its confines as well as its own people in charitable/societal areas. The deacon, as one who is particularly authorized and empowered by ordination

---

1. Pope Paul VI, *Laying Down Certain Norms Regarding the Sacred Order of the Diaconate (Ministeria Quaedom)*, issued *motu proprio*, August 15, 1972, printed in *The Deacon, Minister of Word and Sacrament*, Study Text VI, prepared by the Bishops' Committee on the Liturgy (Washington, D.C.: U.S. Catholic Conference, 1979), 4.

to be the icon of *diakonia,* is the minister to lead in raising the consciousness of all the baptized for such ministries.

Ministry of the Word

The use of a separate category for the deacon's ministry of the word empha-sizes the importance of the word in the Church's ministry. The symbol of the deacon's ministry of the word is the high privilege of reading the Gospel at the Eucharist. Liturgically, this is the apex of the ministry of the word as is shown, indeed proclaimed, by processional candles preceding the gospel book and/or the deacon to the place from which the Gospel is read, preferably an ambo[2] or pulpit, and by the people standing. The deacon is thereby associated with the word in a way different from but equally distinctive and liturgically more im-portant than that of the presbyter, who preaches, or the lector, who reads the Old Testament or the other New Testament lesson. This is not to depreciate the value of the other Scripture readings or the sermon, but the other readings are prelude to the Gospel and the sermon is only the exposition of the Scriptures. The Reformation emphasis on preaching was profoundly needed, but it should not mislead us into placing a diminished value on the reading of the Gospel in the Liturgy. This reading of the Gospel signifies the genuine and important min-istry of verbal witness deacons make to Christ as they carry out their particular pastoral and charitable ministries.

Preaching in the liturgy is essentially a presiding function and, as we have seen, belongs historically to the episcopate and presbyterate. Although there are practical reasons involving the need for more extensive theological train-ing which mitigate against the authorization by ordination for deacons to preach liturgically, the more important argument against this function being made in-herent in the diaconal office is the resultant confusion of the orders of presbyter and deacon. It is more important today, when the Church is restoring its original organic character in which ministry is seen to belong to all the baptized, than it may be in the future to draw boundaries between the functions of the deacon and the presbyter due to the now centuries-old concept that the totality of ministry essentially belongs to the presbyter. Conveying authority to preach liturgically to all deacons through ordination is a vestige of the transitional diaconate and gives credence to the notion that the ordained offices are much the same, dea-cons simply being a lesser version of the presbyterate in contrast to a distinctive order with a glorious heritage and its own particular functions.

At Baptism

Much the same thing may be said of the authorization by the Roman Catholic Church for deacons solemnly to baptize infants with all rites and ceremonies of the office without qualification, an authorization that appears to be due to a

---

2. "Ambo" is the ancient name, being revived today, for the platform or reading desk used for the proclamation of the Word: all the Scripture readings and the sermon.

shortage of priests and should be reserved for cases of necessity. The Episcopal Church authorizes deacons to preside over the baptismal liturgy only when a priest is not available and with the bishop's authorization. Although in the early Church deacons had an important place in Baptism, the bishop, and later the presbyter, as the leader of the congregation, presided at this signal event in the life of the Church and of the Christian. Aidan Kavanagh writes of the centrality of Baptism:

> The experience of baptism in all its paschal dimension, together with the vivid memory of it in individuals and the sustained anamnesis of it in every sacramental event enacted by the community at large, constitute not only the touchstone of Catholic orthodoxy but the starting point of all catechesis, pastoral endeavor, missionary effort, and liturgical celebration in the Church. The paschal mystery of Jesus Christ dying and rising still among his faithful ones at Easter in baptism is what gives the Church its radical cohesion and mission, putting it at the center of a world made new. That world is a paschal world, and baptism in its fullness is the compound process of act and reflection by which one enters such a world, leaving behind an obsolete world where death is lord. The latter world was made by us all. The former is meant and made by God no less for all.[3]

The presbyter (or bishop, if he is present) presides over the liturgical observation of the paschal mystery at Easter and is the normal presider over both Baptism and the Eucharist whenever they take place. Full initiation into the life of the Church includes not only Baptism but the Eucharist over which the Church has required a presbyter or a bishop to preside since these offices became normative in the late third- and early fourth-century Church. Further, the central importance of Baptism dictates that the community's leader presides. It follows that the function of presiding over the incorporation of a person into the life of the Church is that of the presbyter, except in an emergency, when any baptized person may administer the Baptism. Any baptized person may administer Baptism not because it is of lesser importance than some other things reserved to the ordained but the opposite, because it is of the greatest importance. Deacons may appropriately do the actual submersion, immersion, or pouring for those they have prepared for Baptism or in assisting either a presiding presbyter or bishop. Hippolytus is clear that a bishop or presbyter baptizes but probably means that he remained beside the font while a deacon went into the water, asked the questions, and did the actual immersion:

> Let the candidates stand in the water, naked, a deacon going with them likewise. And when he who is being baptized goes down into the water, he who baptizes him, putting his hand on him, shall [ask the three questions, each a section of a version of the Apostles' Creed, with the response, "I believe"]. Then holding his hand placed on his head, he shall baptize him [three times — immerse the person after each response].[4]

---

3. Kavanagh, *Shape of Baptism*, 162–63.
4. *Apostolic Tradition of Hippolytus* 21:11–18, trans. Easton, 46–47.

Infants are appropriately being baptized by immersion naked today, but some form of clothing in which the individual candidate will be comfortable is the rule today when Baptism is administered by immersion. As was previously pointed out, there was then no sense of impropriety in the ancient world for non-Jews due to their being accustomed to the public baths. It may be difficult for some presbyters to allow deacons to do the immersion, especially since getting into the water is not required, but that role for the deacon does better express the theology that Baptism is an act of the community.

At Marriages

Officiating at marriages is also a presiding function and, therefore, presbyterial in nature. The principle is recognized in both the Roman Catholic and Episcopal churches by provisions requiring special authorization, implying exceptional circumstances. The Roman deacon must be specifically delegated to preside at marriage celebrations by the bishop or pastor. Episcopal deacons may so function only when no bishop or priest is available and may not use the nuptial blessing. Both Roman and Episcopal churches require authorization of civil law for deacons to solemnize marriages.

Deacons Presiding at Quasi-Eucharists

"Communion Services," as some Roman Catholics call them, or "Deacons' Masses," in the terminology of some Episcopalians, are a phenomenon coming about largely as a result of the shortage of priests in Roman Catholicism and of transitional deacons being put in charge of churches in Anglicanism, the practice carrying over into the restored diaconate of today. The motivation behind them is laudable even if the theology is not. They are quasi-Eucharists presided over by a deacon and are not uncommon when an ordained presbyter is not available. However, they raise serious theological questions. Forms of these services are more acceptable at least when they do not resemble a eucharistic rite.

The Deacons' Mass normally includes the Liturgy of the Word and the administration of communion with related items, omitting the eucharistic prayer and those parts, such as the offering of the elements, related to it. Communion Services may less resemble a Eucharist. One Roman Catholic deacon, who regularly officiates at weekday Communion Services when the Mass is scheduled but a priest cannot be present, includes an extemporaneous prayer at the outset, then the Gospel, an act of contrition, the Lord's Prayer, and the administration of communion with a concluding prayer and dismissal.

It is doubtful if any precedent can be found for this phenomenon in the early Church. In the late third century in situations that were probably similar to ours so far as need was concerned (when a bishop, the normal president, could not be present), deacons did preside at the Eucharist in some places until the practice was forbidden. But it was the Eucharist, not the anomaly of a Eucharist without the eucharistic action and prayer in which the community "does this" in *anamnesis* (recall, re-presentation, remembrance, memorial, reenactment) of

Christ and his sacrifice, so that he is made present with his people. Councils forbad deacons so presiding because it was not in accord with the character of the diaconal order.

In Deacons' Masses and Communion Services the deacon is, first of all, serving in the role of a presider as a substitute priest. Of greater importance, the implication is that Christ is only barely present in his Word and would deny his grace to his people simply because an ordained priest is not present, reducing the Eucharist, or nearly so, to Christian priestly magic. Although the Great Thanksgiving is omitted, deacons have been known to substitute some other prayer in its place, certainly creating confusion in the minds of worshipers not only about what is being done but who or what the deacon is. The Eucharist is an action of the community gathered about the Lord's table through which he becomes present with his disciples according to his Word.

This theology is seen in the eucharistic prayer of the second-century Acts of Thomas:

> Jesus, you have deemed us worthy to draw near unto your holy Body and to partake of your life-giving Blood, and because of our reliance upon you we are bold and draw near and invoke your holy Name which has been proclaimed by the prophets as your godhead willed:...we beg of you that you would come and have fellowship with us for help and for life....Come, holy Spirit;...come, power of the Father and wisdom of the Son, for you are one in all; come, and partake with us in this Eucharist.[5]

Jungmann recalls the custom of erecting a throne and placing the gospel book on the throne at councils of the early Church, giving Ephesus in 431 as an example, "to show that Christ is presiding."[6]

This eucharistic theology was still present at the beginning of the ninth century. At the Vatican Pavilion of the New Orleans World's Fair in 1984 I purchased a precise computer-generated copy of a beautiful ninth-century reliquary cover made for Pope Paschal I, 817–824. It was discovered early in this century in a cypress-wood box under the altar of the Oratory of San Lorenzo. The center panel depicts a communion scene with a small, almost square altar upon which loaves of bread and a chalice are visible. But the focus is on the figure of Christ standing at the center behind the altar, symbolizing his presence at the Eucharist. The integrity of the Eucharist does need to be maintained.

Are there not natural, dedicated leaders in even small congregations who could be ordained presbyters without a seminary education or extensive theological training so that the faithful may have the Eucharist? Does not every Christian community have a right to both presbyteral and diaconal leadership? But when presbyters are not available, does not the God revealed by Jesus Christ give his grace to his people gathered in his name? One wonders how

---

5. *Acts of Thomas* 49–50. Based on the edition of A. F. J. Klijn, *The Acts of Thomas* (Leiden: E. J. Brill, 1962). Quoted in Hatchett, "Seven Liturgies," 23.

6. Jungmann, *The Mass of the Roman Rite*, 1:446.

the Church could have spread like wildfire through the Roman world if the first Christians had had such a narrow view of God and his grace. Deacons taking the Eucharist from the celebration to the sick or disabled and others unable to be present is quite a different matter. This distribution should normally follow directly the community's Eucharist. It asserts and strengthens the unity of the body of Christ, extending his presence to the absent and incorporating them into the celebration as parts of the body.

At times in Eastern Orthodoxy, when the reserved sacrament has been administered at the close of the day, it has been distributed at the end of the evening office.[7] In the absence of a priest when communion is desired from the reserved sacrament, a clearer and sounder statement would be made by a deacon's distributing it after Morning or Evening Prayer, preferably with a lay person officiating at the office. The deacon, appropriate to the character of the diaconal order, would not then appear to be substituting for a priest as the presider but serving the community according to his or her office.

Presbyters, Deacons, Laity — Each in Proper Role

Clearly, presiding at the official sacramental liturgies of the Church has been presbyterial or episcopal in nature throughout the ages and is today. Exceptions to this rule should be seen as allowed because of pressing need and should be limited so far as possible to such occasions. The demarcations in the ordained ministries show forth the organic nature of the Church, just as confusing the orders blurs an understanding of the Church as an organic society, the body of Christ.

In all of the Church's rites every effort should be made to have presbyters, deacons, and lay persons present and participating in their proper roles to set forth visibly that the Church, like a body, needs all of its members to be and to do that for which its Lord sent it into the world to be and to do. The symbolic statement made by the priest or pastor assuming virtually all of the functions at liturgies perpetuates the idea that ministry really belongs to that order and that order is alone sufficient. During rites in parishes such as the Daily Office, when it is as appropriate for a lay person to officiate as for one ordained, the laity are affirmed by taking this role while the clergy may either take their place among the people or, on occasion, take their customary places. A presbyter as president of the congregation or a bishop as leader of a diocese would appropriately assume his or her customary place at major liturgies, and it is fitting that the diaconate be similarly represented. At such liturgies vested clergy in the procession and seated together symbolize the Church's universal nature.

Full-time Employment

A review of the pastoral and charitable functions of the diaconate quickly indicates that full-time salaried deacons are not only possible but highly desirable in

_____

7. Marion J. Hatchett reported this in a conversation with me.

some situations. Large parishes and dioceses have many needs that could best be provided by deacons working as full-time employees, trained and skilled in their specialized ministries. Such ministries range from diocesan or parish administrators or Christian education specialists to parish visitors or prison chaplains. As the diaconate grows and as resources become available, these ministries will undoubtedly become more numerous both in numbers and variety.

Symbols of the Unity of Life

The deacons of the early Church, and now, are the ones above all others who bring together the worship (*leiturgia*) and the service (*diakonia*) of the Church, symbolizing the unity of worship and all other forms of ministry, proclaiming the sacredness of all. It is, therefore, important that the functions of liturgy and service, both pastoral and charitable/societal, be given balance in the ministry of individual deacons and of the diaconal community. In that way the essential relationship of liturgy and service is visibly expressed.

Liturgical Functions

The following may be listed as among the proper liturgical functions of the deacon. Related pastoral and/or charitable/societal functions are put in the second column.

1. To carry the paschal candle, chant the Exultet, and assist at Baptism and the Eucharist at the Easter Vigil.	Ministry as servants of the Church.
2. To assist in the administration of Baptism and in cases of necessity to officiate at Baptism.	Readiness to assist others. Ministry in precatechumenate, catechumenate, and postbaptismal catechesis.
3. To announce the stages of the eucharistic Liturgy.	Ministry of representing the Church in helping God's people.
4. To read the Gospel at the Eucharist.	Ministry of the word in teaching, bearing witness in the world, and counseling.
5. To bid the prayers of the people.	Ministry to the sick, the poor, the aged, the unemployed, prisoners, and others who suffer.
6. To prepare the people's oblations at the Eucharist.	Ministry of serving humbly in whatever way is needed and of offering to God the needs, concerns, and lives of his people.

7. To administer the Bread and the Wine of the Eucharist.

Ministry to provide food, clothes, and other physical needs to the poor.

8. To perform the ablutions at the Eucharist.

Ministry of servanthood.

9. To take the eucharistic Bread and Wine to the absent.

Ministry to the sick and disabled.

10. To assist at marriages and to solemnize marriages in the absence of an ordinary minister (bishop or priest) of marriage.

Ministry of premarital instruction, marriage counseling, and to families.

11. To administer Holy Unction to the sick.

Ministry to the sick.

In the Roman Catholic Church today deacons may not anoint. In the Episcopal Church they may do so in case of necessity but using oil blessed by a bishop or priest.

15. To preside at noneucharistic prayer services, such as the Daily Office and nonsacramental penitential rites.

Ministry of prayer.

13. To conduct services in homes for the aged and disabled.

Ministry of visiting the aged and shut-ins.

14. To read services in congregations without a priest or pastor.

Ministry of pastoral concern.

15. To lead the Church's music.

Ministry of glorifying God and of pastoral care and concern for choir members. Ministry to the liturgical needs of a congregation.

16. To officiate at burial rites, except the Eucharist.

Ministry to the dying and their families.

17. To deliver homilies when officiating at a Baptism, marriage, burial, or other liturgical services in place of a priest or pastor.

Ministry of pastoral concern for special needs.

The Roman Church authorizes deacons presiding at such services to preach. On occasions where the deacon is not presiding, he must have the authorization of the bishop. A deacon not trained for preaching could use a sermon prepared by one who is, perhaps adapting it. Burial homilies should focus on Christ's resurrection and ours through him. Ecologies are inconsistent with the Christian understanding of original sin, manifest in all. Numerous homiletical aids are available.

18. To act as master of ceremonies for liturgies.

Ministry of pastoral assistance.

Deacons should be prominently in evidence as normal and necessary ministers in the Church's worship, and especially at Baptism and the Sunday Eucharist. Only in this way can they give visible expression to their dual role, which serves to give unity to their total ministry and that of the Church.

Ceremonial Notes

One of the problems with liturgical reform is the superimposing of old ceremonial accretions on the new rites, sometimes obscuring important aspects of the meaning of the rites. For example, the presence of Christ in the Eucharist and its character as a meal is obscured by treating the eucharistic Sacrament as an object to be worshipped. Although many assume genuflection as a reverence to the Sacrament to have been an ancient practice, it originated as a princely ceremonial and was taken into the liturgy as an honor the clergy paid to bishops. Jungmann reports that the first evidence of a priest genuflecting at the consecration is in the late fourteenth century; and a slight bow of the head, which appears to have begun in the thirteenth century, was prevalent in the fifteenth and continued into at least the sixteenth century in some areas.[8] Liturgical reform has brought about the minimizing or elimination of genuflections during eucharistic celebrations today, implying as they do that the Eucharist is an object and obscuring the meaning of the Eucharist as a meal.

Perhaps the first rule of good ceremonial is that it expresses the theology of the Church and of the particular rites. Good liturgy makes good sense both liturgically and culturally. Good liturgy enhances meaning and deepens faith. It is not sufficient to do something because it has "always" been done that way. There is said to be a church in Italy that had a blank, painted wall near the entrance toward which the people genuflected as they entered, although no one knew why. In doing some renovation it was discovered that underneath the paint on the wall there was a picture of the Virgin, which had been painted over in the distant past and forgotten, that is, except for the genuflections. Obviously, that ceremonial made no sense. In Episcopal churches it was common practice to face the east (or the liturgical east) during the recitation of the creeds and the "Glory to the Father" (Gloria patri), although either practice was difficult to rationalize and few could give any reason for it. I have actually seen Episcopal choirs kneeling in full view of the congregation during the singing of a canticle suddenly stand and face the east at the end of the song in order to be in the "proper" position to add the "Glory to the Father."

In accord with the teaching of Ignatius of Antioch, the custom of one chalice and one loaf on the altar for the Great Thanksgiving is being restored.[9] In the preparation of the altar deacons should place only one chalice and, if needed, one flagon or decanter of wine on the altar. The single chalice and flagon symbolize the oneness of the body of Christ. If additional chalices are needed, they

---

8. Jungmann, *The Mass of the Roman Rite*, 1:123, 2:212, 213.
9. Ignatius, *To the Philadelphians* 4.1, in *Early Christian Fathers*, ed. Richardson, 105.

should be brought to the altar at the time of the communion of the people, wine then being poured into them from the flagon or decanter. Cut-glass decanters, widely available today, serve well as containers for the additional wine. Cruets suggest vinegar, not wine. The mixing of the wine with water comes from our Jewish heritage of the ancient world, in which self-respecting people always added water to their wine. The same symbolic value setting forth our oneness in Christ is given to loaf bread, preferably a single loaf, which must be broken and divided to be distributed among the people of God. Real bread, in addition, helps to connect the Eucharist with daily life and is generally recommended by liturgical authorities today. The use of leavened bread restores the practice of the early Church. Ambrose of Milan wrote, "The bread I have received in Communion is the bread I am accustomed to use every day."[10] Jungmann says that various ordinances appeared in the Western Church in the ninth century directing the use of unleavened bread but that this "new custom" became universal only in the eleventh century.[11] Deacons, if asked, may appropriately assist in the breaking of the Bread and in the elevation of the sacrament inviting the people to receive, as well as in the distribution.

In the early Church the primary time for Baptism was at the Great Vigil of Easter, when the events of salvation history from the creation to the redemption were recalled and made present. Appropriately Pentecost, celebrating the gift of the Spirit to the Church and to the baptized, was also such an occasion. Other times recommended today are All Saints', celebrating the victory of Christ in his people; the Baptism of Christ; and the bishop's visitation, setting forth the association of the baptized with the bishop and the whole Church. Baptism is normally done at the community's primary services at these special times, enabling the community to celebrate Baptism both liturgically and afterwards socially, welcoming the newly baptized into the community.

Large baptismal fonts in which immersion or submersion[12] is possible are needed to express the theology of Baptism, particularly of death and resurrection and of the new birth in Christ. The word "baptize" derives from the Greek *baptizein,* meaning "to dip."[13] Hippolytus reflects the teaching of the early Christians on the desirability of abundant water. He says, "The stream shall flow through the baptismal tank or pour into it from above when there is no scarcity of water; but if there is a scarcity, whether constant or sudden, then use whatever water you can find."[14]

The font should be a major symbol in the building, equal in importance to

---

10. Ambrose, *De sacramentis*, IV, 4 (Quasten, *Mon.*, 158). Quoted in Jungmann, *The Mass of the Roman Rite*, 2:32.

11. Jungmann, *The Mass of the Roman Rite*, 2:33–34.

12. "Immersion" is being used today to mean Baptism with a person being at least partially immersed in water with water poured over the person. Many of the ancient fonts were two and a half to three feet deep, indicating that adults were often not submerged in Baptism. "Submersion" is being used to indicate complete covering by water, as in the *Apostolic Tradition* of Hippolytus.

13. *Webster's Ninth New Collegiate Dictionary*, s.v. "baptize."

14. Hippolytus, *Apostolic Tradition of Hippolytus* 21:1, trans. Easton, 45.

the ambo (pulpit-lectern) as the symbol of the Word and the altar as the symbol of the Eucharist. Anita Stauffer provides an outstanding resource in her video presentation with commentary, *Re-Examining Baptismal Fonts,* showing ancient fonts followed by contemporary examples providing the proper symbol.[15] When inadequate fonts must be used, they should be used with as much water as possible, some of the water being poured with sound and splash prior to its being blessed and then copious amounts poured over the person's head.

The deacon's dismissal should follow the final hymn, or if there is none, the final prayer, so that the congregation can actually leave immediately after it is given.

Liturgy is an action of the community. It follows that, regardless of one's own knowledge or personal preference, the direction of the liturgical leader should be gracefully followed. This leader is normally the presiding presbyter or pastor of a congregation. Some larger congregations have "liturgists" with special knowledge and training in liturgics to act in this capacity. There is certainly precedent from the early Church for deacons to function as the master of ceremonies at liturgies. In the Apostolic Constitutions (c. 380) the deacons facilitate the progress of the Eucharist by announcing its various stages. By so doing the deacon relieves the eucharistic president of responsibility for the flow of the Liturgy and demonstrates the organic nature of the Church. However, to act as "liturgist" for a parish with responsibility for planning and directing the rites, the deacon needs in-depth knowledge both of theology and liturgy.

The norm for the Church's liturgies should be the participation of deacons and laity along with the presbyter in order that the fullness of the Church be evident. Generally, the more who are actively involved in the doing of a liturgy the clearer is the true, corporate nature of the Church set forth. This concept needs to be emphasized today as we strive to recover the principles incorporated into the reformed rites. For centuries the presbyter or priest "did it all." Although we recognize today that such a liturgical monopoly is both inconsistent with the theology and practice of the early Church and of the reformed rites and is detrimental to the life of the Christian community, old customs often subtly persist to undermine the teaching. This means that deacons and lay lectors should be included in such rites as weddings and funerals as well as the Sunday Liturgy. Altar servers (acolytes in Anglicanism) are also desirable.

It is far better to err on the side of simplicity than elaboration or exaggeration. Thus, if it is customary to make some reverence toward the altar, bowing or genuflecting upon entering and again upon leaving the church for a liturgy is sufficient. Ostentation and unnatural actions are to be avoided. For example, it is both ostentatious and unnatural for crucifers to hold the staff of a processional cross with the backs of their hands held toward their bodies and their elbows

---

15. Stauffer traces the history of Baptism and baptismal theology through an impressive collection of video pictures of ancient fonts and contemporary examples: S. Anita Stauffer, *Re-Examining Baptismal Fonts: Baptismal Space for the Contemporary Church,* 36 minutes (St. John's Abbey, Collegeville, Minn.: Liturgical Press, 1991).

horizontal to the floor, some also wearing white gloves, or for others to swing a censor in full circles or produce clouds of incense. The same applies to the deacon carrying the gospel book overhead at arms' length. The size of a building is to be considered. A gesture that might be appropriate in a large building could look ostentatious or unnatural in a small church.

Documents from the third and fourth centuries mention an elevated place from which the Gospel and other Scripture were read. The Council of Laodicea (343–381) uses the term "ambo" for the reading desk or lectern placed on this podium, the word being derived from a Greek verb meaning "to mount or climb." A single place for the reading and preaching of the Scripture provides a unified symbol for the word and is recommended. In churches today using both a lectern and a pulpit the Gospel should be read from the pulpit, creating a visual, symbolic connection between the reading and preaching of the Gospel. There is also ancient precedent for the prayers of the people to be bid from the ambo, an ancient function of the deacon, and for the gradual psalm to be said or sung from there as well.[16]

A gospel procession to the ambo with the deacon being preceded by torch-bearers, who stand on either side facing the deacon for the gospel reading, is appropriate, honoring Christ who is as present in his word as he is in his sacrament. Its ancient origin, Jungmann says, is to be seen in the testimony of Jerome (d. c. 420) that lights were lighted in all the churches of the east for the reading of the Gospel. A crucifer in this procession, a development of the later Middle Ages, is unnecessary and frequently obtrusive during the reading. Originally incense was simply carried in the procession to the ambo, censing of the gospel book being mentioned only since the eleventh century.[17] The gospel procession to the midst of the congregation for the proclamation of the Gospel was an experiment of the 1950s which proved unsatisfactory, although it continues in many churches. The practice, first of all, separated the Gospel from the sermon and the other readings, symbolically dividing the symbol of the word. In addition, the reading is less effective due to many being unable to see the person reading. The principle here, that the people be able to see the person speaking, is equally applicable to the deacon leading the prayers, and to others. Even in small groups where there is great simplicity in a liturgy, it is appropriate that those reading Scripture or leading prayers stand where they may be easily seen, usually at the front of the group.

The custom of the deacon seeking a blessing from the presiding celebrant before reading the Gospel, found in the eleventh-century Missa Illyrica and frequently afterwards in other documents,[18] raises serious theological questions regarding the theology of Baptism and by extension of the laity. In Baptism all receive the Holy Spirit and are incorporated into the royal priesthood of

---

16. Jungmann, *The Mass of the Roman Rite,* 1:411–12.
17. Ibid., 1:445, 446, 451–52.
18. Ibid., 1:454.

Christ. Although the Church authorizes and empowers presbyters and bishops to exercise certain functions of its priestly ministry on behalf of all and the Spirit gives grace for these, the ordained minister is not made holier than others among the baptized. All stand before God as priests and as equals. The Church today affirms this theology and calls its people to live into its full meaning. The theology of Baptism, of the laity, and of the diaconate is denigrated by this Medieval custom.

The Church's liturgies are expressions of its theology. At a national conference of Episcopal diocesan liturgical leaders in 1982, Louis Weil pointed to a significant problem in the Episcopal Church, where priests may vest as deacons for diaconal roles in the liturgies, a practice prohibited in both the Eastern Orthodox and Roman Catholic traditions. Weil observes,

> In both the Eastern Orthodox and Roman Catholic traditions an ordained person is inhibited from vesting with the signs of another order. A priest may not vest as a deacon. Liturgical ministries are seen as integrally linked to the Church's pastoral ministry. The liturgical expression corresponds to a real pastoral relationship with the community. These are not merely roles for which one puts on one costume one time and another costume another time. This practice among Orthodox and Roman Catholics is not liturgical fussiness. It is based in a theological understanding of ordained ministry. Yet in the Episcopal Church we do not take this matter seriously and we continue to have priests playing the role of deacon or other variations on the theme.[19]

Weil cites several examples that were not uncommon and continue in many places. One was of a liturgy that he attended at which the bishop presided, a priest took the role of deacon, a deacon was the server, the bishop read the epistle, and the priest read the Gospel. He observed that "if we believe in a threefold ministry that has some kind of authenticity, then we really can't play that kind of charade."[20] The ministry of each of the orders is articulated in the Liturgy by a particular set of relationships. "It's not what you are wearing" but rather the theology behind it that concerns him. He speaks of the relationships established by liturgical roles,

> When I have presided at the Eucharist and placed the Eucharist into the hand of the person over any period of time, my pastoral identity for them is linked to those acts. And then suddenly I put on a costume which says for now I'm pretending I can't do those things. It's intolerable....It's a confusion of signs. Are we serious about the threefold orders or is it merely liturgical charade to permit fancy vesture to distinguish roles which really have no true connection with our theology of orders?...The orders are an expression in the Liturgy of the

---

19. Louis Weil, lecture at the conference of the Association of Diocesan Liturgy and Music Commissions, Chicago, November 8–11, 1982, taped by the author. Later printed in *Open* (the newsletter of Associated Parishes), Alexandria, Va. Weil is a professor of liturgics at the Church Divinity School of the Pacific (Episcopal) and the consortium associated with it, Berkeley, California.

20. Ibid.

reality of distinct forms of service within the Christian community, and they must signify with consistency and integrity, or else we are playing a liturgical game.[21]

Weil's words deserve the attention of the Episcopal clergy and perhaps others. There is no place in the Church for this kind of "charade," whether it is based on power or a sentimental attachment by priests and bishops to their transitional diaconate.

Pastoral Functions

The pastoral and charitable functions of the diaconate are usually considered together, and certainly no absolute distinction exists. There is a sense in which what is pastoral is charitable and vice versa. However, in the Church over the centuries we have become far too accustomed to think of ministry primarily in terms of the Church's ministering to its own people. Much of this attitude stems from the time when Church and State in the Western world were two names for the same society in which virtually everyone belonged to both. But today, this is far from true. There are large numbers of unbaptized adults in Western society, and many who are baptized are at best nominal Christians. Modern communication and transportation have also brought the peoples of the world much closer together. Christians urgently need to reform their habitual way of thinking. Therefore, in order to give greater emphasis to ways in which the Church's ministry can and should reach out beyond the confines of the Church into the world, a division is made here between its pastoral and charitable functions, the former having more to do with the Church's care for the welfare and nurture of its own people and the latter more with its concern for those in the world outside.

The proper pastoral functions of the deacon are broad and varied. The following functions are ordinarily primarily focused upon ministry to the Church's own people and illustrate the kinds of things they might encompass:

1. To visit the sick and the shut-ins.

2. To care for and about the parish's poor.

3. To coordinate programs for visiting and integrating newcomers.

4. To visit prospects for entering the Church.

5. To instruct adults in the precatechumenate, catechumenate, and postbaptismal catechesis, which is sometimes called mystagogy, and others, who come baptized, on parallel tracks.

6. To instruct parents and godparents for baptisms.

7. To lead small study/prayer/sharing groups.

---

21. Ibid.

8. To organize and head groups and activities to serve special needs within the Christian community.

9. To train acolytes or altar servers.

10. To work with student groups.

11. To teach the children of the Church.

12. To lead parish discussion groups.

13. To organize and coordinate retreats, workshops, and similar activities.

14. To coordinate ushers or "parish hosts."

15. To develop youth programs and activities.

16. To counsel those with problems.

17. To coordinate and train lectors.

18. To assume responsibility for some aspect of parish or diocesan administration.

19. To fill in the "gaps" in a parish.

Charitable/Societal Functions

In a highly sophisticated, complex industrial society such as ours, Christian ministry can be and increasingly is exercised in numerous and sometimes imaginative ways. However, categorizing and listing such functions, as we have in the liturgical and pastoral areas, does not do justice to *diakonia* with the special character here classified as charitable or charitable/societal. Such a list might include the following, again simply as illustrative:

1. To help and befriend the powerless who are in need, both individually and through political action and social programs: prisoners, minorities, the poor, the rejected.

2. To counsel the troubled.

3. To work in referral programs to help those in crisis situations.

4. To lead or work in community action groups to effect social change.

5. To organize and promote community activities or programs to meet special needs: unwed parents, single parents, people with AIDS, community "soup" kitchens, food pantries, released prisoners, addictive behavior such as drug, alcohol, or food dependencies, and so on.

6. To work with juveniles and adults in hospitals, prisons, orphanages, half-way houses, and other institutions.

7. To serve youth in various educational and recreational programs, as AIDS or chemical abuse awareness, athletic programs in inner-city neighborhoods, tutoring disadvantaged youth, foster care, counseling pregnant teenagers.

8. To care for the needs of the elderly and disabled: providing in home meals or nursing care, transportation, visiting, minor home repairs, promoting handicapped accessibility to public buildings and rest rooms, promoting adequate health care.

9. To visit the lonely and neglected, especially those in prisons, nursing homes, and other institutions.

10. To work with the handicapped.

11. To provide halfway houses and employment assistance to those leaving institutions, such as prisons and treatment centers for addictive behavior.

These activities serve to illustrate the kinds of charitable/societal functions that are proper to the diaconate. However, the possibilities for these functions seem far more numerous, challenging, and creative than a list such as this might imply.

The diaconate should serve to enable and encourage those in varied occupations and life situations to develop special ministries of service, although these do not lend themselves to precise categories. Some of these ministries would be natural outgrowths of occupational vocations. A nurse or a lawyer might give part of his or her time to service in a free clinic on a regular and continuing basis. Such service, enlightened and informed by the Holy Spirit, is a *diakonia* of love and rises above the level of mere social service.

A teacher might offer special classes or personal instruction to children with learning problems. A salesperson could offer time and expertise to teach volunteers how to "sell" charitable organizations to prospective supporters to raise needed financial support. A carpenter, an electrician, or a "handyman" might use his or her particular knowledge and skills by setting aside time to help the elderly, and especially the elderly poor, maintain their homes or, perhaps, to work with the younger poor to upgrade theirs. I was delighted to be picked up at the airport by one such "handyman" deacon in his tool-filled van when I was to speak at a conference on the diaconate. A psychologist might offer counsel or lead a support group for men and women who befriend children of single-parent homes. Another might conduct classes in child-rearing for young couples.

Others may develop ministries in other ways. A woman who has recovered from breast cancer could have a real ministry in teaching groups of women the procedures urged for early detection. One woman who battled breast cancer for fourteen years became as an angel of light as she visited others, bringing them faith, hope, and inner peace, especially to those with cancer, but also to others. She is the only person I recall who would offer prayer for me after I prayed for her. A "recovering" alcoholic could help others similarly afflicted, as has been repeatedly demonstrated by members of Alcoholics Anonymous. "Recovering" drug abusers can be equally effective. A father or mother whose children have left home might offer much to boys or girls from single-parent homes over the years as a "big brother" or "big sister" to them or as a foster parent to children needing placement or to more troubled youth in other programs of this nature.

Many have hobbies or knowledge and/or special talents that may be utilized in the service of others. Using one's talents to teach crafts and hobbies in such places as regional mental health centers or senior citizen centers can constitute an important and vital ministry. Offering one's services in continuing work with youth in sponsoring a basketball team or coaching wrestling, swimming, karate, or judo at a YMCA or community center can be equally the work of Christ.

The kinds of service that might properly be seen to be appropriate functions for the charitable/societal ministry of the deacon seem almost endless, so many and varied are the needs of people in modern society. However, it is not simply in the doing of these things that we find either diaconal or Christian ministry. The work becomes a true ministry when it is motivated by the desire to serve Christ in those ministered to under the tutelage of the Holy Spirit and is done with caring love. There comes to it a quality of joyful love and perseverance that often is not otherwise present. Although the person involved in such work tends to find it rewarding and fulfilling, he or she is motivated more by the needs of others than by self-satisfaction. If duty is involved, it is a duty transformed by love. Christian *diakonia* tends to have a distinctive character, flowing as it does from a life committed to Christ, empowered by his Holy Spirit, informed by his word, made loving through prayer, and made humble through Christ-like service.

Why Ordination

Ordination to the diaconate of some of those who render such service in the name of Christ, or seek to do so, serves a number of important purposes. Some of those which come to mind are these. First, ordination is the certification that this person represents the Church in his or her ministry. Second, the Church officially affirms that the things done in this ministry are expressions of its concerns. Third, in the ministries of many deacons, the concept of Christian ministry is broadened both in the eyes of Christians and of the world, bringing reality to the love the Church professes. The diaconate asserts that we who call ourselves by the name of Christ are called to be servants. Fourth, the symbol of *diakonia* is embodied and made real in areas that are meaningful to contemporary society. The Church is visibly reaching out into the world and is seen to care about the needs of all humanity. Fifth, the distinctive Christian workstyle and lifestyle of these deacons provides a model and witness to inform others of what it can mean to live and work as a Christian in their world.

Symbolically, each of these deacons by virtue of the diaconal office asserts the unity of the "sacred" and the "secular," of all of life, another witness much needed in the midst of our fragmented world. And last, but of great importance, such ministries are "strengthened by sacramental grace," as Pope Paul VI has affirmed.[22] The quality of these ministries is enriched and their vitality enhanced.

It is readily apparent that a corps of deacons in a parish could not only relieve the overwhelming burden borne by the clergy today but would multiply the ef-

---

22. Paul VI, *Approval of a New Rite*, 5.

fective ministry of the Church both among its own people and in the community around it manyfold.

Training for the Restored Diaconate

The character of the diaconate as a full and equal order requires a radically different philosophy of training than that which shapes and informs training programs of the seminaries for the "transitional deacon" aspiring to the priesthood or of those programs essentially based on the seminary model. The fundamental problem with these programs for the restored diaconate is that their underlying philosophy defines ministry in terms of the traditional ministry of the presbyter or pastor. Such programs perpetuate the Medieval notion that ministry is clerical, a gift of ordination, not of Baptism, and that ministry is for most intents and purposes exercised in and for the Church. They encourage, if not create, the image of the deacon as a reduced version of the priest or pastor. If indeed all the baptized are ministers of the Church engraced by the Holy Spirit with differing gifts for varied ministries, as the early Church so clearly understood, then what justification is there for insisting that every order of the clerical ministry, regardless of its function, be theologically trained with the same model, even if differing in degree? Why, in fact, should deacons have more theological formation than lay men and women should?

The guidelines for the formation and ministry of Roman Catholic deacons in the United States clearly recognize the distinctive role of the diaconate and advocate a different model for deacons:

> The priesthood and the diaconate are neither identical nor competitive, but, rather, complementary ministries. The diaconate is not an abridged form of priesthood, but a distinct and full order in its own right. Both priests and deacons should understand, then, that the diaconate is not to be thought of or exercised on the model of the priesthood.[23]

The fundamental problem here does not lie in theological training for the diaconate. Rather, as we have seen, it is a lack of Christian formation among the baptized. Were Christian formation generally adequate, as it was through the formation process of the early Church, notably the catechumenate, further theological training of lay persons for most diaconal ministries would be as unnecessary as it was in the early period. Is not the needed solution for both the renewal of lay and of ordained diaconal ministry to correct the deficiencies in basic Christian formation? More adequate Christian formation of the baptized would greatly facilitate our seminaries in fulfilling their proper role of preparing candidates for clerical office and of providing advanced theological education for others who need or desire it instead of expending much time and energy on basic formation. In fact, would not such formation for the baptized in itself also

---

23. Bishops' Committee, *Permanent Deacons*, 1984 rev., par. 121, p. 45.

dilute the belief that full commitment leads to ordination, a belief that results in significant numbers seeking ordination whose gifts are for lay ministry?

When the ministry is conceived of functionally with all members having a ministry, it is apparent that what might be called professional theological training and qualifications are neither required nor desirable for most. This principle is recognized in the report of a group of sixty bishops, other clergy, and lay people of the Episcopal Church who met in 1964 to consider the requisites of a "self-supporting ministry." The group asserts that seminary training for most of those entering self-supporting or nonstipendiary ministry is not necessary and probably not desirable.[24] The guidelines of the Roman Catholic U.S. Bishops' Committee regarding theological training or formation for the diaconate also state that "the needs of the Church and the diaconal ministries envisaged as a response to them must direct the preparation of men for this ministry."[25] This philosophy is reinforced by the guidelines in the section on "Theological Formation." After observing that the program is designed to prepare candidates for pastoral ministry, the guidelines state:

> The theological program should therefore be oriented toward ministry, providing the candidate with the knowledge and appreciation of the faith that he needs in order to be able to carry out his ministry of Word, sacrament, and service.... Theological formation should take into account the general needs of diaconal service in the communities for which a man is to be ordained. It should be constructed in such a way that a candidate is helped to evaluate his society and culture in light of the Gospel and to understand the Gospel in light of the particular features of the society and culture in which he will be serving. This permits and requires a certain amount of latitude in the construction of theological programs and in the evaluation of candidates' performances.[26]

When the subjects enumerated in the guidelines for theological formation are interpreted in this context, the process becomes one tailored for diaconal, not priestly, ministry.[27]

The character of diaconal ministry is *service.* Careful consideration of this representative ministry of *diakonia,* embodied in the ordained deacon, leads to the conclusion that professional training in the theological disciplines is neither designed for nor needed by most forms of this ministry. Although in recent years many training programs have moved away from the seminary model, the most serious error in the training programs continues to be the use of that model. This is as might be expected, the image of the deacon having been that of the transitional diaconate for many centuries and no other model being available. The character and nature of the diaconate is not yet clear or well defined even

---

24. *A Self-Supporting Ministry*, 5. Though this statement appears in a section of the report relating to "a Self-Supporting Priesthood," the report later states that this applies also to deacons.

25. Bishops' Committee, *Permanent Deacons*, 1984 rev., par. 69, p. 30.

26. Ibid., par. 75–76, pp. 31–32.

27. Ibid., par. 78, p. 32, for listing of subjects required.

among the clergy. In the minds of most there is a real, if unconscious, picture of the deacon as a somewhat diminished version of a priest or pastor.

This error was tacitly acknowledged in a letter written to me in 1977 from the Roman Catholic director of the Permanent Diaconate Program of the Archdiocese of Omaha and President of the Association of Permanent Diaconate Directors, a priest, Patrick McCaslin. He wrote regarding the weakness of their program:

> We have gone from a seminary model of education, with a teacher talking at them, to our present methodology which utilizes facilitators directing and guiding but with the men and women doing all the reading, reflecting and responding in small groups of eight.[28]

A personal visit to one such group in early 1979 did reveal that at least in this archdiocese the seminary model had given way to the small study/sharing group model. The group and the meeting observed were apparently typical of the program. The group consisted of five men, one already a deacon who had been ordained in an earlier program, and their wives. They met in the home of a parish priest, who acted as group facilitator. One couple was responsible for the opening prayers or prayer time. Most of the evening was devoted to discussion-type study based on two chapters of a book currently in use in a religion course in one of the diocesan high schools. A series of study questions in mimeographed form, originally prepared for the high school class, formed the basis for discussion, which had considerable depth and revealed profound understanding of and concern for the gospel.

The diaconal candidates were learning to think theologically. In many, perhaps most, ways it was typical of small group meetings of committed lay people concerned with Christian growth which occur in parishes throughout the United States today. The study course, in this instance on Christian ethics, was presented in nontechnical terms. It provided the input needed to prevent the group from being what has become all too common in American Christianity of recent years, a sharing group of what has been termed "pooled ignorance." The Omaha program has been altered to some extent with a change in directors but follows much the same pattern.

Although the approval and support of a spouse is essential for married diaconal candidates, there is no compelling reason that the spouse be required to participate in the training or formation program. In churches with centuries of experience with married priests or pastors, the spouse is not required to be involved on this level. The spouse may not be called to the diaconate and may have other interests and obligations to pursue, while at the same time able to be supportive and enthusiastic of the diaconal ministry.

The School of Theology of the University of the South, an Episcopal institution, has developed a somewhat unique training program designed for

---

28. Letter dated July 8, 1977, to me.

ecumenical use in training for lay ministry called "Education for Ministry" (EFM).[29] A considerable number of Episcopal dioceses have recommended the program for diaconal candidates. Although it presents what is called the "core curriculum" of a seminary, the program is not that of a seminary model. In four years the traditional disciplines of a theological seminary are interwoven within the framework of following the story of the people of God. The content is imparted through individual study each week from books prepared for the program with optional supplemental reading suggested. The weekly group meetings are concerned with theological reflection on incidents from the lives of participants. Problem solving is not permitted. Content is of a high caliber and is ecumenically oriented, so that the program is used by other denominations as well and has spread to several continents. Such training programs as that described of the Archdiocese of Omaha and Education for Ministry are far more appropriate for the functions of the diaconate than those based on the seminary model provide.

It should be recognized that although most deacons are not full-time paid employees of the Church a restored diaconate does include deacons professionally trained to serve the Church as full-time salaried workers. In some areas, such as diocesan directors of Christian education, a seminary program might be desirable. In others, for example, parish administration, stewardship promotion, secretarial work, evangelism promotion, Church music, or Christian counseling (such as family or penal), their training might consist of a specially designed program combining appropriate seminary and college work. Seminaries should develop and offer suitable programs to provide for these needs.

The canonical requirements of the Episcopal diaconate, revised in recent years, have moved in the direction of diaconal training on a nonseminary model by providing for the ordination of "local priests and deacons."[30] This category is designed to meet the needs of small or remote communities or those with distinct ethnic character which cannot be adequately provided with the sacraments and pastoral ministries by clergy who have met the requirements of the more demanding, traditional process. However, the canon specifies that deacons ordained through this process may be called by a congregation of the type described and its bishop even though the sacraments are regularly available. Local priests and deacons are to be more mature than those ordained in the more traditional process and are to be called to the offices by their congregations and bishops, normally being members of the congregations calling them. The requirements for theological study are significantly modified and are those appropriate for lay people generally. After ordination, local deacons and priests are licensed to serve the communities for which they have been ordained and are expected to remain there, although a process is provided for their being licensed elsewhere.

However, the educational requirements set forth by the Episcopal canons for the diaconate in its communities of mainstream America, those not falling

---

29. Education for Ministry (EFM), School of Theology Extension Center, Sewanee, Tenn.
30. *Constitutions and Canons (1991)*, III.9, pp. 72–74.

under the description applicable to "local priests and deacons," continue to be based on the seminary model but suggest reduced proficiency. A possible saving grace of the requirements is that the bishop is to determine the time and the extent of the course of study of diaconal candidates. Deacons ordained under the provisions of this canon are not transitional deacons and, should any wish to become a priest, must comply with the more extensive educational requirements of transitional deacons before ordination to the priesthood.[31]

Implications of Training Models

A diaconate that no longer accommodates those called to the presbyterate is clearly seen to have different qualifications and requirements. Not only is there no inherent suggestion of the priesthood, but a deacon who did afterwards feel called or was called by a Christian community to the ordained ministry of priest or pastor would clearly and canonically be required to undergo appropriate training for that ministry, training that would certainly usually mean the seminary itself or, at least, that based on its model.

All Christians need theological training. But it is difficult to justify the need for deacons to have extensive training beyond that of properly formed laity unless such training is directly related to the special ministry a particular deacon is to perform. Certainly, if a deacon is to lead a Bible study group, he or she would benefit by special training in that area, as would any other. But the principle involved here is to train deacons for their *diakonia,* not to make them a kind of "paraprofessional" similar to the "paramedics" in the medical profession.

Training programs that tend to make the deacon a "paraprofessional" or quasi-priest are actually disparaging to the order. They involve an implied assumption that the priesthood is the higher order and forms the essential model for the diaconate, a view that is increasingly being recognized. So long as the transitional diaconate remains, the diaconate will not be the full and equal order that will hold the image of the servant-Christ before the Church and the world as the model for all ministry.

Were preaching an inherent function of the diaconate, as it has often been thought to be, then significantly more comprehensive theological education would be important in the training of diaconal candidates. Undoubtedly, part of the impetus for seminary-type preparation has been due to this assumption. However, as has been conclusively shown, preaching was never a function belonging to the diaconate in the early Church. To make it so now is neither helpful nor desirable, confusing as it does the diaconate and the presbyterate, but in fact is counterproductive. Of course, there will be some deacons along with some lay people who are eminently qualified and possess a charisma of the Spirit for preaching. These should by all means be specially licensed by the Church.

---

31. Ibid., III.6.4(a), p. 65. Compare with the requirements of the transitional diaconate, III.6.10, 7.5(a), p. 68.

The Roman Catholic Church in the United States currently authorizes deacons to preach on occasions when they officiate or preside at a sacramental or liturgical rite. But it is to be remembered that they preach then because they preside, not because they are deacons. Presiding is a presbyteral or episcopal function. The Bishops' Committee on the Liturgy's Study Test VI, *The Deacon, Minister of Word and Sacrament,* lists these occasions on which the deacon may preach when presiding: Baptism of infants and some of the adult rites of Christian initiation, matrimony, benediction of the blessed Sacrament, a wake or Christian burial service apart from the Eucharist or in a cemetery, Morning or Evening Prayer or other rites of the liturgy of the hours, and the visitation of the sick.[32] When the deacon presides at such services, preaching is often desirable, but provision might better be made by providing the deacon with a homily prepared for the purpose by one properly trained in theology and homiletics. Deacons should, of course, make adaptations for the particular occasion and should not feel compelled to follow the text slavishly, giving it vitality by making it as much their own as possible. Would it not be generally better for the deacon, the congregation, and the Church to meet this need in this way?

Liturgical preaching by the deacon on occasions such as the Eucharist requires the bishop's authorization or approval by "diocesan norms" in the Roman Church.[33] The ordination rites of the Episcopal Church clearly designate liturgical preaching as a function of the priest or the bishop. The deacon is to assist bishops and priests in the "ministration of God's Word and Sacraments."[34] The character of the diaconate is servanthood, not the role of leadership expressed through presiding and its accompanying activities. Further, the Church needs the *diakonia* in its ordained diaconate of persons with real gifts for diaconal ministry who would hesitate, perhaps rightly so, to be ordained to an office carrying with it the obligation of preaching. As Paul says, we have differing gifts. We should honor the differences in the body of Christ.

Wilhelm Schamoni writes in relation to the problem of diaconal training that a "genuinely spiritual man," who has demonstrated by the "way he brings up his children and presides in his home that he could just as well preside in the House of God," does not necessarily need to acquire special knowledge or undergo any special training and could be ordained without lengthy preparation. Boone Porter emphasizes the same point when he observes, "indeed it is the depth of personal commitment to Jesus Christ, compassion, love of the scriptures, and the ability to communicate the faith to others, that are primary needs for a deacon."[35]

Those earning their own living with family and social responsibilities frequently do not have sufficient time for extensive diaconal training. As Richard Rashke affirms, too much training will keep qualified individuals away while

---

32. Bishops' Committee on the Liturgy, *The Deacon, Minister of Word and Sacrament,* 46.
33. Ibid.
34. *Book of Common Prayer and Administration of the Sacraments,* 531, 543.
35. Schamoni, *Married Men as Ordained Deacons,* 36; Porter, *Canons on New Forms of Ministry,* 7.

too little will give the program a bad reputation.[36] Is not the kind of Christian formation most would consider reasonable and desirable for lay persons actually sufficient today as it was in the early Church? Formation or training that is beyond this and not related to the functions of the diaconate will inevitably prove burdensome and exclude many who are qualified and who would enhance and enrich the Church by using their special gifts and abilities in the specific ministry of the deacon.

In writing of the restored diaconate Karl Rahner advocates this type of religious training. He recognizes that there need to be differences in different areas and situations. The religious training of what he terms the "absolute" deacon (not transitional) should "correspond to what is customary and possible in the case of an educated Christian layman in a particular region." He also speaks of the need for professional training for the particular work they will do, as a welfare or social worker, a catechist, or an ecclesiastical administrator.[37]

Cardinal Suenens of Belgium, who enjoys the respect of Christians of all communions throughout the world, has recommended that those who are already doing diaconal services should be ordained.[38] The "Decree on the Missionary Activity of the Church" of Vatican II affirms Cardinal Suenens's belief and recommends the ordination of those so serving the Church. The council urges the restoration of the diaconate where episcopal conferences approve this and goes on to say

> For there are men who are actually carrying out the functions of the deacon's office, either by preaching the Word of God as catechists, or by presiding over scattered Christian communities in the name of the pastor and the bishop, or by practicing charity in social or relief work. It will be helpful to strengthen them by that imposition of hands which has come down from the apostles, and to bind them more closely to the altar. Thus they can carry out their ministry more effectively because of the sacramental grace of the diaconate.[39]

In the Episcopal Church one of its leading scholars of this century, Massey Shepherd, similarly suggested that there are lay readers doing such diaconal service who should simply be ordained.[40] Additional preordination training seems unnecessary for these.

The Content of Programs

Diaconal training programs should center upon the liturgical, pastoral, and charitable/societal functions of these ministries. They should include the following:

---

36. Rashke, *The Deacon in Search of Identity*, 69.
37. Rahner, *Later Writings*, 5:312.
38. Echlin, *The Deacon in the Church Past and Future*, 117.
39. "Decree on the Missionary Activity of the Church" 2.3.16, in *Documents of Vatican II*, ed. Abbott, 605.
40. Personal communication to me.

1. A study of the diaconate itself.

2. An examination of the meaning of personal commitment. The biblical view of the Christian as one totally committed to God, offering all one is and has to God, should be examined and applied in depth.

3. Emphasis on spiritual development. Instruction should include discussion of prayer and the spiritual life. Each candidate should be committed to using the means of spiritual growth. Special attention should be given to the Sunday Eucharist, daily prayer, regular personal use of the Scriptures, and participation in the total life of the Christian community.

4. A review of the Church's basic teaching. Primary areas of instruction in this adult-level review would be the Holy Scriptures; Christian doctrine particularly relating to the Creeds, the Sacraments, and the nature of the Church and its ministry; prayer and Christian worship; the history of the Church; and Christian conduct or ethics.

5. A general knowledge of the Bible. Although this is included under item 4, it is of sufficient importance to list separately. Deacons as adult members of the Church generally should have a sound knowledge of its Scripture and know how to use it responsibly. Training in this area should include how to think theologically about any problems presented to them, whether in the Church or in the world.

6. Specific training in the particular ministry or ministries anticipated for the respective diaconal candidate, when appropriate. This may be practical or theoretical or both.

7. Participation in a "support group" within the parish structure, if possible. The primary emphasis here should be on the Christian community. Any tendency toward an "elitism" or "exclusivism" that could occur if such a group is composed of deacons from a single parish should be avoided.[41]

8. Participation in a continuing support program for deacons. This program would include meetings of deacons on a regular basis, as need indicates, in both parishes and regional or diocesan areas.

Length of Training

The time needed for the training and testing of the more mature diaconal candidate prior to ordination could well be less than the three years called for in the U.S. Roman Catholic program or perhaps the year and nine months normally required in the Episcopal Church,[42] providing adequate Christian formation has taken place earlier and candidates have demonstrated their Christian

---

41. Interestingly, the diaconal candidates I visited in their two-year preordination training program in the Archdiocese of Omaha began apparently as members of a nonchanging diaconal group but afterwards were shuffled at regular intervals.

42. Bishops' Committee, *Permanent Deacons*, par. 73, p. 31. *Constitutions and Canons* (1991), III.5.1(b), p. 64, and III.6.2, p. 65. The Episcopal canon provides that "under special circumstances" the time may be shortened to fifteen months: nine months in a program of preparation (though only six months as a postulant) and six months as a candidate.

commitment, fitness for this ministry, and stability by their life in the Christian community over a period of at least several years. The minimum age for ordination of "local deacons" of the Episcopal Church, referred to above, is 32 years and standards of learning are modified. "Local deacons" need not fulfill the minimum time for study or preparation required of other deacons, so that their ordination could take place in as little as one year. For such candidates a year would, in many instances at least, give ample time both for adequate preparation and for testing the vocation to this form of ministry.[43] However, until basic Christian formation is more adequate and more experience is gained with the diaconate, it is probably better normally to require a two-year process for diaconal training and testing prior to ordination, more to allow time for testing than for training.

Examination and Admission to Candidacy

Examination of those in the diaconal program should be more concerned with sincerity of commitment and purpose than content of knowledge. The quality of ministry being done by individuals is more indicative of whether they should move on in the process than the answers they might give to examination questions. Following approval, it is fitting and proper that formal admission take place at a public service, one that would best take place in the candidate's parish church when the congregation is gathered, as in the context of the Sunday Eucharist. A comparable type of public commissioning of lay people to lay ministries would also be singularly appropriate, giving visual expression to the fullness of the Church's ministry.

Continuing Education

Continuing education should be an on-going process so long as the deacon remains active in this ministry. In this connection it should be emphasized that one of the most important aspects of postordination training and sustenance involves participation where possible in a support system involving other deacons, as has been previously suggested. Conferences led by scholars and other authorities in areas ranging from Scripture, contemporary ethical questions, or the spiritual life to church architecture and music can benefit not only the deacons but those to whom they minister and the Church at large. Although not considered "education," traditional retreats with conducted meditations and silence may add depth to the spiritual life.

Experience in diaconal training or formation will lead to deeper insight into the content and character needed in these programs and facilitate molding those of the future. At the present time those responsible for formulating diaconal programs need beware of the seminary model and think in terms of the diaconate as a distinct ministry in and of itself constituting a major component of the

---

43. *Constitution and Canons* (1991), III.9.1(a), (b)(1), p. 72, and 2(b), p. 73; Porter, *Canons on New Forms of Ministry*, 7.

ministry of the baptized. Realistically, deficiencies in Christian formation need be addressed, but beyond that the emphasis should be on training related to the diaconal ministries of the candidates. The training of devout and committed lay people, which puts training for their *diakonia* at the heart of the program, will encourage a broad spectrum of candidates with many diverse gifts, often already developed, to seek the diaconate and will provide the Church with an abundance of Christ-like symbols to recall all the people of God to their servant ministries.

Chapter 13

The Wholeness of the Church

The renewal of the diaconate envisioned here involves no less than its restoration as a full and equal order. This does not, of course, mean a reconstruction of the office as it was in the early Church but rather its renewal in the modern world to serve the Church in terms of our own day and our particular needs. The deacon will again be the symbol par excellence of the servant-Christ and the whole mission of service given by him to us his people. The office of the deacon will then again be the measure by which all ministry is taken, it being the representative form of the whole.

The implications of the restoration of the integrity of the diaconate are so far-reaching and profound that we can only begin to see them. No less than the nature of the Church and its wholeness is involved.

The restoration of the diaconate as a full and equal order would go a long way toward recovery of a truly organic conception of the Church and its ministry as is found in the New Testament. Probably no single step could do more to bring about expansion of lay ministry in the Church today than making deacons of those who will in the minds of most remain "lay people." Perhaps we shall begin to recover the original and total ministry of the apostolic and pre-Nicene Church in which all are "laity." Perhaps we shall find again the essential oneness of creation seen in Jesus' incarnation as the "sacred" and the "secular" are united in the deacon of today. Perhaps the Church shall again be a servant people who will astound the world and bring forth the accolade, "See how they love one another!"

Could it be that the form of ministry the Church chose so long ago to designate by the lowly term "servant" will be that form which will again make us and the gospel we bear of our Servant-Lord credible to the world?

Appendix

The Archdeacon

The office of archdeacon appears in the latter part of the fourth century. The first reference to the office is that of Optatus, bishop of Milevis, writing c. 365.[1] It is significant that the term was originally used to designate the "bishop's deacon" and not the chief deacon.[2] The importance of recognizing the meaning of the designation is the clear implication that at this time in the latter half of the fourth century one deacon in particular was assistant to the bishop, not all the deacons as is frequently assumed. Jerome mentions archdeacons as an order and says that every church has a single archdeacon. After his time they are common in both the East and the West.[3] However, the direction of the Spanish Council of Merida in 666 that "every bishop shall have in his cathedral an archpresbyter, archdeacon, and primiclerus" suggests that the practice may not have been universal.[4] The archdeacon was, for many centuries, in deacons' orders.

As the diaconate in general declined in the early Middle Ages, the position of the archdeacon increased in importance. Although the letters of Pope Leo, 453, in which he objects to Bishop Anatolius of Constantinople removing Archdeacon Aetius from office by making him a presbyter "under the pretense of promotion" may not be genuine, they serve to illustrate the importance of the office in the fifth century.[5] Archdeacons were assistants and sometimes representatives of the bishops, particularly in the administrative and governmental affairs

---

1. *The Work of St. Optatus*, trans. Vassall-Phillips, 31. Although Vassall-Phillips dates Optatus's first edition c. 373 (xxii), Berthold Altaner (in *Patrology*, 435) prefers 365.

2. Hardy, "Deacons in History and Practice," 21. Cf. Bligh, "Deacons in the Latin West Since the Fourth Century," 426.

3. Jerome, *Epistle 146 to Evangelus*, and *Epistle 125 to Rusticus* 15, in *Nicene and Post-Nicene Fathers*, 2d ser., 6:249, 288; Maclean, "Ministry (Early Christian)," 667.

4. Hefele, *History of the Councils*, 4:483. The primiclerus was the superintendent of those in minor orders including the subdeacons. In the fourth century the title of archpriest was given to the presbyter who presided in the bishop's place over parishes uniting for the principal Sunday Eucharist. In the fifth century the archpriest was the senior presbyter either in years or by appointment of a city bishop who performed many of the bishop's functions in his absence. His importance declined with the establishment of separate parishes.

5. Leo, *Epistles* 111–113, in *The Letters and Sermons of Leo the Great*, trans. Feltoe: *The Book of Pastoral Rule and Selected Epistles of Gregory the Great*, trans. Barmby, in *Nicene and Post-Nicene Fathers*, 2d ser., 12:82. Cf. *St. Leo the Great, Letters*, in *The Fathers of the Church*, trans. Glimm et al., 34:198. The translator notes that these letters are said to be spurious by Silva-Tarouca, *Nuovi Studi*, 183.

of the Church.[6] As the bishop's principal assistant, he had jurisdiction over other deacons and those in the minor orders in the West, but never in the East. In the East during a vacancy in a see the archdeacon appears to have been its guardian or coguardian, but evidence for this function in the West is lacking.[7]

Often they administered the charitable distributions of the Church, as can be seen in the collection of canons compiled prior to the end of the sixth century under the name of the Fourth Council of Carthage. Its seventeenth canon directs that "the affairs of widows, orphans, and strangers shall not be transacted personally by the bishop, but through the archpresbyter or archdeacon."[8] Such legislation as that of the Fourth Council of Toledo, 633, which defines the role of the archdeacon in the meetings of councils, indicates the importance and extent of his position.[9] In 774 Bishop Heddo of Strasburg divided his diocese into three archdeaconries, and from that time on in the West dioceses were divided into archdeaconries to relieve the bishop of administrative duties.[10]

However, by the ninth century priests began to hold the office, and in the twelfth century in the West the archdeacon was generally a priest and had therefore passed out of the history of the diaconate. In the East the archdeacon has never been a priest. They may still be found with some bishops, but they do secretarial work, such as keeping registers and accounts and taking care of correspondence.[11]

Diaconal Vestments

It is to be noted that the Church did not invent vestments for its clergy. For a long time the clergy wore the same dress as others in the society in which they lived and worked. Pope Celestine wrote to the bishops of the province of Vienne and Narbonne, c. 428, condemning the use of special dress for the clergy. He stated, "We should be distinguished from the people by our learning not by our clothes,"[12] an admonition the Church might well follow today. A picture of Gregory the Great (d. 604) with his father, Gordianus, and his mother, Silvia, shows that as late as the end of the sixth century laymen continued to wear the dalmatic and chasuble over the alb, which had for a long time been

---

6. Emil Albert Friedberg, "Archdeacon and Archpriest," in *The Schaff-Herzog Encyclopedia of Religious Knowledge*, ed. Samuel M. Jackson (New York: Funk & Wagnalls, 1908), 1:260. Cf. Bligh, "Deacons in the Latin West Since the Fourth Century," 426, and Bingham, *The Antiquities of the Christian Church*, 1:275–81.

7. Bingham, *The Antiquities of the Christian Church*, 1:275–76. Cf. Bligh, "Deacons in the Latin West Since the Fourth Century," 426; Edwin Hatch, "Archdeacon," in *Dictionary of Christian Antiquities*, ed. William Smith and Samuel Cheetham (Hartford: J. B. Burr, 1880), 1:138.

8. Hefele, *History of the Councils*, 2:409–12.

9. Ibid., 1:65. It is to be noted that his function here is liturgical and administrative, not deliberative.

10. Hatch, "Archdeacon," 1:136.

11. Bingham, *The Antiquities of the Christian Church*, 1:280; Gillet, "Deacons in the Orthodox East," 417.

12. Dearmer, *The Ornaments of the Minister*, 26. Cf. Duchesne, *Christian Worship*, 381.

the dress of Roman society. The only difference between the dress of Gregory and that of his parents is the pallium that distinguishes the pope.[13] However, in time the influence of the barbarian invaders, with their shorter garments, altered the classical dress of ancient Roman society, classical dress gradually becoming vestments worn by the clergy.[14]

Christian vestments are then derived primarily from the customary dress of the people of the late Roman Empire. But before considering the specific vestments of the deacon, a brief statement by Gilbert Cope giving an overview of an often complex and confusing subject is helpful in providing a frame of reference:

> The basic garments are: (1) an *indoor tunic;* (2) an *outdoor cloak.* The classical form of the tunic is the white *alb,* while the cloak exists as both the *chasuble* and the *cope.* Derivatives and variations of the tunic include the following garments: tunic, dalmatic, rochet, surplice, and cotta. Obviously, in clement weather, indoor clothing may also be worn outside without an overgarment, just as, conversely, for ceremonial reasons, outdoor robes may be worn indoors. It should be remembered that, though worn under a chasuble, or *cope,* the tunic is an outer-garment rather than an under-garment.[15]

The Alb

The alb originated from the *tunica alba* of antiquity, which existed in two forms: first, a knee-length garment sometimes without sleeves, called in Greek *chiton;* and, second, the longer *chiton poderes* or, in Latin, *tunica talaris,* reaching to the feet with either narrow or wide sleeves. This tunic was made of linen or wool and was frequently decorated with a dark russet or purple stripe on either side reaching from the shoulder to the hem or sometimes a single stripe down the middle in front and back, an ornamentation that disappeared as the dalmatic came to be worn over the tunic.[16]

Although some have thought that the *tunica alba* was originally an undergarment,[17] it is more likely that it was simply an indoor garment. It is uncertain when it came to be worn under the dalmatic, but it is definitely present as an undergarment in the sixth-century mosaic of Archbishop Maximianus and two deacons in the Church of St. Vitale at Ravenna.[18] The narrow-sleeved alb is clearly visible protruding at the wrist from under the wide sleeves of the dalmatic on the figure of the archbishop. It is not in evidence on the deacons, but it is possible that the dalmatics of the deacons were worn "doubtless over albs,"

---

13. Pocknee, *Liturgical Vesture,* 14, and plate 2, opposite p. 21. The picture is believed to be contemporary. Cf. Dearmer, *The Ornaments of the Ministers,* 29.

14. M. McCance, "Alb," in *New Catholic Encyclopedia,* 1:245.

15. Cope, "Vestments," 365.

16. Ibid., 366. Dearmer, *The Ornaments of the Ministers,* 41; Pocknee, *Liturgical Vesture,* 25; Cope, "Vestments," 366.

17. Dearmer, *The Ornaments of the Ministers,* 21; Pocknee, *Liturgical Vesture,* 25. Dearmer inconsistently tells us that the ornamentation disappears from the tunic, which he says was originally an undergarment, when the dalmatic came to be worn over it (41).

18. Pocknee, *Liturgical Vesture,* plate 1, opposite p. 20. See also Dearmer, *The Ornaments of the Ministers,* plate 8, p. 28. Dearmer states that this portrayal is typical of others.

as Dearmer thinks,[19] particularly since the deacons were men of considerable prestige at that time. But in the event the alb was not yet customarily worn by the deacons at this time, it soon came to be.

The alb was worn by all clerical orders until the eleventh century. At that time a transition occurred in the West. The surplice began to develop, as we shall shortly discuss, for use both in choir and in noneucharistic worship. It was also at this time that an ornamental border or orphrey came to be put around the border of the alb, which was soon reduced to two oblong pieces called apparels on the hem and one on each sleeve.[20]

The Girdle

In antiquity the tunic was normally gathered at the waist by a girdle of some sort for the sake of convenience. The girdle then, as a matter of course, continued to be used with the tunic as that garment acquired the character of a vestment. However, in the Eastern Orthodox churches the girdle is not worn by the deacon with the *sticharion,* as the version of the alb there is called, although bishops and priests do wear it in the form of a belt called a *zone.*[21] In the West it has in the past been a belt, sometimes called a cincture, of varied color and material,[22] but today it is usually a long rope with knotted or tasseled ends.

The Amice

The amice, which has never been classed among the official vestments of the Eastern Orthodox churches, was originally a neckerchief in use in the ancient world as an optional article of apparel to protect other clothing. Dearmer reproduces the picture of a sculpture from the second century of the sailor, Blussus, showing him in tunic, amice, and chasuble. Mosaics of clergy from the sixth century do not show the amice. By the eighth century it had come into common use among the clergy in the West, although it seems still not to have been used invariably as late as the beginning of the ninth century. Evidence for the decorated amice comes from the tenth century, this ornamentation taking the form of a strip of material called an apparel in the twelfth century. These apparels were in the color of the stole and maniple, contrasting with that of the chasuble or dalmatic.[23]

Originally this rectangular linen garment was put on over the alb, a practice which still survives at Lyons and Milan, although elsewhere the custom of

---

19. Dearmer, *The Ornaments of the Ministers,* 56. Pocknee, *Liturgical Vesture,* 25–26, seems to agree.

20. Cope, "Vestments," 367; Dearmer, *The Ornaments of the Ministers,* 41–42.

21. Cope, "Vestments," 368; cf. Pocknee, *Liturgical Vesture,* 26.

22. Christa C. Mayer-Thurman, *Raiment for the Lord's Service: A Thousand Years of Western Vestments* (Chicago: Art Institute of Chicago, 1975), 30. Cf. Cope, "Vestments," 368.

23. Cope, "Vestments," 367–68; Dearmer, *The Ornaments of the Ministers,* 80, and plate 4, p. 15; Pocknee, *Liturgical Vesture,* 18.

beginning with the amice, which arose in the tenth century due to longer hair styles, is prevalent.[24]

The Stole

The origin of the stole is uncertain. Some have thought that it was originally simply the ancient handkerchief or neckcloth, which was modified to become part of the ceremonial dress of the clergy.[25] However, more recently, it has been maintained that it derives from a scarf worn over the tunic and chasuble in ancient Rome by senators and consuls as an insignia of their status. This latter view is more probable and could indicate a common origin with the pallium worn by the bishops.[26]

The original name of the stole was the *orarium,* which appears to come from the Latin *oro,* meaning "to pray," thus implying that it is the special ensign of those who lead public worship. The term *orarion* is still used for the stole in the Eastern Orthodox churches today. In the West the change in terminology from *orarium* to stole appears to have commenced in the ninth century as a Franco-Germanic innovation but was not apparently used throughout the West as the preferred designation until the thirteenth century.[27]

It is probable that the stole was worn as a distinctive mark of the clergy first in the fourth century. The Council of Laodicea, 343–381, states that the sub-deacon has no right to wear the stole. Since it is not mentioned in the previous canon respecting the place of deacons, clearly it is worn by them. However, as time passed certain of the minor orders adopted the stole as well. Records of the ninth century reveal that subdeacons and acolytes as well as bishops, priests, and deacons were wearing the stole at that time. Interestingly, Jungmann says that legislation of the ninth and tenth centuries made the wearing of the stole by priests both at home and while traveling obligatory.[28] But the diaconal stole apparently was not used at Rome until the ninth or tenth century, although it had been adopted universally elsewhere.[29]

The stole appears originally to have been white. Although in the West the material of the deacon's stole is uncertain, in the East it was made of linen. Isidore of Pelusium, d. c. 435, records that it was like the bishop's pallium except made of linen instead of wool. In the Middle Ages in the West the diaconal stole came to be made from richer materials and was heavily embroidered in colors like

---

24. Cope, "Vestments," 368.

25. Both Duchesne, *Christian Worship,* 390–91, and Dearmer, *The Ornaments of the Ministers,* 62, maintain this origin for the stole.

26. Pocknee, *Liturgical Vesture,* 21–22. Cf. Cope, "Vestments," 368 and Duchesne, *Christian Worship,* 391.

27. Pocknee, *Liturgical Vesture,* 22–23; Cope, "Vestments," 368.

28. *Council of Laodicea,* Canon 22, in *Nicene and Post-Nicene Fathers,* 2d ser., 14:140; Duchesne, *Christian Worship,* 390; Jungmann, *The Mass of the Roman Rite,* 1:280.

29. Dearmer, *The Ornaments of the Ministers,* 63, indicates its adoption at Rome in the ninth century. Duchesne says it was unknown for the deacon and the priest at Rome in the tenth century (*Christian Worship,* 390).

those of the apparels and in contrast to the colors of the dalmatic. The long, narrow stole of the Middle Ages became the shorter, less graceful stole with wider ends which we find in use at the close of the Medieval period.[30]

The Council of Braga, 563, directs the deacons to wear the stole over the shoulder and outside the tunic (dalmatic), so that they will not be confused with the subdeacons.[31] It is probable that deacons wore their stoles outside their dalmatics and hanging straight down from the left shoulder, as is still the custom in the Eastern Orthodox churches today.[32] The Council of Toledo, 633, mentions the stole in connection with bishops, priests, and deacons only and specifies that it be worn by the deacon over the left shoulder, "because he *orat, id est praedicat.*" It continues, "The right side of the body he must have free, in order that he may without hindrance, do his service."[33] This is of importance because here we see the primitive emphasis on *diakonia* asserted and symbolized in the deacon's stole. Canon 28 of this council refers to the stole and the alb as the special marks of the deacon in contrast to the stole and chasuble of the priest.[34] Later, when the stole was finally adopted at Rome, it was worn over the left shoulder by the deacon but under the "dalmatic or chasuble."[35]

Although the chasuble is not usually considered to be a diaconal vestment, for many centuries it apparently was worn by acolytes and subdeacons as well as deacons, priests, and bishops. Duchesne and Dearmer both report that it is still worn in Europe by deacons and subdeacons during penitential seasons.[36] Wearing the stole under the dalmatic may account, as Duchesne believes, for its coming to be caught together on the right side at the waist.[37]

The Dalmatic

The dalmatic appears to have originated as a garment of ordinary dress in the province of Dalmatia, being made from the fine wool for which the province was noted. It was a long white tunic, reaching almost to the ankles, and had wide sleeves.[38] At an early time it came to have a stripe on each side reaching from the shoulder to the hem in both front and back and two similar stripes around

30. Duchesne, *Christian Worship*, 391, 394; Pocknee, *Liturgical Vesture*, 23–24.

31. Council of Braga, Disciplinary Canon 9, in Hefele, *History of the Councils*, 4:385.

32. Dearmer, *The Ornaments of the Ministers*, 64. Cf. Pocknee, *Liturgical Vesture*, 23. Dearmer says that the Orthodox deacon sometimes brings one end round over his right shoulder.

33. Council of Toledo, Canon 40, in Hefele, *History of the Councils*, 4:454. Canon 41 of Toledo is the first synodical legislation ordering a tonsure in the form of a *corona*, which is to be worn by all clergy, "even lectors," as well as priests and deacons (Landon, *A Manual of Councils of the Holy Catholic Church*, 2:158). Heretofore, the clergy have worn long hair like the laity, only having shaved a little circle in the middle of the head (Canon 41, in Hefele, *History of the Councils*, 4:454).

34. Council of Toledo, in Hefele, *History of the Councils*, 4:453. The canon deals with the restoration of deposed clergy and directs that these vestments be presented before the altar in restoring the lost degree.

35. Duchesne, *Christian Worship*, 392.

36. Ibid., 380–81. Dearmer, *The Ornaments of the Ministers*, 46–47.

37. Duchesne, *Christian Worship*, 392n.

38. Pocknee, *Liturgical Vesture*, 37.

the wide sleeves near the border. Such ornamentation is seen in the picture of a woman praying in the catacomb of Callisto in Rome dating from the middle of the third century.[39] The stripes seem generally to have been either linen or wool. The dalmatic continued for a long time to fit this general description in many places, though by the seventh century other richer materials and colors were beginning to be used.[40]

It is uncertain when the dalmatic came to be a distinctive clerical vestment.[41] Although it has been thought that Cyprian wore a dalmatic to his martyrdom, the evidence does not support this contention.[42] There is conclusive evidence that in the time of Pope Damasus, 368–384, bishops and deacons at Rome, and perhaps elsewhere in that region, wore the dalmatic. But as Dearmer points out, "This early mention of the Christian use of the dalmatic can only refer to its general everyday use." There is no indication that others at Rome had ceased to wear the dalmatic. It appears to have been during the sixth century that deacons and bishops wore the dalmatic as a distinguishing mark of their dress with the bishops adding the chasuble and pallium, although it was probably during the seventh century that the dalmatic finally became obsolete in general usage.[43]

The origin of the dalmatic as an ecclesiastical vestment is particularly associated with the Church at Rome. The evidence indicates that the dalmatic was not worn by deacons in Africa, Spain, and Gaul at least in the latter part of the fourth century, when we know it was at Rome. Not only did it come to be worn by the pope and the Roman deacons, but in time the Roman bishops came to award the use of the dalmatic as a special privilege to certain bishops and deacons of other places. The first recorded instance of this practice is thought to be that of Pope Symmachus, who granted this right to the deacons of Arles c. 500.[44] However, by the ninth century the dalmatic had come to be worn everywhere in the West.[45]

---

39. A picture of this fresco is reproduced by Dearmer, *The Ornaments of the Ministers*, plate 13, p. 55.

40. Dearmer, *The Ornaments of the Ministers*, 13, 57; Pocknee, *Liturgical Vesture*, 37, 38; Cope, "Vestments," 376.

41. Duchesne, *Christian Worship*, 382n. He states that ascribing the introduction of the dalmatic to Pope Silvester (314–335), as Herbert Norris and others have done, even as late as 1949, is due to the legendary account of his life written in the fifth century. See Herbert Norris, *Church Vestments: Their Origin and Development* (London: J. M. Dent & Sons, 1949), 46.

42. Duchesne says that Cyprian wore "a linen tunic, a dalmatic, and an overgarment, answering to the paenula, or planeta" to his martyrdom c. 259 (*Christian Worship*, 382). Joseph Bingham is probably correct in asserting that this idea is due to a corruption in the text, since the dalmatic was not at that time a common garment among the Romans and there is no other mention of it among the clergy (*The Antiquities of the Christian Church*, 2:299).

43. Dearmer, *The Ornaments of the Ministers*, 24, 28. Cf. Pocknee, *Liturgical Vesture*, 37. Duchesne maintains (*Christian Worship*, 382) that this had happened by the end of the fifth century, when he says the dalmatic was no longer worn by others, but this is probably too early.

44. Dearmer, *The Ornaments of the Ministers*, 24, 28, Cf. Pocknee, *Liturgical Vesture*, 37.

45. Phillips, "Dalmatic," 6:994. Cf. Cope, "Vestments," 376.

The Surplice

The surplice, as noted earlier, is derived from the alb. In the unheated churches of northern Europe in the Middle Ages a gown lined with furs was worn during the winter, making it difficult to wear the narrow-sleeved alb over it. As early as the eleventh century there is evidence for the *superpelliceum,* a word meaning a garment worn over the *pelliceum* or fur coat, which has been contracted into the English "surplice." It apparently became a liturgical vestment in the twelfth century and gradually displaced the alb as clerical attire in choir. In the fourteenth century it had come into wide usage. It was "everywhere established as the essential choir-habit, the substitute for the alb in procession, in the ministrations of Sacraments and all rites outside the actual service of the altar: it was also the official (though not the only) vestment of the lower orders of the ministry."[46]

The early form of the surplice reached, like the alb, almost to the feet and had sleeves shaped much like the alb except somewhat broader and extending beyond the fingers. The sleeves soon became much fuller, as they have remained until the present time. Although the length of the surplice seems to have varied somewhat prior to the sixteenth century, it remained quite long until the latter part of that century. It was at that time that it began to be abbreviated, except in England where its length and simplicity tended to remain unchanged. In the seventeenth century lace came into use as an embellishment.[47]

In Anglicanism in the latter half of the nineteenth century surplices in some places began to be shortened both in the sleeves and the skirt,[48] although most of the clergy continued to wear knee-length or sometimes longer garments. Lace surplices have been a relative rarity in Anglicanism. A marked trend toward the restoration of the simpler and fuller surplice is evident in the liturgical churches of the West today.

Letters of Agreement

The following letters of agreement are included to illustrate the form such letters might take. The first is that currently suggested as a guide in the Roman Catholic Archdiocese of Omaha. Its simplicity is commendable.

Letter 1

CONTRACT OR WORK AGREEMENT AND APPOINTMENT

After ordination a contract or work agreement similar to the following is written by the deacon and agreed upon by his wife and the priest with whom he is establishing the work agreement:

---

46. Dearmer, *The Ornaments of the Ministers,* 94.
47. Ibid., 94–95. Also, see plates 17 (p. 68), 19 (p. 73), and 20 (p. 74) showing fourteenth- and fifteenth-century examples of clerical dress including the surplice.
48. Pocknee, *Liturgical Vesture,* 42.

[Addressed to the Archbishop]

The following is my service agreement to _____ Parish, _____. Agreed upon [by] Fr. _____, the pastor, as well as my wife, _____, and myself.

Liturgically, I will be minister at the altar at one mass on Sunday as deacon. Also, I will minister at the altar, as deacon, at the 5:30 P.M. weekday Mass. Possibly, at a later date and after further training, to preach on occasions approved by the pastor. Also reading Scripture of the day and helping share the Eucharist with the faithful when the pastor is not present to the community. I will minister at Baptism on occasions approved by the pastor.

I will continue to serve the sick as an active member of the local community's rest home. I would also like to work with the young adults in our parish (ages 18–30) in developing meaningful programs for their spiritual growth.

Realizing that I have priorities in my life, i.e., my family, my work, and the Diaconate, I agree to minister to the people in this parish according to the above description. I wish, therefore, to be appointed to share in the ministry in _____ parish and elsewhere, to the best of my ability, with the time I have available, and keeping my priorities straight. I ask not only for canonical appointment, but also your prayer for God's help.

Attest

Wife _____

Pastor _____

The directions with the agreement state that the contract is reviewed by the director and submitted to the archbishop for approval and for the official appointment. It is recommended that the contract be reviewed and updated yearly.[49]

Letter 2

The following is a combination and to some extent a condensation of several longer and more detailed letters from Episcopal sources.

LETTER OF AGREEMENT FOR DEACONS

We, Deacon _____ and Fr. _____ Rector of _____ Church, agree on this the _____ day of _____ (year), that the exercise of this diaconal ministry related to this parish will be in accord with the terms set forth in this letter.

---

49. "Basic Philosophy of the Permanent Diaconate Program for the Archdiocese of Omaha."

1. The deacon accepts the following principles of ministry:

   a. The Church is a body with many members, each sent by Christ with special gifts to serve first one another and then others.

   b. Every parish rector by virtue of his or her order and the good order of the Church as set forth in its canons has been given the ministry and authority to function in the role of primary leadership in the parish.

   c. The ministry of the deacon is an assisting role in the parish structure and is always to be exercised in harmony with the rector, lending support, and seeking to build up the body of Christ.

   d. Under the present canons the deacon is also subject to the authority of the bishop and is assigned to his or her ministry by the bishop.

2. The bishop's approval of this agreement constitutes assignment to this ministry in this parish.

3. The deacon shall serve in these pastoral and/or charitable ministries:

   [The particular ministry or ministries are enumerated.]

4. The deacon shall assist at the Church's liturgies including Baptism, the Eucharist, marriage, and burial when possible, as requested by the rector.

5. The deacon will use the style or title of his office, "Deacon," and dress in the manner of the baptized. Clerical attire may be used only under extraordinary circumstances and with the approval of the rector and the bishop.

6. Preaching is a presiding function of the priest. The deacon may preach his or her own homily only with a license by the bishop.

7. The deacon's ministry is nonstipendiary. The parish may reimburse expenses incurred by the deacon in service to or for the Church at its discretion. (Full-time service would normally be compensated, the terms set forth here in place of this statement.)

8. The deacon will participate so far as possible in diocesan gatherings for deacons and in continuing education.

9. The deacon will (will not) have a seat and voice on the parish vestry.

10. This agreement automatically terminates if and when the deacon moves to another place or at the end of (each year) (every two/three years). It may be terminated at any time either by the deacon, the rector, or the bishop,

provided written notice is given to the other two, first, of the intention to terminate and, second, within sixty days of the termination.

(Signed and dated)

Deacon _____

Rector _____

Bishop _____

Select Bibliography

Abbott-Smith, G. *A Manual Greek Lexicon of the New Testament*. Edinburgh: T. & T. Clark, 1937.

Albright, W. F., and C. S. Mann. *Matthew*. Anchor Bible Series 26. Garden City, N.Y.: Doubleday, 1971.

Alexander, J. Neil. "A Call to Adventure: Seven Propositions on Ministry." In *This Sacred Story: Anglican Reflections for John Booty*, ed. Donald S. Armentrout. Cambridge, Mass.: Cowley Publications, 1990.

Altaner, Berthold. *Patrology*. Translated by Hilda C. Graef New York: Herder & Herder, 1960.

Ambrose. *Duties of the Clergy*. In *Nicene and Post-Nicene Fathers*, 2d ser., vol. 10.

————. *Saint Ambrose, Letters*. Translated by Mary Melchior Beyenka. vol. 26 of *Fathers of the Church*, ed. Roy J. Defarrari. New York: Fathers of the Church, 1954.

Ambrosiaster. Pseudo-Augustine. *Quaestiones Veteris et Novi Testamenti CXXVII*. Translated by Alexander Souter. *Corpus Scriptorum Ecclesiasticorum Latinorum* 50. 1908; rpt., New York: Johnson Reprint Corp., 1963.

The Ante-Nicene Fathers: Translations of the Writings of the Fathers Down to A.D. 325. Edited by Alexander Roberts and James Donaldson. American reprint edited by A. Cleveland Coxe. Grand Rapids: Eerdmans.

    Vol. 1. *The Apostolic Fathers with Justin Martyr and Irenaeus*. 1956.

    Vol. 2. *Fathers of the Second Century: Hermas, Tatian, Athenagoras, Theophisbus, and Clement of Alexandria*. 1956.

    Vol. 3. *Latin Christianity: Its Founder, Tertullian*. 1957.

    Vol. 4. *Tertullian, Part Fourth; Minucius Felix; Commodian; Origen, Parts First and Second*. 1956.

    Vol. 5. *Fathers of the Third Century: Hippolytus, Cyprian, Caius, Novatian, Appendix*. 1951.

    Vol. 7. *Lactantius, Venantius, Asterius, Victorinus, Dionysius, Apostolic Teaching and Constitutions, Homily, and Liturgies*. 1951.

    Vol. 8. *Fathers of the Third and Fourth Centuries: The Twelve Patriarchs, Excerpts and Epistles, the Clementina, Apocrypha, Decretals, Memoirs of Edessa and Syriac*. 1951.

    Vol. 9. *Documents, Remains of the First Ages; Biographical Synopsis; Index*. 1951.

Audet, Jean-Paul. *Structures in Christian Priesthood: A Study of Home, Marriage, and Celibacy in the Pastoral Service of the Church*. Translated by Rosemary Sheed. New York: Macmillan, 1967.

Augustine. *The City of God*. vol. 2. Translated by John Healy. Edited by R. V. G. Tasker. London: J. M. Dent & Sons, 1945.

————. *City of God*. In *Nicene and Post-Nicene Fathers*, 1st ser., vol. 2.

————. *The City of God*. Translated by Henry Bettenson. Harmondsworth, Middlesex, England: Penguin Books, 1972.

————. *De haeresibus ad Quodvultdeum*. Edited by Lambert Daneau. Geneva: Evstathivm Vignon, 1576.

————. *On the Good of Marriage*. In *Nicene and Post-Nicene Fathers*, 1st ser., vol. 3.

————. *St. Augustine's City of God*. Abridged and translated by J. W. C. Wand. London: Oxford University Press, 1963.

Ayer, Joseph Cullen, Jr. *A Source Book for Ancient Church History from the Apostolic Age to the Close of the Conciliar Period*. New York: Scribner's, 1948.

Barrett, C. K. *A Commentary on the Epistle to the Romans*. New York: Harper & Brothers, 1957.

————. *A Commentary on the First Epistle to the Corinthians*. Edited by Henry Chadwick. Harper's New Testament Commentaries. New York: Harper & Row, 1968.

————. *The Pastoral Epistles in the New English Bible*. London: Oxford University Press, 1963.

"The Basic Philosophy of the Permanent Diaconate Program for the Archdiocese of Omaha." Mimeographed. n.d.

Beare, F. W. *A Commentary on the Epistle to the Philippians*. New York: Harper & Brothers, 1959.

Beasley-Murray, George R. "The Diaconate in Baptist Churches." In *The Ministry of Deacons*, ed. Department of Faith and Order.

Bede. *Bede's Ecclesiastical History of the English People*. Edited by Bertram Colgrave and R. A. B. Mynors. Oxford: Clarendon Press, 1969.

Bingham, Joseph. *The Antiquities of the Christian Church: The Works of Joseph Bingham*. New ed. Edited by R. Bingham. Oxford University Press, 1855.

    vol. 1. Books 1–3 of *The Antiquities*.

    vol. 3. Books 8–10 of *The Antiquities*.

Bishops' Committee on the Liturgy. *The Deacon, Minister of Word and Sacrament*. Study Text VI. Washington, D.C.: U.S. Catholic Conference, 1979.

Bishops' Committee on the Permanent Diaconate. *Permanent Deacons in the United States: Guidelines on Their Formation and Ministry*. Washington, D.C.: U.S. Catholic Conference, 1971.

Bishops' Committee on the Permanent Diaconate, National Conference of Catholic Bishops. *Permanent Deacons in the United States: Guidelines on Their Formation and Ministry*. (1984 Revision.) Washington, D.C.: U.S. Catholic Conference, 1985.

Blenkinsopp, Joseph. *Celibacy, Ministry, Church*. New York: Herder & Herder, 1968.

Bligh, John, S.J. "Deacons in the Latin West Since the Fourth Century." *Theology* 58 (1955): 421–29.

Bokser, Ben Zion. "Halakah." In *An Encyclopedia of Religion*, ed. Ferm.

Bonansea, Bernardino M. "Celibacy." *Encyclopedia Americana*. International ed., vol. 6. New York: Americana Corp., 1977.

Bonner, Gerald. *St. Augustine of Hippo, Life and Controversies*. Philadelphia: Westminster Press, 1963.

The Book of Common Prayer and Administration of the Sacraments and Other Rites and Ceremonies of the Church. New York: Church Hymnal Corp. and Seabury Press, 1979.

The Book of Common Prayer and Administration of the Sacraments and Other Rites and Ceremonies of the Church According to the Use of the Protestant Episcopal Church in the United States of America. New York: Church Pension Fund, 1945.

The Book of Discipline of the United Methodist Church, 1980. Nashville: Abingdon Press, 1980.

Borgen, Peder. "God's Agent in the Fourth Gospel." In *Religions in Antiquity: Essays in Memory of Erwin Ramsdell Goodenough,* ed. Jacob Neusner. Studies in the History of Religions 14. Leiden: E. J. Brill, 1968.

Bowden, John William. *The Life and Pontificate of Gregory the Seventh.* New York: J. R. Dunham, 1845.

Bradshaw, Paul F. *The Anglican Ordinal: Its History and Development from the Reformation to the Present Day.* Alcuin Club Collections, no. 53. London: SPCK, 1971.

Bridel, Claude. "Note on the Diaconal Ministry in the Reformed Churches." In *The Ministry of Deacons,* ed. Department of Faith and Order.

Brockman, Norbert. *Ordained to Service: A Theology of the Permanent Diaconate.* Hicksville, N.Y.: Exposition Press, 1976.

Bruce, F. F. *Commentary on the Book of the Acts.* The New International Commentary on the New Testament. Grand Rapids: Eerdmans, 1956.

Callebaut, André. "Saint François levite." *Archivum Franciscanum Historicum* 20 (1927): 193–96.

Calvin, John. *Institutes of the Christian Religion.* Translated by Ford Lewis Battles. Edited by John T. McNeill. Library of Christian Classics 21. Philadelphia: Westminster, 1960.

Canons and Decrees of the Council of Trent. Translated by H. J. Schroeder. St. Louis: B. Herder Book Co., 1941.

Carey, George, and John Hind. "Ministry, Ministries, and the Ministry." In *Stepping Stones: Joint Essays on Anglican Catholic and Evangelical Unity,* ed. Christina Baxter, John Scott, and Roger Greenacre. London: Hodder & Stoughton, 1978.

The Catholic Encyclopedia: An International Work of Reference on the Constitution, Doctrine, Discipline, and History of the Catholic Church. vol. 4. Edited by Charles G. Herbermann et al. New York: Encyclopedia Press, 1908.

Chrysostom, John. "De Beato Philogonia" 6. In *Contra Anomoeos. Patrologia sive Latinorum, sive Graecorum* 48, ed. J. P. Migne. Turnholt, Belgium: Brepols, n.d.

———. *Homily 14. On Acts 5:34.* In *Nicene and Post-Nicene Fathers,* 1st ser., vol. 11.

The Church, the Diaconate, the Future. The Report of the Diaconate submitted by the Council for the Development of Ministry to the House of Bishops, the General Convention (Episcopal Church), Denver, 1979.

Clement. "The Letter of the Church of Rome to the Church of Corinth, Commonly called Clement's First Letter." Translated by Cyril C. Richardson. In *Early Christian Fathers,* ed. Richardson.

Cockin, F. A. "Ministers of the Priestly People." *Theology* 65 (January 1962): 7.

Collins, John N. *Diakonia: Re-interpreting the Ancient Sources.* New York: Oxford University Press, 1990.

Constitution and Canons for the Government of the Protestant Episcopal Church in the United States of America. N.p., 1958, 1964.

Constitution and Canons for the Government of the Protestant Episcopal Church in the United States of America Otherwise Known as the Episcopal Church Adopted in General Conventions, 1789–1979, Together with the Rules of Order. New York: Seabury Professional Services, 1979.

Constitution and Canons for the Government of the Protestant Episcopal Church in the United States of America Otherwise Known as the Episcopal Church Adopted in General Conventions, 1789–1991, Together with the Rules of Order Revised by the Convention 1991. N.p., n.d.

Consultation on Church Union. *A Plan of Union for the Church of Christ Uniting.* Executive Committee of the Consultation on Church Union. Philadelphia, 1970.

Cope, Gilbert. "Vestments." In *A Dictionary of Liturgy and Worship,* ed. J. G. Davies. New York: Macmillan, 1972.

Craig, Clarence F. "Introduction and Exegesis," "The First Epistle to the Corinthians." In *The Interpreter's Bible,* vol. 10. New York: Abingdon-Cokesbury Press, 1953.

Cullmann, Oscar. *Peter, Disciple — Apostle — Martyr.* Translated by Floyd V. Filson. Philadelphia: Westminster Press, 1953.

Dale, Alfred W. W. *The Synod of Elvira and Christian Life in the Fourth Century.* London: Macmillan, 1882.

Daugherty, Ruth A. "Changes in Our Ministry: What's Being Proposed in '92?" In Pohl, ed., "Circuit Rider."

"Deaconess." *The Encyclopedia Americana.* International ed. vol. 8. Danbury, Conn.: Grolier, 1992.

"The Deaconess Community of the Evangelical Lutheran Church in America." Gladwyne, Pa.: The Deaconess Community, Evangelical Lutheran Church in America, n.d.

Dearmer, Percy. *The Ornaments of the Ministers.* New ed. London: A. R. Mowbray & Co., 1920.

De Ecclesia: The Constitution on the Church of Vatican Council II Proclaimed by Pope Paul VI, November 21, 1964. Edited by Edward H. Peters. Glen Rock, N.J.: Paulist Press, Deus Book, 1965.

Delhaye, P. "History of Celibacy." In *New Catholic Encyclopedia,* vol. 3.

Denzer, George A. "The Pastoral Letters." In *The Jerome Biblical Commentary,* vol. 2. Englewood Cliffs, N.J: Prentice-Hall, 1968.

The Diaconate Now. Edited by Richard T. Nolan. Washington, D.C.: Corpus Books, 1968.

Dibelius, Martin, and Hans Conzelmann. *The Pastoral Epistles.* Translated by Philip Buttolph and Adela Yarbro. Edited by Helmut Koester. Philadelphia: Fortress Press, 1972.

A Dictionary of Christian Biography and Literature to the End of the Sixth Century A.D. with an Account of the Principal Sects and Heresies. Edited by Henry Wace and William C. Piercy. Boston: Little, Brown, 1911.

The Didache or Teaching of the Twelve Apostles. Translated by Francis X. Glimm. In *The Fathers of the Church,* vol. 1, *The Apostolic Fathers.* Translated by Francis X. Glimm, Joseph M. F. Marique, and Gerald G. Walsh. New York: Cima Publishing, 1947.

Didascalia Apostolorum: The Syriac Version. Translated by R. Hugh Connolly. Oxford: Clarendon Press, 1929.

Directory of Deacons: Episcopal Church, Anglican Church of Canada, Evangelical Lutheran Church in America. Providence, R.I.: North American Association for the Diaconate, 1991.

Dix, Dom Gregory. "The Ministry in the Early Church c. A.D. 90–410." In *The Apostolic Ministry: Essays on the History and the Doctrine of Episcopacy,* ed. Kenneth E. Kirk, 183–304. London: Hodder & Stoughton, 1946.

———. *The Shape of the Liturgy.* Westminster: Dacre Press, 1945.

———. "Textual Materials." In Hippolytus, *The Treatise on the Apostolic Tradition of St. Hippolytus of Rome.* New York: Macmillan, 1937.

The Documents of Vatican II, All Sixteen Official Texts Promulgated by the Ecumenical Council, 1963–65. Edited by Walter M. Abbott. Translation edited by Joseph Gallagher. New York: Guild Press, 1966.

Donlon, S. E. "Pontiff." *New Catholic Encyclopedia.*

Dorris, Tom. "Lutheran-Episcopal Pact Includes Deacons." *Diakoneo* (March 1991): 1.

Duchesne, L. *Christian Worship, Its Origin and Evolution: A Study of the Latin Liturgy Up to the Time of Charlemagne.* 5th ed. London: SPCK, 1923.

Duckett, Eleanor Shipley. *Alcuin, Friend of Charlemagne.* New York: Macmillan, 1951.

Dunlap, E. Dale. "Consecration or Ordination: A Critical Look at the Proposal." In Pohl, ed., "Circuit Rider."

Early Christian Fathers. Edited by Cyril C. Richardson. Library of Christian Classics 1. Philadelphia: Westminster Press, 1953.

Easton, Burton Scott. *The Pastoral Epistles.* New York: Scribner's, 1947.

Echlin, Edward, S.J. *The Deacon in the Church Past and Future.* Staten Island, N.Y.: Alba House, Society of St. Paul, 1971.

Elders'-Deacons' Manual. Compiled by P. A. Willis. Cincinnati: Christian Restoration Association, 1968.

An Encyclopedia of Religion. Edited by Vergilius Ferm. New York: Philosophical Library, 1945.

Ennodius. *Opuscula miscella* 9 and 10. "Benedictio Cerei." *Corpus Scriptorum Ecclesiasticorum,* vol. 6. *Magni Felicis Ennodii: Opera Omnia.* Recensuit et commentario, Guilelmus Hartel. Vendobonae: Apud C. Geroldi Filium Bibliopolam Academiae. 1882.

Eusebius. *The Church History of Eusebius.* In *Nicene and Post-Nicene Fathers,* 2d ser., vol. 1.

———. *Life of Constantine.* In *Nicene and Post-Nicene Fathers,* 2d ser., vol. 1.

Evans, Ernest. *Tertullian's Homily on Baptism: The Text Edited with an Introduction, Translation, and Commentary.* London: SPCK, 1964.

Farrar, Frederic W. *Lives of the Fathers,* vol. 2. Edinburgh: Adam and Charles Black, 1884.

Filson, Floyd V. *A Commentary on the Gospel According to St. Matthew.* Edited by Henry Chadwick. Harper's New Testament Commentaries. New York: Harper & Brothers, 1960.

———. "Exegesis" and "The Second Epistle to the Corinthians." In *The Interpreter's Bible,* vol. 10. New York: Abingdon-Cokesbury, 1953.

Fine, Benjamin. *The Stranglehold of the I.Q.* Garden City, N.Y.: Doubleday, 1975.

Fiske, E. B. "Finding Fault with the Testers." *New York Times Magazine,* November 18, 1979.

Fitzmyer, Joseph A. "The Letter to the Philippians." In *Jerome Bible Commentary,* 2 vols., ed. Raymond E. Brown, Joseph A. Fitzmyer, and Roland E. Murphy. Englewood Cliffs, N.J.: Prentice-Hall, 1968.

Florovsky, George. "The Problem of Diaconate in the Orthodox Church." In *The Diaconate Now,* ed. Nolan.

Ford, J. Massingberd. *A Trilogy on Wisdom and Celibacy.* The Cardinal O'Hara Series. Studies and Research in Christian Theology at Notre Dame. Notre Dame: University of Notre Dame Press, 1967.

Foshee, Howard B. *The Ministry of the Deacon.* Nashville: Convention Press, 1968; rev. 1974.

Fox, J. J. "Papacy." In *Encyclopedia Americana,* vol. 21. New York: Americana Corp., 1938.

Frere, Walter Howard. "Early Forms of Ordination." In *Essays on the Early History of the Church and the Ministry by Various Writers,* 2d ed., ed. H. B. Swete. London: Macmillan, 1921.

Friedberg, Emil Albert. "Archdeacon and Archpriest." In *The Schaff-Herzog Encyclopedia of Religious Knowledge,* vol. 1, ed. Samuel M. Jackson. New York: Funk & Wagnalls, 1908.

Fuller, Reginald H. "Church." In *A Theological Word Book of the Bible,* ed. Alan Richardson. New York: Macmillan, 1951.

————. "Early Catholicism in the New Testament." Lectures at the Graduate School of Theology, Sewanee, Tenn., 1970.

————. *Preaching the Lectionary: The Word of God for the Church Today.* Rev. ed. Collegeville, Minn.: Liturgical Press, 1984.

Gillet, Leo. "Deacons in the Orthodox East." *Theology* 58 (1955): 415–21.

Goodspeed, Edgar J. *The Apostolic Fathers — An American Translation.* New York: Harper & Brothers, 1950.

————. *A History of Early Christian Literature.* Revised and enlarged by Robert M. Grant. Chicago: University of Chicago Press, 1966.

Gregory, Bishop of Tours. *De Gloria Confessorum. Patrologiae Latinorum* 71, ed. J. P. Migne. Paris, 1879.

————. *History of the Franks.* Translated by Ernest Brehaut. New York: Columbia University Press, 1916.

Gregory Nazianzen. "Oration on St. Basil the Great." In *Funeral Orations by St. Gregory Nazianzen and St. Ambrose.* Translated by Leo P. McCauley. vol. 22 of *Fathers of the Church.* New York: Fathers of the Church, 1953.

Gregory the Great. *Pastoral Care.* Translated and annotated by Henry Davis. Westminster, Md.: Newman Press, 1950.

Gwatkin, Henry M. "Deacon." In *A Dictionary of the Bible: Dealing with Its Language, Literature, and Contents,* vol. 1, ed. James Hastings. New York: Scribner's, 1911.

Haddan, Arthur W. "Chorepiscopus." In *A Dictionary of Christian Antiquities,* vol. 1, ed. William Smith and Samuel Cheetham. Hartford, Conn.: J. B. Burr, 1880.

Haenchen, Ernst. *The Acts of the Apostles, a Commentary.* Philadelphia: Westminster Press, 1971.

Hanson, A. T. "Shepherd, Teacher, and Celebrant in the New Testament Conception of the Ministry." In Paton, ed., *New Forms of Ministry.*

Hardy, Edward R. "The Deacon in History and Practice." In *The Diaconate Now,* ed. Nolan.

Hatch, Edwin. "Archdeacon." In *Dictionary of Christian Antiquities,* vol. 1, ed. William Smith and Samuel Cheetham. Hartford: J. B. Burr, 1880.

Hatchett, Marion J. *Commentary on the American Prayer Book.* New York: Seabury Press, 1980.

————. "The New Book: A Continuation of or a Departure from the Tradition?" *Open* (June 1977): 7.

————. "Rites of Ordination." Lectures at the School of Theology, University of the South, Sewanee, Tenn. Summer 1975.

————. *Sanctifying Life, Time, and Space: An Introduction to Liturgical Study.* New York: Seabury Press, 1976.

————. "Seven Pre-Reformation Eucharistic Liturgies." *St. Luke's Journal of Theology* (now *Sewanee Theological Review*) 16, no. 3 (June 1973): 13–115.

Hebert, A. G. *Apostle and Bishop: A Study of the Gospel, the Ministry, and the Church-Community.* New York: Seabury Press, 1963.

Hefele, Charles Joseph. *A History of the Councils of the Church.*

    Vol. 1. *A History of the Christian Councils, from the Original Documents to the Close of the Council of Nicaea, A.D. 325.* 2d ed., rev. Translated by William R. Clark. Edinburgh: T. & T. Clark, 1894.

    Vol. 2. *A History of the Councils of the Church, from the Original Documents, A.D. 326 to A.D. 429.* Translated by Henry N. Oxenham. Edinburgh: T. & T. Clark, 1876.

    Vol. 3. *A History of the Councils of the Church, from the Original Documents, A.D. 431 to A.D. 451.* Translated by the Editor of Hagenbach's *History of Doctrines.* Edinburgh: T. & T. Clark, 1883.

    Vol. 4. *A History of the Councils of the Church, from the Original Documents, A.D. 451 to A.D. 680.* Translated by William R. Clark. Edinburgh: T. & T. Clark, 1895.

Henderson, Robert W. "Notes on the Diaconate in American Presbyterianism." In *The Ministry of Deacons,* ed. Department of Faith and Order.

Hippolytus. *The Apostolic Tradition of Hippolytus: Translated into English with Introduction and Notes.* Translated and edited by Burton Scott Easton. Cambridge: University Press, 1934; rpt., 1962.

Holmes, Urban T., III. *The Future Shape of Ministry: A Theological Projection.* New York: Seabury Press, 1971.

————. *Ministry and Imagination.* New York: Seabury Press, 1976.

Ignatius. *The Apostolic Fathers.* Translated by J. B. Lightfoot. Edited and completed by J. R. Harmer. 1891; rpt., Grand Rapids: Baker Book House, 1956.

————. *The Apostolic Fathers.* Translated by Kirsopp Lake. Cambridge: Harvard University Press, 1912; rpt., 1970.

————. "The Letters of Ignatius, Bishop of Antioch." Translated by Cyril C. Richardson. In *Early Christian Fathers,* ed. Richardson.

————. "The Letters of St. Ignatius of Antioch." Translated by Gerald G. Walsh. In *The Fathers of the Church,* vol. 1, *The Apostolic Fathers.* Translated by Francis X.

Glimm, Joseph M. F. Marique, and Gerald G. Walsh. New York: Cima Publishing, 1947.

Innocent I. *Epistle 37 to Felix.* In *Patrologiae Latinorum* 20, ed. J. P. Migne. Paris, 1845.

Irenaeus. *Against Heresies.* In *Ante-Nicene Fathers,* vol. 1.

Jaffé, Philip. *Regesta Pontificum Romanorum,* vol. 1 (A. S. Petro ad A. MCXLIII). Leipsig: Veit et Comp., 1885; rpt., Graz: Akademische Druck-U. Verlagsanstalt, 1956.

Jalland, Trevor G. "The Doctrine of the Parity of Ministers." In *The Apostolic Ministry: Essays on the History and the Doctrine of Episcopacy,* ed. Kenneth E. Kirk, 305–50. London: Hodder & Stoughton, 1946.

————. *The Life and Times of St. Leo the Great.* London: SPCK, 1941.

Jasper, R. C. D., and G. J. Cuming, trans. and eds. *Prayers of the Eucharist: Early and Reformed.* 2d ed. New York: Oxford University Press, 1980.

Jeremias, Joachim. *Jerusalem in the Time of Jesus.* Philadelphia: Fortress Press, 1969.

Jerome. *The Dialogue Against the Luciferians.* In *Nicene and Post-Nicene Fathers,* 2d ser., vol. 6.

————. *Epistle 28 Ad Praesidium. De Cereo paschali. S. Hieronymi, Tomus undecimus. Patrologiae cursus completus* 30, Series latina, ed. J. P. Migne. Paris, 1846. Published on microcards, 1960. Fo-60 M359-2, Microcard V. 30 — Card 1 (of 6). Washington, D.C.: Microcard Foundation.

————. *Letter 146.* In *Early Latin Theology,* trans. S. L. Greenslade. Library of Christian Classics 5. Philadelphia: Westminster Press, 1956.

Jungmann, Joseph A. *The Mass of the Roman Rite: Its Origins and Development.* Translated by Francis A. Brunner. Replica Edition, 2 vols. Dublin: Four Courts Press, 1986.

Justin. "The First Apology of Justin, the Martyr." Translated by Edward R. Hardy. In *Early Christian Fathers,* ed. Richardson.

Käsemann, Ernst. *Essays on New Testament Themes.* Studies in Biblical Theology 41. London: SCM Press, 1964.

————. *New Testament Questions of Today.* London: SCM Press, 1969.

Kavanagh, Aidan. *The Shape of Baptism: The Rite of Christian Initiation.* New York: Pueblo Publishing, 1978.

Keller, Rosemary Skinner, Gerald F. Moede, and Mary Elizabeth Moore. *Called to Serve: The United Methodist Diaconate.* Edited by Rosalie Bentzinger, assisted by Joyce King, Martha Wagner, and Margaret Gregory. Nashville: Division of Diaconal Ministry of the General Board of Higher Education and Ministry, 1987.

Kelly, J. N. D. *A Commentary on the Pastoral Epistles: 1 Timothy, 2 Timothy, Titus.* New York: Harper & Brothers, 1963.

————. *Jerome: His Life, Writings, and Controversies.* New York: Harper & Row, 1975.

Klauser, Theodore. *A Short History of the Western Liturgy: An Account and Some Reflections.* Translated by John Halliburton. London: Oxford University Press, 1969.

Khodr, George, "The Diaconate in the Orthodox Church." In *The Ministry of Deacons,* ed. Department of Faith and Order.

Knox, John. *The Early Church and the Coming Great Church.* New York: Abingdon Press, 1955.

Krimm, Herbert. "The Diaconate in the Lutheran Church." In *The Ministry of Deacons,* ed. Department of Faith and Order.

Küng, Hans. *The Church.* Translated by Ray and Rosaleen Ockenden. New York: Sheed & Ward, 1967.

————. *Structures of the Church.* Translated by Salvator Attanasio. New York: Thomas Nelson & Sons, 1964.

Lake, Kirsopp. "The Communism of Acts 2 and 4–6 and the Appointment of the Seven." In *The Beginning of Christianity,* vol. 5, pt. 1, *The Acts of the Apostles,* ed. F. J. Foakes Jackson and Kirsopp Lake. Grand Rapids: Baker Book House, 1979.

Lambert, J. C., and George Johnston. "Deacon" and "Minister." In *Dictionary of the Bible,* ed. James Hastings. Rev. ed. Frederick C. Grant and H. H. Rowley. New York: Scribner's, 1963.

The Lambeth Conference 1958. The Encyclical Letter from the Bishops together with the Resolutions and Reports. London: SPCK, and Greenwich, Conn.: Seabury Press, 1958.

Lampe, G. W. H. "Acts." In *Peake's Commentary on the Bible,* ed. Matthew Black and H. H. Rowley. London: Nelson, 1962.

————. *Some Aspects of the New Testament Ministry.* London: SPCK, 1949.

Landon, Edward. *A Manual of Councils of the Holy Catholic Church,* vol. 1. London: Griffith Farrar & Co., n.d.

Latourette, Kenneth Scott. *A History of Christianity,* vol. 1, *To A.D. 1500.* New York: Harper & Row, 1975.

Lawrence, Raymond J., Jr. *The Poisoning of Eros: Sexual Values in Conflict.* New York: Augustine Moore Press, 1989.

Lawstuter, W. J. "The Pastoral Epistles: First and Second Timothy and Titus." In *The Abingdon Bible Commentary,* ed. Frederick Carl Eiselen, Edwin Lewis, and David G. Downey. New York: Abingdon Press, 1929.

Lea, Henry C. *The History of Sacerdotal Celibacy in the Christian Church.* New York: Russell & Russell, 1957. (First published under the title *An Historical Sketch of Sacerdotal Celibacy in the Christian Church.* Philadelphia: Lippincott, 1867.)

Lee, Jeffrey D. "A View from the Omnivorous Presbyterate," an address delivered at the Biennial Conference of the North American Association for the Diaconate, Spokane, Wash., June 13, 1991. Providence, R.I.: North American Association for the Diaconate, 1991.

Lemaire, André. "The Ministries in the New Testament: Recent Research." *Biblical Theology Bulletin* 3, no. 2 (June 1973): 133–66.

————. "Pastoral Epistles: Redaction and Theology." *Biblical Theology Bulletin* 2, no. 1 (February 1972): 25–42.

Leo. *The Letters and Sermons of Leo the Great.* In *Nicene and Post-Nicene Fathers,* 2d ser., vol. 12.

Lietzmann, Hans. *A History of the Early Church. I: The Beginnings of the Christian Church. II: The Founding of the Church Universal.* Translated by Bertram Lee Woolf. New York: World Publishing, Meridian Books, 1961.

Lightfoot, J. B. *St. Paul's Epistle to the Philippians.* 1913; rpt., Grand Rapids: Zondervan, 1963.

Lowrie, Walter. *The Church and Its Organization in Primitive and Catholic Times: An Interpretation of Rudolph Sohm's Kirchenrecht.* New York: Longmans, Green, 1904.

Lupton, J. M. *Q. Septimi Florentis Tertulliani — De Baptismo.* Cambridge: University Press, 1908.

Lutheran Church in America. *Bulletin of Reports, Eighth Biennial Convention of the Lutheran Church in America.* July 21–28, 1976.

———. *Minutes, Fifth Biennial Convention.* Minneapolis, June 15–July 2, 1970. Philadelphia: Board of Publication of the Lutheran Church in America, 1970.

———. "Report on the Ministry of Deacons." Mimeographed, n.d.

McBain, John M. "What On Earth Are Deacons For?" *The Deacon,* April–June 1977. Nashville: The Sunday School Board of the Southern Baptist Convention.

McCance, M. "Alb"; "Dalmatic"; and "Stole." *New Catholic Encyclopedia,* vols. 1, 4, and 13, respectively.

McCaslin, Patrick, and Michael G. Lawler. *Sacrament of Service: A Vision of the Permanent Diaconate Today.* New York: Paulist Press, 1986.

MacDonald, A. J. *Hildebrand: A Life of Gregory VII.* London: Methuen, 1932.

Macgregor, G. H. C. "Exegesis" and "The Acts of the Apostles." In *The Interpreter's Bible,* vol. 9. New York: Abingdon Press, 1954.

McKee, Elsie Anne. *John Calvin on the Diaconate and Liturgical Almsgiving.* Geneva: Librairie Droz, 1984.

Maclean, A. J. "Ministry (Early Christian)." In *Encyclopedia of Religion and Ethics.* vol. 8, ed. James Hastings. New York: Scribner's, 1916.

Martimort, Aimé Georges. *Deaconesses: An Historical Study.* Translated by K. D. Whitehead. San Francisco: Ignatius Press, 1986.

Mayer-Thurman, Christa C. *Raiment for the Lord's Service: A Thousand Years of Western Vestments.* Chicago: Art Institute of Chicago, 1975.

Michael, J. Hugh. *The Epistle of Paul to the Philippians.* The Moffatt New Testament Commentary. New York: Harper & Brothers, n.d. (Preface dated 1927).

The Ministry of Deacons. Edited by the Department of Faith and Order. Geneva: World Council of Churches, 1965.

Moore, Peter S., and Herman Hausheer. "Peter Lombard." In *An Encyclopedia of Religion,* ed. Ferm.

Moorman, John R. H. *A History of the Church in England.* 2d ed. New York: Morehouse-Barlow, 1967.

———. *Saint Francis of Assisi.* London: SPCK, 1963.

Moule, C. F. D. "Deacons in the New Testament." *Theology* 58 (1955): 405–7.

Müller, Jacobus Johannes. *The Epistles of Paul to the Philippians and to Philemon.* The International Commentary on the New Testament. Grand Rapids: Eerdmans, 1955.

Neale, John Mason. *A History of the Holy Eastern Church.*

Vol. 2. *The Patriarchate of Alexandria.* London: Joseph Masters, 1847.

Vol. 3. *The Patriarchate of Antioch.* Edited by George Williams. London: Rivingtons, 1873.

New Catholic Encyclopedia. Prepared by an Editorial Staff at the Catholic University of America. New York: McGraw-Hill, 1967.

The New Oxford Annotated Bible with the Apocrypha: Revised Standard Version Containing the Second Edition of the New Testament with an Expanded Edition of the

Apocrypha. Edited by Herbert G. May and Bruce M. Metzger. New York: Oxford University Press, 1977.

The New Oxford Annotated Bible with the Apocryphal/Deuterocanonical Books: New Revised Standard Version. Edited by Bruce M. Metzger and Roland E. Murphy. New York: Oxford University Press, 1991.

Nicene and Post-Nicene Fathers of the Christian Church, A Selected Library of the. 1st ser. 14 vols. Edited by Philip Schaff. Grand Rapids: Eerdmans, 1956.

    Vol. 1. *St. Augustin: Prolegomena, Confessions, Letters.*

    Vol. 2. *St. Augustin's City of God and Christian Doctrine.* Translated by Marcus Dods.

    Vol. 3. *St. Augustin: On the Holy Trinity, Doctrinal Treatises, Moral Treatises.*

    Vol. 4. *St. Augustin: The Writings Against the Manichaeans and Against the Donatists.*

    Vol. 7. *St. Augustin: Lectures or Tractates on the Gospel According to St. John.*

    Vol. 11. *St. Chrysostom: Homilies on the Acts of the Apostles and the Epistle to the Romans.*

    Vol. 13. *Saint Chrysostom: Homilies on Galatians, Ephesians, Philippians, Colossians, Thessalonians, Timothy, Titus, and Philemon.*

Nicene and Post-Nicene Fathers of the Christian Church, A Select Library of the. 2d ser. 14 vols. Edited by Philip Schaff and Henry Wace. Grand Rapids: Eerdmans.

    Vol. 1. *Eusebius: Church History, Life of Constantine the Great, and Oration in Praise of Constantine.* Translated and edited by Arthur Cushman McGiffert. 1952.

    Vol. 2. *Socrates, Sozomenus: Church Histories.* 1952.

    Vol. 3. *Theodoret, Jerome and Grennadius, Rufinius Historical Writings, etc.* 1953.

    Vol. 4. *St. Athanasius: Select Works and Letters.* Translated by Archibald Robertson. 1953.

    Vol. 6. *St. Jerome: Letters and Select Works.* Translated by W. H. Fremantle, assisted by G. Lewis and W. H. Martley. 1954.

    Vol. 7. *St. Cyril of Jerusalem. St. Gregory Nazianzen.* 1955.

    Vol. 10. *St. Ambrose: Select Works and Letters.* Translated by H. de Romestin. 1955.

    Vol. 12. *The Letters and Sermons of Leo the Great.* Translated by Charles Lett Feltoe. *The Book of Pastoral Rule and Selected Epistles of Gregory the Great.* Translated by James Barmby. 1956.

    Vol. 14. *The Seven Ecumenical Councils.* Edited by Henry R. Percival. 1956.

Nicetas David of Paphlago. *Vita S. Ignatii. Patrologiae sive Latinorum, sive Graecorum* 105, ed. J. P. Migne. Turnholt, Belgium: Brepols, n.d.

Norris, Herbert. *Church Vestments: Their Origin and Development.* London: J. M. Dent & Sons, 1949.

Optatus. *The Work of St. Optatus, Bishop of Milevis, Against the Donatists.* Translated by O. R. Vassal-Phillips. London: Longmans, Green, 1917.

O'Rourke, J. J. "Deacons — In the Bible." *New Catholic Encyclopedia,* vol. 4.

O'Shea, W. J. "Easter Vigil." *New Catholic Encyclopedia,* vol. 5.

The Oxford Dictionary of the Christian Church. 2d ed. Edited by F. L. Cross and E. A. Livingstone. London: Oxford University Press, 1974.

Paredi, Angelo. *Saint Ambrose: His Life and Times*. Translated by M. Joseph Costelloe. Notre Dame: University of Notre Dame Press, 1964.

Parker, Pierson. "Violence in the Gospels." Lectures at the Graduate School of Theology, University of the South, Sewanee, Tenn. Summer 1972.

Paton, David M., ed. *New Forms of Ministry*. Research Pamphlets No. 12. World Council of Churches, Commission on World Mission and Evangelism. London: Edinburgh House Press, 1965.

Paul VI. *An Apostolic Letter in Motu Proprio Form Laying Down Certain Norms Regarding the Sacred Order of the Diaconate, An Apostolic Letter in Motu Proprio Form By Which the Discipline of First Tonsure, Minor Orders and Subdiaconate in the Latin Church Is Reformed*, issued August 15, 1972. Washington, D.C.: U.S. Catholic Conference, 1972.

————. *Approval of a New Rite for the Ordination of Deacons, Priests, and Bishops. Apostolic Constitution*, June 18, 1968.

————. *General Norms for Restoring the Permanent Diaconate in the Latin Church (Motu Proprio)*. Washington, D.C.: U.S. Catholic Conference, June 18, 1967.

Paul, Robert S. "The Deacon in Protestantism." In *The Diaconate Now*, ed. Nolan.

Paulinus. *Life of St. Ambrose*. Translated by John A. Lacy. In *Early Christian Biographies*. vol. 15 of *Fathers of the Church*, ed. Roy J. Deferrari. New York: Fathers of the Church, 1952.

Phillips, Walter. "Dalmatic." In *Encyclopaedia Britannica*, vol. 6. Chicago: William Benton, 1961.

Philostorgius. *Ecclesiastical History*. In *Patrologiae Cursus Completus Omnium SS. Patrum, Doctorum Scriptorumque Ecclesiasticorum Sive Latinorum, Sive Graecorum* 65, ed. J. P. Migne. Turnholt, Belgium: Brepols, n.d.

Plater, Ormonde. *The Deacon in the Liturgy*. Boston: National Center for the Diaconate, 1981.

————. *Many Servants: An Introduction to Deacons*. Cambridge, Mass.: Cowley Publications, 1991.

Pocknee, Cyril E. *Liturgical Vesture: Its Origins and Development*. London: A. R. Mowbray, 1960.

Pohl, Keith, ed. "Circuit Rider" (brochure). Nashville: United Methodist Publishing House, November 1991.

Polycarp. "The Letters of Polycarp, Bishop of Smyrna, to the Philippians," trans. Massey H. Shepherd Jr. In *Early Christian Fathers*, ed. Richardson.

"Pontifex." *Encyclopedia Americana*, International ed. (Danbury, Conn.: Grolier, 1992).

Porter, H. Boone, Jr. *Canons on New Forms of Ministry*. Kansas City: Roanridge, n.d.

————. "Modern Experience in Practice." In Paton, ed., *New Forms of Ministry*.

————. "Ordained Ministers in Liturgy and Life." *The Living Church*, January 9, 1977.

The Proper for the Lesser Feasts and Fasts together with the Fixed Holy Days. 3d ed. New York: Church Hymnal Corp., 1980.

The Proper for the Lesser Feasts and Fasts. 1991 together with the Fixed Holy Days. New York: Church Hymnal Corp., 1991.

Prosper of Aquitaine. *Chronicon*. In *Monumenta Germaniae Historica*, vol. 1, ed. G. H. Pertz and others. Berlin, 1826.

Quasten, Johannes. *Patrology*. Westminster, Md.: Newman Press, 1950.

    Vol. 1. *Beginnings of Patristic Literature in Patrology*.

Vol. 2. *The Ante-Nicene Literature after Irenaeus.*

Vol. 3. *The Golden Age of Greek Patristic Literature from the Council of Nicaea to the Council of Chalcedon.*

Rackham, Richard B. *The Acts of the Apostles.* 13th ed. London: Methuen, 1947.

Rahner, Karl. *Bishops: Their Status and Function.* Translated by Edward Quinn. Baltimore: Helicon Press, 1964.

————. *Theological Investigations.* vol. 5, *Later Writings.* Translated by Karl H. Kruger. Baltimore: Helicon Press, 1966.

Rashke, Richard L. *The Deacon in Search of Identity.* New York: Paulist Press, 1975.

Reicke, Bo. "Deacons in the New Testament and in the Early Church." In *The Ministry of Deacons,* ed. Department of Faith and Order.

A Religious Encyclopaedia or Dictionary of Biblical, Historical, Doctrinal, and Practical Theology, vol. 1. Edited by Philip Schaff. New York: Funk and Wagnalls, 1882.

Rengers, Christopher. "Liber Pontificalis." In *An Encyclopedia of Religion,* ed. Ferm.

"The Report of the Consultation." Part 2 of *The Ministry of Deacons,* ed. Department of Faith and Order.

"A Report on the Restoration of the Office of Deacon as a Lifetime State." By a Committee of the Catholic Theological Society of America, Edward Echlin, Chairman. Made at the request of the Bishops' Committee on the Permanent Diaconate (Roman Catholic). Published in *American Ecclesiastical Review* 164, no. 3 (March 1971): 190–204.

Research Report, Women in Church and Society. Edited by Sara Butler. Bronx, N.Y.: Catholic Theological Society of America, 1978.

Richardson, Cyril C. Introduction to "The Letter of the Church of Rome to the Church of Corinth, Commonly called Clement's First Letter." In *Early Christian Fathers,* ed. Richardson.

————. Introduction to "The Teaching of the Twelve Apostles, Commonly Called the Didache," trans. and ed. Richardson. In *Early Christian Fathers,* ed. Richardson.

Riley, T. J. "Deacons — In the Church." *New Catholic Encyclopedia,* vol. 4.

Robinson, John A. T. "Taking the Lid Off the Church's Ministry." In *New Ways with the Ministry,* ed. John Morris. London: Faith Press, 1960.

The Roman Missal, the Sacramentary. New York: Catholic Book Publishing, 1974.

Ross, J. M. "Deacons in Protestantism." *Theology* 58 (1955): 429–36.

Schaff, Philip. *History of the Christian Church,* vol. 2, *Ante-Nicene Christianity A.D. 100–325.* New York: Scribner's, 1924.

Schamoni, Wilhelm. *Married Men as Ordained Deacons.* Translated by Otto Eisner. London: Burns & Oates, 1955.

Schillebeeckx, Edward. *Celibacy.* Translated by C. A. L. Jarrott. New York: Sheed and Ward, 1968.

Schweizer, Eduard. *Church Order in the New Testament.* Translated by Frank Clarke. London: SCM Press, 1961.

Scott, Ernest F. "The Epistle to the Philippians." In *The Interpreter's Bible,* vol. 11. New York: Abingdon Press, 1955.

A Self-Supporting Ministry and the Mission of the Church. By a Group of Sixty Bishops, Other Clergy, and Lay People of the Episcopal Church. The Division of Christian Ministries of the National Council of the Episcopal Church, and the Overseas Missionaries Society, 1964.

Serapion. *Bishop Serapion's Prayer Book: An Egyptian Sacramentary Dated Probably about A.D. 350–356.* 2d ed. Translated by John Wordsworth. London: SPCK, 1923.

Shepherd, Massey H., Jr. "The Christian Year." Lectures at the Graduate School of Theology, University of the South, Sewanee, Tenn., Summer, 1970.

———. "The Church in the Fourth Century." Lectures at the Graduate School of Theology, University of the South, Sewanee, Tenn., Summer, 1970.

———. "Deacon" and "Deaconess: KJV Servant." In *The Interpreter's Dictionary of the Bible,* vol. 4, ed. George A. Buttrick. New York: Abingdon Press, 1962.

———. "Ministry, Christian" and "Priests in the NT." In *The Interpreter's Dictionary of the Bible,* vol. 3, ed. George A. Buttrick. New York: Abingdon Press, 1962.

———. *The Oxford American Prayer Book Commentary.* New York: Oxford University Press, 1950.

———. "Prayer Book Revision." Lectures at the Graduate School of Theology, University of the South, Sewanee, Tenn. Summer 1970.

———. "Smyrna in the Ignatian Letters: A Study in Church Order." *Journal of Religion* 20 (1940): 141–59.

Simpson, E. K. *The Pastoral Epistles: The Greek Text with Introduction and Commentary.* Grand Rapids: Eerdmans, 1954.

Siricius. *Epistle 1 to Himerius.* In *Patrologiae Latinorum* 13, ed. J. P. Migne. Paris, 1845.

Socrates. *Ecclesiastical History.* In *Nicene and Post-Nicene Fathers,* 2d ser., vol. 2.

Sozomen. *Ecclesiastical History: A History of the Church in Nine Books from A.D. 324 to A.D. 440.* Translation. In *The Greek Ecclesiastical Historians of the First Six Centuries of the Christian Era.* London: Bagster & Sons, 1846.

———. *Ecclesiastical History.* In *Nicene and Post-Nicene Fathers,* 2d ser., vol. 2.

Stamm, Raymond T. "Exegesis" and "The Epistle to the Galatians." In *The Interpreter's Bible,* vol. 10. New York: Abingdon-Cokesbury, 1953.

The Standing Liturgical Commission of the Episcopal Church. *The Ordination of Bishops, Priests, and Deacons: Prayer Book Studies 20.* New York: Church Hymnal Corp., 1970.

The Standing Liturgical Commission of the Protestant Episcopal Church in the United States of America. *Prayer Book Studies VIII: The Ordinal.* New York: Church Pension Fund, 1957.

Stauffer, S. Anita. *Re-Examining Baptismal Fonts: Baptismal Space for the Contemporary Church* (video). St. John's Abbey. Collegeville, Minn.: Liturgical Press, 1991.

Stepping Stones: Joint Essays on Anglican Catholic and Evangelical Unity. Edited by Christina Baxter. London: Hodder & Stoughton, 1987.

"Steps into Diaconal Ministry." Nashville: Division of Diaconal Ministry, General Board of Higher Education and Ministry, The United Methodist Church, n.d.

Stevenson, J., ed. *Creeds, Councils, and Controversies: Documents Illustrative of the History of the Church A.D. 337–461.* London: SPCK, 1966.

———, ed. *A New Eusebius: Documents Illustrative of the Church to A.D. 337.* New York: Macmillan, 1957.

"Stole." In *Encyclopaedia Britannica — A New Summary of Universal Knowledge,* vol. 21. Chicago: William Benton, 1961.

Symonds, R. P. "Deacons in the Early Church." *Theology* 58 (1955): 404–14.

Tally, Thomas. "The Liturgy of the Bishop." A lecture recorded by the author at the conference of the Association of Diocesan Liturgy and Music Commissions in Chicago, November 8–11, 1982. Later printed in *Open* (the newsletter of Associated Parishes), Alexandria, Va.

Teegarden, Kenneth L. *We Call Ourselves Disciples.* St. Louis: Bethany Press, 1975.

Tertullian. *Tertullian's Homily on Baptism.* The text edited with an introduction, translation, and commentary by Ernest Evans. London: SPCK, 1964.

Thomas, Donald F. *The Deacons in a Changing Church.* Valley Forge, Pa.: Judson Press, 1969.

Thomas of Celano. *The First Life of St. Francis.* Translated in Marion A. Habig, ed., *St. Francis of Assisi: Writings and Early Biographies: English Omnibus of the Sources for the Life of St. Francis.* Chicago: Franciscan Herald Press, 1972.

Thurston, Herbert. "Deacons." In *The Catholic Encyclopedia,* ed. Herbermann et al., 4:649.

Titus, Eric Lane. "The First Letter to Timothy." In *The Interpreter's One-Volume Commentary on the Bible,* ed. Charles M. Laymon. Nashville: Abingdon Press, 1971.

Toynbee, Arnold J. *A Study of History.* 2 vols. Abridgement by D. C. Somervell. New York: Oxford University Press, 1957.

Turner, C. H. "The Organization of the Church." In *The Cambridge Medieval History,* vol. 1, ed. H. M. Gwatkin. Cambridge: University Press, 1936.

Tyrer, John Walton. *Historical Survey of Holy Week: Its Services and Ceremonial.* London: Oxford University Press, 1932.

Tytler, Donald. "Each in His Own Order." In *New Ways with the Ministry,* ed. John Morris. London: Faith Press, 1960.

"Varieties of Diaconal Ministry." Nashville: Division of Diaconal Ministry, General Board of Higher Education and Ministry, The United Methodist Church, n.d.

Vischer, Lukas. "The Problem of the Diaconate." In *The Ministry of Deacons,* ed. Department of Faith and Order.

Walker, Williston. *A History of the Christian Church.* New York: Scribner's, 1947.

Wallach, L. "Alcuin." In *New Catholic Encyclopedia,* vol. 1.

Wallis, Ernest. "Introductory Notice to Cyprian." In *Ante-Nicene Fathers,* vol. 5.

Wand, J. W. C. *A History of the Early Church to A.D. 500.* 3d ed. London: Methuen, 1949.

Ware, Timothy. *The Orthodox Church.* Baltimore: Penguin Books, 1964.

Webster's New Collegiate Dictionary. Springfield, Mass.: G. & C. Merriam, 1979.

Webster's Ninth New Collegiate Dictionary. Springfield, Mass.: Merriam-Webster, 1991.

Weil, Louis. Lecture recorded by the author at the conference of the Association of Diocesan Liturgy and Music Commissions (Episcopal) in Chicago, November 8–11, 1982. Later published in *Open* (the newsletter of Associated Parishes), Alexandria, Va.

Williams, George H. "The Ministry of the Ante-Nicene Church (c. 125–325)" and "The Ministry in the Later Patristic Period (314–451)." In *The Ministry in Historical Perspective,* ed. H. Richard Niebuhr and Daniel D. Williams, 27–81. New York: Harper & Brothers, 1956.

Wilson, Frank E. *The Divine Commission: A Sketch of Church History.* New York: Morehouse-Gorham, 1946.

Winter, Gibson. *Elements for a Social Ethic: Scientific Perspectives on Social Process.* New York: Macmillan, 1966.

Wordsworth, John. *The Ministry of Grace: Studies in Early Church History with Reference to Present Problems.* London: Longmans, Green, 1901.

Wright, J. Robert. "The Distinctive Diaconate in Historical Perspective." June 1979. Available from the Centre for the Diaconate, Providence, R.I.

———. "Ministry in New York: The Non-Stipendiary Priesthood and the Permanent Diaconate." *St. Luke's Journal of Theology* 19 (December 1975): 18–50.

Zosimus. *Epistle 9 to Hesychius.* In *Patrologiae Latinorum* 20, ed. J. P. Migne. Paris, 1845.

Index

Abraham, 10
Acts of Thomas, 194
Aetius, deacon of Antioch, 82
Aetius, archdeacon of Constantinople, 218
Agde, Council of, 182
agentry, in Judaism, N.T., 16–18
agreement, with deacon, 177–79, 225–28
Alcuin, 84, 110
Alexander, bishop of Alexandria, 88
Alexander, Neil, 135, 142
Alexandria, bishop of, 100–101 n.51
altar, 200
ambo, 95, 200–201
Ambrose, bishop of Milan, 63, 108, 117, 144, 199
   Duties of the Clergy, 63
Ambrosiaster, 43, 90, 103
   "On the Boastfulness of the Roman Deacons," 90
Anatolius, bishop of Constantinople, 218
Ancyra, Council of, 80, 97, 99–100, 115
Andrieu, Michel, 110
Andronicus of Alexandria (Jacobite), 67
Anglican Church of Canada, 151
Anglican–Roman Catholic International Commission, 9
Anicetus, 56
Antioch, Council of, 66, 87, 93, 104
Antonius, 109
Apocalypse (or *Vision*) of Paul, 65
Apostles, married, 114
Apostolic Canons, 116
Apostolic Constitutions, 72–73, 84, 86, 102, 111, 116, 200
apostolic succession, 46
Apostolic Tradition (Hippolytus), 60–64
Aquinas, Thomas, 118

archdeacon, 72, 100, 155, 218–19
   as "the bishop's deacon," 95, 218
   in every church, 218
   as reader of Gospel, 72
archpresbyter, 218
Ariald, 91
Arianism, 66, 82
Arles, Council of, 43, 75, 88, 89, 101
Associated Parishes, Council of, 152
Association of Diocesan Liturgy and Music Commissions, 152
Athanasius of Alexandria, 66, 88, 109, 187
Audet, Jean-Paul, 39
Augustine, 10, 79, 101, 117
   On the Good of Marriage, 117
Aurelius, reader, 70

Baptism, 90, 112
   being replaced by ordination, 13, 112
   centrality of (Kavanagh), 191–92
   confused with ordination, 185
   by deacons, 74–75, 191–93
   formation for, 207–10
   by immersion and submersion, 199
   infant, 92 n.15
   and ontological change, 134–45
   presider at, 192–93
   as primary sacrament of ministry, 3, 13, 23, 133, 164
   as sacramental prerequisite for ordination, 84, 106, 108, 111, 112, 152–53, 163–64
   special days for, 199
   and status, 22
   theology of, 201–2
baptismal font, 199–200
Barmby, James, 110
Barnabas, 18, 25, 35

Moser, James E., 185
Moses, 10

Narcissus, bishop of Jerusalem, 78
National Association of Permanent
    Diaconate Directors, 186
National Conference of Catholic Bishops
    in the United States, 145
Nature of Ministry (United Presbyterian),
    160
Nectarius, patriarch of Constantinople,
    107
Neocaesarea, Council of, 99
New York Times Magazine, 186
Nicaea, Council of, 43, 88, 89, 93, 95, 96,
    101, 104
Nicolaitans, 57
Nicolas, 56
North American Association for the
    Diaconate, 152
Notebaart, James, 156

Oakerhater, David Pendleton, 85
oil, 63, 64
Optatus, bishop of Milevis, 99, 218
orders
    clearly delineated, 191, 195
    confusion of, 139
    each with proper functions (Episcopal),
        133
    indelibility of, 93 n.21
    "religious," 112
    Roman Catholic, 103
    and symbols of power and authority,
        137
ordination, 23, 70
    of Calvin's deacons, 158
    conferring grace, 134–35
    conferring no absolute right for a
        ministry, 179–80
    in *Didache,* 47
    difference made by, 140–41
    direct (*per saltum*), 66, 91, 110, 143,
        152–53, 163
    greater order containing others
        (Ambrosiaster), 103
    and laying on of hands, 25–26, 60

ontological change with, 134, 166–67
    in Paul, 34–36
    presbyterial, 100
    reason for, of deacons, 206–7
    replacing Baptism as initiation, 13, 112
    required by ministry (Collins), 22
    Roman Catholic restoration of, 146
    of women, 183
organic nature of church, 3–12, 14–15, 73
    all are *laos,* 3
    as "body of Christ, 5
    and community, 6–7
    created by Baptism, 3
    demonstrated in taking Eucharist to
        absent, 55
    as meaning of *ecclesia,* 7
    as reflection of God, 7
organic structure, 97–98, 103–11, 131–36
Origen, 92
Orleans, Council of, 116, 182
Orthodox Creed of the General Baptists,
    160
Otto I, pope, 111

pallium, 94, 222
papal states, 86
Paphnutius, bishop and confessor, 116
Paschal I, pope, 194
paschal candle, 77–80
pastor. *See* presbyter
Paul, 4, 5, 10, 11, 15
Paul, Geoffrey, bishop, 134
Paul of Samosota, 66
Paul VI, pope, 103, 121, 182, 190, 206
    *Approval of a New Rite for the
        Ordination of Deacons, Priests, and
        Bishops,* 146
    *General Norms for Restoring the
        Permanent Diaconate in the Latin
        Church,* 131, 145, 146, 182
    *Laying Down Certain Norms Regarding
        the Sacred Order of the Diaconate,*
        190
    Sacerdotalis caelibatus, 121
Pauline churches, 34–36
Pelagius, 102
Pelagius I, pope, 119